*The*

# Book

*of the*

# Goddess

## Past and Present

*An Introduction to Her Religion*

# Carl Olson
*Allegheny College*

WAVELAND

PRESS, INC.

Prospect Heights, Illinois

For information about this book, contact:
Waveland Press, Inc.
P.O. Box 400
Prospect Heights, Illinois 60070
(847) 634-0081
www.waveland.com

*For Holly and Kelly,*
*two living goddesses*

# Contents

# Preface 2002

Beautiful and ugly, violent and benign, sexually aggressive and sexually passive, terrifying and soothing, awe-inspiring and capricious, loveable and terrible, close and remote, violent and peaceful—these adjectives and many others characterize goddess figures. Often, these seemingly contradictory features can be discovered in the same goddess. Although scholars had neglected goddesses as subjects of serious study for some time, this is no longer the case, as evidenced by the many studies on them in the past few decades. When I wrote the original preface to this book in 1982, I referred to the return of the goddess to our purview, by which I implied the Western viewpoint. Little did I realize then that the goddess's return would be so overwhelming and dramatic. The recovery of interest in various goddesses accompanied the rise of feminist scholarship and its challenges to the field of religious studies and beyond.

The re-publication of this book comes at the urging of many scholars of religious studies conveyed to me personally over the past few years. Some of these scholars had published books on goddesses themselves. Numerous people combined their encouragement with comments about *The Book of the Goddess* still being the best thing available for students of the subject. Encouraged by such supportive statements by well-meaning professional colleagues, I decided to look into the possibilities of making the book available once again to students for course use. After returning from my research fellowship at Clare Hall of the University of Cambridge, I decided to take the advice of others and to seek to re-issue a very successful book.

Through the contribution of the scholars represented in this book and other fine studies, goddesses are much less strangers to those in the West. These many scholarly contributions about various goddess figures have enabled readers to broaden their religious horizons and understanding. The re-publication of this book continues the arrival of the goddess to the religious awareness of Westerners.

# Preface 1983

While teaching a course on goddesses in the history of religions a few years ago, I discovered that there was no common source book available to my students. The lack of an adequate source book for classroom use led me to outline a work that would be faithful to the diverse religious cultures and periods of history in which goddesses have played an important role.

Without trying to be exhaustive or encyclopedic in scope, this book includes examples of ancient and modern goddesses, encompassing Eastern and Western religious traditions, major world religions and tribal religions, living religions and those that have passed into historical memory. Besides serving students of religion as an introduction to the subject, this volume is intended to help the reader understand the various manifestations of the goddess and her often complex nature.

Throughout the course of the history of religions, the goddess has manifested herself in numerous ways. She has been a source of creativity and destruction, a passionate lover and a pure virgin, a temptress and a repeller, beautiful and ugly, terrible and benign. She has been a vivid symbol of fertility, prosperity, and wealth, as well as a symbol of loss and death, both beckoning and repulsing the religious devotee. Since I felt that it was practically impossible for one individual to master the numerous and varied cultures in which goddesses have appeared, I invited an international group of scholars to elucidate various goddesses, thereby making a vast range of information about goddesses available in a single source.

Besides discussing the manifestations of the goddess and her complex nature, this book is also an invitation to the reader to share in a renewal of interest in the goddess and in a celebration of her return to the religious consciousness of those who have forgotten her. The arrival of the goddess brings with it her message concerning the earth, society, culture, the individual's place in the world, the meaning of existence, and the nature of the divine. Finally, this book attempts to discern the significance of the goddess for contemporary feminist thinkers.

There are a number of people who have given me their encouragement, help, and friendship. There are three chairmen who took care of me like fathers: John Hayward of Southern Illinois University; George Frein of the University of North Dakota, an outstanding host; and James Day of Allegheny College, who unofficially adopted an orphaned teacher of religious studies and helped smooth the transition to a new institution. I also want to thank my colleagues at Allegheny College—Brownie, Bill, and Don—for their good humor, encouragement, and friendship. Thanks go to Dean Andy Ford of Allegheny College for generously approving a typing grant, and to the typists, Karen Holzerland and Audrey Onspaugh. My thanks also go to President David B. Harned and Jonathan E. Helmreich for giving me an opportunity to teach at the college on the hill. Finally, I want to thank Craig McVey for his expert editorial assistance, helpful criticism, and friendship.

# Introduction

With the possible exception of the Virgin Mary, the goddess as a viable religious symbol is a stranger to most contemporary Westerners. We are disposed to conceive of the divine in masculine terms and images, whereas other cultures still worship goddesses who are living realities and not simply museum curiosities. Among some feminist writers and thinkers, as well as a number of male scholars, the goddess is receiving renewed interest as she emerges in the consciousness of contemporary religious individuals. This emergence calls into question the basic assumptions that Western people have held about the nature of the divine, and thereby shakes their confidence in the validity of their habitual way of conceiving of the divine. Since contemporary Western individuals have not in general been able to experience the goddess as part of their own personal biography, the essays in this volume are intended to fill this void by enabling the reader to share the history of the goddess in a cross-cultural context.

The essays in this book often depict the goddess as a creative figure with a strong, powerful, and dynamic character. The figure of the goddess as represented in religious history often stands in sharp contrast to the mistaken concept that the feminine is tranquil, passive, or inferior. The goddess is associated with life-giving powers, renewal, rebirth, transformation, and the mystery of death. She also attracts us with her alluring charms, arouses our curiosity about her powers, and tempts us with her pleasureful and unbridled nature.

Another aspect of her nature that many of these essays depict is her demonic or destructive power (a power also possessed by male deities)—a virtually inconceivable, overpowering aspect that threatens death and darkness. Even though her surface may appear benign and beautiful, beneath this facade is a terrible, destructive aspect. Thus, like the process of time, the goddess can be irrational, merciless, and destructive. Sometimes her outward appearance is horrible, like Kālī with her disheveled hair, dark appearance, necklace of severed human heads, waistband of severed human hands, fanglike teeth, and blood-dripping mouth. However, for those who truly love her, Kālī is also, like many other goddesses, the loving, protective, warm, nourishing mother.

The roots of goddess devotion are to be found in prehistoric culture. Anne L. Barstow finds one goddess with many roles in the prehistoric period. Although she was associated with many things, the goddess was primarily a symbol of fertility, as well as a source of material and spiritual power. The prehistoric goddess was depicted as faceless, without feet, unclothed, often large-breasted, sometimes pregnant, nursing a child or exposing her genitals. Besides her concern with the goddess, Barstow examines female roles in prehistoric cultures by using the archaeological discoveries at Çatal Hüyük, a city in Anatolia. She notes that agriculture was replacing hunting as the preeminent source of food and wealth in that culture and that women controlled it. The society was matrilocal and the priestly class contained women; the goddess cult predominated over the male gods. Although we cannot return to the prehistoric goddess and the culture over which she presided, Barstow argues that the evidence can serve as an inspiration to contemporary women.

A popular goddess of ancient Mesopotamian religion was Ishtar. Judith Ochshorn places Ishtar in her cultural and historical context, in which divine activity was viewed as immanent in natural and cultural events. In this ancient culture neither goddesses nor gods were viewed as particularly benevolent or malignant owing to their sex. Within this polytheistic religion, we find the unrestricted participation of women in every phase of the cult. Ishtar was responsible for fertility and for victory in war, neither of which was viewed as a particularly feminine or masculine trait. Ishtar's close relationship with kingship reminds one of Śrī Lakshmī, of the Hindu tradition, and Isis, of ancient Egypt. Ochshorn's essay concludes with an important reevaluation of the position of temple prostitutes.

C.J. Bleeker examines Isis and Hathor and notes that women were held in high esteem in ancient Egypt. Besides her intimate relationship with divine kingship, Isis is known as a goddess of wisdom, and of a kind of magical power, and also as the wife, who searches for her dead husband, Osiris. Bleeker notes the significance of Isis's lamentation for Egyptian mortuary practices, her part in the birth of Horus, and her role as patroness of sailors. After becoming hellenized, Isis gains universal importance as a savior figure. Appearing with the sun disc between her horns, Hathor, the cow, sky, and tree goddess, is connected with fertility, love, death, inebriety, dance, music, and song. Hathor's independent, martial, benevolent, wrathful, and tumultuous nature is manifested in her cult.

The Greek and Roman goddesses are discussed, respectively, by Christine R. Downing and M. Renee Salzman. The former examines

Gaia, the primordial mother goddess of the earth, of which later Greek goddesses like Athene, Aphrodite, and Artemis are specialized forms. Gaia is rebellious matter, the unsubdued earth, manifested as the earthquake and volcano and representing life as becoming, renewing, and changing. She becomes subordinated to the male Olympian order with her dominion and powers more limited. Downing concludes with a fascinating and suggestive look at the goddesses' childhoods and their roles as mothers. Salzman traces the historical development of the Magna Mater in Rome and indicates that her official adoption was due to a combination of religious, political, and social factors. Salzman examines the frenzied nature of this cult; the roles played by Roman aristocrats, women, and eunuchs; and the importance of Attis, the unfaithful lover of the goddess.

The Caananite-Hebrew goddess is discussed by Steve Davies, who focuses his attention on Anath, the warlike, virgin wife of Baal, and on Asherah, the wife of El, and the Yahwist struggle on behalf of the Israelites to obliterate this cult. Davies also discusses the problem of a Hebrew goddess within the context of a radical monotheistic religion and notes the significance of Sophia and of the Shekinah in Jewish mysticism.

Concerns raised by Davies about the status of the goddess in a monotheistic religion are also examined by E. Ann Matter in her article on the Virgin Mary. Matter uses a historical, theological, and anthropological approach to her subject. From the picture of Mary in the New Testament through the pseudepigraphical writings, which fill in some of the gaps in the Marian story, to the medieval period of Christianity, and to the Marian apparitions at Guadalupe, Lourdes, and Fatima, Matter seeks to discern the meaning of Mary for the faithful. She concludes by reviewing some of the significant contemporary interpretations of Mary's place in Christianity and discovers that many authors agree that Mary fills a deep need and that devotion to her is ultimately directed to God. Thus Mary has an important place in the Christian concept of divinity.

Pheme Perkins examines Sophia, a goddess in the Gnostic tradition, by attempting to discern the philosophic origins of the female divine principle, the role of Sophia in the origins of the world, her ordering and providential role, and her creative and soteriological activity. Sophia, the perfect consort of God, plays a complicated role in the origin of the world due to the Gnostic separation of the divine and material worlds. Her responsibility for the devolution of the cosmos from the heavenly world is embodied in such negative imagery as a sexual flaw or a desire to imitate the father. The most important part of her creative activity relates to providing spirit to the human realm. As a redemptress, she protects her offspring from destructive powers.

Three essays on goddesses in Hinduism have been included in this volume because these goddesses have played a significant part in the history of Hinduism and still function as living symbols of the divine. Probably the most fascinating goddess in the Hindu tradition is Kālī, the fierce goddess of death and destruction. C. Mackenzie Brown captures the spirit of Kālī when he discusses her nature and her creative and destructive activities. Brown notes that the key to understanding her nature is to be found in the concept of *māyā*, a deceptive, magical, beguiling power through which she plays the game of life and death. Brown notes that Ramprasad and Ramakrishna, two Bengali saints, were able to see through her terrifying exterior to her merciful, maternal aspect.

A very different image of the Hindu goddess emerges in my consideration of Śrī Lakshmī and Rādhā, the consorts respectively of Vishnu and Krishna. Besides surveying their historical development and associated symbols, I examine them as representing two different kinds of feminine sexuality and spirit. Rādhā is the more independent, free, lustful lover, and Śrī Lakshmī represents the obsequious wife and inferior to her consort, the proper position for any Hindu spouse. From a once unpredictable and uncontrollable fertility goddess, Śrī Lakshmī comes under the domination of her husband, who acts to control her sexuality. A very different relationship exists between Rādhā and Krishna, whose relations are characterized by passionate, violent, erotic, and comic features, as seen in the poetry of Jayadeva and Śrī Hit Harivamś, the performances of *rāsa līlā* (circle dance), and in the colors associated with the goddess.

In contrast to the Hindu goddesses with consorts, the village goddesses on whom villagers depend for protection are independent figures with powerfully ambivalent natures. After discussing the divine hierarchy, the village cosmos, regional differences between goddesses, and the importance of the lower castes in maintaining the purity-ranked system, Richard L. Brubaker considers the festival of the village goddess and how it expresses communal solidarity, dedication to the goddess, and defense against and expulsion of demons. Village goddesses are closely associated with disease: they defend against it, inflict it, manifest themselves in its symptoms , and are themselves its victims. Finally, Brubaker examines the sexuality and violence of the village goddesses, and the symbolism of heat, which illustrates that the goddess is not a bundle of contradictions but rather is surrounded by multifarious symbols forming a web of connected meanings. As also intimated in the essay on Śrī Lakshmī and Rādhā, an uncontrolled goddess is viewed as dangerous. This threat derives from male fears of feminine sexuality and of the depths of the sacred.

East Asian goddesses are represented by Kuan-yin and Amaterasu. Diana Paul traces the historical development of the cult of Kuan-yin, a celestial bodhisattva endowed with powers and compassion to aid individuals in distress. Paul investigates the Buddhist notion of savior and the redefinition of faith by Mahayana Buddhism, from faith in Buddha as a teacher and commitment to follow his teaching and his monastic community, to faith in a celestial bodhisattva as a way of acquiring personal merit. Consideration is also given to the doctrinal reasons for the inclusion of the savioress Kuan-yin in Pure Land Buddhist cult practices. Kyoko Motomochi Nakamura traces the origins of Amaterasu in Japanese mythology, where she was originally androgynous. The problem of her sexuality arose when she was made the ancestor of the imperial family. Nakamura discusses the origin of the sun goddess's shrine at Ise and the fact that women originally monopolized the cult. These shamanistic women were gradually relegated to the more informal and popular spheres of religious life only to be revived with the increasing knowledge of Amaterasu and Japanese mythology in the modern period. Nakamura gives three examples of modern shamanistic women and indicates why their teachings were viewed as a threat to the established faith and why they were persecuted by authorities. The tradition of these shamanistic women has survived, however, despite suppression and sexist prejudice.

Examples of goddesses from tribal religions are offered by Joseph M. Murphy and Åke Hultkrantz. From her origins among the Yoruba of Nigeria, Murphy traces the development of Oshun, the river-born, enchanting African goddess. Murphy discusses Oshun's myths and rites as they are celebrated in Cuba, where she has come to be identified with the Virgin Mary and plays an important role in spirit possession. Oshun is the great coquette, the flirtatious adulteress, who reminds one of the promiscuous Rādhā of the Hindu tradition. Hultkrantz concentrates on various Native American goddesses among the Eskimo, Sioux, Shawnee, and other tribes. He discusses the manifestations of the goddess as Mother Earth and guardian of animals, her association with vegetative life, her role as patroness of womanhood, and her link with the realm of the dead. Hultkrantz argues that it is a common misconception to assert that male deities predominated among the tribes of North America.

The final two essays are concerned with the relevance of the goddess to contemporary Western religion. Rita M. Gross looks to a second coming of the goddess and suggests that Hindu female deities have much to teach in order to assist us in reimaging the goddess. Gross examines six basic aspects of the goddess in Hinduism: bisexuality, strength and beauty, symbolism of the coincidence of opposites, mother imagery, cultural activities, and sexual symbolism. Carol P. Christ examines the symbols of "goddess" and "god" from the perspective of feminist theology. From her criticism of Tillich and Jung and her assertion that god as a symbol has outlived its usefulness, Christ argues for the creation of a new symbolism that will make feminist goals easier to achieve and will enrich modern feminist lives. Christ surveys feminist work on divine symbolism and finds agreement among feminist theologians on the critique of God symbolism.

According to Christ, the symbol of the goddess forces the recognition of female power, body, and finitude that can transform deeply held attitudes and beliefs.

Although the main objective of this book is to serve as an introduction to goddesses and to present an understanding of their complex natures, another goal is to continue the task of opening up religious horizons for the second coming of the goddess and, in doing so, to speak her name. At the very least, this book bids welcome to the goddess, who remains a stranger to most contemporary devotees of monotheistic religions. Her personal biography is an ancient story that begins before the dawn of recorded history.

# 1

## ANNE L. BARSTOW

## *The Prehistoric Goddess*

Goddesses have been worshiped since earliest times, far longer than have male deities. Evidence of female figurines placed in sacred settings, as in circles of stones found on floors of caves, dates as far back as ca. 25,000 B.C.E. Traces of this worship have been found from Siberia to southern Africa, from the Indus to Ireland, and all over the New World as well. In caves, on mountaintops, at home altars, and in the earliest shrines, the goddess appeared, carved from stone, modeled from clay, etched in plaster.

Because these manifestations of the worship of a female deity begin long before recorded history, we call her the prehistoric goddess. She was the forerunner of the great goddess familiar to us from the written records of ancient Egypt and Mesopotamia, of ancient Greece and Rome. Because her worship antedates the invention of writing, we learn about her through archaeology. Who was she and why was she worshiped? The answer lies in archaeological records that reveal many richly varied and complex cults.

"She" is many goddesses: from the settings in which her likenesses are found we know that she was worshiped variously as the guardian of childbirth, the source of wisdom, the dispenser of healing, the Lady of the Beasts, the fount of prophecy, the spirit who presided over death. But preeminently she was the symbol of fertility, the guarantor of crops, animals, and humans. In this role she was the great mother, the earth mother, whose magical powers assured the food supply and the continuance of the human race.[1]

Since evidence of her worship is found across the world, she must have been known by many names, of which our earliest written records give us hints—Cybele, Inanna, Isis. But despite her various names and her different purposes, she is a single goddess. The multiple roles created for her can be seen as different facets of one power, as expressions of one basic belief of these early Stone Age societies: that the female represented the principle of creativity and of power over both life and death. Prehistoric people expressed their deepest questions about life by constructing various cults that centered around a female deity.

What was she like? Were there common characteristics among the goddess figurines of the many cults over the centuries? Yes, despite differences in style, one can discern common traits. The goddess was faceless, as if to accentuate her universality, her ability to "stand for" the power of the female. Lacking feet, she appeared to come straight up out of the earth, with which she was identified. Unclothed, her very body seemed to have an efficacy. Often—but not always—she was big-breasted, and her hands were frequently placed under her breasts as if to display them. Many figurines show her entire body as ample, with huge breasts, belly, and buttocks, as if the very plenitude of her body would insure plentiful crops and herds. Sometimes she is pregnant, her enlarged belly emphasized by special markings. Sometimes she was sculpted nursing a child. Then again, she may be slender, the emphasis falling not on her procreative potency but on her sexual powers. In this case, her genitals received particular emphasis. In other representations she appears in a regal pose, often holding or supported by an animal or wearing jewelry, perhaps indicating that she was patroness of artisans. But regardless of manifestation or setting, it is clear that she was seen as a chief magical source of power, both spiritual and material.

I became interested in the prehistoric goddess when I first asked myself, "What would a religion created, at least in part, by women be like? What values would it express? What needs would it meet?" I knew that the Western religious tradition in which I had been raised, with its narrow patriarchalism, did not meet my spiritual needs,[2] but I had no knowledge of alternative religious ideas. Although I was drawn to the ancient female figurines as expressions of female power, I could not appropriate them as meaningful symbols in my own religious life because they were from cultures totally alien to my own. The hunting and gathering groups and the early agricultural settlements that had produced the cults of the goddess were unknown to me. I discovered that I needed to understand the societies that had produced these female cults before I could appropriate the meaning of the prehistoric goddess for myself.

One must start with the question of women's roles in prehistoric cultures, a topic which, given the lack of textual evidence, is controversial among scholars. How much power did women wield in prehistoric societies, in the earlier hunting and gathering economies or the later agricultural settlements that emerged in the Neolithic period?

It has been argued widely that although artifact and myth may suggest that females held important roles in early societies, the actual power of women was illusory. It has been contended in addition that the projection of female images (by men, presumably) can be in itself a sign of women's subjugation. Whether woman is depicted as a sex object (Astarte or Eve) or as a magical virgin mother (the cult of Mary, for instance), the symbol serves as the projection of male needs, not as the expression of female experience or values.

Some scholars have agreed that women have never held dominant positions in any society,[3] and thus have never been able to shape institutions to their own needs. I maintain that, although this analysis is true for many cultures, including our own, it may not apply to all early societies. In the first place, we simply do not know enough about the political organization of prehistoric groups to say for sure what was the balance of power between the genders. It seems premature, therefore, to close the door on the possibility that prehistoric women might have had the power to express themselves in an autonomous way in some areas of their lives.

It should be clear, however, that I am not talking about matriarchy. In acknowledging that matriarchy was a myth, we are free to ask a more realistic question about prehistoric societies: Did men and women perhaps relate in ways other than dominance/subjection? Male-dominant modes of social organization, after all, may not be the only types that humans have devised. Eleanor Leacock, for example, has shown that in some hunting and gathering societies women *share* political authority *when they have control over economic resources,* a point pertinent to the study of Neolithic women because the new wealth of that society was based on agriculture, domestication of animals, weaving, and pottery making—all activities associated in some degree with women's invention and control.[4]

Our problem lies, at least in part, in the word dominance, for it is, in fact, foolish to judge this material by our common definitions of power. When we apply the usual Western concept of centralized power or of "power over" to tribal or early urban societies, we may well be led to ask the wrong questions. Power can be seen as power *with* rather than power over, and it can be used for competence and cooperation, rather than dominance and control. In reflecting on the dependence on nature that prehistorical people had to contend with, it occurred to me that a cooperative use of power may have been necessary, indeed crucial, for them: it is this different concept of power which I want to use. It is possible that neither patriarchy nor matriarchy describes the methods of early community control, and that these terms, which come from nineteenth-century comparative religious studies, are useless in analyzing many preliterate cultures.

However the issue of gender relations is decided, an understanding of the roles prehistoric women played is essential to an analysis of their religion, dominated as it was by powerful female imagery. We must learn what we can about their economic roles and their family arrangements, matters which varied according to the natural resources and level of technology of each society. For this reason, rather than surveying goddess cults over the centuries and vast geographical areas in which they were found, I will focus on the evidence for a female cult in one society, an early urban center of Anatolia that thrived during the sixth millennium B.C.E. This site, called Çatal Hüyük and rich in evidence of a female cult, was excavated by the British archaeologist James Mellaart. By studying its burial customs, its family organization, the sources of its wealth, its shrine decorations and carved figurines, we will be able to reconstruct much of the social, economic, and religious life in a Neolithic town.[5] Then, and only then, can we answer whether it was possible for women there to assert themselves autonomously, that is, to express their spiritual needs directly through the public channels of power.

What was this culture like? To begin to answer this question, one must first picture a town built like a beehive: no streets, no large plaza, no palace; the homes were one-story abodes entered from the roof by a ladder and showed very little variation in wealth or possessions. Inside each one-room mud-brick house was a hearth and an oven. Every house had a large sleeping platform, always along the east wall, accentuated by wooden posts painted red; the skeletons of women and of some of the children were buried under this platform. Smaller platforms were scattered about the room in varying positions, children buried under some, men under others, but never children and men together. The houses were kept immaculately clean; refuse and sewage were disposed of in small courtyards.

This tightly constructed mass of housing was apparently a perfect defense: there is no evidence of invasion or violent destruction in the entire 1,000-year period of occupation.

The textiles and pottery found on the site are the earliest known and indicate a remarkably high level of specialization. Weaving of wool, flax, and grass; chipping and polishing of stone tools and weapons; and manufacture of beads, copper, lead jewelry, fine wooden vessels, and simple pottery were performed with such artistry that Mellaart assumes they were carried out by specially trained workers. Only gold and silver are missing from the materials he had hoped to find.

Trade was carried on far and wide in order to bring these raw materials to Çatal Hüyük. Timber was imported from the Taurus Mountains, shells from the Mediterranean, obsidian from the volcanic peaks near Çatal Hüyük, flint from south of the Taurus. But the wealth of these people lay primarily in their abundant farm produce. They ate plentifully from their crops of barley, peas, wheat, almonds, apples, and pistachios; they may have had yogurt and honey. They made wine from the hackberry and procured both milk and meat from domesticated sheep, cows, and goats.

Impressive as the economic production is, what is most extraordinary about this Neolithic town is that it has revealed a surprising number of shrines, one for every four or five homes in the area so far excavated. Because they are so numerous, they were most likely family shrines for extended family groups. We can identify them as sanctuaries by the ritual themes painted on their walls, their extravagant decorations of bulls' horns, bulls' heads, plaster goddess reliefs, cult statues, and evidence of elaborate burials. The practices of painting a handprint on sacred objects (the child's handprint on the breast of a goddess, for instance) and of destroying the sacred objects when a shrine fell into disuse offer conclusive proof that these buildings were set aside for a cultic purpose. However, there are no provisions for sacrifice, no altars or pits for blood or bones, such as later Bronze Age sites would lead us to expect. Although offerings were made to the deity—gifts of grain, stamp-seals, weapons, and votive figurines— there were no burnt offerings. Whatever the cult was, it was not bloody. What then was the religion that was celebrated here? Can we speculate without written records? Mellaart believes not only that we can speculate but that we must. He bases his decision on the wall paintings, which are the earliest-known frescoes painted on constructed walls. Admitting the difficulty of understanding these reliefs without an accompanying text, he maintains that we must interpret them, for if ever an early society tried to communicate through its art, this society tried, through these lively, natural, lifelike figures.

The earliest shrines have no goddesses, but are dominated by animal paintings and bulls' horns. Mellaart assumes that the hunt was then still an important food source and was seen as the great, magical source of power in the people's lives. Then, around 6200 B.C.E., the first goddess appears, in plaster outline on the wall, her legs spread wide, giving birth; below her, rows of plaster breasts, nipples painted red, are molded over animal skulls or jaws that protrude through the nipples. Already at her first appearance she is the deity of both life and death. She is the goddess of crops as well, as is suggested by the many statuettes of the goddess found in grain bins. Mellaart concurs with scholars who claim that women were the primary discoverers of agriculture and assumes therefore that women controlled this activity. He concludes that at Çatal Hüyük, agriculture was replacing hunting as the preeminent source of food and wealth, that the women controlled the new form of wealth and status, and that they introduced the new female religious images.

The goddess is faceless, usually naked, sometimes covered with a robe. She may be shown as a maiden (that is, not pregnant) who is running or dancing and whirling, her hair streaming behind her in the wind. Many times she is shown big-bellied with pregnancy, or actually giving birth. She is portrayed as the twin goddess, one of whom gives birth to an enormous bull. A human figure is pictured doing homage to a triple-goddess figure, the human covering her face as she approaches the deity. We may ask if the goddess shrines were special sanctuaries for women having difficulty in childbirth, for in one shrine, the skeletons of a woman and a baby were found buried together, and the body of a prematurely born child was carefully deposited nearby. One of the shrines is decorated entirely with floral patterns or textile designs, indicating that the goddess was the patroness of weaving. As the goddess of wild animals, she is shown flanked by leopards or holding leopard cubs.

As is true of many early goddesses, she is the deity of death as well as of life. Statues show her as a grim-faced goddess accompanied by a vulture. Many of the shrine wall paintings portray huge vultures attacking small headless human figures. In one such mural, painted above a row of four human skulls, the vulture in the painting appears to have human legs. Mellaart speculates from this that "priestesses" dressed themselves as vultures in order to preside over funeral rites. Because the care with which the dead were deposited indicates a belief in life after death, the goddess of death is in reality the goddess of another kind of life.

Mellaart is convinced that there was a priestly class at Çatal Hüyük, and that many of its practitioners were female. He observed that many abodes in what he calls the priestly quarter did not contain the usual equipment for weaving, spinning, reaping grain, or chipping stone. Lacking these standard tools, the occupants must have purchased essential items ready-made from the bazaar. He calls this professional priestly caste "elegant sophisticates."

Further evidence for a priesthood lies in the wall paintings, in which women and men dressed in leopard skins are shown chasing and dancing around deer and bulls. Mellaart assumes that only special persons could dress in rare leopard skins, and so concludes that some persons were set aside as priests and priestesses. His strongest evidence, however, comes from burials within shrines, where skeletons were buried with more care and with somewhat finer gifts than most of the home burials, although without indication of a wide differential in wealth. A number of the female skeletons are painted with red ochre (this does not occur outside shrines) and are buried with costly obsidian mirrors. Males are accompanied by belt-fasteners, perhaps those born with the leopard-skin costumes. These burials represent a privileged class of people, possibly a priestly class. The majority of these shrine burials are of females.

Statues of male gods, found only outside shrines, show either a very young or a bearded male, usually riding on or standing beside bulls or leopards. But except for these figurines, the male is not depicted; he is represented only by bulls' or rams' horns. Mellaart assumes that the bull or ram was considered "a more impressive exponent of male fertility" than the human form. Another statue shows two scenes: on one side, two figures embracing, and on the other, a woman holding a child. Mellaart interprets the child as the product of the embrace and surmises that the population of Çatal Hüyük understood the role of the male in human conception. Although the male is represented in far fewer carvings (usually in connection with hunting) and although he appears to be strictly subordinate to the goddess, Mellaart believes that the male deity was still an object of "confidence, pride, and virility" at Çatal Hüyük. He may have been both the goddess's son and her consort, but he was not sacrificed—the dying god was probably not yet known in neolithic Anatolia. Mellaart concludes that men at Çatal Hüyük were figures still to be reckoned with, and that whatever forms of community control existed were shared by women and men.

Some statues show the goddess with a daughter, others show a son. Her daughter may be her successor; there may have been a religious hierarchy of females.

In the last period in which Çatal Hüyük was occupied, a shrine devoted to the hunt, decorated with hunt murals, was painted over with white paint. A bit later it was destroyed in order to build over it a shrine dedicated to agriculture and weaving, containing nine statuettes of the goddess. Mellaart speculates:

> Sometime in the fifty-eighth century B.C.E. agriculture finally triumphed over the age-old occupation of hunting and with it the power of the woman increased: this much is clear from the almost total disappearance of male statues in the cult, a process [observable elsewhere in Anatolia later.][6]

What conclusions, then, can be drawn about the roles of women in this society? Looking at women in the family, Mellaart interprets the family burial customs, in which the woman is always, the man never, buried under the main platform, to mean that the family centered around the woman, was matrilocal and probably matrilineal, and that women chose their mates. In the public sphere, the usual public leadership roles appear not yet to have existed: there is no evidence of central political organization, no major role for the military (no evidence of warfare whatever for a one-thousand-year period), and finally, no hunting ritual. Therefore, the positions of power that men usually hold did not exist. But in contrast to our lack of knowledge about male authority, we have evidence that women exercised certain kinds of power at Çatal Hüyük, because its chief source of wealth was agriculture and women were in charge of its development. They controlled the home and the economy, and eventually they molded the religion, incorporating into it their concerns about the fertility of crops and humans.

Mellaart makes a case for an impressive female status in this Neolithic society, a status that enabled women not necessarily to control the society but to express their own values and experiences in it. One of Mellaart's arguments for female creation of the religion is a bit farfetched. He posits that eroticism in art is "inevitably connected with male impulse and desire"—a dubious premise—and that because the art shows no erotic symbolism, no phallus or vulva, but instead stresses breasts, navel, and pregnant belly, it must have been commissioned by women.[7] Whatever may have seemed erotic to the people of Çatal Hüyük, male or female, my own feelings are that the female representations convey a sense of dignity and great strength, more like objects of awe than sex objects. I agree with Mellaart, therefore, that the artwork does not appear to be erotic, and I would add that, with the exception of the ambiguous vultures, it does not relate to the demonic; it does not, therefore, express two of the themes commonly associated with the female in art. It is, rather, a celebration of fecundity and rebirth, and of the beauty and strength of textiles, animals, and women. And it is powerful.

More convincing is Mellaart's argument that Çatal Hüyük women created Çatal Hüyük religion by performing or controlling many of the economic tasks. In that way women gained authority in the community and became predominant in the priestly class. From this base they created the community's religion, a religion devoted to the conservation of life in all forms, devoted to the mysteries of birth and nourishment and life after death.

I know what I felt when I first saw the ruins of a shrine at Çatal Hüyük: the goddess figure above the rows of breasts and bulls' horns, her legs stretched wide, giving birth, was a symbol of life and creativity such as I had not seen in the Western church. But fertility symbols are no longer a sufficient image for twentieth-century women, just as the impressive agricultural society that produced those symbols no longer relates to our day. We cannot, therefore, go back to the ancient goddess cults.

But neither can we ignore these alternatives to the images of Western religions. Here is ample evidence that female deities were predominant in the religious lives of many peoples for millennia, and they raise the possibility that female values and experiences were expressed in the cults. They are thus an inspiration to women today who struggle to take their lives seriously (that is, gain economic independence) and to express their spirituality in new ways.

## Notes

1. Merlin Stone, *When God Was a Woman* (New York: Dial Press, 1976), chaps. 1 and 2.

2. See Carol P. Christ, "Why Women Need the Goddess," in *Womanspirit Rising*, ed. Carol P. Christ and Judith Plaskow (New York: Harper & Row, 1979), pp. 273–86.

3. Sherry Ortner, "Is Female to Male as Nature Is to Culture?" in *Women, Culture and Society*, ed. M. Rosaldo and L. Lamphere (Stanford: Stanford University Press, 1974).

4. Eleanor Leacock, "Women in Egalitarian Societies," in *Becoming Visible: Women in European History*, ed. K. Bridenthal and C. Koonz (Boston: Houghton Mifflin, 1977).

5. This material is based on discoveries made on the Anatolian plateau of Turkey by the British archeologist James Mellaart. He recorded his interpretation of the findings in *Çatal Hüyük* (London: Thames & Hudson, 1967). Some of my comments appeared earlier in my article, "The Uses of Archeology for Women's History: James Mellaart's Work on the Neolithic Goddess at Çatal Hüyük," in *Feminist Studies* 4, no. 3 (October 1978): 7–18. My thanks to the editors for their permission to use that material.

6. Mellaart, p. 176.

7. Ibid., p. 202.

# 2

JUDITH OCHSHORN

## Ishtar and Her Cult

Through all the fluctuations of historical change in the ancient Near East, during the ascendance and decline of civilizations that flourished and then were conquered or even supplanted, the great goddess Ishtar was so widely and continuously worshiped for thousands of years by so many different peoples throughout Mesopotamia that she is often referred to as the generic goddess. Indeed, although there were some variations in the ways in which her attributes were emphasized by different cultures over time, the preeminence of Ishtar is well-attested in divine pantheons that included literally hundreds of greater and lesser goddesses and gods.

Temples were built in her honor in many parts of Mesopotamia—in the city Alalakh alone, it appears that each of the fifteen levels excavated contained temples of Ishtar.[1] In one temple, oaths were sometimes taken to settle legal disputes in the belief that litigants would not dare to swear falsely in the presence of the goddess. In royal treaties, she was usually listed among the divinities who presumably would destroy those who broke their agreement. Seen by her supplicants as invincible in battle and as the source of fertility, she was prayed to by kings and commoners alike. Indeed, Ishtar was one of the paramount official and national deities, she was at the center of some of the most widespread popular cults, and, by the second millennium, had come to be portrayed as intensely involved in the personal lives of her worshipers, endowed by them with many ethical qualities.

Ishtar's name is etymologically identical with that of the West Semitic goddess Astarte, the South Arabian god 'Athtar, or Astar, who in Ethiopia was the god of heaven and who also appears in Ugaritic or Canaanite myths as both the female Athtart and the male 'Athtar 'Arīz. Perhaps her most significant designation is as the Semitic version of Inanna, "queen of heaven," the multifaceted and most enduring of all the powerful Sumerian goddesses. In addition, the association of Ishtar with male as well as female deities reveals an important ingredient of Mesopotamian conceptions of the divine that spilled over into cultic practices.

To see Ishtar through the eyes of those who venerated her requires a quantum leap of consciousness, in which both the goddess and her cult must be placed in the context of the outlook, concerns, values, and historical circumstances of their own time and locale. While it is of course impossible to measure the depth of individual religious faith from such a great distance in time, the extant literature suggests that from ca. the third through the first millennium B.C.E. the view prevailed that the divine was always present and in constant interaction with the secular in everyday life, or that these ancient societies were religion-centered.

## Conceptions of the Divine, and Divine-Human Relationships

The geography and climate of Mesopotamia heavily influenced perceptions of the nature of divinities and of divine-human relations. Often subject to violent extremes of weather that threatened the food supply—scorching winds, torrential rains, recurrent drought, devastating floods—Mesopotamians understood much of the inconstancy of the natural environment as the outward face of immense, violent, cosmic conflicts among divinities who, on the whole, were kindly disposed toward people but also behaved in unpredictable ways.

Thus, the early religious literature of Mesopotamia reflects the rather fatalistic comprehension that humans were created almost as an afterthought by goddesses and gods in order to serve them in menial fashion, to feed and clothe them. Slaves to the caprice of the divine, people apparently felt that the best they could hope for was that, through proper performances of rituals and sacrifices, divinities could be sufficiently conciliated to ensure an adequate food supply, avert natural and social disasters, and enable people to experience the immediate future as not too discontinuous with the past.[2] It is not surprising, then, that throughout the centuries of warfare from the third millennium on, victory was believed to signify the intercession of the divine on behalf of the victors, while the defeated attributed their loss to abandonment by their special goddesses and gods. On a more personal level, sickness and pestilence were believed to be caused by sin or by the failure to observe prescribed rituals for the propitiation of deities; by the second millennium, personal adversity and misfortune were lamented as consequences of the desertion of individuals by their "personal" goddesses and gods.[3]

In other words, the divine was seen as immanent in nature, and all events in the natural and social universe were considered a manifestation or result of divine activity and intervention. Goddesses and gods were endowed with a plurality of attributes, sometimes regarded as personifications of specific natural phenomena, such as the sun or thunder, or as responsible for a host of more general conditions, such as the creation and organization of the universe; the existence of social order, disorders, justice, and wisdom; dominion over the dead, and so forth.

All of these attributes appear to have been shared in rough equivalence by goddesses and gods: apparently the source, extent, and nature of divine power was not grounded in gender, except when divinities acted sexually or reproduced. No single goddess or god was believed to encompass all divine attributes, and neither goddesses nor gods were viewed as particularly benevolent or malignant on account of their sex. Therefore, the later elevation of the importance of gender in biblical texts represents a radical departure from both polytheistic conceptions of the divine and prescriptions for divine-human relationships.

Above all, divinity was conceived in anthropomorphic terms. Though incomparably more powerful than people and usually (though not always) immortal, goddesses and gods ate, drank, slept, loved, reproduced, hated, fought, and exhibited jealousy, anger, wisdom, compassion, remorse, deceit, and bereavement. Their affectional and familial relationships occasionally mirrored some aspect of social reality; for example, in the second millennium the great goddess of Elam was portrayed in serially, polyandrous, incestuous relationships with two of her divine male siblings, reflecting the practices of incest and levirate marriage in the Elamite royal family. But for the most part, relationships between divinities were different and far more inclusive than those prevalent in the human community.

Frequently, divine sexual liaisons and "marriages" occurred between mothers and sons or brothers and sisters, less frequently between fathers and daughters. Often these relationships were not monogamous, and sometimes they involved mortals and animals as well as deities. The notion of divine incest or illegitimacy as pejorative was foreign to the ancient mind; divine sexuality was considered normal, and female sexuality in particular was most often considered beneficial in its consequences for the human community; divine "body" and "spirit" were not dichotomized or valued differently. Maternity did not inhibit the ambition for power or the active sexuality of divine mothers, and there was no association of ritual impurity or uncleanness with the normal sexual and reproductive functioning of deities of either sex.

Further, irrespective of whether a female or male deity was credited with the creation of the universe—in Mesopotamia, the creator was usually female—it was most often the sexual unions of goddesses and gods that organized the universe. In addition, the protection and intervention of divinities of both sexes were solicited by communities of worshipers in order to assure the provision of an abundant harvest, the continuity and stability of society from year to year, and the success of community and individual ventures. While the models of divine behavior were not precisely replicated by humans, they were matched on earth by the fairly unrestricted participation of women as well as men in virtually every phase of polytheistic cult, even in positions of leadership, and by social sanctions for the active and open exercise of female sexuality in the service of the divine.

In sum, the worship of Ishtar developed out of a milieu that saw the individual as part of society; believed that society was part of the ordering of nature; interpreted cosmic phenomena as signs of divine immanence and activity; regarded human history as the product of divine intervention; looked to the content of divine-human relationships as the basis for the survival and prosperity of the community and the individual; and was characterized by attitudes toward the importance of gender and the nature of female sexuality that were substantially different from those encountered in Western monotheistic religions.[4] It was just such an outlook that pervaded the complex, highly developed civilization of Sumer, whose goddess Inanna came to be invoked interchangeably with the mighty Ishtar.

## The Influence of Sumer: Inanna and Ishtar

Situated around the confluence of the Tigris and Euphrates rivers, each of the city-states of Sumer was dominated architecturally and spiritually by a many-storied temple, or ziggurat, constructed to house a tutelary deity under whose auspices the city was thought to live out its destiny and to prosper. Where the deity of the main temple was female, the *en* ("high priest") was male, and where the diety was male, the *en* was female. By the end of the third millennium, Sumer was conquered by the Semites or Akkad to the north and, except for a brief renaissance, its political existence came to an end and its people vanished as a discrete ethnic group, or, more likely, were assimilated into what was later to become Babylonia.

However, though Sumerian ceased to be spoken, it continued to be used as the religious and literary language of the Semitic conquerors. In addition, Sumerian goddesses and gods were incorporated into the Babylonian pantheon along with the sacred and mythic literature that testified to their power over human affairs. The study of the Sumerian language and literature persisted in schools that trained scribes; this study was pursued for a very long time in the places that constituted the intellectual and spiritual centers for the Babylonians, Assyrians, Elamites, Hurrians, Hittites, Canaanites, and, it now seems, for the Eblaites as well.[5]

The incantation literature used by exorcists to rid the sick of evil spirits was written in Sumerian and was employed in essentially unchanged form throughout Mesopotamia for several thousand years. Thus, as the Sumerian goddess Inanna was fused with her Semitic counterpart Ishtar, Ishtar's cult was spread in part by the diffusion of Sumerian beliefs and practices through the continued use of its language and literature by diverse civilizations.

The spread of Ishtar's cult was facilitated in ca. 2300 B.C.E., when, in an attempt to consolidate his political control over all of Sumer and Akkad, Sargon the Great appointed his daughter Enheduanna as *en*, or high priestess, of the moon god Nanna at Ur (and possibly later as the high priestess of the heaven god An at Urak, as well). Though these appointments helped to unify both nations by the cultic union of the sacerdotal offices of Ur and Urak in the person of Enheduanna, it was her own lifelong devotion to the goddess Inanna—contrary to the usual cross-sex assignments of high priestesses to male deities—that helped the process of political union by her fusion of the Sumerian Inanna with the Akkadian Ishtar.

The first in a long line of royal high priestesses who presided over temples in Sumer and Akkad for the next five hundred years, Enheduanna was also a brilliant poet and hymnographer whose influence on subsequent sacred literature was so great that she was almost deified. Her hymn "The Exaltation of Inanna," one of the earliest-known Akkadian examples of this genre and part of a great cycle of hymns to the temples of Sumer and Akkad, contributed significantly to Mesopotamian theology. In it, Enheduanna eulogizes the vast powers of Inanna as a martial goddess and fertility goddess, both primary fields of power for Ishtar as well. While the identification of Ishtar with Inanna remained very close, with the passage of time a number of modifications in the character of Ishtar were elicited by the emergence of new needs and values in the human community, and the similarities and differences between these towering goddesses may be noted in some of the major literary and sacred writings of those early epochs.

For example, in "The Exaltation of Inanna" that goddess is described as of equal rank with the god An, head of the Sumerian pantheon, and in possession of all the divine ordinances. Even deities cringe in the face of Inanna's fury when people fail to pay her proper homage as a fertility goddess, and the vengeance she takes on the land and its inhabitants is terrible when she judges the latter and gives them "their just desserts" or decrees their fate.[6] In the startlingly androgynous vision of ancient Near Eastern polytheism, it is interesting to note how those awesome powers to judge people, decree their fate, initiate violence, and control fertility were all, in large measure, shared by some male divinities, among them the Sumerian Enlil and Ninurta and the Akkadian Shamash. This may help explain the seemingly contradictory responsibilities of Ishtar, for fertility and for victory in war, neither of which was seen as an essentially feminine or masculine trait, and both of which were crucial to community survival.

Centuries later, in "The Hymn to Ishtar"[7] written during the First Dynasty of Babylon (ca. 1600 B.C.E.), like the autonomous Inanna, Ishtar is shown as exalted, even supreme, among deities in the power of her words and decrees, and in her power over fate. But unlike Inanna, her physical charm and sexuality are also praised, foreshadowing a gradual diminution in the roles of most goddesses among Semitic peoples. Here is a theme that was to merge the identities of Ishtar and Inanna when the former was named as the source of the king's secular power, common (as shall be seen) to all the celebrations of the sacred-marriage rite.

Still later, "The Prayer of Lamentation to Ishtar"[8] from the neo-Babylonian period repeats her exaltation among divinities and her supremacy in battle. However, unlike Inanna, Ishtar is prayed to here as a goddess of compassion (not fertility), appealed to as one who will be moved by a litany of individual misfortune and will act mercifully. It may be argued that whether the goddess was seen as a source of judgment (as in "The Exaltation of Inanna") or as a source of compassion (as in "The Prayer of Lamentation to Ishtar"), both of these qualities represent some sort of ethical consensus on the character of justice and mercy in the community of believers, and both indicate a conception of divinity, in this instance female divinity, as concerned with moral issues.

"The Epic of Gilgamesh"[9] is one of the oldest, most widely proliferated literary works recovered from ancient Mesopotamia, dating in some of its versions to the beginning of the second millennium. Ishtar is described by the semidivine protagonist, King Gilgamesh, as sexually promiscuous and predatory. Paralleling the ferocity of Inanna when her sexual advances are rebuffed by the king, Ishtar entreats the supreme god An to unleash the bull of heaven in order to destroy Gilgamesh and his city, Urul. Her power is here shown as enormous when she threatens that if she does not have her way, she will release the dead from the netherworld so that they will outnumber the living. In her other guise as fertility goddess, she promises to provide enough food to sustain people in the wake of the divine bull's destruction.

In a tale of a flood (similar in many details to the Old Testament story), Ishtar is pictured in her compassionate aspect and is shown as equal in power to the active head of the Sumerian pantheon, the god Enlil. Out of disgust with people, Enlil inundates the world, and only one family, craftsmen, and animals are able to survive on a stout ship built under the direction of the god of wisdom, Ea. After the flood subsides and Utnapishtim, the Sumerian Noah, offers material sacrifices to divinities in thanksgiving, Ishtar finally and majestically appears. She accepts her moral responsibility for the disaster by deploring her assent to it in the Assembly of the Gods, laments its consequences for her "children" (humanity), and forbids Enlil to partake of the sacrifice because of his destructiveness.[10]

## The Sacred-Marriage Rite

It was perhaps in the sacred-marriage rite that the identities of the goddesses Inanna and Ishtar became indistinguishable. One of the most widely attested rituals performed throughout Mesopotamia for two thousand years, it was based on a sacred fertility drama described in poetic and priestly accounts that originated in Sumer early in the third millennium and focused on how to assure fertility to the land and its people.

The first instance of the sacred marriage involved the king Dumuzi (later deified for his participation in that rite) and an avatar of Inanna, most likely her high priestess. In its many reenactments, a king, representing Dumuzi, had sexual intercourse with "the goddess," consummated in an elaborately ceremonial and public setting, the temple of Inanna. Despite variations in accounts of the rituals surrounding the sacred marriage and the feast that celebrated it afterward, the substance of the sacred rite remained constant, even in later renditions when the Semitic goddess Ishtar and the deified king Tammuz replaced Inanna and Dumuzi.

What is common to all of the sacred-marriage literature is the dominance of the goddess, who selects the ruler privileged to cohabit with her, and actively and explicitly enjoys him sexually. The issue of this union is not her offspring but luxuriant vegetation and the fertility of the land (or a bountiful harvest), the goddess's endorsement of the king's fitness to rule (or the stability of the throne), and the goddess's promise that she will lead the king to victory in battle (or the survival of the social order). The reaction of the community was marked by jubilation and bliss, and while it is not certain how often this sacred marriage (*hieros gamos*) occurred, the evident meaning of this rite to the people of those times clarifies how Mesopotamians perceived Ishtar as satisfying some of their most basic requirements for survival and prosperity.

Unlike the Egyptian pharaohs, who were seen as literal incarnations of the god Horus in life and of the god Osiris after death, the rulers of Mesopotamia were viewed as mortals. The king was seen as an intermediary for the community in winning the favor of the divine; the welfare of society was believed to hinge on the good fortune of the king, who claimed the throne not through direct inheritance or succession but by divine election. Thus, when rulers were chosen as the "bridegroom" of the goddess, their self-designation was as "the overseer of Ishtar"; Sumerian and Old Babylonian royal inscriptions describe the king's relationship to Ishtar when they refer to that goddess as "the carrier, the fountainhead, of his power and prestige."[11] Indeed, not only is Inanna/Ishtar the source of the king's power, but the personal intervention of the goddess to guarantee his success, especially in war, also guarantees the continued welfare of the community.

Thus the sacred-marriage texts rapturously portray the active sexuality of the goddess as purely good, as yielding blessings for the king and the whole community. At least with reference to divine female sexuality, it held no connotations of evil or danger to the pursuit of righteousness by men. The goddesses' sexuality was celebrated as nonmonogamous, extrafamilial, and not linked to their reproductive capacity. The heart of the sacred-marriage rite resided in Inanna/Ishtar's great power over fertility, war, and the destiny of peoples and cultures; in her commanding role in actively choosing and sexually enjoying the king; in the energizing and beneficient nature of her sexuality in her aspect as goddess of love and fertility, and in the consequent good fortune for the human community which it, in turn, fervently commemorated.

Related to the sacred-marriage rite, but different from it in content and emotional affect, was the widespread cultic observance of the annual death of the younger Mesopotamian vegetation god after the harvest, marking the cycle of seasons and the onset of the earth's barrenness. Mourned variously as Dumuzi, Tammuz, Adonis, or Baal, his cult consisted chiefly of women, and the most complete account of its basis may be found in two myths, the Sumerian "Inanna's Descent to the Netherworld," inscribed at the beginning of the second millennium and the prototype for the Akkadian version, "Descent of Ishtar to the Netherworld," inscribed a thousand years later. The differences between them illuminate a change in attitudes toward the power of goddesses in Mesopotamian religions.

The older myth is more complete. It relates how Inanna, for unknown reasons, descends to the netherworld and leaves identical messages for the gods Enlil, Nanna, and Enki should she not return within a few days. In fact, she is divested of her divine power and prerogatives as she passes through the gates of the netherworld, and is then killed by her sister-enemy, the goddess Ereshkigal. While Enlil and Nanna tell her messenger that they can do nothing to save the "queen of heaven" in violation of the decrees of the netherworld, Enki, the god of wisdom, understands the full import of Inanna's message, namely that she will reverse the progress of civilization in Sumer to its primitive stages if she is not rescued from the realm of the dead.[12] Enki therefore devises a way to revive and rescue Inanna, but when she returns to the land of the living, even she must abide by the laws of the netherworld and provide a substitute to take her place. Dumuzi alone shows neither proper deference to his dominant partner in the sacred marriage or nor sorrow for her suffering. In retaliation, Inanna consigns Dumuzi to the netherworld as her surrogate, and it is only through the self-sacrifice of his sister that the deified king is doomed to spend but half the year among the dead, corresponding to the time between harvests.[13]

There are important differences in the myth of Ishtar's descent to the netherworld. Though she threatens to raise the dead to out-number the living if she is denied admission, she, too, is slain by Ereshkigal. However, Ishtar sends to the gods no messages or threats about what she will do to Akkadian civilization should they not rescue her. Instead Ea, the god of wisdom, notices that people, animals, and the land are sterile in her absence. That is why he arranges to restore her to life, and Ishtar does not herself choose her replacement in the netherworld. Hence, the scope of Ishtar's power is shown here as considerably more constricted than that of Inanna. Unlike Inanna, Ishtar is valued only for her power over fertility. She does not autono-mously set the conditions for her release from death. She is not the commanding bride in the sacred marriage but the faithful wife, for there is no mention of her dooming Tammuz to the netherworld for his failure to show her proper respect. Rather, when he surprisingly appears there at the end of the myth, Ishtar expresses compassion and concern for his presumably untimely demise, and she even requests that he be provided with courtesans to ease his death.[14]

## The Holy Women of Ishtar

The worship of Ishtar in one form or another was nearly universal and continuous in every part of Mesopotamia, and there is fairly general agreement among scholars that women's participation in cult was extensive, at least during the Old Babylonian period (the first half of the second millennium), when, like men, they served the temples as scribes, priestesses, judges, oracles, prophets, diviners, witnesses of legal documents, and the like. There is yet another area of agreement, namely, the designation of those women attached to the temples of In-anna and Ishtar who celebrated the specifically sexual aspects of the goddesses as temple harlots or sacred prostitutes. (It is the use of culturally loaded terms like harlots and prostitutes that seems prob-lematic and warrants reevaluation.)

Until very recently, most of our information about ancient Meso-potamian religious beliefs and practices came from allusions to them in the Bible and in the works of late classical authors (for example, Herodotus and Lucian) and Christian historians and com-mentators (for example, Clement of Alexandria). The problem inherent in all of these sources is that they either express a theologi-cal perspective antagonistic to polytheistic religions that, after all, competed with Judaism and Christianity for the spiritual allegiance of people; or they interpret the customs of alien populations through the biases of their own cultural attitudes and customs; or they professed to convey the meaning of much earlier cultic rites from random information available in later, hence different, times. In short, what had been lacking until only a century ago were firsthand accounts of polytheistic beliefs and sacred rites in Mesopotamia recorded by those who lived at the time they evolved, were engaged in these sacred rituals, and shared the widespread belief in their efficacy.

From the profusion of firsthand accounts to which we now have access—hymns, epics, myths, liturgies, lamentations—it seems inappropriate to use terms like "harlots" and "prostitutes," albeit sacred ones, to describe the *Ishtaritu*, or holy women of Ishtar. Early documents from Sumer indicate that temples dedicated to Inanna had a full complement of hierodules, or temple "prostitutes." However, in *The Exaltation of Inanna* and elsewhere, that goddess is referred to as "the hierodule of An," the supreme god of Sumer. Its theological significance, the elevation of Inanna to equal stature with An, seems to derive from the appearance of that phrase in the earliest Sumerian royal inscriptions where it signifies a throne name for the queen-consort.[15] By analogy, the temple hierodules of Inanna may have enjoyed enhanced status in the celebration of her sacred rites. Also, the evidence from the Sacred Marriage literature, in which the active sexuality of Inanna/Ishtar results in prosperity for the king and the community, and the joy of the latter at the consummation of the Sacred Marriage in which real women, as representatives/priestesses of the goddesses, must have participated, suggests the unlikelihood that people of those times (as different from our own) regarded the hierodules of Inanna/Ishtar as prostitutes in our modern sense of the word.

Likewise, in "The Epic of Gilgamesh" one of the characters is a harlot, presumably from the temple of Ishtar in Uruk, since the goddess assembles her "votaries," the "pleasure-lasses and the temple harlots," after the bull of heaven is slain there. However, except for the harlot's open sexuality, her behavior hardly corresponds to our own conception of harlotry in the context of the narrative. When Gilgamesh abuses the people of Uruk, the goddess Aruru compassionately fashions a hero, Enkidu, to tame and subdue him. This hero, half-human, half-animal, lives in innocence with animals until the harlot is sent from the city to have intercourse with him and lead him back to Uruk in order to challenge Gilgamesh.

Though ostracized by his animal companions after his sexual experience, Enkidu is also humanized and made wise by the harlot. She treats him like a son, teaches him how to eat and dress like a man, and makes him long for human companionship. Enkidu goes with her to Uruk, fights Gilgamesh to a draw, and the two become fast friends. As Aruru intended, Enkidu humanizes Gilgamesh. He ceases to abuse his subjects, becomes susceptible to a wide range of emotions and philosophical concerns, and together with Enkidu embarks on an adventure to achieve fame and benefit the city. Thus the active sexuality of the harlot (not unlike that of Inanna/Ishtar in the sacred-marriage rites) results in good fortune for both the ruler and the community.

Sometimes dedicated to the service of deities other than Ishtar, these ritual prostitutes were often called *quadištu,* and there are bits of evidence, some linguistic, some historical, which point to their importance in the cult in ways that seem irreconcilable with what we associate with prostitution. In Sumerian, the word *quadištu* simply means "set apart or taboo," and in Sippar during the Old Babylonian period (1894–1595 B.C.E.), there is no evidence that the *quadištu* attached to the main temple complex engaged in prostitution.[16] Moreover, the word seems related to the Hebrew *qdsm* ("holy' or "hallowed"), and there are references in their own times to priestesses of Ishtar in Babylonia and Assyria who sexually served the goddess in her rituals as "the sacred ones" and "the holy ones."[17]

It seems probable that at least early in the second millennium the status of some of these *quadishtum* was high, insofar as some of them were daughters of aristocratic families among the Hittites, Luwians, Hurrians, and Semitic Amorites. And Akkadian wisdom literature refers to a sacred prostitute only as "an Ishtar woman vowed to a god," a poor choice for a wife because she was not monogamous.[18]

## Some Scholarly Dilemmas

Part of the difficulty in assessing the roles of these priestesses and female votaries of Ishtar, who celebrated in their rites the sexual aspect of the goddess, stems from our own attitudes toward female sexuality, which are very different from those that prevailed in ancient Mesopotamia. It seems clear that these *Ishtaritu* were not prostitutes as we understand the word today.

All scholarship is culturally bound, and much of modern scholarship is marred by a cluster of unexamined ethnocentric assumptions. For instance, if one believes that the emergence of monotheism in the ancient Near East meant the discovery of the true divinity and marked an ethical advance for all humanity, the logical corollary is to trivialize and denigrate goddess worship insofar as it was an integral component of polytheism, and to see divine-human relations based on polytheism as somehow morally deficient. This position is reinforced by a number of other legacies from the past that burden and obscure our capacity for disinterested analysis.

Among these legacies are the elevation of the importance of gender, the emergence of a dichotomy between body and spirit, the emphasis on female chastity and monogamy, as well as a distinction between "good" and "bad" women on the basis of their sexual behavior, and the formulation of a double sexual standard for women and men. Most of these ideas are found in biblical writings, in the legal and familial structure of ancient Athens and Rome, and in much of the literature and philosophy these influential cultures produced.

Obviously, the religious vision of ancient Mesopotamia, which created goddesses like Ishtar who held captive the destinies of rulers and nations and which attributed all kinds of blessings enjoyed by the human community to the exercise of that goddesses' active, open, nonmonogamous sexuality, does violence to our own notions of the proper place and nature of the feminine. And while the spread of profane prostitution by the beginning of the first millennium clouded the cultic roles of sacred prostitutes somewhat, it may be more than accidental that up to now we have been unable to see Ishtar, her cult, and the sexual roles of her priestesses and female votaries in her sacred rites, through the religious vision of their own times. It may be well to remember that part of our own sacred literature equates idolatry, the worst of all sins against Yahweh, with female sexuality and promiscuity (cf. Ezek. 16:1–49, 23 and Rev. 17:15; 18:2–8, 21; 19:3).

## NOTES

1. Nadav Na'aman, "The Ishtar Temple at Alalakh," *Journal of Near Eastern Studies* 39 (1980): 209–14.

2. Cf. H. and H.A. Frankfort, John A. Wilson, and Thorkild Jacobsen, *Before Philosophy: The Intellectual Adventure of Ancient Man* (1946; reprint ed., Middlesex, England: Penguin Books, 1963), pp. 137–39, 216, 237–41; Henri Frankfort, *Kingship and the Gods: A Study of Near Eastern Religion as the Integration of Society and Nature* (1948; reprint ed., Chicago: University of Chicago Press, 1971); Thorkild Jacobsen, *The Treasures of Darkness; A History of Mesopotamian Religion* (New Haven: Yale University Press, 1976), pp. 25–27, 36–37, 43–44.

3. Cf. Edmund I. Gordon, *Sumerian Proverbs: A Glimpse of Everyday Life in Ancient Mesopotamia* (Philadelphia: The University Museum, University of Pennsylvania, 1959), p. 45, 1.7; Jacobsen, *The Treasures of Darkness*.

4. Judith Ochshorn, *The Female Experience and the Nature of the Divine* (Bloomington: Indiana University Press, 1981), chaps. 2, 3.

5. Samuel Noah Kramer, *Sumerian Mythology: A Study of Spiritual and Literary Achievement in the Third Millennium B.C.*, rev. ed. (Philadelphia: University of Pennsylvania Press, 1972), pp. 28–29; Giovanni Pettinato, "The Royal Archives of Tell Mardikh-Ebla," *The Biblical Archaeologist* 39 (1976); 44–52; Paolo Matthiae, "Ebla in the Late Early Syrian Period: The Royal Palace and the State Archives," *The Biblical Archaeologist* 39 (1976); 94–113.

6. Enheduanna, *The Exaltation of Inanna*, trans. William W. Hallo and J.J.A. VanDijk (New Haven: Yale University Press, 1968).

7. James B. Pritchard, ed., *Ancient Near Eastern Texts Relating to the Old Testament*, 3rd ed. with supplement (Princeton: Princeton University Press, 1969), p. 382.

8. Ibid., pp. 383–85.

9. *The Epic of Gilgamesh*, trans. N. K. Sandars (Middlesex, England: Penguin Books, 1960).

10. Ibid., pp. 105–9.

11. Cf. Jorgen Laessoe, *People of Ancient Assyria: Their Inscriptions and Correspondence*, trans. F.S. Leigh-Browne (London: Routledge and Kegan Paul, 1963), p. 24; A. Leo Oppenheim, *Ancient Mesopotamia: Portrait of a Dead Civilization*, rev. ed. (Chicago and London: The University of Chicago Press, 1977), p. 205.

12. Ochshorn, *The Female Experience and the Nature of the Divine*, pp. 82–87.

13. Samuel Noah Kramer, *The Sacred Marriage Rite* (Bloomington and London: Indiana University Press, 1969).

14. E. A. Speiser, trans., "Descent of Ishtar to the Nether World," in Pritchard, *ANET*, pp. 106–108.

15. Enheduanna, *The Exaltation of Inanna*, p. 50.

16. Rivkah Harris, *Ancient Sippar: A Demographic Study of an Old Babylonian City* (1894–1595 B.C.) (Belgium: Nederlands Historisch-Archaeologisch Instituut Te Istanbul, 1975), p. 328.

17. Cf. Addison Walter Jayne, *The Healing Gods of Ancient Civilizations* (1925; reprint ed., New York: University Books, 1962), p. 123.

18. *Cambridge Ancient History*, 3rd ed. (Cambridge: Cambridge University Press, 1973), 1, pt. 2: 715–18; Robert H. Pfeiffer, trans., "Akkadian Proverbs and Counsels," in Pritchard, *ANET*, p. 427.

# 3

## C. J. BLEEKER

# Isis and Hathor,
# Two Ancient Egyptian Goddesses

The culture and religion of ancient Egypt demonstrate several remarkable features. A significant feature is the favorable position occupied by women both in ordinary life and in state affairs. The texts and the sepuchral monuments show that the ancient Egyptians treated their wives and mothers with great respect. As a rule, a man had only one legal wife, though he might possess several concubines. The relationship between husband and wife is described as being cordial and close. On funerary monuments they stand or sit beside each other, the wife folds her arms around the neck of her man, accompanies him when he goes to his work, and is present when he goes hunting or fishing. Special respect is paid to the mother. The books of Wisdom, for example, teach that one should never forget the care that a mother has bestowed on her children. Sometimes, during the Middle Kingdom, for instance, descent is reckoned through the maternal line. It is difficult to ascertain whether this represents a final trace of a prehistoric matriarchate; at any rate, it is testimony to the important position that women generally occupied in ancient Egypt. They were not obedient slave-women, but the equals of their husbands.

This was true of the queen to an even greater degree. By marrying the pharaoh, officially called "the good god" and considered to be the son of the sun god, the princess or lady of lower rank who became queen acquired a new and very important status. She was raised to the position of an actress in the drama of divine kingship and thereby placed in an influential position that is evident in her titles: she is called not only "the king's wife," "the great or principal wife of the king," but also *itj.t* and *nswj.t,* names that are the feminine form of the official titles of the king. Their literal translation is ruler, or queen. They show that the queen had her share in the prestige of her royal husband.

Apparently she had occupied this position since the dawn of Egyptian history, for the queen already appears in this position on a relief of the sepuchral monument of Pharaoh Sahure, a king of the fifth Dynasty. To her name is even attached an elaborate set of titles that sometimes have a poetical flavor and in other cases give the impression of being juridically formulated.

As the consort of the divine king and the mother of the divine prince, the queen naturally possessed a certain amount of power. No wonder that ambitious queens used their influence for all kinds of intrigues. It is known that King Pepi II of the Sixth Dynasty had to encounter a palace revolt in which the queen took part. Many centuries later an analogous case is recorded of a plot against Pharaoh Ramses II. However, there were also many queens of a different character. It is a remarkable fact that in the Eighteenth Dynasty several royal women came into the foreground whose personalities are better known than that of any other women of antiquity. During the life of Ahmose, the founder of the Eighteenth Dynasty, three women played an important role: his grandmother Tetishezi, whom he remembers with great respect; his mother, Ahhotep, the ancestress of the Eighteenth Dynasty; and his wife, Nofretete, whose role as his good counselor appears in a text that gives a touchingly human picture of the way in which the royal couple solved certain questions in harmony. No queen had as much influence on the affairs on the state as Tiye, the wife of Amonhotep III. Though she was not of royal descent, she managed to acquire an influential position—apparently thanks to her strong character, her intellect, and the esteem in which women generally were held in ancient Egypt. Though the beautiful face of queen Nofretete is better known than her character, it becomes clear from the texts that she occupied a very favorable position at the court of her husband, Pharaoh Amonhotep IV.

The part that the queen played in the drama of the birth of the royal child has already been hinted at. The famous birth scenes of Queen Hatshepsut in the temple at Der el-Bahri describe how the sun god visited the queen mother in the shape of her husband and wooed her, resulting in the princely offspring. Playing an important role in this drama, the queen functions as the vehicle that conveys the divine substance to the royal child. The god, acting as the father, was an invisible figure in the background and the human father officially played no part at all. Thus the queen was the sole person who could actually guarantee the divine nature of the crown prince. No wonder that pharaohs who were not of royal descent, like General Haremheb, the founder of the Nineteenth Dynasty, married princesses of royal blood in order to strengthen their position. From this evidence we can see that the Egyptian queen occupied a sacral position. This view is corroborated by texts that inform us that the queen participated in the cult both in the daily order and during great festivals.

Considering the favorable position of women in general and the pivotal function of the queen in ancient Egypt, no one can doubt the importance of the feminine element also in the divine realm. There we encounter a number of goddesses with a more or less prominent character. Considering some of the most famous ones, an imposing figure was Nut, the góddess of the sky and as such the partner of Geb, the earth god. Next comes Ma-a-t, the goddess of truth, righteousness, social order, and cosmic order. It can be said without exaggeration that she held a dominant position in ancient Egyptian religion. Very ancient goddesses were Buto and Nechbet, who respectively had the shapes of a vulture and a snake, and who were connected one with the northern and the other with the southern parts of Egypt. Nut increased her renown by marrying Amon, the mighty god of Thebes. She manifests a martial nature, like Sachmet, who had her residence in Memphis. The complement of Sachmet was Bastet, who had the head of a cat. A well-known saying concerning certain goddesses is: She is kind like Bastet and terrifying like Sachmet. Another imposing figure was Neith of Sais, a cosmogonic goddess, the patron of victorious weapons and of the art of weaving. Furthermore, Seshat was the valuable aid of Thoth in furthering the art of writing and of scholarship. Nephthys, the sister of Isis, is a rather pale figure. Nevertheless, her part in the drama of the death and resurrection of Osiris is essential. The two goddesses who surpass all their female colleagues are Isis and Hathor, who in later centuries were partly amalgamated with other goddesses, although they were originally independent deities.

The ancient Egyptians worshiped many goddesses, as did other peoples of antiquity, such as the Greeks. There is, however, a striking difference. The late Dutch historian of religions G. van der Leeuw correctly remarks that in Greek religion all goddesses were mere figurations of the great mother goddess who was connected with the earth. The ancient Egyptian goddesses have a quite different nature in two respects: first, each originally possessed her own separate character that was maintained over the course of centuries so that the goddesses were not figurations of one and the same type; second, they were not intrinsically related to the earth, conceived as a divine, motherly being. Moreoever, the deity of the earth, Geb, was male. That Isis and Hathor were gradually understood as divine and motherly beings does not contradict this statement. Their motherly care for human creatures was a result of the part they played in the piety of their adherents.

## Isis: Her Name and Her Manifestation as Wisdom

In ancient Egyptian hieroglyphics Isis is called *s.t.* (It hardly needs to be recalled that the vowels of Egyptian words are unknown.) In

Coptic, Isis is named Ese or Esi, from which the Greek form of the name Isis originated. These linguistic facts provide the key to the original character of Isis. For *s.t* means "chair" or "throne." In the hieroglyphic writing it is represented as a simple, high seat with a short, straight back and a small footstool. There is reason to assume that this hieroglyph expresses the original nature and function of the goddess.

This means that Isis probably represents the throne, the holy seat of the pharaoh. This in itself is not surprising. It is a well-known fact that people of antiquity took important objects of daily use as divine beings, of which Egyptian religion offers several examples. The royal scepter was, for example, a kind of fetish. And hymns were dedicated to the crown that the king wore. In this context the royal seat gained its significance. The king received his authority by taking his place on the throne. The throne, so to speak, makes the king. In other words, the throne is his mother. The ancient Egyptians understood this idea not symbolically, but literally. This appears from a relief in the temple of Abydos depicting King Seti I seated on the lap of Isis, who in turn sits on the typical Egyptian throne. Since the beginning of Egyptian history, pharaohs called themselves sons of Isis. In the Pyramid Texts it is stated that Isis gave birth to the king, that she suckled him, and that she attended him as a mother. This conception has its mythical prototype in the care that Isis took for her son Horus. What Isis did for Horus, she is willing to do for the king, who bears the Horus name. It is true that there is a difference between Horus, the son of Isis and Osiris who defended his father, and Horus, the martial sky god. However, the two Horus gods have already in ancient times become mixed so that they could replace each other.

Isis is characterized by her wisdom. Curiously enough, the Egyptians indicated this quality of the goddess by calling her "great in magic power," hence, wise. According to the religious conceptions of antiquity, real wisdom consisted of insight into the mystery of life and death. This knowledge is creative; it evokes life from death. Thus wisdom was to the Egyptians equivalent to the capacity of exerting magical power. Isis possessed this gift to a high degree.

This appears, for instance, in a curious text relating how Isis obtained knowledge of the secret name of the god Re. It is well-known that in antiquity a name was considered to include the very nature of the person who bore the name. Thus the secret name of Re contained the mystery of his creative power. According to the myth, as Re grew old his mouth trembled and his spittle dropped on the ground. Isis mixed his spittle with a bit of earth and shaped a snake, which she placed on the path on which Re used to walk. When Re approached the snake bit him. Re cried out in pain, but he did not know what caused his illness. Isis, along with other deities, pitied him. She offered to cure him by her wisdom and her magic art on the condition that he would reveal his real name. Immediately, he listed a series of impressive names, but Isis was not deceived and insisted on knowing his secret name. Finally, Re was forced to comply with her demand and whispered his name in the ear of Isis so that nobody could hear the secret except the goddess. This myth means that the creator god is unknowable; Isis alone, the wise goddess, has insight into his being.

## Osiris, Horus, and Lamentation

Isis became famous as the wife of Osiris and as the mother of Horus. Perhaps she was originally an independent deity who patronized a city, either Buto or Behbet, which were both situated in the Nile Delta. Because the neighboring city Busiris was one of the centers of the cult of Osiris, it has been suggested that Isis had become associated with this god in prehistoric times. However, there is no solid proof for this theory; when Isis enters history she is already the wife of Osiris and in this capacity she gained great renown.

It is worthwhile to pay attention to the manner in which the famous myth of Osiris and Isis has been handed down. One would look in vain in the Egyptian texts for an unabridged version of the tale. What we find are allusions to the myth, which are meant to sanction certain cultic acts. The Greek author Plutarch was the first to render a coherent story of the adventures of Osiris and Isis. Rather than extensively depicting the myth of Osiris, it is sufficient to relate the part that Isis plays in the mythical drama.

After the murder of Osiris by Seth, Isis immediately became active by seeking the corpse of her beloved husband. Sometimes she was alone in her searching, but mostly she was helped by her sister Nephthys. As the death of Osiris was considered to be a dreadful mystery, the ominous words "to die" and "death" were evaded. In the Pyramid Texts it is stated that Seth cast Osiris to the ground in *Ndjt*, the mythic place of the murder, or that Osiris was drowned and that he lay on his side on the bank of *Ndjt* where Isis and Nephthys found him. A beautiful Osiris hymn from the Eighteenth Dynasty describes the search of Isis in the following way: "Isis sought for him [Osiris] without tiring, passing through the country in sorrow; she did not take rest until she had found him; she made shadow with her feathers, she produced air with her wings [she is here represented as winged, so that she could wave vivifying air to him], she rejoiced when she brought her brother to the bank." All these actions were intended to cause the resurrection of Osiris. Actually the two sisters succeeded in their efforts; Osiris arose from the dead. However, he did not return to the earth, but became the king of the netherworld.

Plutarch offers a few additional details to this story. He relates that Seth lured Osiris to lie down in a beautiful sarcophagus. Thereupon, his helpers suddenly rushed in, locked the coffin, bore it to the Nile, and let it drift off through one of the mouths of the river. Finally it was cast ashore at Byblos. After intensive searching, Isis obtained the coffin. As soon as she was alone with the coffin she opened it, laid her face on that of her dead husband, kissed it, and wept in a heartbreaking way. Her lamentation has special significance both in this myth and for Egyptian mortuary belief and practice.

After finding the body of her dead husband, Isis performed an act of great importance. She provided the dead Osiris with an offspring by giving birth to Horus. The Osiris hymn says that: "She raised the slackness of the weary [i.e., the phallus of the dead Osiris], received his seed, and formed his heir." Thus Isis took the initiative in the act of procreation. In a late Osiris ritual Isis takes pride in this "manly" deed by speaking the following words: "O Osiris, the first of the westerners, I am thy sister Isis; there is no god who has done what I have done, nor a goddess: I made myself to a man, though I am a woman, in order to make thy name live upon earth." The act is also depicted by showing Isis in the form of a bird descending upon the phallus of Osiris in order to impregnate herself.

After Horus was born, Isis educated her child in a hidden place in order to protect him against the evil designs of Seth. As soon as Horus became mature, she brought him to a hall that contained the divine court of justice. There a lawsuit against Seth was initiated, with the result that both Osiris and Horus were vindicated and Seth was condemned and punished. Thereupon, Horus received the office and the throne of his father. According to the hymn, this decision of the gods restored the cosmic order (Ma-a-at) and universal joy prevailed among gods and humans.

From time immemorial two figures took part in the funerary procession that conducted the dead person to the grave. They were the official wailing women, generally distinguished as "the big wailing woman" and "the small wailing woman." At an early age they were identified with Isis and Nephthys. During the journey to the tomb, they uttered not a single word, but we may assume that in the house of mourning they exercised their profession.

It is interesting to note that the same two wailing women also played a part in the cult of Osiris. Two papyruses have been preserved with the litanies of this cult. They have been published under the titles "The Songs of Isis and Nephthys" and "The Lamentations of Isis and Nephthys." The two women who recited these lamentations represent the mythic wailing women, Isis and Nephthys. Their activity goes back to the gesture of Isis, weeping over the dead Osiris. In the opening passage of "The Songs of Isis and Nephthys" instructions for the choice of the women is found: "Two women should be fetched, pure of body, virgins, the hair of whose body has been shaved off, round whose heads braids have been plaited, whose hand holds a tamborine and on whose upper arms their names have been written, viz., Isis and Nephthys." This is clear proof of the link between the funerary ritual of the ordinary dead and the cult of Osiris. The usual name of these cultic officials was *dr.tj*, a word indicating a soaring bird of prey. It was believed that the high pitch of the funerary lamentations reminded people of the shrill cries of these birds. This identification was likely the reason that the two divine sisters were often thought to be winged.

In order to understand the tendency of the lamentations one should know that besides expressions of grief, they were also evocations. They possessed the constraining power innate in the magical word and particularly in the magical song. They were meant to call Osiris back to life. In this sense they were indispensable to Osiris. By lamenting Isis—and, to a lesser degree, Nephthys—they rendered him the greatest service which they could bestow on him. For the two sisters do not sit down passively and give free course to their tears. They take care of the battered body of Osiris. The Pyramid Texts say concerning the dead Osiris, "You are washed by Isis, you are purified by Nephthys, your two great sisters who unite your flesh, who raise your members." In a later text Isis exclaims, "I gave wind to his nose, so that he should live"; that is, she waves with her wings to him the refreshing wind that in the hot climate of Egypt was considered the breath of life. Furthermore, it is said, "Isis provides you with life." Together the wailing women exclaim, "Raise yourself, you are risen, you are not allowed to die, your soul shall live." The chorus of this text concludes, "You triumph, O Osiris, prince of the westerns [i.e., the dead]." The striking feature of the quotations is that Isis acts as an energetic loving woman who by her care for the body of the murdered Osiris and by her magical word restores her husband to life. In this respect also she functions as the goddess of wisdom.

## The Universal Goddess and Her Mysteries

It has been noted that Isis was originally closely related to symbols of royalty, especially to the throne. This means that she was not directly connected with any part of the cosmos like other well-known gods, such as Re and Geb. Neither did she possess a chthonic background. However, by her function in the Osiris myth she was associated with cosmic events and natural phenomena. Accordingly, her significance grew and diversified, and she became gradually a beneficial goddess of nature. Thus she was identified with Thermuthis, the goddess of the harvest, and also with Hathor, the great patroness of Dendera. Furthermore, the Egyptians connected her with Sothis, the goddess of the star Sirius; she was viewed as the eye of Re, the sun god. The main center of her cult was in Philae, at the southern border of Egypt. From there her influence extended southwards to the temples of north Nubia and even to Meroë. In the last period of Egyptian civilization, when horizons were opened and people traveled over long distances, she acquired popularity in the countries around the Mediterranean Sea. Already in the fourth century B.C.E. she had a sanctuary in Piraeus, near Athens. Her cult spread also to the Greek islands. Next she conquered the western part of the Roman Empire, and traces of her cult can be found, for example, in Sardinia, North Africa, Switzerland, Germany, and Spain.

As the goddess of the harbor of Alexandria, she became the patroness of sailors. In her honor the so-called *navigium Isidis* was celebrated annually. It consisted of the launching of a small ship in order to open a favorable season for journey over sea. Thanks to Apuleius we possess a colorful description of the rite celebrated in Corinth. He describes how a gay company marched out to the seashore where the ship was launched. At the front of the procession there walked a group of oddly dressed people; next came women in white clothes strewing flowers, "stolists" with what was necessary for the goddess's toilet, so-called *dadophores* with torches, and *hymnodes* who sang with flute and *sistra*; and at last a group of initiated and priests who bore the images and symbols—including the golden jar, containing water of the Nile— stopped at the seashore. The ship of Isis was consecrated by certain rites and was loaded with gifts. Accompanied by good wishes, the ship put to sea. In this picture of the extension of the cult of Isis it should not be forgotten that her presence in Rome was particularly important.

In the course of time Isis became to a certain extent hellenized. This appears from a late image of her in the Greek style. Moreover, she was identified with goddesses such as the Greek Demeter and the Anatolian Cybele, both of whom belong to a type of great mother goddess. Thus Isis became a goddess of universal importance.

Some consideration should be devoted to Serapis (or Sarapis) because Isis gained in popularity partly through her partnership with this god. The name of the god is supposed to be a combination of Osiris and Apis, which is an actual historical possibility. However it arose, Serapis and Isis became the principal figures of a new cult that is alleged to have been introduced by King Ptolemaeus I (323–284 B.C.E.). This ruler, a general in the army of Alexander the Great, acquired Egypt at the partition of the empire. It seems that he introduced the new cult in order to offer a common belief both to his Egyptian and Greek subjects.

Considering the introduction of the worship of Serapis, both Plutarch and Tacitus provide us with interesting information, even though it can not be fully trusted. Ptolemaeus is reported to have witnessed in a dream an image of an unknown god who ordered him to transfer his big statue to Alexandria. Worried by the dream, the king consulted with his friends. One of them, Sosibos, a traveler of wide experience, told him that he had seen such an image in Sinope, a city at the border of the Black Sea. The king sent two ambassadors to this place, and with much difficulty they managed to transport the statue to Egypt. When it arrived Timotheus from Eleusis, and Manetho, an Egyptian priest who became famous for his book on the history of Egypt, drew from some of the emblems the conclusion that it was an image of Pluto, the god of the netherworld. They convinced Ptolemaeus that it represented the god Serapis. The center of his cult soon became the Serapeum in Alexandria. From its commencement the new cult showed a distinct Greek influence. Greek was the liturgical language. Artists shaped beautiful statues of Serapis, representing him as a dignified seated person with a friendly, somewhat melancholic face wreathed by curly locks and a full beard.

The cult of Serapis soon spread throughout the Roman Empire. Nevertheless the attitude of the Greeks and Romans towards the Egyptian cults was ambivalent. On the one hand, they were impressed by the high wisdom that the Egyptian priests possessed; on the other hand, they abhorred the typical Egyptian veneration of animals. The cult of Serapis therefore tried to avoid the objectionable features and was esoteric enough to kindle curiousity. Thus Serapis and Isis invaded Italy. In 105 B.C.E. there was already a Serapeum in Puteoli and at the same time an Iseum in Pompeii. However, now and then the animosity towards the foreign cults exploded. Isis chapels were repeatedly demolished. Not until the period of the later emperors did Isis get the unconditional support of these rulers. Her influence reached its peak in the beginning of the third century C.E., when her cult was a serious competitor of the Christian church. Isis was particularly popular with women. Though Serapis enhanced the popularity of his consort, it is remarkable that Isis gradually surpassed her partner. This is proven by the fact that the Egyptian mysteries that fascinated many people bear the name of Isis only.

All the new oriental religions introduced into Greece and Rome had a twofold feature. Besides the secret rites, there were daily services and festivals in which everyone could take part. This latter feature pertained also to the Isis cult. The daily service followed the ancient Egyptian pattern: with solemn gestures the priest opened the sanctuary in the morning, kindled the fire, shed water, and awakened the deity, who was carefully dressed and remained the object of worship during the day. In the afternoon or evening the sanctuary was closed with a short service. Two frescoes from Herculanum give a good impression of the sphere of the official Isis cult. The Romans were captivated by this type of religion because it appealed to their personal piety, which was neglected by the impersonal religion of the state. In addition other festivals were celebrated; the principal one was the launching of the ship of Isis. It took place on the fifth of March. But more important than these solemnities were the mysteries.

About 300 B.C.E. the cult of Isis took the form of a mystery religion. This means that there arose a closed society of adherents of Isis who celebrated secret and sacred rites into which one could be initiated in order to acquire the deep wisdom and the full salvation that the goddess could offer. Apparently the mysteries were a religious-socio-logical type of religion, which strongly appealed to the people of those centuries. The ancient national religions had in those days partly lost their authority and did not offer the personal care that people craved. In general there reigned a widespread spiritual uncertainty. People longed for a new religious truth. A number of oriental cults tried to fulfill this longing. Besides Isis, the Persian Mithras and the Anatolian Cybele, for example, won many followers.

According to the official doctrine, Isis herself had instituted the mysteries. In a great hymn in which she enumerates her virtues, she declares, "I taught people the mysteries." Plutarch discloses the mo-tives for this deed: "When the sister and the wife of Osiris, as his avenger, had tempered and extinguished the fury of Seth, she desired that the struggle, the danger and the wanderings which she passed through, being so many acts of courage and wisdom, should not be forgotten. Therefore, she wove into the most secret mysteries the images, indications of previous sufferings, and she instituted a doc-trine of piety and a consolation to men and women who find them-selves in the same misfortune." The last sentence is particularly note-worthy in that it reveals a side of the character of Isis which in that age became more and more prominent. She is a savior goddess, serving as a comforting example to the faithful in distress. She is able to redeem because she herself, through the courage with which she bore her suffering, had once obtained salvation.

The best information about the nature of the mysteries and about the part that Isis played therein is drawn from a book by Apuleius. It is a curious book that combines comical and scabrous stories with deep and profound ideas. Lucius, the principal character of the story, was changed into an ass by the misuse of a magical unguent. In this form he underwent a series of adventures. Finally he was released by the favor of Isis. By her instruction he ate from the wreath of roses that the high priest bore in the procession already described of the *navi-gium Isidis* in Corinth. Thereby he assumed the obligation to become a follower of Isis and to be initiated into her mysteries.

The people of antiquity expected that initiation into the mysteries would afford insight into esoteric wisdom with the hope of immortal-ity. The decisive act seems to have been the *epopteia*, a vision of the highest truth that was likely a dramatizing representation of some crucial events in the myth on which the mysteries were founded. It is evident that *epopteia* was a secret that the initiated was not allowed to divulge. Thus when Apuleius in his narrative reaches the moment of the initiation he lets Lucius affirm that he was not permitted to reveal what happened when he entered the inner chamber of the sanctuary. But in order to satisfy the curiosity of the reader, he relates what even the noninitiated are allowed to hear. Thereupon follow the famous enigmatic words: "I approached near unto hell, even to the gates of Proserpina, and after that I was ravished throughout all the elements, and I returned to my proper place; about midnight I saw the sun brightly shine. I saw likewise the gods celestial and the gods infernal, to whom I presented myself and whom I worshiped." These veiled words have become the object of various interpretations. Without offering another explanation, I might add that Lucius does not accurately describe certain mystery acts, but rather records his experience of the emotional hours of his initiation. Furthermore, one should keep in mind that for the people of antiquity initiation meant to die. During the preparations the priest declares that the initiation is "like a voluntary death and a difficult restoration to health." He adds that the goddess has the power "to let the initiated, as it were, be reborn and to bring them back on the path of salvation." Lucius himself celebrated the initiation as his birthday by arranging a banquet.

The initiation took place during the night. The next morning Lucius appeared, dressed in twelve stoles, having a precious cape on his shoulders, whereon beasts in various colors were wrought. This garment was called the Olympian stole. He carried a lighted torch in his right hand and wore a garland of flowers on his head. The text relates that he was thus adorned like the sun *(ad instar solis exornatus)*. He was ordered to stand upon a platform of wood in the middle of the temple in front of the statue of the goddess. After the curtain had been drawn, people assembled to behold him in his glorified form.

The reader of Apuleius's book will be surprised to learn that Lucius had to undergo a second and a third initiation. The second initiation took place in Rome. The goddess warned him in his sleep that he had to receive a new order and consecration. It was required because Lucius had become an adherent of Isis but was not yet a follower of Osiris. Apparently there were differences of order and ceremony in the cults of the two gods. The reason for the third initiation was alleged to be the fact that he left the stola in which the goddess dressed him in Corinth. The significance of this garment of initiation can be understood from a communication of Plutarch which says that "the dead followers of Isis are dressed in the holy garment, as a sign that they enter the hereafter with nothing else than this doctrine." These words reveal how great an impact the service of Isis had on the piety of her adherents.

In these three cases the initiation is performed at the command of the goddess. This fact calls for close attention. Isis proves to be a gracious goddess, but she is also a severe one. Her sternness manifests itself in the strict regulation that nobody can be initiated before being deemed worthy and called by the goddess. Moreover Isis ordered abstinence during the preparations for the initiation. Lucius was obliged, for example, to fast for ten days. In other respects, too, Isis exerts a severe discipline. It is said that she required the Roman ladies who followed her to cut a hole in the ice on the Tiber in midwinter and to plunge into the river three times. She also desired that at the entrance of the temple people should openly confess their offenses against her rules. While it is evident that Isis kept her followers under strict discipline, she also proved to be a gracious savior goddess, winning the devotion of the initiated.

## Hathor:  Her Name and Her Manifestations

The Egyptian Hathor is called *Ht.Hr,* usually translated as "the house of Horus." The hieroglyphic rendering of the name is the sign for a large house or a temple containing a falcon, the bird of Horus. The Horus represented here by a falcon is undoubtedly the sky-and-sun god and not Horus the child of Osiris and Isis. The two gods are inextricably linked, but typologically they are easily distinguished. Horus the sky god is a martial figure who combats his enemies; Horus the child of Osiris and Isis is the faithful son who stands up for and defends his father. By virtue of her name and its relation with Horus, Hathor is characterized as a sky goddess, a feature that will be discussed more fully later.

From time immemorial and particularly in later ages, Hathor was surnamed "the Gold" and "the Golden One." Gold, the noblest of metals, evokes thoughts of immortality and eternity. The Golden One is therefore an apt epithet for a goddess whose imposing personality and inexhaustible strength give the impression that she defies transience. Perhaps Hathor was given this epithet because gold glitters and because Hathor is described as a radiant figure.

Hathor is portrayed in three main ways. These representations are so similar that they may be termed variations of the same notion. First, she is portrayed as a female personage bearing headgear with two horns embracing a sun disc and ornamented with the uraeus, the snake that protects gods and kings. Sometimes this Hathor figure wears a cap in the shape of a vulture. She evidently borrowed this headgear from the goddess Nut, who appears as a vulture or as a female personage with a vulture cap. Second, she is depicted as a cow wearing the headgear of the first figure and also the *mnj.t* as a necklace. Apart from being a jewel that enhances the charm of Hathor, the *mnj.t* is also a musical instrument and a cultic object. By shaking this ornament and making noise with it, it was possible to win the favor of an eminent person, such as the pharaoh, or of the god-head. Actually the *mnj.t* was used on occasions not connected with the cult of Hathor, but it is and remains the special ornament of Hathor. Third, Hathor is shown as a female visage with cow's ears and a wig—or else crowned with the sistrum, the musical instrument typical of Hathor—which serves as the capital of a pillar. A striking feature of this representation is that here the goddess is seen full-faced. This is an unusual manner of portrayal, for the Egyptian gods are normally portrayed in profile. The unusual shape of Hathor's head, of course, is partly due to the fact that it forms the uppermost part of a pillar. Nevertheless, this shape accentuates the special position of the goddess in the Egyptian pantheon.

The wholly or partially theriomorphic shape of Hathor's effigy requires further explanation. It is a well-known fact that Egyptian gods can be recognized not from their physical traits, but from the emblems they bear or from the head of their sacred animal placed on their bodies. The relation between deities and their sacred animal is polyvalent. Sometimes the deity appears completely as an animal, as when Horus is portrayed as a falcon; sometimes the deity has an animal head, such as the ibis head of Thoth; often the god is accompanied by a sacred animal, such as Amon and the ram. The explanation of this relationship must be sought in the appreciation felt for animals. The animal is a fascinating creature because of its nature and habits that give the impression that it belongs to an entirely different order. This explains why it was possible to conceive of the animal as a manifestation of the deity.

It has already been noted that Hathor can appear as a cow goddess. To understand the meaning of this representation it is important to note that the Egyptians attached substantial value to the cow. The possession of a healthy herd was a matter of pride. The cow became a symbol of prosperity and even of vitality and immortal life. Secondly, it should be noted that as a cow goddess Hathor does not represent the peaceful, domesticated animal, but rather the wild cow that lived in the originally marshy region of the delta. This magnificent, semi-mysterious cow became a divine being, the symbol of fertile, abundant life. A vignette in the Book of the Dead shows Hathor as a cow emerging from a mountain on which stands the sign of the west, representing the realm of the dead.

Hathor is not the only cow goddess, others have also taken on this shape. The most important of these are Nut and *Mht wr.t.* Nut, the typical sky goddess, is sometimes portrayed as a cow. In a famous drawing she is arched as a gigantic sky cow above the earth, while the sun god sails across her back in his ship. *Mht wr.t*, the great flood, arose out of the primeval waters and gave birth to the sun god, who is placed between her horns. Immediately the question arises as to which goddess can claim to have the original cow form. There are grounds for awarding priority to Hathor. Ideologically, Nut is linked with her partner, the earth god Geb, both of whom are depicted anthropomorphically. As for *Mht wr.t* she has remained a purely mythological figure who never developed her own cult, unlike Hathor who was worshiped in many temples in Egypt where sacred cows were kept in her honor. The cow figuration of Hathor evidently appealed more strongly to the religious imagination of the ancient Egyptians, for Hathor eclipsed *Mht wr.t* completely.

As the goddess who promotes fertility, one of her epithets is *nb.t htp.t*, mistress of the vulva. She is the goddess who helps conception and birth. That is why women in childbirth pray to her for help. Hathor is expected to promote fertility in general. She is "she who, by her fertility, brings abundance in all Egypt." More particularly she is called "mistress of love." The term love, when applied to an ancient goddess, generally means that she stimulates sexuality. But Hathor also fosters affection between young people. The hymns testify to people in love turning to Hathor with the prayer that she may fulfill their amorous yearnings. A hymn directed to Hathor from a person in love affirms this conception:

> *I send a prayer up to my goddess* [*Hathor*].
> *That she may give me the present of my sister*
> [*the beloved*].
> *When two lovers are united, they acknowledge that*
> *this joyful event is a disposition of Hathor. A woman*
> *cries:*
> *Brother, oh, I am among the women*
> *destined for you by the goddess.*

The conclusion to be drawn from this hymn is obvious: Hathor is a mother goddess only in a restricted sense. She possesses no chthonic nature. Clearly, she promotes all forms of life in the animal, the vegetable, and also in the human world. In the last domain, however, she not only stimulates procreation, but also furthers affection.

## The Tree Goddess and Goddess of the Dead

The tree cult dates from earliest times and was widespread among the people of the ancient world. Even in ancient times there were no forests in Egypt. Thus a sturdy tree was valued for the shadow it cast in a country where the sun shone mercilessly and also as an embellishment of the landscape. In ancient Egypt trees were considered sacred, especially the sycamore and the acacia. It is not surprising that the tree plays a role in mythology. It is only a short step from a sacred tree to a tree goddess.

Although Hathor can be called a tree goddess, she is not the only tree goddess, sharing this honor with other goddesses, particularly Nut, Isis, and Saosis. Nut, the goddess of the sky, became patroness of the dead in later times. One way in which she performs this function is that she leans forward from a tree and gives food and drink to the deceased. The personification of Nut as a tree goddess is certainly not original, nor is that of Isis, which is analogous to it. Saosis, or Jusas, a goddess who was identified with Hathor, was associated with the acacia, although she is a numen of less importance.

It is evident that Hathor is a dominating personage as tree goddess. She appears to have absorbed in her person all sorts of nameless tree goddesses, eclipsing Nut, Isis, and Saosis. She became the tree goddess par excellence. She manifests herself in one tree in particular—the sycamore—and is therefore called *nb.t nht,* the mistress of the sycamore.

Not only does Hathor reveal herself in the tree, but she sits under her sycamore. The dead wish to keep her company. In the Book of the Dead the wish is often expressed that the dead may sit under Hathor's tree, in which she reveals her power of renewal.

The Egyptians were firmly convinced that the dead could conquer death and could reach a happy afterlife. Therefore they mummified the dead, celebrated an elaborate funerary ceremony, built solid graves, and instituted a cult of the dead.

In regard to fate after death, the Egyptians also placed their hope in Hathor. The goddess who granted abundant life on earth was also expected to take care of the departed. The texts give many instances of this conviction. In the Coffin Texts it is said of the dead: "Hathor has anointed him, she will give him life in the west (the realm of the dead) like Re, daily." From time immemorial Hathor was called *nb.t smj.t,* the mistress of the (western) desert, the necropolis and the realm of the dead. In this role she was especially venerated in the Theban necropolis. In the region she was associated with Amentet and Meresger. As her name indicates, Amentet is the typical goddess of the west. Meresger means "she who loves silence," a typical epithet, because the Egyptians called the land of the dead "the place of silence."

It is no wonder that Hathor appears in the royal Theban tombs. She is also present at the so-called "beautiful festival of the desert valley," of which we possess a clear description. It consisted of a visit of the sacred bark of Amon to the Theban necropolis. During the festivities Hathor was constantly present.

What do the dead expect of Hathor? First, the deceased hopes that Hathor will give the benefit that she can offer as tree goddess, that is, a refreshing drink from her tree. Second, the deceased wishes to sit under her tree and to be admitted to her retinue, declaring proudly, "I am in the retinue of Hathor." The deceased takes pride in being in the service of Hathor as her secretary and in being allowed to attend to part of her toilet by fastening the *tstn,* a garment or ornament of unknown form and purpose.

The relationship of the deceased to Hathor is so close that the former often identifies with her. In a spell in the Coffin Texts we read: "I am Hathor, I have appeared as Hathor, who is descended from primeval age, the queen of the All." Women in particular were identified with Hathor. This does not mean that they placed themselves on the same level as the goddess. It implies the hope and the conviction that the dead might participate in the creative and renewing life of the godhead.

## The Sky Goddess and the Sun-Eye

Hathor's many-sided nature is further manifested as a sky goddess when she is called "mistress of the sky." In the Pyramid Texts it is stated that the king will ascend "to Hathor, who is in the sky." In the Coffin Texts the dead say: "Hathor, reach me thy hand, [so that] thou takes me up to the sky." In the Book of the Dead the deceased says "I am a distinguished beautiful person; prepare my path to the place where Re, Atum, Kheprer, and Hathor are." Since Hathor is mentioned together with Re, Atum, and Kheprer, it seems logical to conceive of her as a deity of the diurnal sky. There are also, however, good reasons for considering her to be primarily the goddess of the nocturnal sky. In this way she functions as the goddess of the dead, for the nocturnal sky is often viewed as the netherworld, called *Dw 3t*. In this case *Dw 3t* is localized in the nocturnal sky. The proof of this is that Hathor sometimes is pictured as a cow with stars on the points of her horns and on her body.

Paradoxically, Hathor, goddess of the nocturnal sky, also plays the role of the sun-eye. This apparent contradiction is resolved when we realize that according to the Egyptians the sun god originates from the dark night. We find this idea expressed in the picture of Hathor as sky cow, bearing the sun disc between her horns.

The sun-eye is connected with a myth that we know in various versions. In this short article only the main features can be sketched. The myth has two main variations: in one, the sun-eye is sent forth to seek Shu and Tefnet (or to chastise rebellious enemies of Re); in the other, the sun-eye is enraged, removes itself, and is reconciled to Re by Thoth. To these versions can be linked the story of Tefnet, the savage lioness in the Nubian Desert, whose fury is calmed by Thoth and Shu and who is brought to Egypt, where she changes into a benevolent deity.

The behavior of Hathor as the sun-eye is clearly depicted in a remarkable myth that deals with an earthly revolt against Re, who had become old and feeble. Re called together the most venerable gods and asked for their advice. Nun, the oldest of the gods, proposed that Hathor, the sun-eye, should be sent out in order to chastise the rebels. Hathor did her work thoroughly. Thereupon, Re became afraid that she would exterminate mankind and he hurriedly ordered that a red dye should be fetched and mixed with a thousand urns of beer. This beverage was poured and the next morning Hathor saw the flood of beer, drank great quantities, became drunk, and forgot all about her instructions. Thus humankind was saved. In this myth Hathor is depicted as a martial goddess with a fiery temperament. Since she does not despise intoxicants, she is called "mistress of inebriety." Besides her association with inebriety, Hathor is also the mistress of dance, music, and song.

## The Cult of Hathor

Although Hathor was worshiped in many places from very ancient times, we have only scant information about most of these cult places. Only three centers of the Hathor cult are colorfully depicted: Memphis, the necropolis of Thebes, and Sinai. Moreover, thanks to the beautiful Hathor temple at Dendera it is possible to form some idea of the way in which the goddess was worshiped at the daily service and on festive occasions. The temple dates from the time of King Cheops of the Fourth Dynasty, but its present state was completed under the reign of the last of the Ptolemaic monarchs.

There is no extant record of the daily cult. Nevertheless, we may assume that the worship was conducted according to the pattern of the ritual of the daily cult in the Egyptian temple of which we possess the text. Moreover, certain representations in the temple give an idea of how the cult was performed. The main service was held in the morning and consisted of a rather elaborate ritual. The afternoon and evening services were simpler. It is not too bold to assume that the daily morning service of Hathor developed according to the same lines as that of Horus of Edfu, of which we now have evidence. The following elements can be distinguished: The bringing in of the water, introduction of the offering, purification of the offering, consecration of the offering, daily service at the sanctuary (this service consisted of entering the sanctuary, during which the following rituals were performed: preliminary rites, revelation of the countenance of the god, gazing upon it, and paying homage to it; a subsequent second entrance included the meal of the god, the toilet of the god, and finally the purification rituals), the service held in the temple while the high priest was engaged in the sanctuary, and the bringing outside of the offerings.

This rather fragmentary sketch of the daily cult can be supplemented by the testimonials of personal devotion provided by a number of texts. First, it appears that personal names are formed by a compound with Hathor, a testimony to her popularity. Second, there are series of hymns composed in honor of Hathor that prove that the goddess was highly loved as well as held in awe, as is seen in this quotation:

> *Worship Hathor, the Lady of Dendera, in all lands,*
> *for she is the mistress of fear.*
> *Worship Hathor, the Lady of Dendera, in all lands,*
> *for she dispatches the gods of vengeance against the foe.*

But gratefulness for her benevolence is also voiced, especially for the children she gives. Thus a poet exhorts the worship of Hathor:

> *So that the goddess lets your wives*
> *bear sons and daughters.*

*So that they may not be barren*
*and you may not be impotent.*

The cult of Hathor evokes among the people an optimistic joy and enthusiasm that lifts mortal beings into a higher sphere.

Attention should be focused next on the festivals of Hathor. Their number increased considerably over the course of time. Part of our information about them is drawn from the great festival calendar of Dendera. It appears that although Hathor plays a leading role on certain occasions, the festival as such is not held in her honor exclusively. For the sake of brevity we can skip such festivals and concentrate our attention on four festive rituals that can be considered as ritual manifestations of some of her characteristics.

The first ritual of this category is the festival of the plucking of the papyrus for Hathor. Opinions differ as to the origin and significance of this festive act. Some think that it originated from the poetic custom of plucking flowers, especially the papyrus, for a beloved. But it must have had a deeper meaning, because the papyrus was the token of renewing life. According to a second explanation, the real meaning was not the plucking, but the rustling of the papyrus. This playful shaking of the papyrus is supposed to be the invocation and propitiation of Hathor, who, as the savage cow was supposed to live in the marshy regions of the Nile Delta.

The second festival to be recorded was celebrated on the twentieth day of the month of Thoth and was called "the festival of inebriety for Hathor." People drank wine in great quantities in honor of the goddess. This habit created a sacral drunkenness—not the same as an ordinary befuddling of the senses, but rather a kind of ecstasy that suited the nature of Hathor. This goddess was known to become wrathful at times and needed to be pacified by intoxicants. Moreover, Hathor liked gladness and her adherents were not slow in following her example.

The third festival is the ceremony that took place on certain days of the month of Tybi known as the festive voyage of Hathor. The motivation for this festival is as follows: "The ceremonial was inaugurated for the goddess by her father [in this case, Re]; it was celebrated for her when she returned from *Bwga* [in Nubia]." These words hint at the myth, already recorded about Hathor and the sun-eye, that relates how the savage goddess Tefnet, with whom Hathor is identified, was induced to return to Egypt. This explanation does not fully cover the significance of the ritual. The voyage by boat, on waters potentially symbolic of chaos and death, is actually an expression of the victory of the goddess over these destructive forces.

The fourth festival is the voyage of Hathor to Edfu, where she visited the god Horus. It is generally believed that Hathor celebrated in Edfu the so-called "holy marriage" with Horus. In my study *Hathor and*

*Thoth: Two Key Figures of the Ancient Egyptian Religion* I tried to prove that this idea is highly questionable. Hathor is an independent personality; she does not have a fixed partner, though several gods on various occasions act as her companions. Hathor's visit to Edfu was a friendly meeting of two neighbor gods. The festival at Edfu in which Hathor participated had a complex nature. First, it was a commemoration of the victory of Horus over his foes. Second, it had an agrarian tendency, and third, the dead were involved. As sun-eye, as goddess of fertility, and as patroness of the dead, Hathor appeared as a figure whose presence was almost indispensable.

## Conclusion

When Isis entered history, she moved in the sphere of sacred cultic objects. Her name indicates that she is the royal throne. There is no chthonic feature in her being. She developed an almost humanlike personality in the myth of Osiris. Many texts throughout the history of Egypt testify to the fact that the actors of this mythic story were extremely popular: Osiris, the wise king of humankind; Seth, the treacherous brother who killed him; Isis, the devoted wife who, together with her sister Nephthys, succeeded in attempts to revive Osiris; Horus, the faithful son who defended his father; Anubis and Thoth, the faithful friends and helpers. Compared to the rather passive Osiris, Isis is an energetic and resourceful deity. No wonder that her dignity and importance increased over the course of time. When her cult spread in the Roman Empire she became a universal goddess, a great motherly figure. It is a natural consequence that she became the central figure of the mysteries that, as we may assume, gave solace and spiritual guidance to many uprooted people. At that time she revealed herself as a savior goddess, a form that from the beginning belonged to her nature.

Hathor was not directly connected with the earth as the source of creative forces. On the contrary, her name discloses that she had a connection with the sky. She was a mighty goddess with a complex nature appearing in many guises. Alternately she was a cow goddess; a tree goddess; a patroness of dance, music, and song; a bestower of all abundance; a protectress of the dead; a sky goddess, and the sun-eye.

As cow goddess she was the motherly being who promoted fertility. As tree goddess she had the same function, for the tree is the manifestation of renewing life. It is little wonder that she was beloved by both the living and the dead. The deceased hoped to sit under her tree in complete bliss. The living allowed themselves to be captured by the ecstatic trend of her cult. Not withstanding her fiery nature, Hathor remained faithful to the cosmic order (Ma-a-t) by chastising rebellious individuals in her role of sun-eye.

In a polytheistic religion like that of ancient Egypt, it was inevitable that Hathor come into contact with many gods and goddesses. Thus she was called the mother and also the partner of Horus. Actually Hathor did not have a partner. She was too independent to be fettered by conjugal obligations. One might say that she was a true feminist in the divine world.

There is an obvious polarity in Hathor's being. The Egyptians gave expression to this notion by saying that she could be as wrathful as Sachmet and as gay as Bast. On the one hand, she is martial; her wrath is much to be feared. As mistress of drunkenness, she reveals a tumultuous nature. On the other hand, she reveals herself as a lovable, benevolent being, always ready to help and to bestow the goods of life on her adherents.[1]

## NOTES

1. This article is based on the following studies: C.J. Bleeker, "The Position of the Queen in Ancient Egypt," in *The Sacral Kingship* (Leiden: E.J. Brill, 1959), pp. 259–68; *De moedergodin in de oudheid* (The Hague, 1960); "Isis as Saviour Goddess," in *The Saviour God: Comparative Studies in the Concept of Salvation Presented to Edwin Oliver James,* ed. S.G.F. Brandon (Manchester: Manchester University Press, 1963), pp. 1–16; "Isis and Nephthys as Wailing Women," in *The Sacred Bridge: Researches into the Nature and Structure of Religion* (Leiden: E.J. Brill, 1963), pp. 190–205; and *Hathor and Thoth: Two Key Figures of the Ancient Egyptian Religion* (Leiden: E.J. Brill, 1973).

# 4

## CHRISTINE R. DOWNING

# The Mother Goddess among the Greeks

The goddesses of Greece with whom we are most apt to be familiar—Hera and Athene, Aphrodite and Artemis, even Demeter and Persephone—are participants in a polytheistic pantheon dominated by all-father Zeus, whose meeting place is high on Mount Olympus or in the sky. They are complex and vivid personalities, clearly defined, easily distinguished from one another, very human-like creatures whose connections to aspects of the natural world is no longer directly apparent. Yet implicit in some of the myths and more visible in the cults devoted to them is evidence that each of these goddesses has some original connection to vegetation ritual. They are highly developed and specialized forms of the primordial mother goddess. The Greeks called this goddess of the beginning Gaia (or Ge), which means earth.

> The Homeric Hymn to Earth
>
> The mother of us all,
> the oldest of all,
> hard,
>     splendid as rock
> whatever there is that is of the land
>     it is she
>     who nourishes it,
>     it is the Earth
>     that I sing.[1]

Gaia is not simply mother, she is *earth* mother. Indeed she differs from the later goddesses in that she *is* and remains earth, earth recognized as animate and divine. Gaia is never wholly personal, never entirely humanized—not even in Homer or Hesiod. This is not a deficit; it does not mean she is thereby somehow less than the so completely anthropomorphic Olympians (who may wield the thunderbolt or drive the chariot of the sun but are not themselves the lightning flash, the solar disc; who may take on the shape of a bull in sexual pursuit or of a swan in flight but without forfeit of their humanlike personalities). Gaia reminds us that the divine is transhuman and prehuman—there from the beginning—not simply a human projection. Because of this she is the primordial source as no humanlike mother can be.

Yet she is not earth as an abstraction, not the earth but earth, especially that particular expanse of earth that for each of us is earth, from which we know the earthiness of earth. For the Greeks the particular place where Gaia's presence was most evident was Delphi. Most of us probably associate Delphi and its oracle with Apollo, but before Delphi was Apollo's it was Gaia's. The Greeks experienced Delphi as the navel of the earth. The omphalos that marks it as such is its most sacred monument. This is where the world came into being. This is preeminently the place where earth and sky, human and divine, come together. Even in classical times there was still a temple to Gaia near the Castalian spring.

When the oracle was Gaia's it probably took the form of dream incubation, the quest for the kind of knowledge that emerges from hidden depths. Aeschylus suggests that the transition from Gaia to Apollo was a peaceful evolution; Hesiod and the Homeric hymn to Pythian Apollo present a more violent struggle. Python, a female dragon created by Gaia as guardian of the shrine, was slain by Apollo to make possible his usurpation of the oracle. Gaia responded by sending dreams to all those who might otherwise have come to consult Apollo's wisdom, until Zeus was persuaded by Apollo to order her to desist.

Gaia is the living presence of earth; a reminder of the time when matter was still rebellious, long before one could imagine it as terra firma. She reminds her worshipers that matter is *still* rebellious, alive and eruptive. Gaia is earthquake and volcano, molten lava and shifting rock. She is earth as it is in itself, not earth as subdued by humankind. She is goddess of all that grows but never the goddess of agriculture. (Indeed, in Greece the agriculture rites are so entirely civic, political affairs that a goddess as far removed from being a fertility goddess as Olympian Athene can be their patron.) Gaia signifies all that cannot be brought under control. She is divine; she transcends the human. She is that very transcendence but as an earthly, shaped, present, appearing reality.

To understand Gaia as *only* earth, to reduce her to being a personification of an aspect of the natural world, is to miss the point. Gaia is earth made invisible, earth become metaphor, earth as the realm of soul. She is never just vegetal fertility nor even the physical globe at its most volatile and destructive.

She is for life but for ever-renewing, ever-changing life, for life as it encompasses death. Gaia rituals included animal sacrifice as well as offerings of cereal and fruit; they may in archaic Greece as in many vegetation cults have included human sacrifice. The Orphic hymn addresses her thus:

> *Divine Earth, mother of men and of the blessed gods,*
> *You nourish all, you give all, you bring all to*
> *Fruition, and you destroy all.*[2]

There is a within-ness to Gaia; souls live in her body. The Greeks understood that souls inhabit earth, not sky. The dead live in her depths. There is much evidence that Gaia is a chthonic deity. On the Areopagus her statue stands with those of Hermes and Hades. At Athens, Mykonos, and probably Delphi, she was worshiped in association with the dead. Indeed, the omphalos at Delphi was very likely originally a grave mound, clear evidence of a connection to a chthonic cult. The Attic *genesia* (also called a *nekysia* "a descent into the under-world") was an All Souls' festival, when offerings were brought to family graves. The *anthesteria*, which in classical times was celebrated in honor of Dionysos, was probably originally a mournful festival consecrated to Gaia and the dead, and even in the classic period Gaia was still involved. Gaia's rituals, like other chthonic rituals and the rituals of the mystery cults, suggest the possibility of a different kind of identification between the worshiper and the goddess than we find in the worship of her Olympian offspring. Gaia's devotees experienced ecstatic and orgiastic possession (as was also true in the cults devoted to her biforms, Rhea and Cybele).

Gaia is also the giver of dreams and of mantic oracles. Though Hermes is the divinity most closely associated with the interpretation of dreams, Gaia is their source. Her prophecies come not from being able to read the stars or the entrails of birds or beasts, but from her deep knowledge of what is really (and inevitably) going on.

One cannot understand Gaia simply in human or psychological terms. Nevertheless, she is nature moving toward emergence in personal form. The most usual artistic representation of Gaia expresses this beautifully—she is shown as a human woman emerging breast-high from the earth itself.

In Homer, though Gaia has a definite shape, she is more than a vague and inchoate conception of the whole earth as animate and conscious, she is not as concrete and personal as her Olympian offspring and not personally active. She is the presupposition. Because earth is always near at hand and cannot be escaped, she is guarantor of the most serious oaths. Even the gods swear by her.

In Hesiod, though Gaia is still clearly *earth,* she is, nevertheless, more personalistically conceived. According to his *Theogony,* in the beginning there was Chaos, by which he means simply emptiness, pure potentiality, a yawning abyss. Then, by a process of spontaneous emergence, appear Gaia and Tartarus, along with Eros, Erebos (Darkness), and Light. Tartarus represents the within-ness of earth, its dark unknowable interior; Gaia its giving forth; Tartarus its chthonic aspect, earth's relation to death and soul; Gaia its relationship to vegetation, physical life, fertility. But the two cannot really be separated. Tartarus is Gaia's within-ness, Gaia is Tartarus's self-externalization.

## Gaia and Her Offspring

To be creative is Gaia's very essence. To be Gaia is to give birth to something other than herself, to heterogeneity. Her first creations are her parthenogenetic offspring, sea and mountain and sky. Though she then mates with her own dark double, Tartarus, and with sea and sky, she is still their origin. All things begin with the mother, even fathers. Of these primal divine beings only Gaia has a cult. The others belong to mythology, to cosmogonic reflection, but are not experienced by the Greeks as living, active principles, as is she. The others are supplanted, Ouranos by Zeus, Pontus by Poseidon. She is not; indeed, she participates in the supplantation.

According to Hesiod, Ouranos and Gaia co-parented not only the twelve Titans but also a race of one-eyed Cyclops and of hundred-handed monsters. Because Ouranos found these latter creations ugly and terrible, he hid them in Gaia's depths and did not allow them to emerge. But it is Gaia's very nature to give forth. Thus, she is in great distress at having to contain these creatures within her. She solicits the aid of the youngest of the Titans, Cronos, to accomplish their release. When next Ouranos comes to make love to her, Cronos springs forth from his hiding place and, using the sickle his mother had fashioned precisely for this task, cuts off his father's genitals. The falling drops of blood are received by Earth, who conceives and gives birth to the Erinyes, the giants, and the tree nymphs. From the foam surrounding the sea-tossed member Aphrodite emerges. Ouranos is henceforth relegated to the sky, and there serves as the very figure of distance, uninvolvement, abstraction.

Cronos (with his sister Titan Rhea as consort) takes his father's place and gives birth to six children. But Gaia and Ouranos warn that he is fated in his turn to be overcome by one of his children. So, one by one as they are born, he swallows them. Once again it is Gaia who intervenes on behalf of the emergence of life. She deceives Cronos into swallowing a stone instead of his last-born child, Zeus, and she secretly rears her grandson. When Zeus grows up, he tricks Cronos into disgorging the swallowed stone and children and then fights against his father, with his siblings, the Cyclops, the Hundred-handed, and one of the Titans, Themis, as allies. The battles are of truly cosmic proportions—sea and earth and even the wide heavens are shaken by them. Hesiod's descriptions of the clamor, heat, and confusion are magnificent.

But though Gaia sides with Zeus against the Titans, when he next begins to battle them she is on their side. The Titans are Ouranian; they seek to contest the Olympians for heavenly supremacy. The Titans win her support because they are truly earth-born (not at all the huge ogres of fairy tale). It seems to her that Zeus intends to deny his common origin with all her other creations and offspring. This so enrages her that she proceeds to engage in the creation of new monstrous forces to pit against him, most notably the fearsome dragon Typhoeus, from whose shoulders grow a hundred snake heads. Here as always, Gaia shows herself for life and against any stifling order.

It is in her very nature to create, to bring forth variety, heterogeneity. She is ever fertile; a drop of Ouranos's blood or of Hephaestus's semen impregnates her, but she is as likely to give birth to the monstrous as to the beautiful. She groans and protests, feels essentially thwarted when Ouranos forces her to contain her own children in her body (in contrast to Cronos, who swallows his progeny in order to feel safer, who feels threatened by what he does not contain). Gaia's emanations are projections of her own being, each catching one aspect of her own protoplasmic fullness. To know her fully is to see her in that which emerges from her.

Among the pre-Homeric offshoots of Gaia the most important are Themis, the Erinyes, Demeter, and Persephone. Each reflects a different aspect of Earth. Themis, daughter of Gaia and Ouranos, shares many of her mother's functions and attributes, including her knowledge of the future. (It is she, for instance, who warns Zeus against the threat posed by any son born to Metis.) Delphi was hers after it was Gaia's and before it became Apollo's. As bride of Zeus she is mother, among others, of Dike (Justice) and of the Fates. She comes to be associated particularly with righteousness and communal order in society. But it is important to see the significance of its being an earth goddess that thus represents righteousness—for this suggests that right order in the human realm to the Greeks meant harmony with the natural order.

The Erinyes, the Furies, also represent the forces that insist on such right ordering and emerge to reestablish it when it is disregarded. They come into appearance especially to extract retribution for the most heinous crimes—matricide and oath breaking. But the Erinyes are all along also the Eumenides, the consoling ones. The aboriginal conception associated them with marriage and childbirth, with retribution (though the former, too, are bloody events), and as bringers of a gentle death (as to Oedipus), not only as avengers.

Demeter and Persephone in their essential bond with one another represent the two aspects of Gaia, the vegetative and chthonic. But

Demeter is associated more with cultivation than is Gaia; she is the corn mother, not really the earth mother. She is human, too, especially in her bereavement and grief, as Gaia never is. Persephone is the goddess of the underworld but never just a goddess of the world of soul; she is always also the beautiful young goddess of spring as it manifests itself in tender leaf and half-opened bud, in the rushing streams and the freshness of bird song. To hold soul and earth together, the hidden and the appearing—that is Gaia's gift.

Gaia is the all-mother, the mother not only of the gods but of human beings as well. There are many different tales of how the primordial human sprang directly from Earth: one speaks of Erechthionius, whom Gaia conceived when Hephaestus's semen fell to earth; another of Cecrops, who was born from the earth with a snake's body. There is a story to the effect that once in anger Zeus determined to destroy the whole human race with a flood. Only Deucalion and Pyrrha were saved; as they longed for human companionship they were told to throw over their shoulders the bones of their mother. They picked up stones and tossed them behind them: Deucalion's stones became men, Pyrrha's women.

All humans have their source in Gaia. But Pandora, the first woman, is Gaia in human form. Her very name, "rich in gifts," "all-giving" (a name also of Earth itself), suggests this. In Hesiod's account she is fashioned by Hephaestus of earth and water. In vase paintings, where she is often represented as a creation of Prometheus, her iconography is indistinguishable from Gaia's—she is Gaia emerging in human form from the earth, an earth worked up by Prometheus's (or Epimetheus's) hammer. In Hesiod she is associated with the letting loose of many evils into the human world, including sickness and death. Pandora is indeed Gaia's manifestation: the giver of all gifts, both welcome and unwelcome.

## Eclipse of the Goddesses

Probably each of the Olympian goddesses was originally a pre-Hellenic local earth goddess—Hera in Argos, Athene in Attica, Artemis and Aphrodite somewhere in the Near East. In this sense, each *is* Gaia. Nevertheless, Hesiod's attempt to distinguish the Olympians from the original mother derives from a genuinely mythopoetic sensitivity. It is of the essence of the first mother to give birth to a rich variety of daughters. To remember Gaia's relation to these later goddesses is not to say that they are nothing but Gaia herself under other names, but rather that she is the ground out of which their figures emerge.

Today, the most familiar goddesses are, as we are so often reminded, the goddesses of patriarchy. As they are presented to us by Homer, Hesiod, and the tragedians, the Greek goddesses are not very attractive creatures. These texts all exhibit a deep suspicion of feminine power; they all seem concerned to validate the priority of the social over the natural order, and to record the establishment of a "rationally based" policy in which rulership is no longer to be determined matrilineally. The original ties of the goddesses to the natural world have been rationalized or reduced to metaphor. Athene is no longer the Acropolis rock and Artemis no longer the Arcadian wilderness. Aphrodite is no longer the mist rising from sea to sky, or the rain falling from sky to earth, though she may still envelop a favorite hero in a cloud to hide him from an enemy's fatal attack. Some once-potent goddesses (Ariadne and Helen, for example) are in the classical literature reduced to human status. Artemis, the goddess who within the Olympian pantheon is seen as still bound more to the natural than to the interhuman world, is represented in the *Odyssey* as a clumsy child, out of her climate when she leaves her forest haunts. The goddesses' chthonic aspect, their relation to death and transformation, like their relation to the natural world and to vegetal fertility, is emphatically ignored, except in the case of Demeter, the goddess of the grain, and Persephone, the goddess of the underworld (and Homer manages to avoid paying much attention to them).

The establishment of the Olympian order was a revolution, as is made plain in Hesiod's *Theogony* in the account of Zeus's battle against all the generations of divine begins who had preceded him (including eventually even Gaia, the mother who had at first encouraged him against his father). Within the hierarchy thereafter ruled by Zeus (especially in Homer's accounts) the goddesses clearly become subordinated divinities. Aphrodite, who in Hesiod is recognized to be generations older than Zeus, is in the *Odyssey* represented as the daughter of Zeus and Diane. That Hera was known to be a more ancient divinity than Zeus is symbolized in Hesiod by her being his elder sister; in Homer she becomes not only a needy, dependent spouse but a younger sibling. Even Athene, whose stature is less diminished, is made into a goddess entirely dependent on male power, proud to be motherless, Zeus's parthenogenetic creation.

The goddesses are not only subordinated to the god, they are defined as being in their very essence related to men, each in a very particular way: Hera is wife, Athene is father's daughter, Aphrodite is the responsive beloved, Artemis is she who shuns men. Thus they are represented from the perspective of male psychology, and consequently both sentimentalized and denigrated.

Each goddess, too, has had her dominion and powers much more narrowly delimited within the Olympian world than was true earlier. Aphrodite is now only the goddess of physical beauty and human sexual love; Artemis is primarily the goddess of the hunt; Athene the protectress of cities and patron of the arts. Not only is each given a distinct sphere of power but, especially in Homer, the goddesses are represented as implacably hostile to one another. It is the unmitigated rivalry betwen Athene, Hera, and Aphrodite that gives rise to the Trojan War (a rather backhanded recognition of the continued potency of the goddesses).

## Goddesses and Motherhood

It is striking that in the classical presentations the domination of the Olympian goddesses by patriarchal power is symbolized by their being represented as cut off from their mother. Demeter, Hera, and Hestia were swallowed by their father immediately after birth; Aphrodite was born (at least according to Hesiod's account) out of the semen that surrounded her father's severed genitals after Cronos had thrown them into the surging sea; Athene (according to the same source) emerged full-grown from father Zeus's head. Of the major Olympian goddesses only Artemis had a mother—a mother whom she seems to have mothered from almost the moment of her own birth. The newborn daughter immediately sets about assisting with the delivery of her twin brother Apollo, and on many other occasions rescues Leto from insult or danger. There is much that is instinctively motherly in Artemis, especially her tender solicitude for all that is young and vulnerable, animal or human. Indeed, at Ephesus, she was worshiped as the many-breasted great mother. Yet the classical Artemis is a virgin who never bears a child of her own; she shuns the world of men and lives in the forest on the fringes of the inhabited world. She represents the persistence of the natural, the untamed, even within the Olympian hegemony—but a naturalness that had become infertile.

Nor are any of her sister goddesses more whole in their mothering. Like Artemis, Athene and Hestia are childless. Though Hestia can love generously and impartially—and in Rome, as Vesta, becomes a prototype of the good mother—she seems, perhaps in consequence of the early loss of her own mother, to be deeply suspicious of close personal attachments. Athene is a devoted and dependable friend, she is a protectress of the generation of young children on whom the future of the polis depends, but she carefully protects herself from sexual passion and explicitly (in Aeschylus's *Oresteia*) avows an allegiance to father-right and implicitly accepts Apollo's declaration "that the mother is no parent of that which is called her child." Aphrodite's marriage to Hephaestus is sterile; her children are the incidental consequences of the self-indulgence of her passionate attraction to an Ares or an Anchises. She loves Aeneas, the issue of the latter liaison, and tries to protect him as best she can during the Trojan War and his subsequent journey to Italy, but she takes no part in rearing him. In her mothering, she displays the same kind of adventitious dispensation of favors that characterizes her sexual involvements. Though Hera is wife to all-father Zeus, their marriage, too, can hardly be regarded as bounteously fertile; Hera is preeminently wife, not mother. Her daughters (Hebe and Eileithyia) are but pale shadows of herself; her sons, Ares and Hephaestus (who, at least according to some accounts, are parthenogenetic offspring), serve her primarily as pawns in her incessant battles with her husband. Her stepson and namesake, Herakles, is the prototype of the hero who must take on one impossible task after another in the never satisfied hope of receiving her blessing. Demeter's boundless love for her daughter, Persephone, seems at first glance to represent an idealized version of maternal devotion—yet a closer reading suggests it may be her overinvestment in her child that makes Persephone's abduction by Hades a necessary denouement. In these goddesses the Greeks represented in divine proportions the mother who abandons her children or holds them too tight, the mother who uses her children as agents in her marital struggles or to fulfill her own frustrated ambitions.

## Childhoods of the Goddesses

The myths about the childhoods of the goddesses seem to offer us a vision of the sadness and pain, the vulnerabilities and weaknesses, inherent in childhood. To paraphrase Nietzsche: the goddesses justify human life by living it themselves, the only satisfactory theodicy ever invented.

The fantasy element seems evident in the myth of Persephone's childhood. The representation of a primal dyad between mother and daughter, not intruded upon by a father or siblings, could fairly be called "a family romance"—as if the blissful first weeks at the breast could be prolonged forever. Zeus, the most royal and powerful father imaginable, never appears, so the mother never turns away from the child and is never disparaged. This is truly a divine childhood, and though Persephone outwardly becomes a maiden she remains until her abduction a dreamy self-enclosed child.

But Demeter's own childhood is different, spent within her father's body along with the other four children he swallowed as soon as they were born. Robbed of a connection to her birth from birth, she tries to create a fantasy bond with her daughter, overidentifies with her, seeks to give her the childhood she was herself denied. She is childish (not harmoniously childlike) in her raging grief when Persephone is taken from her. Because she had no real childhood of her own, she seems to see childhood sentimentally and to be easily overwhelmed by its negative aspects.

Hera's childhood is essentially the same as Demeter's, but as an adult she lives out her unlived childhood differently. First, she, too, tries living through her children. But whereas Persephone was a more beautiful and vibrant version of Demeter, Hera's daughters, Hebe and Eileithyia, are but pale shadows of their mother. Because they are reduced in her mind to being but pawns in her battles with Zeus, her sons are crippled, Hephaestus physically, Ares psychologically. She had sought to mother Zeus, to make him her well-sheltered son; she had asked him to mother her, wholly enclose her as her father had when she was young. When she discovers the inadequacy of all these modes of asking others to provide her with a childhood, she realizes she must herself go in search of that lost childhood. She returns to her motherland and reimagines the unlived childhood; only then, knowingly carrying her own childhood within her, is she represented as ready for real relationship.

Artemis's childhood has some of the same elements as Persephone's. Zeus is again the absent father; experientially, Artemis has only a female parent, one who is inordinately proud of her. But Artemis is robbed of her childhood by having a mother much more obviously childlike, dependent, and vulnerable than is Demeter. The myths suggest that her childhood midwifery may lead Artemis to be too insistently self-sufficient in her adult form, and to be unwilling ever to renounce the solitude of the child. She remains tender toward children but easily becomes impatient with the childishly dependent adult. There is something eternally *young* in her way of being alone and distant; she, too, carries her childhood with her always.

At first glance Athene seems truly to have no childhood. She emerges full-grown out of the head of Zeus, dressed as a warrior, emitting a triumphant battle cry. She seems to begin life as the adolescent, closely identified with her father, with so-called masculine attributes like self-confidence and courage, intelligence and dispassion, and with the male world. She epitomizes the particular kind of strength that can come by denying childhood and the mother bond. The denial is hers: she seems proud of having had no mother. Yet *we* feel something missing; we feel that until we can connect her to her maternal origins there is something one-dimensional about her. Without her childhood she is incomplete. So we go in search of it and discover Metis, her wise and intrepid mother whose potential progeny threatened Zeus, and we understand Athene differently.

Aphrodite is motherless and fatherless; she is born of the depersonalized phallus immersed in the impersonal oceanic womb. She represents a self-sufficiency that is nontheless warm, receptive, and open. Older than Zeus, coeval with the Titans, she symbolizes a more cosmic beginning than just individual human birth and childhood. She reminds us that the archetype of the child, like that of the mother, pertains not only to personal psychology: part of the divinity inherent in the archetype comes from its transpersonal, cosmic aspect.

The mythological representations of the childhoods of the goddesses evoke the archetype of the divine child and the wonder of all beginnings:

In the image of the Primordial Child the world tells of its own childhood, and of everything that sunrise and the birth of a child mean for, and say about, the world. The childhood and orphan's fate of the child gods have not evolved from the stuff of human life, but from the stuff of cosmic life. What appears to be biographical in mythology is, as it were, an anecdote that the world relates from its own biography.[3]

Which returns us to Gaia, to the beginning of all beginnings, the primordial mother.

### NOTES

1. Charles Boer, *The Homeric Hymns* (Chicago: Swallow Press, 1970), p.5.

2. Apostolos N. Athanassakis, *The Orphic Hymns* (Missoula, Mont.: Scholars Press, 1977), p.37.

3. C.G. Jung and C. Kerenyi, *Essays of a Science on Mythology: The Myths of the Divine Child and the Mysteries of Eleusis* (Princeton, N.J.: Princeton University Press, 1969), p.80.

# 5

M. RENEE SALZMAN

## Magna Mater: Great Mother of The Roman Empire

The worship of a goddess as the earth mother of gods, men, and nature is attested in the Mediterranean world as early as the Paleolithic Age. Mother goddesses were worshiped primarily as fertility powers, for female fertility was associated with agricultural productivity in the natural world; in the human sphere, the mother goddess was similarly associated with aspects of productivity—birth, maturation, fertilization, fruition, death, and rebirth fell under her protection. In the Hellenistic age, the mother goddess was personified as Demeter in Greece, as Isis in Egypt, as Atargatis in Syria, and as Cybele in Anatolia.

It was the Anatolian goddess Cybele (whom the Anatolians worshiped as mighty mother of gods and men, protectress of cities in war, and mistress of animals and of the mountains in which she lived) who was the form of the mother goddess first adopted by the Romans in 204 B.C.E. The goddess Cybele—or "Magna Mater deum Idea," as she was called in Rome—was the first oriental deity officially adopted by the Romans. By studying the history of this cult in Italy—from its inception in 204 B.C.E. until its demise in the fifth century C.E.—we are in a unique position to trace the development and transformation of this oriental mother goddess into the Mother of the Roman Empire; we may also better understand the religious and political mechanisms that enabled Roman pagans to absorb and assimilate foreign beliefs into a peculiarly Roman system of religious thought, an ability which in part explains the vitality of Roman paganism in the Mediterranean world and the success of the Romans themselves as conquerors and rulers of this world. By the third century C.E., the system of beliefs of the cult of the Magna Mater had evolved from its original nature worship into a sophisticated system of spiritual beliefs that represented to contemporary Christians a major competitive religious ideology.

## The Coming of the Goddess to Rome

According to Livy, a Roman historian of the first century, the long war with Hannibal had strained the religious and social fabric of traditional Roman society, and the presence of several foreign religious cults in the city in the years 218–205 B.C.E. led to several outbursts of disorderly conduct. These foreign cults came to be viewed by the Roman aristocrats as a threat to the overall authority of the Roman state; the new cultic rites were officially banned by the magistrates in 213, but the cults themselves could not be suppressed.[1] In 205, when Hannibal was threatening Rome from the mountains of Bruttium, strange supernatural events, "frequent showers of stones," had raised the religious scruples of the people and so frightened them that the leaders consulted the ancient body of Roman oracles, the Sibylline books, for divine advice. According to Livy, an oracle was found saying that "if ever a foreign foe should invade the land of Italy, he could be driven out of Italy as defeated if the Idaean Mother should be brought from Pessinus to Rome."[2] The sanctuary of Apollo at Delphi confirmed the oracle, and a Roman delegation was dispatched to King Attalus of Pergamum to persuade him to allow the transfer of the goddess to Rome.

The Roman aristocrats, unable to eradicate the new oriental cults, turned to a traditional solution. The Romans had introduced other foreign cults into their land by means of an evocation (*evocatio*); most frequently, an attacking Roman general would "call out" the gods of the city under siege with the promises of a new cult and home in Rome, hopefully inducing the foreign god to leave his old city and thereby facilitate the Roman victory. This procedure had been used in cases of extreme emergency, as, for example, when an epidemic in Rome had induced the Romans to bring the Greek god of healing, Aesculapius, to their land in 293 B.C.E.[3] By officially adopting a foreign cult, the Roman aristocrats could more effectively control the cult and its rites. And in the case of the Anatolian goddess Cybele, there were political motivations as well as religious scruples: there were several powerful aristocratic families in Rome in the third century B.C.E. who claimed to be direct descendants of the Trojans who had fled with Aeneas from Troy, and they used this legendary association to support their claims to be the "first families of Rome." Since Cybele was associated with Mount Ida near Troy in Asia Minor (as well as with Mount Ida in Crete), these aristocrats could claim the goddess as a sort of national Roman patroness because of her traditional "Trojan" links. Even beyond these concerns with Rome, the aristocracy found it politically expedient to emphasize Rome's ties with Troy and Asia Minor at this time; the Romans wanted to secure relations with King Attalus of Pergamum to form a common front in opposition to King Philip of Macedon.[4]

This combination of religious, political, and social factors led to the official adoption of the cult of Cybele, now known as the Magna Mater or "Great Mother," in Rome. But would the Anatolians agree to her departure? In Livy's account of this legendary event, King Attalus of Pergamum willingly handed over the goddess, in the form of a sacred black stone (the stone itself must have been rather small since it was later used as the face of Cybele's cult statue in her temple in Rome). Political factors motivated King Attalus to acquiesce willingly, factors which Livy unfortunately does not relate. But the first-century Roman poet Ovid tells us that a minor miracle was necessary to persuade the king to let the goddess leave. After causing a slight earthquake, the goddess speaks:

> 'Twas my will that they should send for me. Tarry not: let me go, it is my wish. Rome is a place meant to be the resort of every god.

To this King Attalus replies in terror:

> Go forth. Thou wilt still be ours. Rome traces its origin to Phrygian ancestors.[5]

Ovid's dramatic description of this legendary event underlines the Trojan associations of the cult that were so important to the Augustan Age in which he wrote.

The goddess was put on a ship bound for Rome, where, in accordance with the mandate of the Delphic oracle, she was to be received by the best citizen of the city; this honor was granted to P. Scipio Nasica, only twenty-eight years old, whose patrician family was no doubt instrumental in the choice. The goddess arrived safely at Ostia, the port city for Rome. The entrance of the goddess into the city gave rise to several legends, one of which, fostered by the Claudian family, is particularly interesting in that it foreshadows the prominent role of Roman matrons in the cult: when the ship bearing the goddess ran aground on the banks of the Tiber and the goddess could not be moved, the patrician woman Claudia Quinta used the opportunity to prove her chastity, for she had been popularly charged with promiscuity, though she had not—and could not—be prosecuted.[6] Claudia merely touched the towline and the ship moved on; her success was taken as divine testimony of her chastity. This legend, indicative of the prominent role of women in the cult, also shows the typical Roman attitude toward female modesty, an attitude that associated chastity in women with the well-being of the family and, in a wider context, of the state: the turmoil of war had led to suspicion of Claudia, and her supposed infidelity was viewed as a threat to the stability of the state that had to be countered by a public demonstration of her chastity. This matrix of ideas is also found in connection with the vestal virgins of Rome, who were similarly charged with the spiritual well-being of the state.

The goddess was carried by Roman matrons into the city on 4 April 204 B.C.E., and was solemnly installed on the Palatine Hill. In the same year, the Roman general Scipio transferred the war with Carthage from Italy to Africa. Hannibal, compelled to meet him there, was defeated in 201. The prediction of the Sibylline books had come true: the foreign enemy, Hannibal, was driven from Italy. The Magna Mater was honored as the conqueror of Hannibal and as the mother of the Trojans, the legendary ancestors of the Romans.

Thus the Anatolian goddess had become a national Roman deity; a temple was erected to her on the Palatine Hill—an extraordinary honor, for foreign gods were not allowed to have their temples within the sacred walls of the city. The temple was dedicated on 10 April 191 B.C.E., and every year thereafter, on 4 April, a celebration in honor of the dedication of the sanctuary and of the goddess's entry into the city was celebrated there.[7] Originally a two-day festival, this celebration expanded until, in the Augustan Age, it lasted from the fourth through the tenth of April.

## The Cult of the Goddess

Ancient accounts of this April festival of the Magna Mater—known as the *ludi Megalenses* —are particularly interesting in that they demonstrate how the cult was intentionally "romanized" to conform to traditional religious practices and to minimize the dangerous, exotic oriental element of the cult. Ovid provides a full account[8] of the festival: a ritual procession (*pompa*) in the circus on 4 April commemorated the goddess's entry into the city with priests and joyous bands of worshipers. On the two main feast days, 4 and 10 April, a Roman magistrate (*curule aedile*) sacrificed a heifer to honor the goddess. On the days between 4 and 10 April, there were the usual games in the circus, and theatrical performances were added as early as 194 B.C.E.; the Roman dramatist Plautus staged *Pseudolus* ("Sly-boots") in 191 for this holiday, and several of Terence's plays were first performed on this occasion.[9] During this week of festivities, the Roman aristocrats held huge banquets to which they invited each other in turn, a practice in keeping with the dominant role that the aristocrats had played in the installation to the goddess in Rome. The role of the Roman matrons was similarly commemorated: Ovid recounts the ritual bathing of the cult statue of the goddess by her female worshipers, followed by her joyful conveyance back into the city. Thus the *ludi Megalenses* were organized as a national celebration, held at public expense with added financial support from the aristocracy.

But alongside of these Roman practices, Ovid notes the oriental aspects of this celebration:

> Eunuchs will march and thump their hollow drums, and cymbals clashing will give their tinkling notes: seated on the unman-

ly necks of her attendants, the goddess herself will be borne with howls through the streets in the city's midst.[10]

On these days, says Ovid, the eunuch priests of the goddess were allowed to run through the streets of Rome, begging for small donations, shouting and dancing wildly to the beat of pipes and tambourines, whipping themselves into a frenzy to the amazement (one suspects) of the Roman onlookers. One can thus understand why the head priest (*pontifex maximus*) of Roman state cult confined the rites of these priests to the temple sanctuary of the goddess on the Palatine Hill.

Moreover, only oriental priests were allowed to serve the Magna Mater; Roman citizens were not allowed to hold priesthoods until the time of Emperor Claudius (41–54 C.E.). The reasons for this proscription are many, but most important was the fact that the priests of the goddess practiced self-castration; their very name, *gallus* ("cock") makes an ironic point of their condition. Several cult myths explain this practice as a ritualized imitation of the fate either of King Gallus, who emasculated himself in a state of frenzy caused by the goddess, or of the young shepherd Attis, beloved of the Magna Mater. Ovid recounts Attis's fate:

> In the woods a Phrygian boy of handsome face, Attis by name, had attached the goddess to himself by a chaste passion. She wished he should be kept for herself and should guard her temple, and she said, "Resolve to be a boy forever." He promised obedience, and "If I lie," quoth he, "may the love for which I break faith be my last love of all." He broke faith; for, meeting the nymph Sagaritis, he ceased to be what he had been before. For that the angry goddess wrecked vengeance... Attis went mad... He mangled, too, his body with a sharp stone, and trailed his long hair in the filthy dust; and his cry was, "I have deserved it! With my blood I pay the penalty that is my due. Ah, perish the parts that were my ruin!" His madness set an example, and still his unmanly ministers cut their vile members while they toss their hair.[11]

The *galli* of the goddess, driven to frenzy by whirling dances and self-flagellation, imitate Attis's act of emasculation in a most primitive and dangerous fashion, using such instruments as a sharp stone, a potsherd, or a knife. To devotees of the goddess, this represented the ultimate act of devotion; the Roman attitude, however, was a mixture of bewilderment and pity for their half-male, half-female state, a state that the *galli* accentuated by dressing conspicuously in long gowns, turbans (*mitras*) on their heads, and masses of jewelry, with hair grown long and bleached like a woman's. The fascination that these *galli* held for the Romans prompted a Roman poet of the first century B.C.E. to describe the experience of one of the *galli* who awakens, horrified to discover the results of his frenzied self-castration. Catullus ends his poem with the fervent prayer:

Goddess, powerful goddess Cybele, Dindyme's sovereign, Protect my home, O mistress, from all this insanity, Let others be enchanted, let others be entranced.[12]

Clearly, it was felt that this was not the way for a Roman to behave. Although Emperor Claudius reformed and reorganized the cult to allow Roman citizens to serve as priests of the cult of the Magna Mater, Emperor Deomitian (81–96) forbade Roman citizens to practice emasculation.[13]

## The Cult of Attis

The worship of Attis, the young male consort or son of the goddess, became increasingly important in the worship of the Magna Mater from the first through the fourth century C.E. In the several legends concerning Attis, one can discern a consistent mythical pattern to explain his religious significance in the cult: Attis is driven mad by the jealous mother goddess; in his frenzied state he commits self-castration and dies; but the mother goddess mourns him so violently that he returns to life and is reunited with her. Attis's fate thus represented triumph over death; and the rebirth of Attis the renewal of life in a happier mode of existence.

Attis's triumph over death and his rebirth was celebrated in a cycle of holidays, introduced by Claudius, that took place from the fifteenth to the twenty-seventh of the beginning of spring and the time of the revival of vegetation, all of which Attis personified. A fourth-century calendar records the series of spring holidays:[14] on 15 March a solemn procession of "reedbearers" in the city probably commemorates the first days of Attis's life, when he was abandoned in the reeds on the bank of Gallus River and miraculously saved by shepherds or by Cybele. A week later, at the time of the spring equinox, was the entry of the pine tree, next to which Attis is often depicted and which is worshiped and mourned as a symbol of the god himself. The tree, decked with purple ribbons and an effigy of Attis, is then laid to rest as the god Attis in the temple of the Magna Mater, and his death is mourned with loud cries and lamentations throughout the next day. The mourning becomes more violent of the following day, 24 March, known as the Day of Blood, when the devotees flagellate themselves until they bleed, sprinkling the altars and the effigy with their blood. This was also the day when certain devotees of the goddess, carried away by their emotion, would perform self-castration. During the "sacred night" of the twenty-fourth, Attis was ritually laid to rest in his grave and the new *galli* would be inducted into the priesthood, presumably symbolizing the rebirth of the god, so that at dawn the Day of Rejoicing *hilaria* would begin. A much needed Day of Rest *requietio* followed these activities, and then, on 27 March, a ritual procession and bathing of the statue of the goddess.

The similarities between the spring rites of Attis, the celebration of his death and miraculous rebirth symbolized by the evergreen tree, and the Easter cycle of Christian holidays are striking: even details appear similar, such as Jesus' entry into Jerusalem surrounded by palm bearers, and the wooden cross as the symbol of his suffering and his chief symbol as well. The intent of both religious groups—worshipers of Attis and those of Jesus—was of spiritual rebirth. This was also the purpose of the most solemn ritual of the Magna Mater cult, the *taurobolium* ("bull sacrifice"): a bull was killed on a perforated platform through which blood dripped down to bathe the initiate standing in a pit below; the less affluent would sacrifice a ram (hence the ritual was also known as the *criobolium*). The *taurobolium*, originally celebrated for the benefit of the emperor, only gradually evolved into a purely personal rite of purification and initiation, as numerous fourth-century inscriptions testify.[15] Indeed, the great quantity of these inscriptions, which record the *taurobolia* in language descriptive of being "born again," vividly points to the concern for spiritual salvation in late antiquity, a concern which was met by the cult of the Magna Mater and Attis.

## Conclusion

The two series of holidays that we have discussed—the Attis festivals in late March and the *ludi Megalenses* in early April—portray the two most outstanding aspects of the cult of the Magna Mater as the Romans worshiped her. On the one hand, a traditional state-supported series of public holidays, celebrated with traditional Roman rites, identified this mother goddess with the very foundations of the Roman state. On the other hand, the March festival of Attis, a cult devoted to spiritual rebirth, to personal psychic renewal, was celebrated with exotic, bewildering, oriental rites. These two very different sets of holidays, joining both public and private worship, held a great attraction for Roman pagans of the late empire; and it is not all surprising that Christian contemporaries, perceiving the nature and popularity of this cult, railed so vociferously against it, both in its traditional Roman and exotic oriental forms: Firmicius Maternus (ca. 350 C.E.) disputed the efficacy of the rite of the *taurobolium*, arguing "that the blood defiles but does not redeem" (in contrast to Christ's blood); while Augustine criticized the traditional public celebrations of the *ludi Megalenses* as "most base and sacrilegious occasions."[16] The appeal of a mother goddess such as the Magna Mater could not, however, be totally eradicated by Christian thinkers, as the role of Mary in the Christian church suggests.

The vitality and enduring appeal of the cult of the oriental mother goddess Cybele, here transformed into the Roman Magna

Mater ("Great Mother" of the Roman Empire), throughout the seven centuries of its known existence demonstrates the strength of the Roman pagan cults when reinforced by the interconnection of public and private rites and beliefs. It demonstrates as well the importance of the mother-goddess figure in the Roman world.

## NOTES

Unless otherwise stated, the translations are my own.

1. Livy *Ab urbe condita libri* 25.1.6 for the situation in 213 B.C.E.

2. Livy (trans. Frank G. Moore) 29.10.5 (Cambridge: Harvard University Press, 1962).

3. Livy 29.11.1

4. For a general history of the period and Roman relations with Asia Minor, see R. M. Errington, *The Dawn of Empire: Rome's Rise to World Power* (Ithaca: Cornell University Press, 1972), pp. 96 ff.

5. Ovid *Fasti* 4.267-71.

6. S. Pomeroy, *Goddesses, Whores, Wives and Slaves: Women in Antiquity* (New York: Schocken Books, 1975), p. 79.

7. Livy 29.37.2; 36.36.3; and the Roman *Fasti Praenestini.*

8. Ovid *Fasti* 4.179-392.

9. Livy 34.54

10. Ovid *Fasti* (trans. James G. Frazer) 4.183-88 (Cambridge: Harvard University Press, 1931).

11. Ovid *Fasti* (trans. James G. Frazer) 4.223-44.

12. Catullus *Carmina* 63.91-3.

13. M. J. Vermaseren, *Cybele and Attis: The Myth and the Cult* (London: Thames and Hudson, 1977), p. 97.

14. The Calendar of Philocalus; see Vermaseren, *Cybele and Attis* pp. 113 ff.

15. R. Duthoy, *The Taurobolium: Its Evolution and Terminology* (Leiden: E. J. Brill, 1969).

16. Firmicus Maternus *De errore profanarum religionum* 27.8; Augustine *De civitate dei* 2.4

# 6

## STEVE DAVIES

# The Canaanite-Hebrew Goddess

Tthis essay may differ substantially from others in this collection for there is considerable doubt as to whether there is or ever was any such thing as a "Hebrew goddess." In thinking about the Hebrew goddess, or various female entities that have been taken to be Hebrew goddesses, we will have the opportunity to discuss a variety of questions as to what constitutes a goddess and what constitutes Hebrew religion.

Nonetheless, there certainly was a Canaanite goddess. Indeed, there were at least two prominent goddesses, Asherah and Anath, and probably a variety of lesser goddesses (for example, Padriya, Talliya, Arsiya, about whom little is known other than that they were wives of Baal and dwelt with Asherah). Even about the leading goddesses of the Canaanite pantheon not much is known. What information we do have comes from guesses concerning the crude clay statuettes in female form found in Palestinian archaeological excavations and from a few tablets on which various myths were inscribed. Those tablets were found in the early 1930s in Ras Shamra. They were written ca. 1350 B.C.E. in the Ugaritic language, a language similar to Hebrew, and can be read in the English translation by H.L. Ginsberg in Pritchard's *Ancient Near Eastern Texts*.

### The Canaanite Goddess Asherah

Unfortunately the Ugaritic Canaanite myths from Ras Shamra do not give us a very good idea of what the Canaanite goddesses were. As most myths, those of Ras Shamra presuppose that the audience will know their deities, and so what little we learn must be inferred from the context of stories. Those stories make it clear that the leading goddess of the Canaanite people was Asherah.

Asherah is called "Lady Asherah of the Sea" but we do not know why. Nowhere in extant Ugaritic mythology is there any evidence that she held dominion over the sea. Asherah is called "Progenitress of the Gods" and, in this sense, is a great-mother goddess. She seems to have been thought to have played a nurturing role for royal infants and was clearly the primary goddess in the pantheon. She was the wife of El, the chief god of the pantheon, and had dwelling with her "perfect brides" who apparently were the wives of the god Baal, son of El.

The longest of the Ugaritic myths we have is the tale of Baal's attempt to gain a palace for himself, to move away from his father El's palace. Baal wishes to gain Asherah's assistance in doing this and comes to her with gifts made from thousands of pieces of silver and gold, a gorgeous table covered with game from all over the world, "gorgeous bowls shaped like small beasts like those of Amurru, stelae shaped like the wild beasts of Yam'an," and other offerings. Asherah, won over by this supplication, eventually intercedes with El on Baal's behalf and he receives the palace he sought.

Asherah is clearly a most important goddess. Unfortunately we know little about her or about her role in Canaanite cult or ritual. She is definitely connected with the sea, she is mother of the gods, she is wife of El, and she is active in mythological lore. This is tantalizing but rather unsatisfying information. Until further texts are discovered Asherah will, in the main, remain mysterious.

## The Caananite Goddess Anath

The other centrally important Goddess of Canaan is Anath, who was also called Ashtoreth and Astarte. Her personality is pronounced and fascinating; about Anath somewhat more is known than about Asherah. Anath is daughter of Asherah, sister of Baal, and (as is not uncommon in mythology) wife of Baal. She is frequently called "virgin" Anath, although she is reported to have had intercourse with Baal and to have conceived a bull (this in a fragmentary Ugaritic text). In the myths, Anath, like Asherah, endeavors to assist Baal in obtaining his palace. Her methods are not those of Asherah. Asherah, to assist Baal, journeys to her husband El and speaks to him kindly and politely. He responds with affection, grants her request, and orders the palace built. When Anath thinks of approaching El she says, "He'll heed me, will Bull El my father, he'll heed me for his own good! For I'll fell him like a lamb to the ground, make his gray hair flow with blood, the gray hair of his beard with gore; unless he give a house unto Baal like the gods."

After Anath has threatened her father, El is justifiably perturbed. He replies, rather unhappily, that when she was weaned she was gentle and that strife did not exist among goddesses. The whole nature of

Anath seems to have been warlike. She seems to have been held respon-sible for some earthquakes (it was said that they occurred when she stamped her foot in anger). She was goddess of war and, hence, of peace: Baal had to plead with Anath to "take war away from the earth, banish all strife from the soil; pour peace into earth's very bowels, much amity into earth's bosom." As goddess of war she played a central role in the consolidation of the Canaanite pantheon's power, for those deities did not achieve their mythological eminence without a struggle.

At one point in the myth Anath fears that Baal is under attack and says, "Crushed I not El's Beloved Yamm (of the sea)? Destroyed I not El's Flood Rabbim? Did I not, pray, muzzle the Dragon? I did crush the crooked serpent (Leviathan) Shalyat the seven headed. I did crush El's beloved Ar [...], cut off El's bullock 'Atak. I did crush the Godly Bitch Hashat, Destroy the house of El-Dhubub, who fought thee and seized the gold; who drove Baal from the Heights of Zaphon ...," and so forth. Anath seems to have personally fought to ensure Baal's primacy and, perhaps, fought to establish the earth from the chaos of primordial waters. It is difficult, of course, to make much sense of myths that we have only in frag-ments. What is clear is that Anath is the most warlike and the most savage of the deities of the Ugaritic myths.

One very curious passage in the myths about Anath concerns her fighting both human foes, and enemies she seems to have conjured from her imagination. We do *not* know why she is doing this; the fragment is too incomplete for us to tell. But her behavior certainly gives substantial insight into her character. The passage in the myth is as follows: "She locked the gates of her [Anath's] house and met the picked fighter in [...]. Now Anath doth battle in the plain fighting between the two towns; smiting the Westland's peoples, smashing the folk of the Sunrise. Under her are heads like sheaves; over her, hands like locusts." (Anath has met a host of enemy heroes and slaughtered them all, slicing them limb from limb.)

> She binds the heads to her back, fastens the hands in her girdle, she plunges knee-deep in knights' blood, hip-deep in the gore of heroes. ...Now Anath goes to her house, the goddess pro-ceeds to her palace. Not sated with battling in the plain, with her fighting between the two towns, she pictures the chairs as heroes, pretending a table is warriors, and that the footstools are troops. Much battle she does and beholds, her fighting Anath contemplates: Her liver swells with laughter, her heart fills up with joy, Anath's liver exults; for she plunges knee-deep in knight's blood, hip-deep in the gore of heroes. Then, sated with battling in the house, fighting between the two tables... She washes her hands of knights' blood, her fingers of the gore of heroes. [Chairs turn back] to chairs, table also to table; footstools turn back into footstools.

This then is Anath, a personality far more striking (in those myths we have) than Asherah. But what a curious personality she has. Apparently her response to all situations is tremendous violence. Her approach to El is to threaten to slaughter him. When she hears that Baal needs assistance she assumes that he wants her to slaughter his enemies, when, in fact, all he wants is a palace of his own. But the most remarkable passage is the long one quoted above. Not only does she slaughter people, but she is dissatisfied with her killing and proceeds to engage in imaginary battle. She conjures enemies out of her household furniture and slaughters them. Finally the corpses become furniture again. Perhaps we may think of Anath as a barely controlled force of deadly primordial chaos, especially if it is true that Anath was responsible for the destruction of the primordial forces of flood, dragon, leviathan. But what sort of rage is it that causes her to battle her furniture? Is Anath a projection into mythology of irrational, unreasoning rage born of frustration?

Anath is a principal wife of Baal, and apparently bears a bull who is the son of Baal. Despite this she is called virgin Anath. Some scholars believe that Baal is principally a god of male fertility and conclude that Anath must be a goddess of female fertility, but the texts we have do not lend much credence to this view. Anath may be in some ways comparable to the Hindu goddess Kālī, but so little is known of Anath that no conclusion can be drawn.

We know some tantalizing facts about Asherah and a few more about Anath, but any effort to make definite statements about the nature and function of these or any other Canaanite goddesses is based mainly on guesswork. It is common practice to call Asherah and Anath fertility goddesses, but there is no conclusive evidence for this claim. Although virtually all deities have something or other to do with fertility, there is nothing in Ugaritic literature to link either Asherah or Anath with fertility generally or with human or agricultural fertility specifically. It is true that Asherah is the mother of the gods, but what of it? The Christian god—the Father—is certainly not a fertility god. It seems that when we do not know much about a religion or about a particular goddess, we claim that the religion was an effort to ensure fertility and that the goddess was a goddess of fertility. This may stem from the fact that some scholars assume that it is the essence of the female to be fertile (a debatable notion at best) and that therefore female deities are deities of fertility. This will not do. One must wonder whether, when reading of a fertility goddess or cult, the term fertility is not just a mask for ignorance.

## The Israelites and Asherah

From the standard perspective, the one developed in the Hebrew Bible, the worship of Asherah should have ceased when the

Israelites invaded and conquered Canaan (ca. 1200 B.C.E.). But it didn't. Asherah was worshiped by the people of Canaan, Hebrew-speaking people, for centuries after the territory was ruled by kings of Israel and Judah. Hence it would be correct to say that Asherah was a Hebrew goddess. There is some evidence, in fact, that Asherah was worshiped even in the temple in Jerusalem as late as 586 B.C.E.

The Israelite invasion of Canaan took place a century or more after the Ugaritic texts we have were written. The biblical accounts of the worship of goddesses were written hundreds of years later and are unanimously opposed to the practice. Virtually all we know about the worship of female deities among Hebrew-speaking people of biblical times is that such worship took place.

The Hebrew Bible occasionally mentions that the people set up "Asherahs" near altars of Baal on hilltops. These Asherahs were, apparently, wooden pillars symbolic of Asherah and were used in the worship of Asherah and Baal. They may have been carved images or may simply have been unadorned stakes. They were of sufficient size that the enemies of Asherah's worship had to chop them down to destroy them.

The history of Israel and Judah from ca. 1200 B.C.E. to the Babylonian exile in 586 B.C.E. is interpreted in the Hebrew Bible as cycles of univocal Yahweh worship alternating with Yahweh worship that included worship of other gods and goddesses. (We have almost no information about the actual practices of worship of deities other than Yahweh).

If we know little or nothing about the nature of Asherah in Hebrew worship we do know something about the popularity of that worship. Before there was a temple in Jerusalem, Asherah was worshiped (Judg. 3:5–7). Solomon, who built the Jerusalem temple, worshiped Asherah (1 Kings 11:5). His son Rehoboam placed an image of Asherah in the temple itself (1 Kings 15:13). The hills of Israel and Judah were surmounted by images of pillars of Asherah. After the reign of Rehoboam there came the first of a series of attacks on Asherah by proponents of the exclusive worship of Yahweh. According to Raphael Patai's close reading of biblical records, the worship of Asherah *in the Jerusalem temple* came and went with the fluctuations of power politics. He reconstructs her career in the temple:

| Asherah in the temple (B.C.E.) | Asherah excluded from the temple |
|---|---|
| 928–893   (35 years) | 893–825 (68 years) |
| 825–725 (100 years) | 725–698 (27 years) |
| 698–620   (78 years) | 620–609 (11 years) |
| 609–586   (23 years) | |

Asherah's presence may mean as little as that a statue or pillar of her was somewhere in the temple court; it may mean as much as that

Asherah's worship was combined with that of Yahweh. Certainly it means that Asherah's existence, importance, and legitimacy were acknowledged by kings, priests, and people for most of 236 years. There was also Asherah worship in the royal court, in the capital of Israel, Samaria. An image of Asherah was set up there sometime during the reign of King Ahab (873–852) and so far as we know remained until the fall of that kingdom (722 B.C.E.).

When Asherah was accepted into the temple we may be certain that "Asherahs" were also set up throughout Israel and Judah on hilltops next to altars of Baal, and that Asherah was worshiped there. Further, we may suppose that homes had individual modes of worship of Asherah. Hundreds of small crudely made clay figurines of female figures have been discovered in archaeological excavations throughout this area. Although archaeologists tend to assume too quickly that human figurines have religious significance surely some of these statuettes represent Asherah and/or Anath. In later Israelite history, incidentally, the distinctions between Anath, Asherah, Ashtoreth, and other goddesses probably disappeared. The existence of figurines indicates that worship of a goddess was conducted within homes as well as upon the high places.

In the Hebrew Bible, substantial evidence about the practice of worship of a goddess is found only in Jeremiah (7:17–18, 44:9, 17–25.). The Yahwist prophet Jeremiah is, not surprisingly, totally opposed to the practices he writes about. He does not even give a name to the goddess, but he does tell us one of her titles, queen of heaven.

The kings of Judah and their wives and the men of Judah and their wives gathered in the streets of Jerusalem and other cities to pay homage to the goddess. They made promises by which they bound themselves to her. They burned sacrifices to her, poured drink offerings to her. At that time, the people said, they had food and contentment and they were free from calamity. However, having left off offering sacrifices and ceremonies to her (probably during the reign of King Josiah) they felt that she had caused them to be in great poverty and to be victims of sword and famine. Jeremiah believed their difficulties sprang from the opposite cause: because they worshiped the goddess they fell on bad times.

The cakes offered to the queen of heaven were, according to Jeremiah, marked with her image. It seems likely that the cakes, which were baked within family groups (possibly in molds in the goddess's form), were consumed by the families themselves. This is an interesting form of communion.

The worship of this goddess was primarily the responsibility of the women, but the men fully participated and, indeed, whole family units participated together. According to Jeremiah even the king and queen participated in, even led, this worship. Under such circumstances was there not a Hebrew goddess?

It is necessary to point out here that we have now virtually exhausted our information about the goddess worshiped from ca. 1250 until 586 B.C.E. The ancient evidence leaves us only hints and, for the Palestinian period after 1250 B.C.E. the hints were left by persons who hated the cult and were devoted to seeing it obliterated. Such evidence is untrustworthy: we cannot assume that information in the Canaanite mythological texts of ca. 1350 B.C.E. has any relevance to belief and worship in Israel or Judah centuries later. Not only do religious beliefs change over the years, but the leaders of worship of the goddess in Israel were peiodically exterminated during times when Yahwists held power. This would lead to the loss or transformation of a great deal of earlier mythology.

## The Problem of a Hebrew Goddess

Some conclude that there was such a thing as a Hebrew goddess or a Jewish goddess. Raphael Patai's well-researched and fascinating book *The Hebrew Goddess* makes a case that there was a female form of deity throughout Hebrew and Jewish history. It seems to have been the case that Hebrew-speaking people regularly worshiped a goddess from 1250 until 586 B.C.E. and perhaps even for some years thereafter. Does this mean that we can meaningfully speak of a Hebrew or Jewish goddess? I think not.

When we speak of a Hebrew goddess are we speaking simply of the fact that Hebrew-speaking people worshiped a goddess? Perhaps so, but that fact means virtually nothing. To speak of a Hebrew goddess seems to make a claim that the Hebrew culture had a goddess. But a language is not a culture. Hebrew culture must be differentiated from non-Hebrew culture for the idea of Hebrew culture to be meaningful. Hebrew culture has consistently been defined in terms of acceptance of the god Yahweh and the rejection of other gods. Anyone who claims that there was a Hebrew goddess because various Hebrew people (probably a majority) once worshiped Asherah and Anath *must* accept that there were Hebrew gods named Moloch, Baal, and Osiris, for at various times these gods were worshiped by Hebrew-speaking people. One cannot simply choose to claim Asherah as a Hebrew goddess and ignore Baal when the Hebrew Bible quite specifically and quite correctly claims that the worship of Asherah and Baal was carried on at the same times and places by the same people.

Was Asherah (whom everyone agrees was worshiped by Hebrew-speaking people at various times) a Hebrew goddess, a Jewish goddess, or was she a Canaanite goddess? This is not a historical question but a question of definition. If Asherah and Baal are Hebrew deities is there any way of defining Hebrew culture as distinct from Canaanite culture? Is Yahweh then simply a foreign god grafted onto Canaanite religion, perhaps replacing or joining with the god El?

Let us turn to a different set of questions. What constitutes a goddess? Is a concept or poetic metaphor a goddess? Obviously, a female divine personage who appears in mythology, who is worshiped as an individual in a cult with established ritual, who has a priesthood or prophethood (the Hebrew Bible mentions four hundred prophets of Asherah at the time of King Ahab of Israel in I Kings 18:19) is a goddess. But what about the times when religious language turns poetic or metaphorical and speaks of God as a being of predominantly male nature with female aspects or attributes? Are such attributes, when discussed in feminine language (use of feminine pronouns and such terminology as wife, daughter, bride), evidence of a goddess? I think not, but an argument to that effect can be made. Let us consider some examples of such a "goddess."

*Sophia* is a Greek word meaning "wisdom" and the "goddess" Sophia was primarily the product of Greek-speaking Judaism. The word *sophia* is feminine in gender in Greek and its Hebrew counterpart, *hochmah*, is also feminine. The greatest biblical passages about Wisdom are in Proverbs. These passages present us with a strange notion: the Wisdom of God is taken to be almost an independent power of God. God is not simply wise but seems to have a Wisdom with whom he interacts, as though that Wisdom were a deity herself. She speaks in the first person in Proverbs 8:22–31 (and elsewhere) and appears there as God's darling and delight. The passage is a lovely one:

> The Lord created me the beginning of his works, before all else that he made, long ago. Alone, I was fashioned in times long past, at the beginning, long before earth itself. When there was yet no ocean I was born, no springs brimming with water ... When he set the heavens in their place I was there, when he girdled the ocean with the horizon, when he fixed the canopy of clouds overhead and set the springs of ocean firm in their place, when he pre-scribed its limits for the sea and knit together earth's foundations. Then I was at his side each day, his darling and delight, playing in his presence continually, playing on the earth, when he had fin-ished it, while my delight was in mankind.

This fine passage, if taken from let us say Hindu or Canaanite literature, would unquestionably be taken to be the statement of a goddess. But in Jewish literature, in a culture which officially main-tains that there is but one God, Wisdom presents a curious problem.

The philosopher Philo, writing at about the time of Jesus, says of this passage, "Thus in the pages of one of the inspired company, Wisdom is represented as speaking of herself after this manner: God obtained me first of all his works and found me before the ages. True, for it was necessary that all that came to the birth of creation should be younger than the mother and nurse of the All," (*De Ebrietato*, 8. 30).

Philo even goes so far as to call God "the husband of Wisdom." Is Sophia (Philo wrote in Greek) then a goddess? Are we to assume that if Sophia is the mother of the world and the wife of God she is only a way of speaking and not a way of worshiping? Philo would very probably have replied yes to the latter question for, despite his occasional overstatements, he had no intention of claiming that the Jews worship or should worship two or more gods. He would have been scandalized at the thought that Jews worship a female god. Still, his writings can seem to hint in that direction.

The Wisdom of Solomon, written ca. 100 B.C.E. speaks of Sophia as a persönage separable from God:

> And with thee [God] is wisdom [Sophia], who is familiar with thy works and was present at the making of the world by thee, and who knows what is acceptable to thee and in line with thy commandments. Send her forth from the holy heavens, and from thy glorious throne bid her to come down so that she may labour at my side and I may learn what pleases thee. For she knows and understands all things.
>
> (Wisd. of Sol. 9:9–11).

Sophia guided human history;

> Wisdom it was who kept guard over the first father of the human race [Adam], when he alone had yet been made; she saved him after his fall and gave him the strength to master all things. It was because a wicked man [Cain] forsook her in his anger that he murdered his brother in a fit of rage and so destroyed himself. Through his fault the earth was covered with a deluge and again wisdom came to the rescue, and taught the one good man [Noah] to pilot his plain wooden hulk.
>
> (Wisd. of Sol. 10:1–4)

Throughout many of the later writings in the Hebrew Bible and in the Greek Apocrypha there is evidence of this kind of serious concern with Sophia. Often it seems as if Sophia were a goddess, but none of the authors who wrote of Sophia ever gives the slightest indication that their *intention* was to write of a goddess.

To say "God in his wisdom created the world" implies the existence of no goddess at all. But to say "Wisdom was present at the creation, she was with God day and night and played upon the newmade earth" seems to imply the existence of a goddess, Sophia, who is an associate of God. Sophia had a role in the mythology of creation, but there was no Jewish cult of Sophia nor did she have any prophets or priesthood. The decision as to whether Sophia was a Jewish goddess rests not on the textual evidence, most of which can be found in the Bible and the Apocrypha, but upon the definition of the term goddess. (Since the Bible and the Apocrypha have been adopted by Christians as sacred texts, Sophia is as much a goddess of Christians as a goddess of Jews, but Christians do not accept her as such any more than Jews do.)

The later career of Sophia is interesting. In maintstream Judaism the wisdom tradition peaked around the years of Jesus' life and rather rapidly faded from view after that. In the Jewish mystical writings of the Kabbalah, the Hebrew word for wisdom, *hochmah* (feminine in gender), is usually considered one of the *masculine* attributes of God. *Hochmah* is at the top of the "masculine" side of the famous Kabbalistic Tree of Life diagram; *binah*, which means understanding, is at the top of the "feminine" side.

Interest in Sophia was carried on by Gnostic Judaism, a religious tradition which postulated that the creation of the external world is something negative, a mistake on the part of divinity. Sophia, in Gnosticism, is much more a goddess than in the Jewish Wisdom tradition. She is thought to have initiated the creation of the world by a mistake and subsequently to have been trapped in the world. Gnostic mythology focuses upon the fall and eventual ascent of Sophia. As Gnostics could not bring themselves to admit that God himself had fallen, although this is implicit in their mythology, the aspect of God which did fall, Wisdom, became virtually independent of God and so became a goddess. After about three centuries of Christianization, Gnosticism faded from the religious scene and, as an independent religious movement, was virtually extinct by 400 C.E.

Sophia continued to exist in another tradition that arose from Judaism. There, however, the attributes and aspects of Sophia were taken from her and given to a male deity. Christians as early as the first century, during the time of the writing of the New Testament, took attributes traditionally assigned to Sophia and applied them to Jesus Christ. His preexistence, participation in creation, descent and presence in the world, all derive from Jewish traditions regarding Sophia. It may be said, in fact, that the prologue to the Gospel of John (the long poem about the Word) was originally a poem about Sophia, the term Logos ("word") being substituted for Sophia ("wisdom"). The gender of Logos is masculine in Greek. Scholars of the New Testament are in general agreement today that many New Testament authors conceived of Jesus Christ in terms previously applied to Sophia. Paul, for example, quite directly states that Jesus is the Sophia of God (1 Cor. 1:24). Does this mean, then, that Christ was a feminine deity prior to the Incarnation? A bizarre notion, but if one wishes to claim that when the Hebrew Bible speaks of God's wisdom personified it speaks of Christ (as many Christians assume), then certainly it is significant that wisdom was conceived to have been feminine.

In what is called the Talmudic period of Judaism (ca. 70–450 C.E.) some Jewish sages wrote of God's Shekinah in ways that may imply that Shekinah is a goddess. The Shekinah of God is the presence of God, the dwelling-with-us of God. Shekinah is a feminine-gender word and so occasionally when sages wrote of the presence of God being with Israel, being exiled with Israel, being present in the temple in Jerusalem, etc., they wrote that *she* is with Israel, *she* is exiled with Israel, *she* was present in the temple. As Sophia was in earlier centuries, Shekinah became a predominant feminine mode of God's activity and, in particularly poetic passages, seemed to take on a will or life of her own.

Similar to Shekinah is Matronit (from the Latin *matrona*, or "lady"), a term used by kabbalists in the thirteenth century and later to denote the presence of God on earth and the feminine qualities of God. Some Jewish writers spoke of Shekinah or Matronit as the bride, of God as bridegroom, of the pair as husband and wife, king and queen, etc.

The goal of human life was seen by Jewish kabbalists to be the return to God and this was allegorically discussed in terms of the reunion of the king and queen or even intercourse between the king and queen. As God was present with his people, and as his people were exiled from Israel and from God, so Shekinah or Matronit was exiled. She was present with her people, assisting them in their difficulties, and occasionally seems to have had the function of interceding with God on their behalf. In some medieval Jewish texts it seems that the community of Israel itself was identified with Shekinah in much the same way that the Christian church identified itself as the bride of Christ.

Should Shekinah, or Matronit, be considered a Jewish goddess? The answer must be no, just as the answer to the question, Is the church of Christians as the bride of Christ a goddess? must be answered no. One who assumes that religious language is to be taken literally simply fails to understand that language. The terms Matronit and Shekinah are used in sentences that imply that they are goddesses apart from god, but the sentences are written by persons who are dedicated to the proposition that there is one God. Therefore, perhaps through the strength of that conviction, they feel free occasionally to speak of the presence of God as distinct from God.

Can we say that some medieval Jews spoke of one God in two persons, male and female? No, that was not their intent. They spoke of one God with various attributes and of one divine reality with various levels. Certain of those attributes and levels were spoken of with feminine language and imagery. This is far from the creation of a goddess.

Religious writing is in a category of its own and cannot be read in the same way as secular writing. It is doubtful, in fact, that there is a single sentence in the *Zohar* (the main kabbalistic book) which should be taken literally. To find in kabbalistic literature poetry and metaphor concerning God as male and female, king and queen, mother and father, presence in heaven and presence on earth, and so forth, does not mean that one is justified in presuming that kabbalists believed that there were two gods of different sexes. It does mean that God was seen to have attributes commonly accorded to both sexes. The Sophia of the Hebrew Bible and the Shekinah and Matronit of the Kabbalah and (to a lesser extent) the Talmud were not Hebrew goddesses or Jewish goddesses. They were ways that Hebrew- and Greek-speaking Jews spoke about one God and that God, fortunately or not, was predominantly male. It is true to say that God was not considered exclusively male, that feminine attributes were accorded to God, but this is not to say that there was a Hebrew goddess.

A Hebrew or Jewish goddess may come into being. It may be the choice of Jewish people to choose to worship Asherah or Sophia or Shekinah as a goddess, although this is certainly unlikely. For at least the past twenty-five hundred years the Hebrew goddess has been a way of speaking, not a way of worshiping.

# 7

E. ANN MATTER

# The Virgin Mary: A Goddess?

As a monotheistic religion with roots in the Judaic tradition, Christianity cannot be said, strictly speaking, to have a goddess. Christian theology testifies to one God in three persons: Father, Son, and Holy Spirit. Insofar as these three persons are understood anthropomorphically (in poetry and art, for example), they are portrayed as male.[1] Beyond the trinitarian godhead, the Christian pantheon is empty. There are no lesser and greater deities; specifically, there is no goddess. Nevertheless, traditional Christian piety has included devotion to holy people, the saints, whose devout lives have earned them a place in heaven. The saints stand in the divine presence and are able to hear the prayers of the faithful and to intercede with God on their behalf. Many women are counted among the saints, and the holiest of all, the head of their company, is the mother of Jesus, the Virgin Mary.

During the nearly two thousand years of Christian history, devotion to Mary has developed in different ways. High points of Marian piety can be found in the medieval and baroque periods, and in the modern Orthodox and Roman Catholic traditions. Where she is venerated, Mary holds a place of such high esteem as to muddle the distinction between divine and human. Although never described as a goddess, she is certainly seen as more than a mere woman, however holy, could hope to be, set above all the saints and only a little lower than God. In contrast, modern Protestantism has tended to minimize Mary's powers and her role in the divine realm; the place of Mary in Christian devotion was one of the hottest issues of the Protestant Reformation.

Perhaps the rejection of Marian devotion by sober Protestantism is testimony to the power of the cult of the Virgin, evidence that she has been perceived, at least in a negative sense, as a goddess. Reformation rhetoric often claimed that Mary had invaded the divine sphere; but the Roman church has consistently maintained that devotion to Mary must be carefully distinguished from the worship due to God alone.[2]

It is likely that no Christian theologian of any confession or century would be comfortable with the idea of an essay on the Virgin Mary in a book about the goddess figures of world religions. But no religion is defined by theologians alone. The practice of the pious often takes its own course, and can sometimes be strong enough to draw theological theory after it. This is the case with devotion to Mary; in no other realm of Christian theology does theory so closely, and it may even be said, so unwillingly, follow practice.

Because I am a historian, this essay will begin with an overview of Christian devotion to the mother of Jesus from the biblical times to the present. However, other disciplines are needed to interpret this phenomenon, so theological explanations of the place of Mary in Christian worship and recent anthropological theories about the widespread and growing appeal of the cult of the Virgin in modern industrial society will also be considered. Through combination of history, theology, and anthropology, I hope to bring the Mary cult into focus as an abiding and still-vital element of Christianity.

## The New Testament

Very little is known about the historical woman Mary of Nazareth. According to the Gospel of Luke (1:26–38) Mary was a virgin engaged to a man named Joseph when she was visited by the angel Gabriel. The angel told her that she had been chosen by God to be the mother of a son conceived by the Holy Spirit, a son who would "be called Son of the Most High...and of his kingdom there will be no end" (Luke 1:32—33). The angel's response to Mary's doubts about this mission makes it clear that the birth of Jesus is to be understood as a union between humanity and divinity (Luke 1:35). It is from this moment, celebrated in Christian liturgy as the Feast of the Annunciation (25 March), that Mary takes the title Virgin. The Christian Scriptures do not indicate whether she *remained* a virgin after the birth of Jesus; but Christian authors until the Reformation upheld the belief that she was ever virgin, before, after, and even during the birth of her son. The idea that, after the birth, Mary and Joseph lived together as a normal married couple was emphatically rejected by the fourth-century Latin author Jerome[3] but was revived during the Reformation and remains the modern Protestant belief about Mary.

Almost all of the biblical references to Mary show her in relation to the divine mission of her son. Immediately following the story of the Annunciation, the Gospel of Luke relates that Mary visited with her relative Elizabeth, then pregnant with John the Baptist, the last prophet of the coming of Jesus. As the two women approached one another, the child in Elizabeth's womb "leaped for joy" (Luke 1:44). Elizabeth cried out to Mary, "Blessed are you among women, and blessed is the fruit of your womb." (Luke 1:42). This story was clearly intended to show the relationship of John the Baptist to Jesus; but Elizabeth's words were later combined with the words of Gabriel at the Annunciation to form the most enduring prayer to the Virgin, the repeated prayer of the rosary, the Hail Mary.

Miracles attending the birth of Jesus also add to the enigma surrounding the Virgin Mary. When the Wise Men from the East followed a star to Bethlehem to present gifts to the newborn child, "they saw the child with Mary his mother, and they fell down and worshiped him" (Matt. 2:11). Images of Mary holding the infant Jesus, both often crowned and jeweled, are the most ancient and consistent representations associated with the cult of the Virgin. In the Middle Ages, the seated-Virgin-and-child motif evoked Mary's role as the *Theotokos* ("the God-bearer") and emphasized the idea that the child Jesus was the second person of the Trinity, and Mary the mother of God.

Shepherds summoned by angels to the site of Jesus's miraculous birth (Luke 2:8–20) related the message that the child was the long-awaited savior, the Christ; the story notes that "Mary kept all these things, pondering them in her heart" (Luke 2:19). When the infant was acclaimed by the prophets Simeon and Anna in the temple of Jerusalem (Luke 2:22–38), and when, as a twelve-year-old boy, he amazed the teachers at the temple with his knowledge and understanding (Luke 2:41–52), Mary's response is the same: "and his mother kept all these things in her heart" (Luke 2:51).

These stories imply more than motherly concern. The idea is that Mary, more than any other human being, was a partner in the mysterious unfolding of the true nature of her son. Even after Jesus had been baptized by John the Baptist and had started to gather disciples about him, only Mary understood the extent of his powers. At the wedding at Cana (John 2:1–11) when the wine ran out, she turned to her son and said simply, "They have no wine." It was clearly a command. Jesus' reply, "O woman, what have you to do with me? My hour has not yet come," was brushed aside by Mary, who said calmly to the servants, "Do whatever he tells you" (John 2:3–4). Jesus obediently ordered six stone jars filled with water; when the servants drew some out, it had turned into the best wine served at the feast. This was Jesus' first miracle, the first demonstration of his powers. Mary's role in the event shows her maternal influence on her son, which is the basis of Marian intercession.

Another biblical passage adds quite a different dimension to Mary's image. Chapter 12 of Revelation describes a "great portent" in heaven: "a woman, clothed with the sun, with the moon under her feet, and on her head a crown of twelve stars" (Rev. 12:1). Like everything else in Revelation, the story line is fantastic and ambiguous: the woman is pregnant, she cries out in pain at the birth of the child; a seven-headed, ten-horned, seven-crowned dragon threatens to devour the child as soon as it is born. But the drama has a happy ending, the birth takes place safely: "she brought forth a male child, one who is to rule all the nations with a rod of iron, but her child was caught up to God and to his throne, and the woman fled into the wilderness, where she has a place prepared by God, in which to be nourished for 1,260 days" (Rev. 12:5–6). Of course, as no name is given to the woman in this passage, it is a matter of interpretation to see the Virgin Mary here. But this was the prevailing interpretation during the Middle Ages; the language describing the child, so reminiscent of the words of Gabriel at the Annunciation, were taken to relate directly to the birth of Jesus. Consequently, Mary was "the woman clothed with the sun," and was often portrayed in radiant clothing, with the moon under her feet, and a crown of stars on her head. Large carved medallions of this scene still hang in many churches in northern Europe; often a dragon or a snake curls around the feet of the Virgin. The fact that Mary is stepping on the beast suggests the curse upon the serpent-devil who led Adam and Eve into sin (Gen. 3:15); this is one of the many ways in which Mary is seen as the female force who overcomes the curse brought upon the human race by the first woman, Eve. So, in the imagery of Revelation, Mary is the queen of heaven, a figure surrounded by heavenly bodies, a mysterious, unearthly woman far from the pensive mother described by the Gospels.

In fact, the biblical references to Mary were found by early Christians to be inadequate testimony to the life of the mother of Jesus. In the first centuries of the common era, as devotion to Mary was finding a place in the body of Christian beliefs, speculation about Mary's life gave rise to a collection of stories that, in effect, fill in the blanks of the biblical accounts. These stories are part of a body of ancient texts known as pseudepigraphical texts, that is, writings that bear an obviously false claim of authorship (usually to a disciple). The Marian pseudepigrapha begins as early as the second century, and is found in a number of languages and forms. Two pseudepigraphical traditions are especially important for the development of Marian devotion: the tales having to do with Mary's birth, and those relating to her death.

## Pseudepigraphical Writings

Legends about the birth and childhood of Mary find classic form in the text known as the Protevangelium of James.[4] This story—purportedly written by James, a son of Joseph by a previous marriage—is an account of two miraculous births: that of Mary and that of Jesus. It opens with Mary's aged parents, Joachim and Anna, mourning their childlessness. Angels appear to both, assuring them that they will have a child "who will be spoken of in the whole world" (4.3). Anna promises that the child, male or female, shall be dedicated to the service of God. This is, of course, an echo of the Annunciation to Mary, it also bears strong similarities to the birth stories of John the Baptist (Luke 1) and the prophet Samuel (1 Sam. 1). The connection to the second story is especially close: Hannah, Samuel's mother, also dedicated her child to the temple. Anna took Mary to the temple at the age of two. The little girl jumped for joy to be placed in the service of God; she was "nurtured like a dove and received food from the hand of an angel" (8.1). To cap this remarkable childhood, the temple priests decided upon an even more remarkable method of finding a suitable spouse for the sanctified child. The widowers of Judea, each bearing a rod, were brought before the temple. A dove flew out of Joseph's rod up to his head; this was a sign that he was to take Mary under his chaste and fatherly care. Such was the answer of Christian legend to the nagging silence of the New Testament about Mary's birth and her exact relationship with Joseph.

The accounts of Mary's death are nearly as fanciful. Of the group of texts known as the Dormition of Mary tradition, the most influential was the one known as the Pseudo-Melito.[5] As this tale relates, after the death of Jesus, Mary was visited by an angel who promised as consolation for her overwhelming grief that she would soon be reunited with her son. Shortly afterward, Mary died, surrounded by the apostles. As her body was placed in the tomb, Jesus and angels appeared in a cloud of light. An archangel brought Mary's soul to be reunited with her body, and she was taken up, physical body and soul, to heaven. Here she remains, incorrupt and eternal.

It is clear that one intention of the Marian pseudepigrapha is to bring the life of Mary more closely into congruence with that of Jesus. The fact that early Christians were motivated to do this suggests that they were concerned with defining the Virgin's nature as sanctified and set apart. Basically, the reasons for this were christological; obviously, the body from which Christ was born must itself have been brought into the world accompanied by special signs. Similarly, this body could not have suffered common corruption after death. The message of the Marian pseudepigrapha is simply that Mary neither was born nor died in the way of other human beings.

That these claims appeared important and logical may be deduced from the tradition of the most ancient Marian feasts: the Nativity (8 September) and the Assumption (of body and soul into heaven; 15 August). For centuries, without official sanction and often against the better judgment of church leaders, Christians enthusiastically marked the anniversaries of Mary's birth and death. Gradually, the idea of Mary's particularity was extended and it became generally believed that the angelic appearance to Anna signaled Mary's special conception. It was not claimed that Mary was born, like Jesus, through an overshadowing of the Holy Spirit, but rather that her normal human conception was marked by a special grace that sanctified her in Anna's womb, freeing her from the original sin borne by all other human beings. By the Middle Ages, a feast celebrating Mary's Immaculate Conception was celebrated on 8 December, in spite of the opposition of such respected theologians as Bernard of Clairvaux and Thomas Aquinas. With the popular acceptance of Mary's Immaculate Conception and Assumption, Marian pseudepigrapha had entered the mainstream of Christian worship.

Eventually, what was professed by the faithful was defined by the church hierarchy. After centuries of debate, the Marian feasts were made official. The Immaculate Conception of Mary was declared dogma (a true and uncontestable teaching of the church) in 1854; the Assumption gained this status in 1950. In a sense, then, official and accepted Marian piety is neither ancient nor medieval, but modern.

## The Medieval Mary

Between the formulation of the Marian pseudepigrapha and the declarations of 1854 and 1950, the cult of the Virgin developed along with the intellectual and theological trends of each place and century. By the High Middle Ages, the major aspects of devotion to Mary were in place. Hymns and prayers to the Virgin were widely used in both Eastern and Western churches, and it was commonly believed that prayers to the mother of Jesus would be passed along to God with a strong recommendation. The power of intercession was attributed to all Christian saints, but Mary's heavenly credibility was especially efficacious, since she was at once the mother of Jesus and the queen of heaven, the most accessible and the most powerful of all who stand in the presence of God. Medieval Marian devotion made much of these contrasting poles of the Virgin's personality. Consider, for example, how the Salve Regina, an eleventh-century hymn of lasting popularity, stresses both the maternal and the majestic nature of Mary:

> *Hail, holy Queen, Mother of Mercy;*
> *Hail, our life, our sweetness and our hope.*
> *To thee we cry, poor banished children of Eve;*
> *To thee we sigh, mourning and weeping in this*
> *vale of tears.*
> *Turn, then, most gracious Advocate, thine eyes of*
> *mercy towards us;*
> *And after this our exile, show unto us the blessed*
> *fruit of thy womb, Jesus.*
> *O clement, O loving, O sweet Virgin Mary.*

The tone of the Salve Regina, a combination of awe, flattery, and childish pleading, is a characteristic of a great many prayers to Mary. In Maastricht, Holland, the Cathedral of Our Lady has a small chapel dedicated to Mary, "Star of the Sea," patroness of sailors. Here, candles burn day and night as signs of the petitions of believers, and the following prayer, an invocation of the Virgin's protection, is posted in several languages:

> O dearest Mother, I come to you now with greatest trust. The manifold wonders that have come to pass here by your intercession fill me, miserable sinner, with the sweetest hope that you, Mother of Mercy, will hear my prayer also. Yes, I supplicate and pray you, O sweetest Mother, O most merciful Star of the Sea, let me not go away from here without being heard. You can help me, you are the most powerful one only after God; you will help me because you are so full of love for all your children. Remember, O most merciful Virgin, that it has never been heard that anyone who came to you full of trust to take refuge in you has been forsaken by you; should I, then, be the first unlucky one to go away unheard by you? No, no, O good Mother, at this holy place may you be, through your omnipotent intercession, my help in my distress and comfort in my suffering.

The loving mother and powerful queen was also invested by popular tradition with the power to work miracles. Latin, Greek, and Coptic tales of wonders worked by Mary flourished from the twelfth to the fifteenth century. One startling but interesting motif that appears again and again in these collections is the power of milk from Mary's breasts to cure blindness, cancer, and other illnesses.[6]

There also remain from the Middle Ages a great many relics of the Virgin, pieces of clothing or bits of hair left behind at the Assumption. These were thought to have the power to work miracles. Most of these relics are now in museums, but some, such as Mary's veil at Chartres cathedral, remain in churches and are still functional. The veil of Chartres was given to the church by the ninth-century king Charles the Bald; it has had a very active career. In 911, the veil was carried in procession to the city gates, where it put an invading Norman army to flight. In 1194, when the cathedral was almost totally destroyed by fire, the veil was found undamaged and taken as a sign that the church was to be rebuilt in the same place.

The new Notre Dame of Chartres, actually built around the relic of the Virgin, is one of the most significant buildings of Christian history. It inspired a wave of soaring Gothic churches dedicated to the Virgin. By the fourteenth century, cathedrals of Mary were to be found in Amiens, Laon, Paris, Reims, and many other cities of northern France. Seen on a map, these churches make up a pattern reminiscent of the constellation of stars known as the Virgin; and the pleasing idea of an earthly constellation of glittering stars in honor of Mary became a part of French popular piety. These great cathedrals are still active centers of the cult of the Virgin. Modern pilgrims to Chartres make the trip from Paris on foot; at the shrine, they kiss the glass case in which the veil relic is held, and embrace the pillar on which stands the statue of the Virgin. The cult of the Virgin of Chartres is one of the best examples of the enduring power of medieval devotion to Mary.[7]

## Marian Apparitions

Marian shrines and pilgrimage sites are by no means limited to medieval Christianity. In fact, the three most famous and flourishing centers of the cult of the Virgin, Guadalupe, Lourdes, and Fatima, came into being in the sixteenth, nineteenth, and twentieth century, respectively. These are "apparitional" shrines, places held sacred because Mary appeared to individuals there, rather than ancient churches dedicated to the Virgin that developed particular cult practices over the centuries. Besides the dramatic circumstances of their founding, these sites have in common the fact that the recipients of the founding visions were humble, theologically uneducated, even naive individuals. Guadalupe, Lourdes, and Fatima are shrines of the common people. Even though all three have been accepted by, and even taken over by, the Roman Catholic hierarchy, they remain some of the best examples of the ways in which Mary is venerated by the most lowly of the Christian community. Their continuing popularity is directly related to their humble origins.

Guadalupe, a shrine in north-central Mexico (now in a suburb of Mexico City), is the site where, in 1531, Mary appeared to Juan Diego, an Indian who had been Christian for only a short time. The miracle occurred on a bleak December day in an isolated mountain spot. Juan Diego was suddenly surrounded by bird song and bright light; he saw a lady clothed in garments as bright as the sun, surrounded by shimmering colors. The lady's message was that a church in her honor should be built on that spot. The message was conveyed to the bishop, who, perhaps not surprisingly, did not find it compelling. Only a miraculous sign would move the unbelieving bishop. The lady instructed Juan Diego to gather roses blooming on a barren winter slope. She put the roses with her own hands into Juan Diego's cloak and told him to take them to the bishop. When the roses were delivered, another sign was revealed: on the cloak was an image of the lady, a portrait imprinted on the cloth by no human means. At that point, the bishop realized that the Virgin Mary herself had appeared to Juan Diego. A church was built at the sight of the apparition, and the miraculous cloak was hung in it as a holy relic. The place was named Guadalupe in honor of a Marian shrine of the same name in Spain, but it is also interesting to note that a phonetic equivalent in Nahuatl, Juan Diego's native language, is *Coatalocpia*, which may refer to the serpent goddess worshiped in the region before the introduction of Christianity.[8]

The apparition at Guadalupe shows the intersection of Christian and pagan cultures in other notable ways: the image on Juan Diego's cloak resembles more closely a Native American woman than a European portrait of Mary. The Virgin of Guadalupe became an important symbol for the developing Catholic culture of Latin America. She is the patroness of the Americas; in the Mexican Revolution, the independent faction marched under her banner. Today thousands of pilgrims visit her shrine each year, many make the last stage of the journey on their knees. The miraculous cloak is still the center of the cult and the focus of the pilgrim's petitions.

The apparition of the Virgin Mary to Bernadette Soubirous at Lourdes, in the French Pyrenees, is the most famous Marian miracle of the postindustrial age, celebrated in popular novels and films. There is a certain romantic charm to the story: in eighteen apparitions between 11 February and 16 July 1858, the Virgin regaled an uneducated peasant girl with messages alternating between simple commands and complex theological statements. The commands seemed intended to test Bernadette's obedience, but each act done in compliance had important consequences for the Lourdes cult. Bernadette was told to kiss the ground at a certain spot, to dig a hole there, to drink from the muddy spring uncovered. The spring soon flowed clear, and was credited with powers of healing. The water revealed by the Virgin is the center of the miracles of Lourdes. Every year, millions of pilgrims, many grievously ill, take the long journey to this isolated spot in the hope that Mary's intercession will cure them. For those who cannot make the pilgrimage, Lourdes water is packaged and sold in containers shaped like a royal lady in flowing robes. These plastic bottles, fitted with blue caps shaped like Mary's crown, may be found in Catholic homes on many continents.

Bernadette was also instructed that a church should be built at the site of the spring, and that pilgrimages should be conducted there, in the spirit of penance, for the sake of spiritual cleansing. This concern for expiation of sin is directly related to the theological revelation of Lourdes; in one of her final messages, the Virgin told Bernadette "I am the Immaculate Conception."

If we recall that the Immaculate Conception had been declared dogma only a few years earlier, in 1854, the message of the Virgin of Lourdes takes on an interesting dimension of religious propaganda. It seemed to the faithful who flocked to the grotto where Bernadette had uncovered the spring that the identification of the lady with the newly recognized but anciently observed Feast of the Immaculate Conception was proof of the objective validity of both the visions and the dogma. To the local clergy, who were skeptical of Bernadette's vision, the introduction of this theme by a theologically unschooled girl was further reason for suspicion that Bernadette was a charlatan.

Bernadette was subjected to the most scathing interrogations and great emotional humiliations. However, she held firmly to her story and was ultimately vindicated by overwhelming popular acclaim for the shrine. In 1866, Bernadette was present at the first mass celebrated in the crypt of the shrine church; in 1933, on the Feast of the Immaculate Conception, she was canonized. By this official concession, the church recognized in yet another way the power of Mary to speak through the most humble members of the Christian family.

Perhaps because of the victories won at Lourdes, the popular devotion to the apparitions at Fatima met with relatively little opposition. The wave of devotion inspired by Fatima is especially remarkable since the details of this apparition were more than usually fantastic. On 13 May 1917, in a poor rural section of Portugal, Mary appeared to three illiterate, particularly irreligious children, Lucia Dos Santos, and her cousins Francisco and Jacinta Martos.[9] At this time, Lucia was ten, Francisco nine, and Jacinta seven. The children were tending cows when, with a flash of light, a lady appeared above a tree. Lucia, who became the dominant figure of the Fatima story, spoke for her younger cousins and asked the lady who she was and what she wanted. The answer was that she had come from heaven, and wanted the children to return to that spot on the thirteenth day of the next five months, over which time her complete message would be revealed.

In spite of Lucia's attempt to keep the story a secret, sixty people from the village were present on 13 June, when the lady once again appeared and spoke to Lucia. By 13 July, the crowd had grown to several thousand, causing the secular authorities to fear a popular uprising. On 13 August, the children were kept in protective custody by the mayor of the neighboring town of Ourem; but the lady appeared to them six days later in a new place, and gave the first instructions for the building of a shrine with the money pilgrims were already leaving at the original site. By 13 September, members of the clergy were present at the monthly apparition. Some of the crowd claimed to have seen signs of the lady's presence in the dimming of the sun, but only the children saw the lady, and only Lucia spoke with her. The message this time was that the October apparition would include a vision of Saint Joseph and the Holy Child, and that the First World War would soon be over.

On 13 October, some twenty thousand people awaited the promised miracle, many weeping and on their knees. The lady appeared and told Lucia "I am the Lady of the Rosary." Immediately after she vanished, Lucia saw a succession of holy images in the sun: various manifestations of the Virgin, Saint Joseph with the infant Jesus, and the adult Jesus, whom she described as "Our Lord." The crowd also saw miracles in the sun, not the holy people seen by Lucia, but strange colored lights, and peculiar dancing movements.

Many aspects of the Fatima apparitions give rise to doubt. In the first place, the statement about the end of the war was a year premature. Secondly, the strange movements of the sun, seen by thousands, are astronomical impossibilities, demanding some scientific explanation. Theories about what really happened at Fatima have drawn on several branches of modern science: some have suggested that Lucia's personality and the high expectations of the crowd caused a mass hypnosis; at least one scientist has related the Fatima miracles to UFO phenomena and hypothesized that the lady was an alien and that the whirling lights were the usual signs accompanying an extraterrestrial contact with human beings.[10]

Whatever the "scientific truth" of Fatima, the story told by Lucia, Francisco, and Jacinta touched a receptive chord in the common people and the clerical hierarchy alike. The parish priest of Fatima had been sympathetic almost from the beginning of the visions; his favorable report was finished in 1919. The study of a commission set up by the bishop of Lisbon, published in 1929, resulted in official sanction of the shrine, confirmed by papal decree. An organization of devotees, the Blue Army of Our Lady of Fatima, is still a thriving concern that sends out literature reiterating the messages of the lady.

As in the case of Lourdes, the messages of Fatima stressed repentance and penance. As befitting her self-given title, the lady encouraged the prayer of the rosary as an especially efficacious tool for overcoming sin. But the Fatima visions included dramatic glimpses of the future torments of the damned: the children were shown the depths of hell, and Francisco, the naughtiest of the three, was specifically warned that he would have to say many rosaries to avoid being sent there.

One of the special concerns of the Virgin of Fatima was for the salvation of Christianity in Russia, newly taken over by Communism. At Lucia's request, Pope Pius XII consecrated Russia to the Immaculate Heart of Mary. Prayers for the conversion of Russia are a major part of the activities of the Blue Army, and were included until recently in the parochial-school training of American children. There was also a secret message from the Virgin that Lucia delivered to the Vatican for safekeeping until 1960, when it was to have been revealed to the world. In spite of the eager anticipation of a generation of Catholic school children, the contents of this message have never been made public.

In this apocalyptic fervor, Fatima fits into a pattern of apparitions described by anthropologists Victor and Edith Turner as phenomena of postindustrial Marian piety. The message of the Virgin to the modern world, delivered to the humble, the poor, the unprepared, is that the world has gone sadly astray but can be saved through the intervention of a loving mother, the only intermediary power with sufficient sympathy and power to restrain the arm of her son.[11] In short, the Virgin Mary of the twentieth century has a more demanding task than ever before—nothing short of the salvation of the world.

A good many other people in the twentieth century have reported visions of the Virgin Mary, but few of these have been met with anything short of censure by church authorities. Nevertheless, Mrs. Van Hoof of Necedah, Wisconsin, sends out regular mailings to a wide following who believe that Mary has warned her of the sure destruction that will be visited upon America unless short skirts and rock music are suppressed; and visions of Mary in Bayshore, Long Island, have inspired an active congregation of devotees whose concerns include the defeat of Communism and the restoration of the old Latin Mass. In June of 1981, the Boston *Globe* carried a front-page story about two women who claimed that a statue of Mary helped them to win two separate prizes in the Massachusetts state lottery. The cult of the Virgin Mary, replete with miracles and apparitions, is alive and well. Mary in the twentieth century is concerned with appropriately modern issues, including Communism, teenage morality, and the struggles of the poor.

## Theories and Interpretations

Does the history of devotion of Mary lead us to conclude that the Virgin was, is, or is becoming a goddess of Christianity? Similarities between the ancient cult of Mary and characteristic devotion to pagan goddesses have been noted by many historians and denounced by many anti-Marian theologians. Mary certainly fits neatly into the protective and sustaining role of ancient Near-Eastern fertility goddesses; her devotees may also have borrowed trappings from classical goddesses to clothe the Christian queen of heaven. This was to be expected in cities such as Ephesus, where fervor for the local Diana of the Ephesians gave way very quickly to equally deep devotion to Mary.

Evidence of this sort was, of course, grist for the polemical mills of the Reformers. However, some modern Protestant thinkers have taken a more favorable view, pointing out that biblical language about God also borrowed motifs from ancient Canaanite deities, paving the way for similar absorption of goddess characteristics into the cult of the Virgin.[12] It could even be argued that a certain amount of eclecticism aided the spread of Christianity, much as the Virgin of Guadalupe bridged a gap between the ancient beliefs of a nation and the introduction of a new religion claiming universal truth.

But, even allowing for influence from non-Christian religions, the cult of the Virgin must finally be judged from what Mary does rather than from what—or whom—she resembles. If she acts like a goddess, is she a goddess? Has Mary's behavior in the past two thousand years been sufficiently puissant to give one pause about the Roman Catholic assertion that she is the head of the saints but not divine, to be venerated but not worshiped?

The figure of Mary has certainly undergone radical change over the centuries. The humble, obedient maid of Nazareth who silently pondered her son's mission became a heavenly queen with the power to influence and even control human destiny in this world and the next. Gradually, she began to take over some of the characteristics of her son. Folk piety attests to this most clearly: in Catholic areas, such as the Austrian Tirol, inns and restaurants are decorated with plaques asking Mary to protect all who pass through the doors, even though, technically, all Mary can offer is intercession for the protection of God. Mary's incursion into the traditional roles of Jesus can be quite explicit: a baroque painting in the parish church of Igls-in-Tirol shows a woman sitting among a flock of sheep; from her shepherd's crook flies a banner reading "Ave, Maria." The woman can only be Mary, but the scene is the most ancient Christian depiction of Christ. Has the Good Shepherd been supplanted by the Good Shepherdess?

The meaning of Mary's prominence in Christian devotional life can be interpreted in a number of ways. Perhaps there is no one answer to the question. Perhaps the Virgin Mary, like the Trinity and the nature of Christ, is a paradox of the Christian faith. Efforts to define a paradox are limited at best, and often they are futile. The Virgin of Ephesus may have been the same goddess as Diana of the Ephesians, Juan Diego's radiant lady may have been the snake goddess of ancient Mexico, but the Virgins of Lourdes, Fatima, Wisconsin, and Long Island draw only on the underlying truths of the Christian tradition. Ultimately, our question comes down to how modern Christians explain the imagery surrounding the mother of Jesus.

For a theologian such as Edward Schillebeeckx, a Dutch Dominican priest, the cult of Mary is a manifestation of the deep truths that the formal, intellectual theology of Christianity too often tries to ignore, but which can never be eradicated from popular piety. Schillebeeckx explains:

> Man has need of props. He feels the need to stroke with his hand the rock where the Mother of God appeared. It is important for him to be able to climb, on his knees or even crawling, up the steps of the stations of the cross. Religion is not simply a question of the interior life. It is not a purely rational matter. Any claim that religion is exclusively rational is contradicted by Bernadette's crawling over the ground and swallowing grass and mud—and doing this on the instigation of the "Lady" who appeared to her.[13]

Even while he recognizes the strength of this need, Schillebeeckx warns of its danger, and recommends firm hierarchical control. The cult of the Virgin touches a primordial human need that can bring the believer to God; but unless it is tempered by the central truth of the Trinity, it can lead away from the One. In Schillebeeckx's view, Christians may desire to worship a goddess, but they should not be allowed to do so.

Andrew Greeley, also a Catholic priest but not a traditional theologian, explores the reasons for this spiritual attraction to Mary. He postulates that the Virgin's role in Christianity fills a deep psychological need without which the true nature of God is hidden:

> Mary is the Catholic Christian religion's symbol which reveals to us that the Ultimate is androgynous, that in God there is both male and female, both pursuit and seduction, both ingenious plan and passionate tenderness. Mary is the Christian symbol which incarnates the sexual differentiation as sacrament, as grace revealing something of someone beyond the horizons of our life, beyond the limits of our daily existence.[14]

For Greeley, Mary is the eternal feminine, the ultimate other. She fills a role similar to that of many pagan goddesses, but goes far beyond them precisely because of her humanity. Just as the event of God becoming human is the deepest truth of Christianity, the fact that God was born of a human woman reveals the completeness and complexity of the Christian truth. Mary is better than a goddess because she reveals the true God, an inclusive, androgynous deity. Greeley's thesis, like much recent writing about Christianity, owes a great deal to the work of Carl Jung, in whose view Mary is not quite a fourth member of the Trinity but is necessary for the understanding of the Trinity because she reveals the feminine side, the anima, of the otherwise exclusively male God of Christianity. Greeley's approach gives us a picture of Mary that is orthodox but ambiguous: Mary is not a goddess, but she is somehow a component of the proper understanding of God. Like Schillebeeckx, Greeley believes that Mary stirs human emotions. He is passionately attached to his view of Mary, defending it against the real and imagined slurs of feminists, Protestants, and other assailants.

Anthropologists Victor and Edith Turner also place great importance on Mary's representation of the feminine in Christianity. Their theory turns on an understanding of the role of icons in religious traditions. All religions, they claim, can be divided into those that accept symbolic representations of the divine (iconicity) and those which do not (iconoclasm). "Marianism has become almost the epitome of iconicity, even iconophily [love of icons], in Christian ritual practice, while contra-Marianism is the most extreme form of iconoclasm."[15] A major factor underlying this division of Christianity is the common view of woman in Western culture as a symbolic and corrective force. On the positive side, woman is the eternal feminine, the good mother; and Mary is the most powerful, the ultimate symbol of the symbolic feminine. In the Turner scheme, Mary's appeal for Christian devotion is culturally determined, and her position has risen and fallen in accordance with the view of women in Western culture as a whole. They explain the last eight hundred years of Marian devotion as follows:

> In the High Middle Ages, Marian representations portrayed mother and son in balance and unity. Then followed several centuries of iconoclasm. In the recent period, new Marian pilgrimage shrines have been founded, associated with visions indicating a tension between mother and son: the mother holds back the son's punishing arm, and yet she upbraids mankind for forgetting religious faith, and promises disasters on earth and hell in eternity if there is not widespread repentance. The recent trend may be one index of a resurgent "female" principle, after centuries of "male" iconoclasm, technical progress, bureaucratization, the conquest by reason and force of all natural vehicles. May we not trace, in the history of Marian pilgrimage, woman's progress from almost anonymous and faceless nurturant vehiclehood to an individuated, liberated femaleness, seen through the "masculine" eyes of Western culture as both nemesis and the coming of a new age?[16]

Different as they appear at first, the theories of Schillebeeckx, Greeley, and the Turners can actually be put together neatly. Together they explain quite a bit about Mary's place in the Christian devotional life. All are agreed that she fills a deep need in Christian spirituality, and that devotion to the cult of the Virgin is ultimately directed beyond herself, to God. Mary nevertheless has a place in the continuum of the Christian concept of divinity. Human beings pray to the woman who has been elevated into the heavenly sphere; she in turn intercedes with her son, Jesus Christ, the God who became human; Jesus remains a part of the transcendent One. It may be that Mary's special appeal originates in a perception about the androgynous nature of God. The cult of the Virgin may flourish in times and places especially inclined to accept what is culturally defined as female.

This leads us to the conclusion that the Virgin Mary is, if not a goddess, a crucial part of the Christian understanding of God. Her devotees may indeed sometimes mistake the part for the whole, but there is an ambiguity in the nature of the Virgin that lends itself to such misapprehension. Mary is, in any case, enigmatic: she is mother, virgin, spouse, daughter, servant, queen.

The all-purpose Mary can be, in the words of a less liberated age, all things to all men.

## NOTES

1. Of course, the very terms Father and Son insist on male gender. The Holy Spirit is a more androgynous figure, but is traditionally called "he." In Christian art, the Father is usually portrayed as an old man, the Son as a young (but adult) man, the Holy Spirit as a dove.

2. For two recent attempts to explain the different views of Mary in Protestant and Catholic theology, see Thomas A. O'Meara, *Mary in Protestant and Catholic Theology* (New York: Sheed & Ward, 1966), and J. de Satgé, *Down to Earth: The New Protestant Vision of the Virgin Mary* (Wilmington, N.C.: McGrath Publishing, 1976). O'Meara works from a Catholic, de Satgé from a Protestant, perspective.

3. Jerome's "On the Perpetual Virginity of the Blessed Mary Against Helvidius" has been translated into English by J.N. Hritzu, *The Fathers of the Church* 53 (Washington, D.C.: McGrath Publishing, 1965) pp. 3–43. For the curious history of belief in Mary's virginity at the moment of the birth of Jesus, see K. Rahner, "Virginitas in partu," *Theological Investigations* 4, trans. K. Smyth (London: Darton, Longman & Todd, 1966) pp. 134–62.

4. E. Hennecke and W. Schneemelcher, *New Testament Apocrypha*, vol. 1, trans. A.J.B. Higgins (London: Lutterworth Press, 1963), introduction to the text, pp. 370–74; selections in English, pp. 374–88.

5. Summary in Hennecke and Schneemelcher, p. 429; English text from the Latin by M.R. James, *The Apocryphal New Testament* (Oxford: Clarendon Press, 1924) pp. 201–16. James also prints Coptic, Greek, and Syriac versions of the Assumption.

6. See the Coptic story "The Virgin Mary of Dalgâ and the Blind Girl of Badramân," trans. E.A. Wallis Budge, in *One Hundred and Ten Miracles of Our Lady Mary* (Oxford: Medici Society, 1933) pp. 53–56. The translator notes parallel stories in Latin collections of Fulbert of Chartres and Vincent of Beauvais. The great twelfth-century monastic theologian Bernard of Clairvaux was also said to have been granted drops of milk from Mary's breast as a reward for his devotion.

7. One of the first modern investigations of the Gothic cult of the Virgin, a classic still well worth reading, is Henry Adams, *Mont-Saint-Michel and Chartres* (Washington, D.C.: Houghton Mifflin, 1904). An extensive and fascinating discussion of marian relics is given by Marina Warner, *Alone of All Her Sex: The Myth and Cult of the Virgin Mary* (New York: Knopf, 1976) pp. 285–98.

8. See Warner, pp. 302–4, especially n.8, for further analysis and bibliography.

9. The earliest accounts of Fatima portray the children in this way; see Hilda Graef, *Mary: A History of Doctrine and Devotion*, 2 vols. (New York: Sheed & Ward, 1965), 2:137–38. Later embroideries of the story turn Lucia, Francisco, and Jacinta into little saints, exemplary children. A popular pamphlet, D. Sharkey, *The Message of Fatima* (Dayton, Ohio: Geo. A. Pflaum, 1947), adds regular angelic visits to their biographies even before the apparitions. Many of these pious details were recalled by Lucia after she entered a convent; but the reports of 1917 describe the children as barely knowing their Rosary.

10. Mass hypnosis is mentioned by Graef, 2:139–40. The imaginative connection between Fatima and UFO communications has been developed by J. Vallee, *Anatomy of a Phenomenon: UFO's in Space* (New York: Ballantine Books, 1965) pp. 160–64, with references to an extensive literature on the subject in *The Flying Saucer Review*. Vallee later expanded his theory to show forty-four parallels, in image, word, and details, between UFO "contactees" and recipients of visions of Mary (both groups made up mostly of children), in *The Invisible College* (New York: Dutton 1976), pp. 161–74.

11. The Turners' theory is developed in *Image and Pilgrimage in Christian Culture: Anthropological Perspectives* (New York: Columbia University Press, 1978); pp. 203–30 deal specifically with the postindustrial age, with special attention to the apparitions at La Sallette and Lourdes.

12. Rosemary Radford Ruether, *Mary—The Feminine Face of the Church* (Philadelphia: Westminster, 1977), pp. 13–18. A similar discussion is given by the Catholic author, Andrew M. Greeley, *The Mary Myth: On the Femininity of God* (New York: Seabury Press, 1977) pp. 73–99.

13. E. Schillebeeckx, *Mary, Mother of the Redemption*, trans. N.D. Smith (New York: Sheed & Ward, 1964) pp. 144–45.

14. Greeley, pp. 216–17.

15. Turner, p. 236.

16. Turner, p. 236.

# 8

PHEME PERKINS

# Sophia and the Mother-Father:
## The Gnostic Goddess

The nature of the Gnostic movement complicates any quest for the function of its mythic figures. Gnosticism did not develop as an indigenous religious movement, closely tied to a particular people whose life, dreams, and customs shaped and were shaped by Gnosticism. Instead, Gnosticism appeared out of the radical syncretism and disruption of religious consciousness that accompanied the ecumenic imperialism of the Greco-Roman age.

Many scholars argue that Gnosticism is better defined as a particular hermeneutic, a radical reversal and revaluation of traditional symbols. They warn us that one cannot expect to find some single Gnostic Urmythos out of which all the variations may be said to have evolved. Though some Gnostic traditions appear to have developed a complex structure of female entities out of a triadic Father-Mother-Son, that triad is usually only an ideal type. Frequently, it appears to have been imposed on other dyadic patterns. Gnostic systems as we find them in the Nag Hammadi codices and the church fathers flourished on amalgamation and complexity.

Though the Gnostics allude to other mythic traditions, they have a special involvement with Jewish traditions. In many cases Gnostic writings deliberately exploit Jewish Midrashic traditions contrary to their original intent. Such reversals appear in the Gnostic Sophia figure, which combines the search of divine wisdom for reception in the world (as in *1 Enoch* 42: 1 f.) with the story of Eve. Sophia often appears farther from divinity in her alienation from the heavenly world. She often receives the epithet *prunikos* (lewd). Eve, on the other hand, frequently appears as a source of divine wisdom and revelation.

Another structural peculiarity of Gnostic speculation is the great distance between the divine world, especially God at the origin of numerous aeons, and this one. This vast system serves to mask the instability that ignorance of God introduces into the heavenly world, an instability that is only manifest in Sophia, the youngest aeon. Sophia's marginality to both the heavenly world and this one suggests that Gnosticism exploits that sense of religious transcendence often found in "liminal" situations. At the same time, the whole system drives toward recovery of the primal androgynous unity. The world fractured by imperialism is recovered in the overwhelming monism of the Gnostic pleroma.[1]

Though we may not be able to speak of a single originating Gnostic myth, the Sophia myth appears in many contexts. It cuts across the fundamental distinction in the Nag Hammadi corpus of Sethian and Valentinian systems.[2] One also finds examples of the later rationalizing interpretation of the Sophia story to bring it into line with philosophical and theological requirements of a particular system. Anthropologists have shown that all idiosyncratic, syncretistic religious symbols go through such processes in order to solidify their claim to belong to the greater religious tradition. Such innovations usually express some instability or shift in the social situation. Consequently, some scholars think that Gnostic mythology reflects the alienation of the growing class of educated tradespeople who had no access to the "educated aristocracy" that governed the cities. Others postulate the struggle of Gnostic Christians against the hierarchical developments of orthodoxy as the foundation for the Gnostic revolt and claims of hidden superiority over the god of this world. Whichever sociological hypothesis one adopts, Sophia's liminal situation reflects the tensions and ambiguities of the Gnostic, who was both caught in this world and superior to its authorities.

## The Feminine Side of God

The highest God often appears with a female (or androgynous) counterpart. Both mythic and philosophical reflection contributes to this symbol. The pair of Elohim and Eden in *Baruch* (Hipp *Ref* V 26,1–27,5) comes close to the mythic sky-god/earth-mother. Humans mediate between the two. Mythic origins might also be suggested for the generation of heavenly aeons from the divine pair, Father-Barbelo, in *Adv. Haer*. I 29,1. But most examples of the divine pair evidence modification from the philosophical tradition. "Self-generation" and the Gnostic concern for the androgynous nature of divine being belong together: "in the beginning the eternal self-engendered aeon, male-female" (Epiph. *Pan*. 31,5,3). Gnosticism takes over and develops "self-engendered" terminology from the philosophical tradition. It serves to permit the development of lower beings from the primordial divine being without destroying divine unity.

While some triadic formulations, especially those with the feminine Spirit in the third position (e.g., *Adv. Haer*. I 30,1), seek to accommodate biblical traditions, most also show evidence of influence from philosophical speculation. The philosophic tradition is presupposed when the female principle is related to matter or to creation of the material world. *ApocryJn* has developed an original pair, a highest-god-father and virginal female (Barbelo), into a triad of Father-Mother-Son.[3] The long version of *ApocryJn* represented by CG II, *1* shows more evidence of philosophic interest than the short version represented by the Berlin Codex. The description of Barbelo makes her cosmogonic role clear:

> *This is the First Thought, His image.*
> *She was the Mother of the All, because she was before*
> *them all,*
> *Mother-Father, First Man, Holy Spirit, triple male,*
> *triple power, triple male-female name, and eternal*
> *aeon of the invisible ones, and first to come forth.*
> *(CG II 5,4 – 11)*

"First to come forth" belongs to the philosophic tradition of the divine as self-engendered. It typically explains the origin of the demiurgic power in the universe. "Mother of the All" belongs to a strand of Platonism that had taken over Stoic gynecological images to describe the origins of the material world. The long version calls Barbelo Mother-Father (CG II 14,19; cp., BG 48,1) and attributes dealings with the lower world to her where the short version simply has "Father." These alterations are philosophically more correct, since the highest divine principle would not take on demiurgic functions (CG II 19,17 f.//BG 51,5 f.; II 20,9 f.//BG 52, 18 f.). However, the short version is not consistent. The Mother-Father's permission for the "opposing spirit" to exist in the universe (II 27,33 f.) is attributed to the Mother (BG 71,6).

Perhaps, the preference for Father in the short version represents an attempt to adapt its picture of divine activity to the divine triad, Father-Mother-Son, which the introductory story equates with Jesus (CG II 2,12 – 15). The divine triad seems to be a regular feature of Sethian traditions, though its location may vary. *GEgypt* overcomes the implication of divine pair as the initiators. The supreme God evolves the Father-Mother-Son triad (CG III 41,7 – 12; 41,23 – 42,4). Both Father and Mother are androgynous (III 42,10 f.//IV 52,2 – 5). The Mother's cosmological functions are evident in her epithets. She "comes forth from herself" and "presides over the heavens" (III 42,12 – 21//IV 52,2 – 14).

A similar pattern appears in *TriProt*, a revelation discourse by each member of the triad. The Father is the image of the invisible spirit and father of all aeons; Mother, the one from whom the all received his image, and the Son, the manifestation of the aeons which come from him. The Mother's revelation is associated with the tree of knowledge. It reveals the ignorance of the lower god (XIII 44,20–29). Her call to gnosis reveals that she is active in shaping and sustaining order in the universe that stems from her, the androgynous Mother-Father (CG XIII 44,29–45,31). The section concludes with a colophon, "On Fate," that indicates that she is associated with the ordering of the world. This function is frequently fulfilled by the Mother or Sophia.

Stead has pointed out that Valentinian traditions have several pictures of Sophia. While Sophia is most commonly the young, "fallen" aeon who must be restored to the pleroma, or Achamoth, the lower Sophia, who will be restored to the aeon along with the Gnostics, there are traditions in which she appears as the perfect consort of God.[4] *Tri-Prot* suggests that the Mother's involvement with the created world and its order can be maintained along with the image of Sophia as divine consort (Epiph. *Pan.* 36,2; Clem. Alex. *Strom.* IV 90,2). Ptolemy, an independent teacher in the Valentinian tradition,[5] modifies a triadic formulation so as to obtain the first Tetrad of an Ogdoad. The triad consists of the Father, the feminine Ennoia, and Nous. The equality between the Nous and the Father provides the possibility for knowledge of God, since only Nous can comprehend him (*Adv. Haer.* I 1,1).

The divine triad is also associated with knowledge of God in a collection of writings that stem from Gnostic circles known to Plotinus. In this tradition, the divine One-Beyond-Existence is "known" by joining in praise of the divine triad. *Zostr* has Barbelo as the one who makes knowledge of God possible. Thus, she is similar to Nous in philosophical triads, the basis for knowledge of the One (CG VIII 83,19–21; 118,10–12; 125,11–16). The goal of the mystic quest is to join in the divine praise (VIII 129,8–16). Similar patterns of joining praise and blessing of the divine triad appear in the other writings of this group, *Mar* (X 8,1–9,25), *Allog* (XI 45,6–49,38; 50,20 f.; 51,12–16; 52,13–15), and *3StSeth*, which gives the praise offered each member of the triad (VII 123,15–124,1; 125,11–14). Unlike their Platonist counterparts, the Gnostic traditions regularly have a female figure as the second member of the divine triad.

## Philosophic Origins of the Female Divine Principle

The Gnostics are not entirely without philosophic support in their presentation of the female second principle. A tradition of philosophical interpretation of mythology combined with the Sophia of Jewish wisdom speculation probably provided the fundamental emphasis on the self-engendered divine Mother and her role in the cosmogonic process. This line of interpretation seems to have played a major role in Valentinian tradition.[6] The Sethian traditions, some of which were used by Valentinian teachers, are more indebted to Jewish Midrashic exegesis. They combine the Sophia figure with Eve traditions.

A tradition of Platonic exegesis, influenced by Pythagorean speculation about the Dyad, used the "feminine principle" to interpret *The Timeus*'s speculations on matter and disorder in the universe. Philo's occasional and somewhat inconsistent use of such traditions suggests that while he knew them, they did not play a major role in his thought. He does not associate these traditions with Eve. She represents "sense perception," the faculty necessary to Mind (cf., *LegAll* II 24, Adam equals Mind) to bring it out of the darkness. Without enlightenment from contact with the material world, Mind would not have any knowledge. This context leads Philo to present the newly awakened mind as arrogant. It thinks that all things belong to it instead of to God, despite its own instability (*Cher* 58–64). This epistemological tradition appears frequently in Gnostic stories of the creation of the lower world by the demiurge. When he sees all the creation, the lower powers and archons, which stem from him, he becomes boastful and arrogant. That boast usually provokes his mother, Sophia, to repentance and initiates the cosmogonic foundations for salvation in the creation of Adam, revelation of gnosis to him, and generation of the Gnostic seed.

The tradition of the Dyad is usually identified with the divine Logos in Philo. Sometimes it appears as matter (*SpecLeg* III 180; *Somn* II 70). Sophia apears with the *Timeus* epithets for matter, "foster mother" and "mother of all things" (*Det* 115f). In that passage, she is presented as an "earth mother" figure nourishing all things with milk from her breasts.[7] The closest one comes to the Gnostic Father-Mother-Son triad is the presentation of the Logos as son of God, Father of All, and Sophia, through whom all things come into being (*Fug* 109). A hint of cosmogonic self-generation appears in the use of the epithet applied to Athene, "motherless," for Sophia (*Ebr* 61) and the Logos (*Opif* 100). That tradition is more directly linked with self-generation by Plutarch a century later. Isis is identified with Athene and the express qualification "I came of myself" makes her self-generation clear. The same passage in Philo attributes to Sophia another attribute that will appear in mythic form in the Gnostic story. She is said to "rise above the material cosmos illuminated by the joy residing in God." The cosmological function of the divine female principle necessarily involves her in the lower world, but her divinity necessitates some form of ascent above that world. *LegAll* II 82 attributes the demiurgic function of "ruling all things" to Sophia. In *Ebr* 30–32, the world perceived by the senses is the beloved son of the union between God the Father and Sophia, his knowledge. A Gnostic cosmology would never have the sensible world so closely linked to the divine. Instead, the divine world of the pleroma emerges from the primary pair or the primary triad. Even Philo usually has the world of ideas as the direct product of God. The rather extraneous and unsystematized character of the references to the feminine as the second principle in Philo suggests that he has not integrated such speculations into his own cosmological reflection.

Plutarch's second-century Platonism is closer both in time and development to that in Gnostic systems. He uses the Dyad/Mother-of-All to exegete the Isis myth (*IsOsir* 372-82). He may also have known a tradition, similar to the development of Jewish Sophia speculation, in which Isis equals Wisdom. *IsOsir* 351 E ff. presents her as *eidesis/phronesis*.[8] Though Isis represents the material vessel of the *Timeus*, imperfect and in need of the ordering Logos, she is not a malevolent principle—just as Sophia and the demiurge are not in many Valentinian systems. The duality inherent in Isis's cosmogonic role is repeated in the Gnostic Sophia figure. She is divided between Eros and a longing for divine order, which can only be brought about through the Logos. Similarly, the ordering activity of the Mother in *TriProt* (XIII 40, 4–42,2) requires completion with the final coming of the son, Logos. All of her activity in the world is aimed at that descent.[9] Gnosticism is not simply a tradition of philosophic interpretation. Its figures take on a mythic tonality that the allegorical interpretations of Philo and Plutarch avoid. But their peculiar shape could never be accounted for simply as the development of mythic stories. Philosophic reflection has already shifted the Gnostic perception of the world and its relationship to the divine.

## Sophia and the Origins of the World

The vast reaches of the pleroma reflect a peculiarly Gnostic concern with separating the divine from the material world and often from its anthropological correlate, the passions of the human soul. This gulf creates difficulties for the role of the divine feminine in creation. Frequently, the mother, who is responsible for the engendering of the divine aeons, appears to have little relationship to the Sophia, who is responsible for the lower world that we know. Some accounts even have more than one Sophia figure. A weak aeon, whose passion or desire for knowledge becomes the source of the god and substance for this world, she may nevertheless return above to the divine world. However, a lower Sophia may remain bound to this world until all of the divine spirit embodied in it returns to its heavenly place. Sophia continues to play an ordering and providential role over against the cosmos, though the various accounts of her responsibility for its devolution from the heavenly world vary in the negative imagery they associate with that act.

One type of flaw is sexual in its overtones. Even in systems that give a different account, it sometimes appears in the epithet *prunikos* (lewd). Sophia wants to conceive without her consort. Since such conception can only produce a material substance without form, the latter being derived from the male, an ugly, abortionlike mass results. It does not even have the image of its mother (cf. *ApocryJn* CG II 9, 25–10,19; *NatArc* II 94, 4–33; *SJC* III 117, 1–119, 7; *PetPhil* VIII 135, 8–136,15). Other less explicit references of this type speak about an "overflow" from Sophia (*OrigWld* II 98, 13–100,29). *Adv. Haer.* I 30,2–4 attributes the overflow to a double impregnation by the Father and the Son of Man.

A second type of flaw is the desire to imitate the Father. Sometimes Sophia is said to seek to create a pleroma like the one created by the Father (*Zostr* VIII 9, 16–11,9). Or, her desire to create without a consort may be a desire to generate as though she were "unbegotten" (Hipp. *Ref.* VI 30,6–8).

Ptolemy has an epistemological interpretation of the Sophia story. God is unknowable by all the aeons except the Mind. This ignorance of God introduces a certain longing into the pleroma which is manifested in the youngest aeon, Sophia. She makes a brash attempt to know the Father. Such a desire would lead to her dissolution. It must be separated from the heavenly world by the Limit (*Adv. Haer.* I 2, 2–4).

Similar diversity appears in the accounts of Sophia's restoration to the divine world and the healing of whatever passion is embodied in the origins of the god/substance out of which the cosmos will come into being. Sophia's divided nature means that she will require divine assistance—often from the consort whose consent she had failed to gain in the first instance. As the "type" of the Gnostic soul caught in a world to which it does not belong, she must remain tied to this world until all have returned to the pleroma. The Sophia story in *ApocryJn* is typical, though once again the long and short versions diverge in important detail. Sophia's repentance is motivated by the arrogant claim to divinity of her offspring. Prayer from the pleroma to the Father brings divine aid. In the short version, Sophia's consort comes to her assistance (BG 47, 4–7; 60, 12–16). In the long version, the Holy Spirit comes from above to elevate her to the Nineth, above her son (CG II 13,8–14,13; cp., *TriProt* XIII 39, 20–40,4). The long version agrees that the deficiency of Sophia must be corrected (by "epinoia," BG 53,20–54,4; CG II 20,27 f.), but it appears to conceive Sophia as identified with the Mother of the highest triad and consequently not possessed of a consort.[10] In Valentinian systems which stress the "passions" of the lower Sophia as the source of the cosmogonic elements, the Savior must rectify the passion of Sophia. Incorporeal matter is often the product of the process (cf., *Adv. Haer.* I 4,5; *ExcTheod.* 44,1–2; 45,1–2; Hipp. *Ref.* VI 32,5–6.

The rest of the story of origins includes both creative soteriological roles for Sophia. She may be assisted by her consort, by a higher Sophia, by the pleroma in general, or by the Spirit. Such divine intervention in the ordering of the cosmos goes undetected by its rulers (e.g., *Adv. Haer.* I 5,3–6; 17,1). Her most important creative/soteriological activity is to provide Spirit to the human, which the lower god has created after an image of the heavenly archetype that had been revealed to silence his boasting. That hidden Spirit makes humanity superior to its creator (e.g., *TriProt* CG XIII 40, 4–42,2; *NatArc* II 87,20–88,15). Sophia, herself, is sometimes the image according to which Adam is created (*GrSeth* CG VII 50,25–51,20; 68,28–31; *ApocryJn* II 19,15–22,9; *ValExpo* XI 33, 35–39,35; *Adv. Haer.* I 5,5–6; *ExcTheod.* 53,1–5; *Adv. Haer.* I 30,6, where the Mother gives Ialdabaoth the "thought of Man" and has the Father breathe in the trace of light). In *GEgypt* (CG III 56,4–60,18), the heavenly seed of Seth is created by a mother-goddess figure with four breasts. It must be transported from the heavens to the vessels waiting in this world, which are the result of the *metanoia* of the hylic Sophia. *OrigWld* gives an even more complex story of the origins of humanity. The Adam story is repeated on each of the three levels–pneumatic, psychic, and hylic. In the middle of the process, Sophia-Life creates Eve, an androgynous instructor for Adam (CG II 107,18–118,6). This heavenly Eve is identified with Sophia (Isis) by the paradoxical "I am" aretalogy, which she proclaims after she comes forth.

The esoteric and elitist side of Gnostic praxis requires that only a small number of humans have the Spirit. In *NatArc* (CG II 96,19–35) the ancestress of the Gnostics is Norea, Seth's sister. She and the Gnostic race have souls from the Father. The Spirit of truth within makes them immortal. They are referred to as the "sown element," which suggests that a process of heavenly creation and divine sowing such as we saw in *GEgypt* might be envisaged. *ApocryJn*, on the other hand, has the Mother intervene in the creation of the Sethians with a special sending of her Spirit (CG II 24,35–25,16). Similarly, the Valentinians associate Sophia with the pneumatics in a special way. She sends seed into them through the angels. Psychics, on the other hand, simply have the "breathed-in likeness" from the demiurge. The pneumatics will enter the pleroma with Sophia; the psychics be exalted to the Ogdoad with the demiurge. Those with only earthly, animal souls will, of course, perish along with the rest of material creation (*Adv. Haer.* I 7,1; *ExcTheod.* 53,5).

## Redemptive Activity by the Mother

The continuation of the stories of the "time of origins" usually establishes a pattern of redemptive intervention by the Mother or Sophia. She must protect her seed/light from destruction by the hostile powers who do not want the truth about their inferiority, ugliness, lack of real divinity to become known among humans. Sophia may rescue her seed from some Old Testament peril (the Sodomites, *Adv. Haer.* 31,1). The flood is particularly common as a hostile incident from which the Gnostic race is saved by some divine agency. *Adv. Haer.* I

30,9−12 has Sophia Prunikos constantly rescuing her light. She saves Noah. She gets around the malicious covenant between the creator and Abraham by having the prophets reveal the future coming of Christ to destroy that convenant. However, she has to enlist the aid of the Mother, the first woman, to prepare a vessel for the coming Christ. Another common time for revelation, as with the Instructor-Eve in *OrigWld*, is at the tree of knowledge. *ApocAd* (CG V 64,5−65,24) has an androgynous Eve-Adam. Eve reveals to Adam the true glory they enjoy and gives him knowledge of the true God. The creator retaliates by dividing them into two sexes. At that point knowledge withdraws.[11] Usually gnosis comes through the tree of knowledge. The Instructor of *OrigWld* (II 118,7−123,31) moves Adam and Eve to disobey the hostile creator and so receive gnosis (cp., *Adv. Haer.* I 30,7). The two versions of *ApocryJn* disagree over who is responsible for the awakening of Adam and rescue from the flood. The short version has Sophia herself. The long version has the heavenly Epinoia, who represents the activity of the highest Mother-Father (CG II 22,19−24,31; 27,31− 30,11).[12]

Another type of redemptive activity has the Mother or Sophia responsible for reordering or controlling Fate (another parallel with Isis). The whole revelation of the Mother's activity in *TriProt* dealt with reordering fate (XIII 42,4−45,20). In other places, one finds general assertions about Sophia's providential ordering of the lower world (e.g., *NatArc* II 87,4−10).

A peculiar development of Jewish Midrashic traditions gave rise to a variant on the reordering theme. Instead of a repentance—lifting-up of Sophia, her rejection of Ialdabaoth's boast leads one of his sons, Sabaoth, to repent (*NatArc* CG II 94,34−96,14; *OrigWld* II 103,3− 106,35). He worships the heavenly Sophia, is exalted in his own heavens above his father, and is given Sophia-Life as a consort to instruct him. The Valentinian tradition has a general version of the instruction of the lower god. Sophia teaches the demiurge that he is not the only god, but he does not reveal the "mystery of the Father and the aeons" to anyone (Hipp. *Ref.* VI 36,2).

With Sophia's activity confined to "holding actions" against the lower god and ordering of the cosmos until the coming of the revealer of gnosis, one might not consider her much of a savior goddess. Yet we have seen that the Instructor-Eve speaks in Isis-like tones to proclaim her identity. The Marcosian ritual attests that one might pray to the Mother in order to defeat the archons, who wish to hinder the soul's ascent into the pleroma (*Adv. Haer.* I 21,5 and the parallel in *I ApocJas* CG V 35, 19 f.). The Mother, who orders fate, in *TriProt* (XIII 45,2− 20) issues a call to awakening and Gnostic baptism.

Both proclamations allude to the functions of the female divine figure in the story of salvation. The long version of *ApocryJn*, which has consistently focused on the Mother-Father as source of salvation, concludes with a proclamation of the threefold coming of the divine Epinoia to aid humanity. The first appears to refer to the awakening of Adam; the second to her activity in ordering fate (the concern with *oikonomia*), and the last to the revealer of gnosis:

> I, the perfect Pronoia of the pleroma, turned myself into my seed, for I existed first, going along every road, for *I am the kingdom of light, I am the remembrance of the pleroma.*
> And I went into the greatness of darkness; I went on until I came to the middle of the prison. And the foundations of chaos shook. I hid myself from them because of their wickedness. And they did not know me. Again, I returned a second time. I went. I came from the light. *I am the remembrance of the pronoia.*
> I came to the middle of the darkness and the inside of Hades seeking my government [*oikonomia*]. And the foundations of chaos shook so that they were about to fall on those in chaos and destroy them. Again I ran up to my root of light, so that they would not be destroyed before the time.
> Yet a third time I went—
> *I am the light which is in the light. I am the remembrance of the pronoia*— so that I came to the middle of the darkness and the inside of Hades. I filled my face with the light of the consummation of their aeon and came to the middle of their prison, that is, the prison of the body, and said, "Let the person who hears arise from the deep sleep." He wept and cried. He wiped away bitter tears and said, "Who is calling my name? Whence comes this hope to me, since I am in the chains of their prison?" I said, "*I am the pronoia of the pure light. I am the thought of the virgin spirit,* who raised you up to the honored place. Arise! Remember that you are the one who has heard and follow your root! *I am the merciful one.* And guard yourself aginst the angels of poverty and the demons of chaos and all who entrap you. And watch out for the deep sleep and the enclosure within Hades." And I raised him and sealed him with the light water of five seals so that death might not have power over him from that time.
>
> (CG II 30,11–31,25)

Here the "I am" predications punctuate a summary of the saving effect of gnosis. The summary would appear to function as a baptismal call to gnosis. But the exhortation to beware of being entrapped also provides a link to another use of the "I am" revelation formula by a female figure. *Thund* uses the paradoxical "I AM" style of the Instructor-Eve as part of a Gnostic wisdom sermon. The hearer is being summoned to follow this Wisdom despite the fact that she is dishonored in the world. Like Isis, this female figure claims to be behind all of human wisdom:

> Why have you hated me in your counsels? For I shall be silent among the silent, and I shall appear and speak. Why then have you hated me, you Greeks? Because I am a barbarian among the barbarians? For I am the wisdom of the Greeks and the knowledge of the barbarians. I am the judgment of the Greeks and the barbarians. I am the one whose image is great in Egypt, and who had no image among the barbarians. I am the one who has been hated everywhere and who has been loved everywhere ... I am she

who does not keep festival, and I am she whose festivals are
numerous. I am godless, and I am the one whose god is great.
(CG VI 15,31–15,11; 15,23–25)

As so often happens, Gnostic rhetoric has intensified the paradox
inherent in the situation of a universal wisdom goddess who goes
unrecognized by most of humanity. Yet she is clearly the source of
salvation for the person who heeds her call.

## Conclusion

This evidence of liturgical acclamation of the Mother, Sophia,
Instructor-Eve, Epinoia as source of gnosis should caution us against
identifying Sophia's fate in the mythic narrative with her place in
Gnostic cult. Further caution is demanded by the fact that most stories
do not attach blame to the devolution of the lower world in which she
plays such a key role. The theological categories of Christianity often
lead interpreters to speak of Sophia's fall and to attribute to it the same
negative evaluations tradition has attached to the fall of Eve/Adam.[13]
Instead, the structure of Gnostic cosmology does not need to explain
fall and alienation from God in terms of sinful disobedience. It needs
to explain the distance between the divine world and this one. That
cosmological structure makes it necessary that some special process of
revelation bring humanity knowledge of that divine world.

The mythic summary of Sophia's wandering fits within the cultic
proclamation of saving gnosis. That gnosis overcomes the ambiguities
and tensions inherent in the Gnostic's experience of the world. *Thund*'s
paradoxes intensify those experiences so as to overcome the disvaluing
effect that they might have on the believer. Though the Mother/
Sophia is not the highest Father or the only revealer of gnosis, she
often appears as the crucial link between the human in this world and
that divinity which constitutes his/her truest identity. The peculiar
amalgamation of mythic and philosophic discourse suggests that her
wisdom also provides a challenge to the claims of human reason
advanced through philosophy. The ultimate image of salvation is
neither male nor female but the restored unity of an androgynous
Mother-Father, who has passed through diversity.

## Abbreviations

GNOSTIC WRITINGS

| | | |
|---|---|---|
| *Allog* | *Allogenes* | CG XI,*3**\* |
| *ApocAd* | *Apocalypse of Adam* | CG V,*5* |
| *ApocryJn* | *Apocryphon of John* | CG II,*1* |
| | | (long version) |
| | | BG 8502,*2* |
| | | (short version) |

| | | |
|---|---|---|
| 1 ApocJas | First Apocalypse of James | CG V,3 |
| GEgypt | Gospel of the Egyptians | CG III,2; IV,2 |
| GrSeth | Second Treatise of the Great Seth | CG VIII,2 |
| Mar | Marsanes | CG X,1 |
| NatArc | Nature of the Archons | CG II,4 |
| OrigWld | On the Origin of the World | CG II,5 |
| PetPhil | Letter of Peter to Philip | CG VIII,2 |
| SJC | Sophia of Jesus Christ | CG III,4; BG 8502,3 |
| 3StSeth | Three Steles of Seth | CG VII,5 |
| Thund | Thunder, Perfect Mind | CG VI,2 |
| TriPot | Trimorphic Protennoia | CG XIII,1 |
| Val Expo | Valentinian Exposition | CG XI,2 |
| Zostr | Zostrianos | CG XIĪ,1 |

PHILO OF ALEXANDRIA

| | |
|---|---|
| Cher | De Cherubim |
| Det | Quod Deterius Potiori insidiari soleat |
| Ebr | De Ebrietate |
| Fug | De Fuga et Inventione |
| LegAll | Legum Allegoriarum |
| Somn | De Somniis |
| SpecLeg | De Specialibus Legibus |

OTHER

| | |
|---|---|
| Adv. Haer. | Irenaeus, Adversus Haeresus |
| Pan. | Epiphanius, Panarion |
| Strom. | Clement of Alexandria, Stromata |
| ExcTheod. | _____, Excerpta e Theodoto |
| Ref. | Hippolytus, Refutatio omnium haeresium |
| IsOsir. | Plutarch, De Iside et Qsiride |

*Italic number refers to the treatise in the codex.

# NOTES

1. E. Voeglin, *Order in History,* IV: *The Ecumenic Age* (Baton Rouge: Louisiana State University Press, 1974), p. 251. On the importance of the element of primordial fusion in Gnostic myth, see M. Tardieu, *Trois Mythes Gnostiques* (Paris: Etudes Augustiniennes, 1974), p. 278.

2. The two main collections of Gnostic writings are the Berlin Codex (referred to by the abbreviation BG) and the thirteen codices found at Nag Hammadi in Egypt, which are in the Coptic Museum in Cairo (referred to by the abbreviation CG). Passages in a Gnostic writing are located by identifying the collection, BG or CG, the codex number (for CG) in roman numerals, and the page and line numbers in arabic numerals.

3. See the discussion of the problem of the dyadic and triadic references to God in Y. Janssens, "L'Apocryphon de Jean," *Museon* 84 (1971):43–48.

4. See G.C. Stead, "The Valentinian Myth of Sophia," *Journal of Theological Studies* 20 (1969):93–95.

5. Ptolemy was an independent Gnostic teacher whose career overlapped with that of Valentinus. Patristic authors present him as Valentinus's successor because they seek to make the Gnostic movement fit into a single chain of traditions; see G. Ludemann, "Zur Geschichte des Eltesten Christentums in Rom. I Valentin und Marcion II Ptolemaus and Justin," *Zeitschrift fur Neutestamentliche Wissenschaft* 70 (1979):102ff.

6. J. Dillon, *Middle Platonism* (London: Dickworth, 1977), pp. 386–89, points out that Valentinians are much closer to Platonic speculation on the imperfection in the material world than they are to any Jewish or Christian speculation on the origin of evil in human sinfulness. The Valentinian system is interpreting the irrational world soul of the *Timeus*. What makes the Valentinian system unusual is the depth of ignorance involved. According to their account the Demiurge cannot see the heavenly forms.

7. Ibid., p. 164, though the language of Sophia's nurturing creation makes her almost an earth mother, she remains a transcendent deity.

8. See G. Quispel, "Jewish Gnosis and Mandean Gnosticism," *Les Textes de Nag Hammadi* (NHS VII; ed. J.E. Menard; Leiden: E.J. Brill, 1975), pp. 80–89.

9. Cp. *GrSeth* CG VII 50, 25–51, 20, Sophia Prunikos prepares monads and places for sons of light; *ExcTheod* 53, 1–5.

10. L. Schottroff, *Der Glaubenden und die feinliche Welt* (Neukirchen-Vluyn: Neukirchner, 1970), pp. 57f., points out the contradictory statement in ApocryJn CG II 14, 7–9.

11. *ApocAd* parodies Jewish salvation history. Though Sophia is not directly responsible, that pattern of salvation history is a series of angelic rescue missions for the Sethians; see my "Apocalypse of Adam: Genre and Function of a Gnostic Apocalypse," *Catholic Biblical Quarterly* 39 (1977):382–95, and, for an alternative reading of the pattern of that salvation history, C. Hedrick, *The Apocalypse of Adam* (Missoula, Mont.: Scholars Press, 1980), pp. 59–84.

12. The short version concludes with a formulaic assertion that the Mother has been active on behalf of her seed despite the fact that the mythic accounts in the short version do not make that activity explicit (BG 75, 10–15, has Mother-Father; 76, 1–6), see Schottroff, pp. 59–66.

13. Schottroff, pp. 42–59. Schottroff observes that the only culpable failure in gnosticism is the failure to respond to the call of revelation (p. 48).

# 9

## C. MACKENZIE BROWN

# *Kālī, the Mad Mother*

**O**ut of the waters of the Ganges arose a young woman of extraordinary beauty, far advanced in pregnancy. With graceful gait she ascended the banks of the river and a few moments later gave birth to a charming baby. She affectionately held the infant and suckled it. Suddenly, the woman was transformed into a cruel and frightening hag. In this terrifying aspect, she seized the child, stuffed it into her mouth, crushed it with her grim jaws, and swallowed it. She then reentered the waters of the river whence she had emerged.[1]

Such was the tender-fierce vision of herself that the goddess Kālī granted to one of her most famous devotees, the nineteenth-century Bengali saint Ramakrishna. In this vision, Kālī revealed not only some of the salient features of her own character, but also intimated something of the nature of reality itself. For it is she, according to her Hindu followers, who creates, governs, and controls the whole of existence. She is the mother of us all, giving us birth from out of her unfathomable depths. She nurtures us and provides us with food, comfort, and the various amusements of life, like any mother with her infant. She bedazzles us with her illusory beauty and consumes us, as she devoured the babe in the vision.

Is the ultimate power of the universe, or God, if you will, really so harsh and uncaring? Can the divine creator be loving, warm, tender, and the next instant indifferent, cruel, devastating? If so, then is God, or Kālī, mad? For many Hindus, the answer to all these questions is yes. What are we to make of Kālī's seeming capriciousness, and of the Hindus' insistence upon her contradictory and bizarre nature? In all of Kālī's works, whether creative or destructive, we can perceive a deceptive quality, what Hindus term *māyā*, a magical, beguiling power. This *māyā* is a key to understanding Kālī's nature, for it is through this delusory power of hers that she plays the game of life, or rather life and death. In her various modes, benign or horrific, Kālī is simply at play. To clarify the meaning of Kālī's entrancing play, we shall need to look deeper into the several aspects of her paradoxical character.

## The Black Goddess

Unlike Ramakrishna's vision, the first impression of Kālī for most Westerners, and for many Hindus, too, begins with the terrifying, bloodthirsty aspects, and only later do the more gentle, maternal qualities become apparent. Kālī, whose name means "the Black One," is commonly described as being dark as the night, naked, and standing on a corpse in the cremation grounds, surrounded by jackals, snakes, and ghosts. She has four arms; her four hands variously hold a bloody sword, a noose or goad, a freshly severed head, and a cup made from half a human skull, filled with blood. From her neck hangs a garland of human or demon heads; newly cut human hands dangle from her waistband; and two dead infants form her earrings. With sunken belly, sagging breasts, and disheveled hair, she stares forward with her three bloodshot eyes, a fitting complement to her gaping mouth with its large fangs, lolling tongue, and blood trickling out of the corners.

As one becomes increasingly familiar with the black goddess, one is ever more impressed by her insatiable thirst for blood. A visit to her temples brings home one dimension of the scriptural statement that Kālī constantly drinks blood, for at her shrines, goats, sheep, buffalo, chickens, and other animals (and formerly humans) are beheaded, until the blood flows like water. The *Kālī kā Purña*, a fairly recent sacred text, affirms in its famous "Blood Chapter" that Kālī receives a month's pleasure from the blood of such animals as fish and tortoises, while by a human sacrifice she is satisfied for a thousand years, and by three human offerings for one-hundred thousand years. The dark goddess, furthermore, takes delight not only in the nectarlike blood, but also in the flesh, especially the heads. At the same time, the text affirms that the "victims" themselves benefit immensely by being offered to Kālī: when sacrificed, humans become pure and free of all sin, they gain the love of the goddess, their blood turns to ambrosia, and they attain the status of divine rulers for many ages. Even here, then, is a suggestion of Kālī's benevolent nature.

The horrific side of Kālī, which initially tends to obscure her benign aspects, was the first to emerge historically within the Hindu tradition.[2] Some fourteen- to fifteen-hundred years ago, Kālī began making her way into the upper ranks of the Hindu celestial hierarchy, largely in the role of a terrible, blood-drinking warrior-goddess. In the *Devī-Māhātyma* of the *Mārkaṇḍeya Purāṇa* (ca. 550 C.E.), Kālī is said to have arisen from the forehead of the goddess Ambikā, or Caṇḍikā, during her battle with the armies of the demon generals, Caṇḍa and Muṇḍa. As Ambikā's face grew dark with anger at the approach of the demons, Kālī suddenly sprang from her furrowed brow, bearing sword and noose, decorated with a necklace of skulls and a tiger skin. Hungry-looking, emaciated, widemouthed, with lolling tongue and sunken, reddish eyes, she was roaring terribly. She proceeded to smash her way through the demon warriors, striking some with her weapons, seizing others with their elephants and chariots and heaving them all into her mouth, grinding them up with her teeth. Howling and laughing in her frightful fury, she finally seized Caṇḍa and Muṇḍa and decapitated them.

This was not the end of Kālī's exploits in the *Devī-Māhātyma*, for soon she came to Caṇḍikā's assistance once again, this time to slay Raktabīja. This fearful demon was endowed with magical power: whenever a drop of blood fell from his body onto the earth, instantly from that drop would spring an exact replica of himself with all his powers. Thus, when Caṇḍikā with her troops succeeded in wounding Raktabīja, she only made her plight worse, as the blood streaming from his gashes at once produced thousands of demons. Caṇḍikā then ordered Kālī to stretch out her mouth to take in the demons and to drink up any blood before it touched the ground. Kālī then devoured all the demons and quaffed the blood flowing from Raktabīja's body until at last he became bloodless and died.

In the *Devī-Māhātyma*, Kālī is not yet the supreme creator and controller of the universe; she is clearly subordinate to another goddess, variously called Ambikā, Caṇḍikā, or Durgā. Kālī, who may well have originated as a fierce tribal deity on the periphery of civilized society, seems to have been incorporated into the main stream of Hindu tradition by being assimilated into or identified with the darker, more violent and destructive aspects of a goddess or goddesses already well-established in the official pantheon. Furthermore, in the ancient accounts of her exploits, Kālī lacks any maternal role, and it is one of the intriguing questions in Hinduism as to how she eventually came to be regarded as mother of the universe. Yet even in the early literature, Kālī is not merely horrific and destructive. After all, her essential purpose in these stories is to serve and protect the interests of the gods and goddesses against the malicious and arrogant demons. To be sure, she seems to take great delight in the carnage and to become intoxicated with the draughts of blood. Her furious laughing in the midst of massacre lends an even more macabre tone. Yet that laugh, reverberating in the hearts of gods and demons, also suggests that Kālī stands above the devastation even while involved in it, that she is aware of her own power, indestructible and irresistible. For most of the combatants, the war is a matter of life and death. To Kālī, it is, as it were, a joke. The battleground of the gods and demons is for her a playground.

While these myths hardly portray Kālī as merciful, another early story brings out something of a horrific-compassionate character. In the *Bhāgavata Purāṇa* (v.9. 12–20), a robber chieftain desirous of a son decided to offer a human victim to the goddess Bhadrakālī, or Kālī. His subordinates captured a wise and saintly man, whom they prepared to sacrifice according to the prescribed rules, washing his body, anointing and adorning it with sandal paste, new jewels, and flowers. They placed him with head bent low before the image of the goddess. When the chieftain, acting as priest, took up the sword to behead the man, Kālī herself, recognizing the extreme saintliness of the victim, suddenly emerged from the image. In an intense rage, she sprang from the altar, lopped off the heads of all the thieves with their own sacrificial sword, and drank her fill of the hot, intoxicating blood streaming from the severed necks. Then she, with her attendants, all inebriated from the blood, singing and dancing, played with the heads, throwing them back and forth. While there is a suggestion that Kālī's compassionate act is, in part, forced upon her by the saint, it is clear that she intends her bloody deeds for the protection of the good. She may get carried away by her gruesome acts, but she is not evil. Also of interest is the attitude of the robber chieftain toward the goddess: Kālī is apparently the granter of children, and thus we find an early hint that she is mistress both of life and death.

One final point in the above story is the reference to Kālī's dancing. In the Hindu tradition, the experience of dance has given rise to rich and varied symbolic meanings. On the cosmic level, dance is seen as the manifestation of the primal vibrations of the universe and as the means by which the absolute brings creation into existence, maintains it, and eventually destroys it. God, the supreme dancer, has no purpose other than the enjoyment of his/her own dynamic movements. Life itself, with its constant transformations of energy, is the dance. When the dance is new and fresh, its perfect rhythm is reflected in the harmony of the cycle of the ages and years, of the seasons, of day and night, and of life and death. When the dance becomes wild and uncontrolled, the whole order of the universe is threatened. Finally, the supreme dancer will rest, before beginning anew. Each human life, furthermore, takes part in the cosmic dance; in rhythm with its own heartbeat, it echoes the tapping feet of God. Thus Kālī's intoxicated dancing comes to be seen as simply one aspect of the pulsing of the universe. Her dancing, though usually uncontrolled and threatening total destruction, contains within it the seeds of new creation, as we shall see. In any case, all dance is an expression of the divine play, which, like dance, has no purpose outside itself.

Kālī's wild dancing was probably an important factor in her developing association with the great god Shiva, Lord of the Dance, who, like her, was noted for his destructive and horrific character. Often the two are portrayed dancing together, inspiring each other to greater frenzy, shaking the worlds with the pounding of their feet and threatening the breakdown of the cosmic order. At times they engage in a sort of dance contest, in which Kālī's wrath is gradually pacified, thereby averting destruction of the world. In a story from the *Liṅga Purāṇa* (I.106), Kālī was so angered after she had slain the demon Darukā, that the universe reverberated with her trembling. Shiva, through his magical *māyā*, assumed the form of an infant in the cremation ground among ghouls and ghosts and began to cry. The goddess, deluded by his *māyā*, cradled him in her arms, kissed and suckled him. As he took her milk, he also sucked out her anger. Then to propitiate her further, he reverted to his previous form and carried out a wild and strenuous dance known as the *Tāṇḍava*. Kālī, much pleased, joined in the dancing. Here, for the first time, we see a clear instance of maternal behavior on the part of Kālī.

Gradually, the black goddess came to be identified as one of the chief spouses of Shiva. One of the common images of Kālī with her husband shows her standing or dancing upon his nude and prostrate body. She is adorned with her usual gruesome attire, and holds a freshly severed head or a blood-filled cranial cup. As she tramples upon her corpselike husband, her energy seems to flow into him, bringing him to life. In some portrayals, not only does he begin to open his eyes, lift his head, and move his arms, but his penis rises, ready for its fecundating act of creating the world. It is Kālī, of course, who will receive the cosmic seed and bring forth the universe from her womb. In such images, it is Kālī who is the dominant figure. She represents Shiva's energy, or *shakti*, and without her he would be a corpse. Her superiority to Shiva is strikingly demonstrated in those scenes where she sits on top of his lacerated and bleeding body receiving his seed.

It was Kālī's association with Shiva, especially in its erotic aspect, that led to the development of her maternal character and thus helped to bridge the gap between her horrific and benign modes. Through Shiva, she becomes the cosmic mother but never completely loses her wild and terrifying nature. Her destructive energies are now perceived as part of her transformative powers, involving both growth and decay. As mistress of blood, she presides over the mysteries of both life and death.

## Kālī and the Tantric Tradition

The expansion of Kālī's personality in close association with Shiva received its most profound impetus within the Hindu Tantric tradition. Tantrism emphasizes the ultimate unity or nonduality of reality, often referred to as Brahman, beyond all name and form. This nonmanifest One, however, becomes two in the process of cosmic evolution and creation. The two primal principles are variously called spirit and matter (*purusha* and *prakṛiti*) or consciousness and energy (*cit* and *shakti*). These two are identified with the god Shiva, and his consort, Shakti (energy personified), whose union represents the ultimate nondual nature of the absolute. Furthermore, there is a hidden correspondence between the divine and human levels of existence; the two mutually interpenetrate each other, and, from the highest Tantric point of view, are one. Specifically, this means that each man and woman not only is a manifestation of Shiva and Shakti, but that each contains within the self both Shiva and Shakti. These have become separated within the individual largely through *māyā*. Here *māyā* is to be understood as an obscuring quality of the absolute that not only hides the real nature of the divine One and makes it appear as split into separate entities, but also causes the apparent fragmentation of the pure, divine consciousness into multiple individual egos. Thus, each of us has forgotten our divine nature and true identity with Shiva/Shakti. Tantric practice aims at the recognition and reunion of the primal consciousness (Shiva) and primal energy (Shakti) within the body through ritual and meditative techniques. This reintegration is the ultimate goal of *moksha*, or liberation, from the cycle of life and death (reincarnation), and is the common goal of Hindu teaching. Necessary to this liberation is the destruction or transcendence of egoistic impulses and desires that perpetuate the obscuring power of *māyā*: it is desire, based on ignorance of our real nature, that impels us to take up new bodies in birth after birth.

It is at this point that Kālī's significance in the Tantric school becomes clear. As Shiva's spouse, she was already identified with his creative and destructive energies on a cosmic level. On a higher, transcendent level, her horrific, terrifying nature comes to be seen as symbolic of her power to destroy *māyā*-induced ignorance, to shatter the delusions of ego. Accordingly, her destructive energies, on this highest level, are seen as a vehicle of salvation and ultimate transformation. The black goddess is death; but to the wise, she is also the death of death. To the liberated sage, her character is wholly benign. Only to the ignorant does she appear terrifying, and with reason, for she threatens destruction of the ego/individual at every moment. It is hardly surprising, then, that Kālī comes to be seen as one of the most important aspects of Shakti, the supreme essence of the universal goddess.

In her Tantric manifestations, Kālī begins to take on a more benign physical appearance, even while retaining much of her grisly form. Her face is sometimes described as beautiful and smiling, her breasts high and youthful, her gauntness gone. Two of her hands still hold the severed head and bloody cleaver but her other two form the gestures of blessing, removing fear and conferring boons.

Especially significant, however, is the reinterpretation in Tantrism of her ancient gruesome and shocking features. As the Dark Night of Destruction, or Time, she is black because she represents the dissolution of the cosmos: all colors and qualities disappear in blackness, just as all beings enter Kālī. Furthermore, as the supreme Brahman, beyond forms, qualities, and colors, she is colorless (black). And for those who have attained final liberation, within her blackness is the dazzling brilliance of illumination. Her disheveled hair, flying free, represents both the entanglements of *māyā* and the loosing of bonds. Similarly, Kālī wields her various weapons to sever the chains of illusion. Her naked body reveals her cosmic powers: her womb, or *yoni*, signifies creation; her full breasts, preservation; her horrible visage, destruction. Her nakedness, like her blackness, shows her to be none other than Brahman the Absolute, free from the covering of *māyā*. Hands are the chief instruments of action, committing good and evil deeds prompted by desires that lead to rebirths. Kālī's waistband of human hands signifies the mergence of all souls and their deeds (*karma*) in her at the end of the world. Kālī as a power of righteousness is revealed in the necklace of freshly cut demon heads. On a deeper level, the fifty severed heads symbolize the fifty letters of the Sanskrit alphabet. These letters represent the universe, as manifested in the various names and forms of material objects. Through divine speech or sound, pure consciousness creates, or evolves into, the gross universe of matter. The necklace of heads thus shows the withdrawal of the objectified world back into Kālī herself, where all duality of matter and spirit, of subject and object, disappears. With her lolling tongue, Kālī quaffs the intoxicating blood-wine of ignorance, thus quenching the thirst for rebirth. She stands on the white, corpselike body of her husband, for he is the illuminating, changeless aspect of consciousness, in pure potential, while she is the activating power of that consciousness. Yet ultimately, she and he are one. She resides or dances in the cremation ground, for in her burning ground all worldly desires are burnt away. Finally, regarding the blood sacrifices performed in her honor (mentioned in the Tantric texts), the whole is interpreted "inwardly" as referring to the sacrifice all individuals must make within themselves. The various kinds of animals are equated with human desires and emotions, all of which must be sacrificed to Kālī before realization can be attained. Thus, one must offer up to the goddess the goat of lust, the buffalo of anger, the cat of greed, the sheep of stupidity, and so forth.[3]

In summary, the esoteric interpretation of Kālī in the Tantra stresses three aspects. On the cosmic level, Kālī is the supreme controlling power bringing forth and withdrawing the universe; she is not really a destroyer, for nothing is absolutely destroyed; the world appears, disappears, and reappears. On the ultimate level, Kālī is the one nondual reality, identical with Brahman, formless and beyond all qualities; or, from a slightly different perspective, she is one with Shiva, the two forming the polar aspects of the universe that at the highest level dissolve in perfect unity. And on the salvific level, Kālī is the transforming-liberating power that breaks through all illusion, destroying the finite to reveal the infinite.

## Interpretative Problems

The question has been raised by various Western scholars as to whether the highly philosophical Tantric interpretation of Kālī is really justified. Some have argued that the Tantric view of Kālī is simply an attempt on the part of an intellectual elite to rationalize the more repulsive aspects of the goddess and her cult. The symbolic and allegorical interpretation of Kālī is regarded by such critics as an unconvincing attempt to transform a cruel, bloodthirsty destructress into a benign mother. It is argued that such Tantric "propaganda" lacks "grass roots" support and thus is forced and graceless.[4] Finally, the Tantric allegorical method of interpretation is said to be entirely arbitrary, as shown by the number of contradictory explanations of some of Kālī's features. One Western author, for instance, points out two very different interpretations of Kālī's dance on Shiva.[5] On the one hand, her wild dance is regarded as symbolizing the dark period of fomentation at the time of the creation of the universe. On the other, it is seen as the tumult of emotions within the individual preceding the moment of divine illumination, when the soul is shocked by realization of the truth, just as Kālī suddenly stops dancing and sticks out her tongue, a sign of embarrassment and surprise. Here, incidentally, is another interpretation of Kālī's protruding tongue, usually seen as an indication of her bloodthirsty nature. According to one story, Kālī was dancing wildly in a corpse-strewn battlefield and threatening the destruction of the world. To pacify her, Shiva threw himself under her feet. She unwittingly stepped on him, and when she realized what she had done, stuck out her tongue in surprise, a gesture once common among Indian village women.[6]

Two points may be made here with regard to the criticisms of the Tantric style of interpretation. First, the Hindu tradition in general recognizes two basic levels of truth: a common, worldly, practical level, and a supreme or absolute level. The latter, by its very nature, will appeal to and be recognized by only a few. The majority will be content with the former, and in fact are not spiritually adapted to take advantage of the higher point of view. For this reason, the supreme truths are often revealed only to initiates. It must be remembered that from the Hindu point of view, such spiritual elitism is based ultimately on radically universalist principles: all beings as they cycle through the chain of bodies in reincarnation gradually attain the spiritual maturity to recognize the highest truths. Most of us are still children. While the presupposition of fundamentally different levels of truth is not well received among many Western academics, an appreciation of such a philosophical perspective is essential to an understanding of most Hindu schools, including Tantrism. The Tantrics are fully aware of the exoteric or popular view of Kālī, but insist that there is also a higher, esoteric significance to the black goddess.

The second point is that Hindu symbolism in general, and Kālī symbolism in particular, is multivalent and multidimensional. It is not surprising to find a specific feature of Kālī, such as her dancing on Shiva, interpreted on cosmic, ontological, and salvific levels. These varying interpretations are not necessarily contradictory, but rather affirmations of the interrelatedness of the different planes of reality. This is especially the case when one encounters the various explanations of Kālī in both an inner and an outer sense. Outwardly, Kālī is regarded as apart from humankind, as mistress over the world. Inwardly, she and the world are not different. She is our own divine, though usually unrecognized, self.

## Kālī and Two Bengali Saints

One final stage in the efflorescence of Kālī is to be found among the poet-saints of Bengal during the last three centuries: the bhaktic, or devotional, elaboration of the goddess as the benign yet indifferent world mother. The Bengali saints were heirs of the rich Tantric philosophical tradition, but they approached Kālī with something of the innocence of a child toward its mother. Two of the most representative and well-known of these saints are Ramprasad (1718–75) and Ramakrishna (1836–86).

Ramprasad affirms the basic unity of all paths to God, but over against the Tantric stress on rituals, yogic meditation, and knowledge (jñāna), he emphasizes the need for total loving surrender of heart, mind, and will to Kālī. A common bhaktic devotional theme in Ramprasad's poems is his own unworthiness as a sinner, with the complementary theme of the greatness of Kālī's mercy of grace in overlooking his faults. Kālī as mother is the supreme saving power. Unlike a father, a mother is ever forgiving her children, or, as Ramprasad says, "mother gives food to her hungry child even if he is guilty at every step."[7] Another standard bhaktic sentiment in Ramprasad is his preference for communion with God over complete mergence in the Absolute Brahman. In a well-known line, Ramprasad declares: "Sugar I love to eat, but I have no wish to become sugar."[8] One should not overstress the dualist elements in Ramprasad, however, for it is a qualified dualism: Kālī and the world are not separate entities, for all things are simply forms of the goddess. She is Brahman and the essence of the individual soul.

Of special interest is Ramprasad's bhaktic interpretation of the ancient and largely horrific features of Kālī. I shall comment on just three: her macabre physical appearance as battle-queen, her intoxication, and her dancing on Shiva's breast. Regarding the first, Ramprasad delights in the battlefields, the swallowing of elephants, the chariots, and the charioteers. In the midst of all this horror, Ramprasad discovers a surprising beauty: her dark complexion is like the splendorous brilliance of fresh blue-black clouds, her face is like the autumnal moon, her teeth sparkle like white flowers, she smiles sweetly. Like the spring adorned with red flowers, her limbs bear stains of bright blood; down her round and smooth thighs flow unceasing streams of blood like flashes of lightning in dark rain clouds. Ramprasad generally refrains from the Tantric type of explicit, philosophic interpretation of Kālī's horrific features, and instead wishes to overwhelm his audience with poetic-bhaktic images of the startling juxtaposition of the graceful and the grotesque. Kālī's beauty transcends earthly norms, confounds the human mind, astonishes the heart. This black beauty is not to be known and understood intellectually: one can only surrender to her. As Ramprasad says, "Fight with the lady is useless."[9]

Kālī's intoxication, for Ramprasad, is significant in a variety of ways. In her wild frenzied dance, she forgets the world and her worshipers. Her indifference is attributed both to her stony heart and to her drunkenness. In many poems the poet complains that Kālī is uncaring and without mercy, yet he asserts that she takes care of him like his own mother. Her loving affection for her child is just one more aspect of her play and is closely related to perhaps the most important meaning for Ramprasad of Kālī's intoxication: he identifies it with the madness of divine love. He calls for Kālī to make him mad with the wine of her love, since he has no more use for reason or knowledge. He likens the world to a lunatic asylum, where "some laugh, some cry, and others dance in excess of joy." "In heaven," he continues, "there is a fair of lunatics," and he concludes, "Who can fathom the mystery of the play of love? /Thou art mad with love, O Mother, crown of lunatics."[10] Kālī's intoxication thus further illustrates her paradoxical nature: she is seemingly forgetful of her devotees in her drunken stupor, and at the same time drunk with love for all beings.

As for Kālī's dancing on Shiva's breast, Ramprasad admonishes her for being shameless, cruel, and hardhearted. She will break her spouse's ribs and even kill him. But the poet also tells us that Shiva is just pretending to be a corpse, because he knows those feet are dispensing divine grace and are none other than Brahman. In Hindu devotionalism, the act of reverencing the feet of a holy person or an image of a god is one of the foremost signs of submission and surrender. Thus, Shiva's holding of Kālī's feet upon his chest signals his taking refuge in her as supreme savior. This theme is developed in various ways. Shiva's corpselike state is said to be, in fact, his trancelike meditation on her feet; he is said to keep his eyes shut, feigning sleep, because he knows that when he "wakes up" he will have to share her feet with her sons (her devotees). Ramprasad even argues that Shiva has stolen those feet: "By what right does He hold my Mother's feet on His bosom, being my Father? ... A child inherits his mother's property; on what right has he usurped it?"[11] Accordingly, the poet threatens to steal back Shiva's ill-gotten treasure, or even to take it by force. The bhaktic interpretation of her bloody, spouse-trampling feet has transformed them into a symbol of the supremely merciful refuge of the universe, granting freedom from fear of death and rebirth in union with her.

Ramprasad also introduces into Kālī devotionalism many new images drawn from ordinary village life to illustrate the nature of his
mother. One example refers to the kite-flying contests in which Indian
boys cover their kite strings with powdered glass so as to cut through
the others. In this verse, the kite set free is the soul released:

> In the market place of this world,
> The mother sits flying Her kite.
> In a hundred thousand,
> She cuts the string of one or two.
> And when the kite soars up into the Infinite
> Oh, how She laughs and claps her hands![12]

Even in granting the soul liberation, Kālī the mother is still at play.

A similar motif is reflected in the thought of Ramakrishna, who was
inspired by Ramprasad and often sang his poems. After singing the
song above and in answer to a question as to why the mother does not
free us all from our earthly bonds, Ramakrishna replied: "She wants
to continue playing with her created beings. In a game of hide-and-
seek the running about soon stops if in the beginning all the players
touch the 'granny.' If all touch Her, then how can the game go on?
That displeases Her. Her pleasure is in continuing the game."[13] Here,
too, like his predecessor, Ramakrishna draws upon the experiences of
village life to explain the nature of his divine mother. Indeed, in the
eyes of Ramakrishna, Kālī takes on much of the character of a village
wife, even in her destructive aspects:

> After the destruction of the universe, at the end of a great cycle,
> the Divine Mother garners the seeds for the next creation. She is
> like the elderly mistress of the house, who has a hotchpotch pot in
> which she keeps different articles for household use .... House-
> wives have pots like that, where they keep "sea foam," blue pills,
> small bundles of seeds of cucumber, pumpkin, and gourd, and so
> on. They take them out when they want them. In the same way,
> after the destruction of the universe, my Divine Mother, the
> Embodiment of Brahman, gathers together the seeds for the next
> creation."[14]

Ramakrishna received his first vision of Kālī around the age of
twenty, while serving as a priest at her temple in Daksinewar, near
Calcutta. He had frequently become absorbed in loving contemplation
of her, singing the songs of Ramprasad and other devotees. But he
became intensely anxious for a direct vision of the mother, complaining that since she had showed herself to Ramprasad, why not to him?
So intolerable became his anguish that one day in the mother's temple
he picked up her sword with the thought of ending his life on the spot.
Suddenly, the mother appeared to him and he was filled with bliss.

Following the vision, his behavior became so inebriated with divine love that many, including his relatives, considered him mad.

Perhaps most striking in Ramakrishna's worship of the mother was his total intimacy with her, often causing him to disregard the "correct" or scriptural mode of worship. He would be found ascending the altar to caress the mother, touching her chin, joking and laughing with her, even catching hold of her hands and dancing. He would take rice curry in his hand and touch it to her mouth, imploring her: "Mother, eat it, do eat it, Mother."[15] In putting her to bed at night he would lie on her silver bedstead and say, "Dost Thou ask me to lie down? All right, I am doing so."[16]

In Ramakrishna, then, we find a simple, innocent, complete self-surrender to Kālī. He is more trusting, less stubborn, petulant, or complaining than Ramprasad in his childlike familiarity with her. For Ramakrishna, Kālī has become the all-merciful and benign mother of all. He did not forget her horrific side, as evidenced by his vision of her quoted at the beginning of this essay. But, like Ramprasad, he saw through her terrifying demeanor, thereby discovering her maternal affection for all humankind, for the whole universe.

## Conclusion

We began by considering the question of Kālī's horrific and benign character, which gives her the appearance of a mad, capricious goddess. We have come to see that the horrific-benign contrast is actually just one of many paradoxes in Kālī's personality. As the good and terrible mother, she represents, or is, the power of the material world—Mother Nature, in her creative, nurturing, and devouring aspects. These really are not separate aspects, for without eating her children, how could she sustain them at her breast? Every nursing mother needs food. She eats what she has given birth to, for she has given birth to everything and thus there is nothing else to eat. Kālī is not only material force, or *prakṛti*, however; she is also spiritual force, *purusha*, or consciousness, *cit*. By many, it is Shiva, her spouse, who is regarded as the "spiritual" principle, but she and Shiva are ultimately one. To her own closest followers, she is both spirit and matter, for she is the universe. As it is sometimes put, the universe lies within, or simply is, her belly. All material forms are transformations of her energy, the gross vibrations of her own consciousness. As consciousness, Kālī also has her negative and positive sides: she is *māyā*, that intoxicating, inebriating force that ensnares beings in the chains of worldy desires by obscuring the divine reality; she is also *vidyā*, knowledge, and *preman*, love, either of which penetrates her veil of *māyā*. Thus she is both the great deluder and great savioress.

Her four primary aspects, as good and terrible mother, deluder, and granter of salvation, are ultimately one. As the cruel hag who dashes to pieces the finite world of individual egos, she teaches humankind the necessity of giving up attachment to ephemeral pleasures and self-centered hopes. Lasting peace can only be gained when one lets go the illusion of personal self-sufficiency, for none of us is truly in control of his or her destiny. Kālī need not frighten us into this realization: she can beguile us into seeing her as the all-merciful and compassionate mother. In either case, she wins us back to her, to whom we ultimately belong. As our two Bengali saints make clear, it is simply her sport, her play, to send us forth, and sooner or later to call us back.

One final question may remain in our minds. Even if we have come tentatively to accept and appreciate the various paradoxes, the negative as well as the positive sides of Kālī, as simply various dimensions of her transformative and salvific powers, still we may ask, Why the play in the first place? If the world is only her play, does this not reduce Kālī to a mere mad prankstress; does it not deprive the world of meaning; does it not finally make our own pains and sufferings pointless in a universe without ultimate purpose? To the worshiper of Kālī, the answer lies in the notion that absolute perfection requires nothing and thus nothing need be accomplished, overcome, transcended. The universe, the "belly of Kālī," when seen by eyes from which the veil of *māyā* has been removed, is understood to be perfect. Only an imperfect god in an imperfect universe has purposes to fulfill. This view expresses an ancient and central theme of Hinduism. In the *Bhagavad Gītā*, God (as Krishna) declares:

> For me ... there is nothing to be done
> In the three worlds whatsoever,
> Nothing unattained to be attained. ...[17]

Accordingly, the world process can best be explained as play—a partial explanation useful to finite human minds in apprehending something of the infinite mystery.

For the Hindu, Kālī has come to reveal the divine perfection, and consequently, perfect freedom also. It is a freedom that transcends the mores of everyday society and the ethical norms of the philosophers. This freedom may appear as capriciousness, until one realizes that perfect freedom embodies the divine bliss that overflows into the universe in an all-affirming love. For the devotee, all earthly sorrows and pains then disappear, merging in that ocean of bliss known as Kālī. We may end with Ramakrishna's words describing the aftermath of his first vision of Kālī: "I did not know what happened then in the external world—how that day and the next slipped away. But in my heart of hearts, there was flowing a current of intense bliss, never experienced before, and I had the immediate knowledge of the Light that was Mother."[18]

## NOTES

1. See M. [Mahendranath Gupta], *The Gospel of Sri Ramakrishna*, trans. Swami Nikhilananda (New York: Ramakrishna-Vivekananda Center, 1942), pp. 21–22; and Swami Saradananda, *Sri Ramakrishna, the Great Master*, trans. Swami Jagadananda, 4th ed. (Madras: Sri Ramakrishna Math, 1952), pp. 201–2.

2. For the following historical survey I am indebted in many ways to the excellent essays on Kālī by David R. Kinsley, in his *The Sword and the Flute; Kālī and Kṛṣṇa, Dark Visions of the Terrible and the Sublime in Hindu Mythology* (Berkeley and Los Angeles: University of California Press, 1975) pp. 81–149. It would be hard, especially in a short essay such as this, to improve upon his organization of materials. I have utilized his historical outline, but have emphasized different aspects and in general provided my own analyses and interpretations, which do not contradict but supplement Kinsley's own.

3. For the various Tantric interpretations of Kālī, see Arthur Avalon [John Woodroffe], trans., *The Great Liberation (Mahānirvāna Tantra)*, 2nd ed. (Madras: Ganesh & Co., 1927), pp. 378–80; Arthur Avalon [John Woodroffe], trans., *Hymn to Kālī: Karpūrādi-Stotra*, 2nd ed., rev. and enl. (Madras: Ganesh & Co., 1953), pp. 39–42; and John Woodroffe, *Shakti and Shakta: Essays and Addresses on the Shakta Tantrashastra*, 3rd ed., rev. and enl. (Madras: Ganesh & Co., 1929), pp. 485–89, 538.

4. Constance Kapera, *The Worship of Kālī in Banaras: An Inquiry* [Delhi: Motilal Banarsidass, 1966?], p. 89.

5. Ernest A. Payne, *The Śāktas: An Introductory and Comparative Study*, Religious Life of India (London: Oxford University Press, 1933), pp. 23–24.

6. See Kinsley, *Sword and Flute*, p. 108; and Sister Nivedita [Margaret E. Noble], *Kālī the Mother*, 2nd ed. (Mayavati, Almora, Himalayas: Advaita Ashrama, 1953), p. 32.

7. *Rama Prasad's Devotional Songs: The Cult of Shakti*, trans. Jadunath Sinha (Calcutta: Sinha Publishing House, 1966), p. 2, no. 3.

8. Edward J. Thompson and Arthur Marshman Spencer, trans., *Bengali Religious Lyrics, Śākta* (London: Oxford University Press, 1923), p. 40, no. 15.

9. *Rama Prasada's Devotional Songs*, p. 152, no. 277.

10. Ibid., pp. 75–76, no. 139.

11. Ibid., p. 65, no. 121.

12. Quote in Nivedita, *Kālī the Mother*, p. tl. Cf. *Rama Prasada's Devotional Songs*, p. 86, no. 160.

13. M., *The Gospel of Sri Ramakrishna*, p. 136. Incidentally, in the Indian game of hide-and-seek, all the players except the leader or "granny" are blind-folded, and it is up to them to find her, an apt analogy for human souls seeking out the Divine.

14. Ibid., p. 135.

15. Saradananda, *Sri Ramakrishna, the Great Master*, p. 145.

16. Ibid.

17. *The Bhagavad Gītā*, trans. Franklin Edgerton, rev. ed. (Cambridge: Harvard University Press, 1972), 3: 22.

18. Saradananda, *Sri Ramakrishna, the Great Master*, p. 140.

# 10

## CARL OLSON

# Śrī Lakshmī and Rādhā: The Obsequious Wife and the Lustful Lover

The Hindu religious tradition recognizes two types of goddess figures: the independent and the nonindependent female deities. This general observation is an oversimplification because one often finds nonindependent goddesses who exert considerable independence in certain religious texts. Nonetheless, independent goddesses are usually unmarried, often unpredictable, erotic, aggressive, fierce, malevolent, and dangerous. These harmful goddesses are frequently depicted as warlike and bloodthirsty. They are often worshiped during times of crisis, such as epidemics and drought. If they are married, they tend to dominate their spouses. The goddess Kālī, or Durgā, is a good example, as are the numerous village goddesses of India, like Mariamma, the goddess of cholera, and Pollamma, the goddess of smallpox. Individuals must continually exercise caution not to offend these malevolent goddesses. These malevolent, dangerous figures are what O'Flaherty refers to as goddesses of the tooth, who are often symbolized by the whore, the mare, or the evil mother.

In distinction to these goddesses are the goddesses of the breast, who are symbolized by the cow, the good mother, and are connected to the life cycle.[1] The nonindependent figures, or goddesses of the breast, are not quick to anger and are not aggressive; they tend to be more pacific and benevolent. Repulsed by the blood offerings frequently made to independent goddesses, they accept only vegetative offerings from their devotees. The goddesses are nonindependent in the sense that they are the consorts of male deities. It is important to note, however, that even nonindependent goddesses are potentially dangerous. What restrains their potentially dangerous character?

Within the later Hindu tradition, the male gods or spouses function as a restraining factor.[2] The nonindependent goddesses are able to release their potentially aggressive natures in satisfying sexual relationships with their male consorts. This is not possible for the independent goddesses, whose sexual abstinence finds no release except in aggressive and often malevolent behavior towards humans.

The subjects of this essay are two nonindependent goddesses: Śrī Lakshmī and Rādhā. The former is the spouse of Vishnu, and the latter the consort of Krishna, an *avatāra* (incarnation) of Vishnu. Actually, Rādhā can be placed somewhere between the two major groups of goddesses. She is often equal to Krishna and sometimes even conceived as superior. The status of Rādhā leads to an ambiguous power relationship with her husband. O'Flaherty aptly summarizes the ambiguity, as she writes, "Soteriologically, the female consort, Rādhā or Pārvatī, may often be greater, but the god is usually ontologically greater. Rādhā has power, but Kṛṣṇa has authority."[3] The historical emergence of Rādhā and Śrī Lakshmī as goddesses is neither entirely lucid nor devoid of scholarly controversy. Rādhā begins as a fully human *gopī* (cowherdess) before becoming deified. Śrī Lakshmī begins as two independent abstract concepts, even though the ancient Indians, as Gonda notes,[4] did not make a distinction between concrete and abstract concepts. Actually, it is possible that Śrī herself represents two different figures: an early abstract concept and a fertility goddess or spirit. Śrī Lakshmī and Rādhā represent a more auspicious, loving, and benevolent aspect of the Hindu understanding of the great goddess.

After summarizing the historical development of Śrī Lakshmī and Rādhā, this essay will present their major functions and some of the differences in their natures. It will be important to call attention to their relationships with their male consorts. This procedure will elucidate their roles as models for female behaviour within Hindu society, and the way in which the male gods function as a restraint upon these goddesses.

## Historical Survey of Śrī Lakshmī's Development

There is a goddess who possesses eyes like a lotus flower (*padmā*, *kamalā*), her thighs are like the lotus, she possesses a lotus face, and her skin is the color of the lotus. She dwells in this aquatic flower, sometimes envisioned as standing erect on the lotus, and often holding the lovely flower in her hands. Once upon a time, she was born from the lotus, her ears delighting to the trumpeting sounds of elephants. Thus eulogizes the Vedic poet in the *Śrīsūkta*, a late supplement of fifteen verses appended to the fifth *mandala* of the *Rig Veda*, about a goddess later to be called Śrī Lakshmī. The poet also describes her garlands of gold and silver, and praises her for abounding in dung and being moist, referring to her connection with the growth of rice. As an earth goddess, she is the mother of all living creatures. The very embodiment of royal splendor, she bestows worldly fame and success by her ability to grant prosperity, long life, health, and offspring. This poetic eulogy, which encompasses many of her major characteristics, actually sings the praises of two goddesses; Lakshmī appears in five verses (1–2, 13–15). Even though Śrī and Lakshmī appear as independent figures, the form of their later characteristics are essentially prefigured in these verses.

The goddess known as Śrī Lakshmī was originally two different independent figures who became merged during the period of the early Upanishads.[5] The term *lakṣmī* originally meant a sign or an omen of good or bad luck. Thus she became the deity representing the signs or prognostications of luck, prosperity, and well-being in the post-Vedic period, and gradually she became accepted as a goddess of wealth or fortune. The term *śrī* denotes well-being, prosperity, luck, and splendor; it is associated with a complete lifetime, offspring, the life sap, honor, glory, and dignity. Thus to lose *śrī* implies hunger, misfortune, and unhappiness. This abstract concept gradually evolved into the goddess Śrī, who does not, however, appear as a distinct female deity before the *Vājasaneyi Samhitā* (ca. 900 B.C.E.). She is a pre-Aryan goddess of fertility, and her origin is probably non-Aryan.

The basic structure of Śrī and examples from Hindu and Buddhist texts contain evidence of her non-Aryan origin. She represents an autochthonous element that became incorporated into early Vaishnavism. It is very likely that Śrī was originally a Yakshinīs, a semi-divine chthonic spirit, because she shares the same fundamental structure as these usually benevolent spirits. The Yakshas and their feminine counterparts, the Yakshinīs, are guardians of wealth, especially treasures hidden in the roots of trees. Possessing the power to assume any shape, they are known as attendants of the god Kubera, with whom Śrī is also associated, acting as powers of wealth and fertility. They are thus closely connected to the essence of the water of life. Like Śrī the Yakshas are often represented holding a lotus, a symbol of the waters of life, or a cup or flask, a symbol of abundance. Śrī is often represented in art with elephants, which serve as vehicles for the Yakshas. Entire cities stand under the protection of Yakshas-like statues of Śrī, which guard towns and villages from evil. There is a very close relationship between Yakshas and kingship, which is also true of Śrī. Yakshas can be cruel and dangerous on occasion. This is especially true of the females, who eat human flesh and drink blood, although there is no evidence of Śrī engaging in such demonic activity. There is, however, a similarity between a late myth of Śrī in the *Padakusalamāṇava Jātaka* and a horse-faced Yakshinī, who is fond of eating men that she captures until she finds a man that she loves and forces him to marry her. In this example, the Yakshinī represents a mare, a symbol of untamed, dangerous, evil, destructive, lascivious, erotic power. Śrī is cursed to become a mare by Vishnu after she lusts for Revanta in the *Devībhāgavata Purāṇa* (6. 17–19), although the curse is mitagated by the promise that she will be released after giving birth to a son. After meditating on Shiva and performing asceticism for a thousand years, Shiva informs her that Vishnu would appear to her in the form of a stallion and beget a son with her. After this promise comes true, both Vishnu and Śrī resume their normal forms and returned home. This myth is an example of a transformation from lustful woman (mare) into a fertile woman (a cow). It also possibly illustrates a remnant of Śrī's early nature, which is similar and possibly even identical to that of a Yakshinī.

Besides the common features of Śrī and the Yakshinīs, the *Mahābhārata* (12. 221. 60f.) informs us that Śrī tells Indra, leader of the gods, that she left the *asuras*, demonic beings, because they not only neglect their cattle, but they also indulge in meat eating. This myth is evidence of her non-Aryan origin and subsequent adoption among Aryan deities. An even earlier example of her adoption by Aryan gods is found in the *Śatapatha Brāhmana* (11.4.3.1–17), where she emerges from the god Prajāpati, who is fatigued from his creating activities. Śrī offends the gods who are envious of her beauty and other attributes. The jealous gods decide to kill her, but they are dissuaded by Prajāpati because she is a female. The angry deities agree to spare her life, but they are given permission to confiscate her attributes, leaving her subjugated. By offering a sacrifice to the gods, Śrī regains all her possessions. Stripping Śrī of her attributes can be viewed as a form of gang rape. If my hypothesis concerning Śrī's Yakshinī-like nature is correct, she probably possessed an originally mysterious, dangerous, and aggressive nature that posed a threat to a male-dominated pantheon. Thus the deities, who with one exception are males in this episode, found it necessary to tame and subjugate her, and this was accomplished by a form of gang rape that initiated her into the Vedic pantheon. In summary, Śrī's development into a goddess was most likely twofold: a combination of an abstract concept with a Yaksha.

In the epic *Mahābhārata*, composed between 300 B.C.E. and 300 C.E., Śrī Lakshmī is often associated with other deities. She is the daughter of Brahmā, her two brothers are Dhātṛ and Vidhātṛ, and her mindborn sons are the horses that fly in the sky (1.60.50). She is one of the ten daughters of Daksha, who gives her in marriage to the god Dharma (1.60.14). And throughout the epic she is also associated with Kubera, the ruler of the Yakshas and lord of wealth. The epic relates the myth of her birth after the gods churned the ocean (1.16.35), similar to the origin myth of the ocean-born Aphrodite of ancient Greek culture. Śrī Lakshmī is known for her fickle nature, which motivates the cows initially to refuse her request to live with them; they finally allow her to dwell in their urine and dung (13.81.1086). Her fickleness confuses others as to whether she is divine or demonic, which may be a clue to her original close association or identity with the Yakshas. Śrī's close association with demonic-like beings is evident in another myth where she leaves the body of the demon Bali, after it is conquered by Indra, who places her for safe keeping in the earth, waters, sacrificial fire, and among truthful men (12.218.1–30). Besides these negative connotations about her nature, Śrī incarnates herself as the heroine Draupadī, the polyandric wife of the five Pāṇḍavas. The most significant characterization of Śrī Lakshmī is, however, as the wife of Vishnu.

Before and possibly even during her adoption into the Vaishnava pantheon (ca. third–fourth century C.E.) Śrī Lakshmī appears to have been worshiped as an independent goddess with her own cult.[6] For the most part, however, she loses her independent status when she becomes the consort of Vishnu. She is very popular among the monarchs of the Gupta dynasty (320–540 C.E.), appearing on nearly all their coinage, which represents the first epigraphic evidence of the union of Śrī Lakshmī and Vishnu. Raychaudhuri views the enthronement of Śrī Lakshmī by the side of her lord as a parallel to the eminent position of royal queens during the Gupta period, indicating an assertion of women's rights. According to Jaiswal, there is no evidence that royal consorts enjoyed any political rights or independent status; they enjoyed social privileges by virtue of their marriage, most often being conceived of as subordinate to and subject to the control of their husbands. Thus the conjugal union of Śrī Lakshmī and Vishnu served as an archetype of ideal married life embodied in the Purāṇic texts.

Around the late fifth century or early sixth centry C.E., Vaishnava texts, such as the *Ahirbudhnya Samhitā* of the Pāñcarātra sect, envision Śrī Lakshmī as the *shakti* (energy, creative power) of Vishnu. Śrī is understood as the material cause *(prakriti)* of the universe. In the *Lakṣmī Tantra*, a Pāñcarātra work composed between the ninth and twelfth century C.E., the worship of Lakshmī is emphasized, as well as her creative and redemptive functions. And Śrī Lakshmī appears as the supreme being—called the Fourth—of the entire universe in the late sectarian *Saubhāgyalakṣmī Upanishad*, which can be dated about the eleventh century C.E.

## Historical Survey of Rādhā's Development

The development of Rādhā into a renowned goddess occurs considerably later than the emergence of Śrī Lakshmī. Some terms in the *Rig Veda* and *Atharva Veda* are similar to the name Rādhā, but these terms are inconclusive and the exact origins of Rādhā remain obscure. Furthermore, the exact period when Rādhā became definitely associated with Krishna is merely conjectural.

Besides her appearing iconically at Pahārapur in the fifth century C.E.,[7] there are a number of literary references to Rādhā, of which the earliest explicit reference is found in the *Gāhāsattasāī*, a Prakrit work by Hāla dated anywhere from the first to the seventh century. Other literary references to Rādhā refer to her beauty, her love making with Krishna, and her emotional states: her pangs of love, her hopes and anger, her anguish and languor, her misgivings, her sulkiness, and her jealousy. Throughout these literary sources, Rādhā appears as a fully human mistress of Krishna.

The *Śilappadikāram*, a Tamil classic written before the second century C.E., contains many of the stories of Krishna that appear in the *Bhāgavata Purāṇa* and other such works. The Tamil work mentions Nappinnai as the wife of Māyan (Krishna-Gopāla). Nappinnai, an incarnation of Vishnu's consort Nīladevī, also appears in the Tamil Ālvār poetry of Āṇḍal and Nāmmālvār. It is possible that the author of the *Bhāgavata Purāṇa* rejected the figure of Nappinnai as she appears in the works of the Tamil poets because she was an embarrassment; another possibility is that Nappinnai forms the source or prototype of the Rādhā legend in Prakrit and Sanskrit literature. Or it is likely that these two female figures represent independent variants due to their different characteristics. The last possibility seems to be the most likely.

There is no explicitly lucid reference to Rādhā in the *Harivaṃśa* (an appendage to the epic *Mahābhārata*), the *Vishnu Purāṇa*, or the *Bhāgavata Purāṇa*, which all contain stories of the birth, life, loves, and heroic exploits of Krishna. The latter two works contain references to a favorite *gopī* (cowherdess). A reason why Rādhā does not appear in the *Bhāgavata Purāṇa* is offered by Katre, who views Rādhā as originating in northern India, while the Purāṇa seems to have been composed in the south. Scholarly speculation concerning Rādhā's ancestry leads Dimock to postulate a Q source for her legend. Based on available evidence, it is safe to postulate that the romance of Rādhā and Krishna was transmitted in the folk tradition and predates the *Bhāgavata Purāṇa*, although the extent to which the legend predates the Purāṇa is uncertain.

Rādhā is specifically mentioned in later Purāṇic works like the *Padma* and *Brahmavaivarta* and other such compositions. In the *Padma Purāṇa*, parts of which can be dated to about 900 C.E., her humble birth as a *gopī* is rationalized by explaining that she is referred to as a *gopī* because she conserves energy. She appears in this work as the *hlādini-shakti* (blissful energy) of Krishna and as Mahālakshmī. Rādhā is married to an unnamed person. Throughout the work, there are numerous traces of a developed Rādhā cult, a description of her birthday festival (*Rādhāṣṭamī*) is given, and her worshipers are glorified. The *Nāradīya Purāṇa* (ca. 875–1000 C.E.) has further traces of a fully developed Rādhā cult where she is called *Mūlaprakriti*. In the

*Brahmavaivarta Purāṇa* (ca. 750–1550 C.E.), which represents a transition from a basically masculine-oriented theology to a feminine theology,[8] Rādhā is active as a creative, life-sustaining, loving, redemptive goddess. The Purāṇa relates that while residing in Krishna's heavenly abode, Rādhā rebukes him for slighting her. Rādhā is admonished by Shrīdāma, whom she curses to become a demon. Thereupon, Shrīdāma curses her to be born as a *gopī* on earth and to suffer the torments of separation from Krishna. Rādhā's earthly parents are Vrishabhānu and his wife Kalāvatī, the latter producing her daughter by means of a virgin birth. After marrying at age twelve and experiencing an earthly life as a *gopī*, Rādhā is married to Krishna in heaven.

Although these Purāṇic works are important, a more profound influence was exerted on Bengali Vaishnavism and Hindu poets of the Vallabha sect by the *Gītagovinda* of Jayadeva, the court poet to Lakshmana Sena, who ruled in the late twelfth century. In this poem Rādhā is Krishna's favorite *gopī*, and it is unclear from the text whether she is the wife of Krishna or of another man. The leading *gopī* of the poem, she symbolizes the perfection of human love for god. In contrast to the frivolous *rāsa* dance, which Krishna performs with other *gopīs*, the love affair of Krishna and Rādhā is a mature relationship culminating in their union and mutual victory over each other. Jayadeva's poem beautifully expresses the various phases of love: amorous advances, disappointment, jealousy, separation, reconciliation, and finally union. By the late thirteenth century, there is epigraphic evidence of a Rādhā cult found on a temple inscription from the reign of Sāraṅgadeva of Gujarat. And before the end of the fifteenth century, Rādhā appears as one of the family deities of a ruling chieftain, according to the *Māṇḍalika-mahākavyam*.

Rādhā plays a prominent role in a number of Hindu sects (*sampradāyas*) and among its poets. In the Vallabha Sampradāya, named after its founder (1479–1531), Rādhā gains a prominent place in the sect only from the time of Viṭṭhalnāth (ca. 1515–1588), the son and successor of its founder. A great influence was exerted on this sect and its acceptance of Rādhā as the divine wife of Krishna by the poet Sūrdas (born ca. 1487), who viewed Rādhā as the legally married (*svakīyā*) wife of Krishna, both having been acquaintances since childhood. Another important figure is Nimbārka, who raised Rādhā to a universal principle at the side of Vishnu around the thirteenth century. Nimbārka's influence extended to Caitanya and Bengali Vaishnavism.

Caitanya, who was born in Bengal in 1485, became the moving spirit of a new religious revival movement centered on devotion to Krishna and Rādhā. Caitanya was conceived by some of his followers as an *avatāra* (incarnation) of Krishna, while others viewed him as an embodiment of Rādhā and Krishna having become one in the body of Caitanya to enjoy the fruits of supreme love. Caitanya served as a model for his followers' own behavior and religious attitude, which included assuming the behavior and attitude of a *gopī*, the only way to gain the pleasure of divine love. Caitanya was influenced by the *Gītagovinda* of Jayadeva and the poems of Caṇḍīdās and Vidyāpati. The latter two poets emphasized *parakīya rati*, or unconventional love, between Krishna and Rādhā unbound by the accepted standards of conjugal love. This unconventional, illicit love was transformed into a model of love between human beings and the divine.

An important source of influence on the theologians of the Caitanya sect was exerted by the *Gopālatāpanī Upanishad*. This text was used by theologians to support their contention that Krishna is the supreme divine being and not merely an *avatāra* of Vishnu. It was also used to prove the antiquity of Rādhā, made possible by a reference in the text (6.5) to a *gopī* named Gāndharvī, who was called the best among the *gopīs*. As the Bengal Vaishnava sect developed, it divided into two factions over the interpretation of Rādhā and her relationship to Krishna—whether she was a mistress or a wife. One faction argued that Rādhā was a *svakīya* woman, which means that she is legally married to her husband and diligently follows the traditional social duties (*dharma*) of her station in life. Neglecting their *dharma*, *parakīya* women enter into love affairs although they belong to another man and have no intention of marrying their illicit lover. There are two kinds of *parakīya* women: married (*parodhā*) and unmarried (*kanyakā*). The former type of *parakīya* women have more to lose when entering into an extramarital love affair. Since they risk the loss of their husband, home, and reputation, they are the best exemplars of *prema* (true love). Those members of the sect who approved of the *parakīya* interpretation of Rādhā won the issue, and Rādhā became the supreme example of an individual who would risk and even abandon everything for her love.

Rādhā also plays a prominent role in two other Hindu sects: the Sakhī Sampradāya and the Rādhāvallabha Sampradāya. Among the former, founded by Haridās (ca. 1600), Rādhā is the legitimate wife (*svakīya*) of Krishna. The members of the sect, called *sakhīs*, or friends, identify with the *gopī* companions of Rādhā by assuming female garb and manners in order to share the *rasa* (emotional mood) experienced by Rādhā in her relationship wth Krishna. The members of the sect act as assistants to Rādhā in preparing for the devotional union with Krishna and serve as witnesses to the divine love making. Rādhā eclipses Krishna in central importance among the Rādhāvallabha Sampradāya, founded in 1585 by Śrī Hit Harivamś. In the theology of this sect, Rādhā is the ground of being, the eternal power, without form or qualities, and the bestower of bliss. She is more powerful than Krishna because he cannot control his profuse passion for her, an inversion of the traditional viewpoint. Her devotees are her companions (*sakhīs*), who act as intermediaries for the union of Rādhā and Krishna.

## The Cosmogonic Function and Its Symbols

Śrī Lakshmī and Rādhā are both conceived as possessing a creative function. Since the creative function of Rādhā is fully explicated in another work[9] and is theoretically very similar to that of Lakshmī, I will concentrate on the creativity of Śrī Lakshmī.

In the *Aitareya* (8.5.4) and the *Śatapatha* (11.1.6.23) *Brāhmanas*, Śrī and the earth are identified. As noted above, the Pāñcarātins identify Śrī Lakshmī with *prakriti*, the material cause of the universe, whereas Vishnu is conceived as the universal *purusha* (self) in the *Lakṣmī Tantra*. Her identification with the material universe implies that she is intimately associated with the very stuff of life and its rhythms of birth, growth, and decay. She is the life-giving womb, the nurturing mother, and the eventual tomb of all living things. From the primordial matter (*prakriti*), creation slowly evolves from subtle to grosser material in six stages called sheaths (*koshas*). Without explicating each sheath, it can be noted that the second sheath is called *māyā* (illusory, creative power), limited, and ordered by it. In fact, Śrī Lakshmī is called *Mahāmāyā* herself (4.45−46). By the extraordinary power of *māyā*, the primal matter is structured and made fit for human beings. The goddess can conceal her transcendental nature, assume other forms, and peform miracles by means of the inscrutable power of *māyā* (9.6−7).

Before the evolution of creation, Lakshmī and Vishnu are regarded as distinct, although they are inseparably connected, like the rays of the moon (1.43). It is Lakshmī alone who acts, even though her creative activity is an expression of her lord's wishes. The initial stage of creation, through the power of the command of Vishnu, manifests the awakening in Lakshmī of her twofold *shakti* (energy, power): *krīya* (action) and *bhūti* (becoming), the former type of *shakti* appears as the universe and the latter form vitalizes and governs the universe. Thus Lakshmī functions as the instrumental and material cause of the universe. She is also the primal source of the pulsating energy and ominous power of the universe.

The creative aspect of Śrī Lakshmī is symbolized by the lotus that she is most frequently depicted as holding in her hand or seated upon. As noted above, the *Śrīsūkta* describes her lotus appearance. In the *Mahābhārata* she is born from the golden-colored lotus that sprang from the forehead of Vishnu (12.59.131−4). The lotus completes within itself the entire life cycle by holding within itself the new seeds and nourishing them until they develop into plants. Thus the lotus represents a maternal womb of self-contained continuity.[10] The lotus also symbolizes the divine transcendent yet immanent, life-giving and life-sustaining waters; its leaf lying on the back of the waters represents the earth.[11] This vegetative symbol of the goddess is indicative of the fertility, wealth, and abundance that she offers to humankind.

Another aquatic representation of the goddess is her appearance as Gaja Lakshmī. After she emerged from the ocean, according to the *Vishnu Purāṇa* (1.9.102), the elephants of the cosmic quarters bathed her with pure water. The goddess is often depicted as standing or seated on a lotus and flanked on either side by two elephants pouring water on her from two jars. Besides being a weapon of war, the elephant is a symbol of fertility, a walking rain cloud. In conjunction with the Gaja Lakshmī motif, the elephants symbolize rain clouds fertilizing the feminine earth.[12] The Gaja Lakshmī motif appears on coins, rock carvings, and over the lintels of temple doorways, where it represents the energy and wealth of the cosmic waters.[13] The Gaja Lakshmī motif is even found on the gates of the Great Stūpa of Sāñcī, of Buddhist fame.

When Śrī Lakshmī is iconographically represented she frequently holds a *bilva* fruit in one hand and a lotus in the other. The *Śrīsūkta* informs us that the *bilva* is her tree. The *Brihaddharma Purāṇa* (1.10) contains a story of Lakshmī worshiping Shiva by offering a thousand lotuses each day. After discovering that a lotus is missing, she offers her breast, which becomes the *bilva*. The trifoliate leaves of the *bilva* are related to longevity and are sometimes identified with the gods Brahmā, Vishnu, and Shiva. The fruit of the *bilva* possesses the power to remove *māyā* (illusion) and all types of misfortune.[14]

Besides the lotus and *bilva*, Śrī Lakshmī is also associated with other plants, such as rice, which is especially sacred to her, and corn. At the Caitra-Gaurī festival[15] (which derives its name from the second month of spring, in which the corn ripens, and from the goddess of the color of corn, named Gaurī, a manifestation of Lakshmī), an earthen image of the goddess is present, as a small trench is dug in which barley is sown until the grain germinates from irrigation and artificially supplied heat. Then women whose husbands are still alive join hands and dance, while invoking the goddess's blessings on their husbands. Throughout the Indian Archipelago, Śrī is the female deity believed to be concerned with the cultivation of rice. Although Śrī Lakshmī gives forth to human beings the bounteous gifts of the earth, her gifts are merely a loan that can be withdrawn or withheld from individuals. For those who greedily covet her gifts, she arouses feelings of even murderous possessiveness.[16] It is important to note that her opposite is Alakshmī, a goddess of drought, scarcity, illness, and death.

In early examples discovered at Bharhut and Sāñcī, Śrī Lakshmī is represented standing or seated on a lotus that rises from a vessel, or the vessel is depicted alone with lotus flowers and leaves rising from it.[17] Sometimes the vessel forms a pedestal sprouting lotus flowers, as in the figure of the goddess from Mathurā dating from the second century C.E. The vessel is a symbol of abundance and is equivalent to the goddess herself. It expresses a wish for well-being, wealth, and long life, serving as a symbol of the *shakti* of Vishnu. Another type of vessel associated with Lakshmī is the cornucopia, the horn of plenty, which yields food. Lakshmī appears holding a cornucopia in her left arm on the coins of Samudragupta, called the *kācha*, and standard types.[18] This representation of Lakshmī is probably due to Greek influence. Eric Neumann, the Jungian psychologist, views the vessel as the central feminine symbol and the cornucopia's major function as containing life-sustaining food.[19] The vessel, a prominent symbol of the goddess, can be understood as both static and dynamic. In the former case it symbolizes openness and passivity; it is the universal receptacle. Yet, it is dynamic in the sense that it represents the source of life because within the vessel, the universal womb, life begins, is formed, is nourished, and is finally discharged.

Śrī Lakshmī's concern with earthly fertility, abundance, and wealth extends more directly to human reproduction. At a Punjabi festival women give gracious thanks to the goddess for giving them a fertile womb by collecting a number of colored cords in accordance with the number of sons the goddess has granted to them and making offerings to her. The Dīpāvali festival,[20] which is celebrated during the last two days of the month of Aṣvīnī (September–October) and the first two days of Kārttika (October–November), consists of five different festivals: the worship of wealth, the celebration of Vishnu's victory over the demon Naraka, Lakshmī *pūjā*, the celebration of Vishnu's victory over the demon Bali, and the expression of brotherly and sisterly affection in celebration of Yama (the lord of the dead) dining with his sister Yamunā. In the first festival, the initial day commences with the participants bathing and anointing themselves with oil. Lakshmī is worshiped by merchants after they have closed their yearly account books and cleared their shops and offices. Collecting their account books and a pile of silver coins, the latter of which are smeared with turmeric and red lead, the merchants worship the giver of wealth. During the evening lamps are lit that burn throughout the festival evenings. This same festival is called the Divālī among the Jainas, although its significance is altered somewhat as a celebration of the day on which Mahāvīra attained liberation. The presence and importance of Śrī Lakshmī is still very evident when women of the Śvetāmbara sect polish their jewelry and other ornaments in honor of the goddess. On the account books of Jaina merchants, a Brahman priest continually writes the name of Śrī—one name on top of another—forming a pyramid, and a priest performs Lakshmī *pūjā* (worship). Since many Jainas are merchants, they are expressing devotion to Lakshmī as the goddess of wealth and the presiding deity of trade and commerce. (During his work in Chhattisgarh, Babb[21] found some different festivals linked together to form the Dīpāvali. The Lakshmī *pūjā* is celebrated by the lighting of lamps to help the goddess way into one's home. The *gobardhan pūjā*, which celebrates Krishna's lifting of the Gobardham Hill to protect his fellow herdsmen from a violent storm, finds Lakshmī incarnated as a cow. After cattle are driven over a replica of the mythical hill made of cow dung, the worshipers apply the cow dung to their foreheads as a gesture of profound humility before the goddess.)

Besides their cosmogonic function, Śrī Lakshmī and Rādhā perform a redemptive role in religious works that tend to emphasize their independent status and activity. The devotees of these goddesses attain salvation by means of the grace of these deities. Both goddesses play the role of a loving mother concerned with the mundane affairs of human life. Since their principal relationship to their devotees is as a mother, the most appropriate mode of adoration is loving service by their children.

## *Śrī Lakshmī and Kingship*

In distinction to Rādhā, Śrī Lakshmī is very closely associated with kingship, especially during the Gupta period (320–540 c.e.). During the pinnacle of the power and influence of the Gupta Dynasty, Śrī Lakshmī appeared on countless coins. On a coin minted by Samudra-gupta (ca. 335–376) referred to as the standard type, a king on one side of the coin holds a standard, and on the reverse side Śrī Lakshmī is seated on a throne with her feet resting on a lotus.[22] A king is depicted relaxing on a couch with a large lotus in his hand on a coin issued by Chandragupta II (ca. 376–415). The reverse side of this coin shows the goddess seated on a throne and holding a lotus in her hand. The intimate relationship between the goddess and kingship is exemplified by the throne. In the *Aitareya* (12.3) and the *Taittirīya* (2.25) *Brāhmanas*, *śrī* (prosperity) is identified with the cushion of the royal throne. The king not only rests on the throne but the *śrī* with which the cushion of the throne is identified contributes to the ruler's prosperity, on which his kingship is based.[23] During the *Rajasuya* (royal consecration ceremony) the throne is addressed in the *mantras* (magical formulas) as the navel and womb of kingship. This conception is very similar to the Egyptian goddess Isis, who is called the seat, or throne, that is the mother of the king. The pharaoh Seti I, for example, is represented seated on the lap of Isis, who sits on the throne. Although any direct connection with kingship is unclear, Rādhā is symbolically represented among the Rādhāvallabhas by a throne cushion (*gaddī*) over which a golden leaf is suspended and upon which is written her name. According to White,[24] the sect members give three reasons for this practice: since Rādhā's beauty is indescribable, no icon can suitably represent her; the throne, which is symbolic of a teacher, also represents Rādhā's role as a teacher; it is improper to depict the eternal *līlā* of Rādhā and Krishna.

The importance of Śrī Lakshmī for kingship and the Gupta monarchs is rooted in ancient Indian tradition. There is an ancient notion of the king being wedded to Śrī. Due to her status as a goddess, Śrī Lakshmī is believed to select a powerful and mighty king as her husband. The relationship of the goddess to the king is so intimate that she is described as residing in the sovereign. In fact, the king refrains from cutting his hair, otherwise he will lose his *śrī* (welfare, majesty). Thus Śrī is the source of the king's power. And she is very concerned about the exercise of royal virtues like truth, generosity, austerity, strength, and *dharma*.[25] Besides playing the queenly role in the heavenly abode of Vishnu, Śrī Lakshmī performed as an earthly queen. Her hairstyle is called *kuntala* in Hindu art, and this style is intended for queens and other royal ladies.

On numerous coins of the Gupta period, Śrī Lakshmī appears in the form of Gaja Lakshmī. This frequent artistic motif of the goddess is similar to the *abhiṣeka* ceremony (a consecration of the king by sprinkling water on him), which is part of the larger *Rajasuya* rite. The sprinkling of water on the king represents his rebirth; his person now acquires sanctity and inviolability, which is only part of the rite's significance. With his arms extended toward the sky, the newborn king impersonates the cosmic pillar of the universe. It is around this cosmic pillar, the *axis mundi*, that the cosmic forces of fertility rotate. Thus he becomes the pivot and source of the forces of fertility, similar in function to Śrī Lakshmī in the form of Gaja Lakshmī.

On a coin referred to as the "King and Lakshmī" type by numismatists, the Gupta king Skandagupta (ca. 454–467) is depicted holding a large bow and standing next to a comely female figure who holds a lotus in her hand. What were the various Gupta monarchs hoping to achieve by their intimate association with Śrī Lakshmī? Since the goddess represents wealth, abundance, prosperity and well-being, she embodies the qualities that the king himself wants to possess. In order for a king to reign successfully, he must possess the same qualities as the goddess; otherwise, his dominion is condemned to failure. If he does not possess the qualities of the goddess and attempts to rule without them, his kingdom and subjects will be subject to strife, drought, famine, sickness, and death. In the *Mahābhārata* (9.18.14), while Duryodhana, the main antagonist of the Pāṇḍavas, falls from power, it is affirmed, for example, that he lost his royal *śrī*. The attitude and objective of a righteous king is succinctly expressed in the *Aitareya Brāhmaṇa* (8.27.7) where the king says, "In this kingdom I make prosperity [śrī] to dwell". Assuming that a king embodies *śrī* and is capable of effecting it in his dominion, it is then his duty to protect it.

## Lustful Lover and Obsequious Wife

Rādhā and Śrī Lakshmī represent two different kinds of divine feminine sexuality. Depending on the text, Rādhā is portrayed as

Krishna's lawful wife or as his lustful mistress. Even when she is depicted as his wife, Rādhā and Krishna's love affair is wild, frenzied, and ecstatic. On the other hand, the love relationship between Śrī Lakshmī and Vishnu is much more sedate and proper, a model of the correct Hindu marital relationship, in which sexual passion is under control. Even though Rādhā is represented by writers as the wife of Krishna, she often assumes a superior position in the relationship. In comparison, Śrī Lakshmī assumes most always a subordinate position to her spouse.

Śrī Lakshmī is a model of the devoted wife. On a Deogarh stone relief (ca. sixth century C.E.) and in the *Matsya Purāna* (117.66–76), Vishnu is depicted as reclining on the coils of the serpent Sesha. While one foot rests on the serpent and the other on the lap of Lakshmī, the goddess massages his foot. Like a devoted and dutiful wife, Lakshmī tends to the comforts of her husband. The great dramatic poet Kālidāsa in his *Raghuvaṃśa* (10.8) describes Lakshmī as sitting on a lotus tenderly caressing the feet of her lord. If one considers that the body is hierarchically ordered in Hinduism, with the head being the superior part of the body and the feet the lowest part, Lakshmī's massaging of her spouse's lower extremities is an act of wifely devotion. It also expresses her obsequious position in relation to her husband, the proper position for all Hindu wives. Thus the humble act of Lakshmī is ideally what a Hindu wife is expected to do for her husband when he returns home after a day of work.

Lakshmī's subordinate position can be viewed in other ways. Rao[26] notes that in the *Śilaparatha* Lakshmī should appear iconographically with only two hands when she is represented at the side of Vishnu. However, she should have four hands when she is worshiped independently in a temple. The representation with two hands indicates her subordinate position. In the Maharashtra region of India, in the city of Paṇḍharpūr, there is a temple dedicated to Viṭhobā, an *avatāra* of Vishnu in the form of Krishna. Within this temple, there is a shrine dedicated to Lakshmī consisting of a porch, a pillared hall, an antechamber, and a *garbhagriha* (womb-house). Significantly, this shrine is located to the south of Viṭhobā's shrine. The southern location represents an inferior direction, being the direction of demonic forces and the realm of the dead. The location of Lakshmī's shrine in the southern direction is indicative of her subordinate position and the fact that she wards off the forces of evil, serving as a guardian to the main shrine dedicated to Viṭhobā. Often Vishnu is represented with more than one wife. In southern India Vishnu is customarily associated with Śrī and with Bhū, an earth goddess, and in the north he is represented with Śrī and with Puṣṭi (prosperity) or Sarasvatī (goddess of speech). When Vishnu is depicted iconographically with his consorts, Śrī stands to his right with Bhū on his left.

Sometimes the goddesses are kneeling on one knee, or they are seated at the sides of the feet of a reclining Vishnu. These latter two images of the goddesses are intended to express their obsequious stance toward their husband. A final example of the subservient status of Lakshmī appears on a piece of sculpture in the Kappe-Chenigarāya temple at Bēlūr in which Lakshmī is seated on Vishnu's lap; the god embraces Lakshmī with his lower left hand. Again, the lap of the god is a position of inferiority, and his left hand represents the inferior or inauspicious hand. The left is the position of a devoted wife in relation to her husband. In Chhattisgarh, an area of eastern Madhya Pradesh, the bride is seated at the groom's left during the marriage ceremony.[27] The left side of the body symbolizes weakness and inferiority in contrast to the right side, which is the more powerful and virile. However, the left side of the body is not merely inauspicious or inferior; it is also complementary to the right side.[28] The polarity of the right and left, as symbolic of a married couple, expresses totality and completeness. In other words, a man and a woman are incomplete without each other. Thus the body language of the icons enables one to understand the result of the taming and domestication of a once unpredictable and uncontrollable fertility goddess. The shapers of the Vaishnava tradition have continued a process begun in the ritualistic texts, as previously noted. In the prevailing Vaishnava tradition, Śrī Lakshmī symbolizes total self-surrender and devotedness to Vishnu. And yet, their conjugal relationship maintains an element of fondness and tenderness, and their love contains a quality of absolute purity and perfection. Their relationship embodies *prema* (ideal love, which rises above mere carnal desire (*kāma*).

In comparison, the love between Rādhā and Krishna is more intense, passionate, violent, and erotic. When she is depicted as the wife of another man, Rādhā's love is more intense than that of Śrī Lakshmī for her spouse because Rādhā's love is not circumscribed by the obedience, discipline, and respect evident in the love of a wife for her husband. The love of Rādhā and Krishna commences in the spring, a time of birth and renewal. Although the love between Rādhā and Krishna begins in the spring, it is not a pacific or leisurely time. According to Jayadeva and Śrī Hit Harivamś, love is an ordeal for Rādhā, often represented as a battle of sexual delight. The battle imagery is instructive and suggestive because the love bouts of Rādhā and Krishna are often violent. Jayadeva writes about the red marks of passion which stain Krishna, the tangled hair of wilted flowers, the nailmarks on Rādhā's breasts, and bodies moist with sweat from the ordeal. As Krishna reaches the height of passion in sexual intercourse, Rādhā's jewel anklets ring out an erotic sound. Śrī Hit Harivamś describes the passionate touching, the meeting of lover's eyes, the disrobing, the resistance of Rādhā, the drops of perspiration on their foreheads, the all-encompassing embraces, and the marks of love made with nails and teeth. The *Brahmavaivarta Purāṇa* (4.28.66.70) expresses similar types of love making: Rādhā, the mistress of *rāsa*, commits eight types of sexual intercourse with her lover, and he kisses her in eight mysterious ways and assails her with his teeth, nails, and hands. Besides the commencement of this erotic and violent love in the spring, Jayadeva writes that Rādhā surreptiously meets with Krishna at night. The darkness of night obstructs prying eyes and forms a dark cloak over the lovers. This springtime, nighttime love takes place apart from the mundane world; it occurs in an ideal world of continual joy and bliss.

The love enjoyed by Krishna and Rādhā is not merely passionate, erotic, and violent; it also possesses a comic quality, which can be seen in the poems of Śrī Hit Harivamś. After a night of blissful love not only is Rādhā's speech confused, but she finds herself wearing her lover's clothing and Krishna wearing her clothing. In other words, their love turns the world upside down by overturning social conventions and accepted norms of behavior. In fact, their love laughs at social conventions. Their mutual amorous laughter is the mirth of the madness of their love as both participants find themselves beyond themselves. They are united to each other like a creeper around a *tamāl* tree, yet their union takes them to a transcendent realm. Their sexual union obliterates time, enabling an evening to become a moment. Not only does it destroy, it also gives life. For example, the divine couple's sexual dalliance restores the life of Kāmadeva (god of love), who had been consumed in the fire radiating from the third eye of Shiva, a symbol in this context of all human life. Where does this love culminate? It terminates in complete self-surrender. In sexual union Rādhā and Krishna become one body, mind, and being.

While culminating in a unitive love, the amorous dalliance of Rādhā and Krishna can be conceived as divine play (*līlā*). As in a frivolous game, there is often a winner. Sometimes, Krishna is viewed as the victor by breaking down Rādhā's defenses, and at other times Rādhā is the victor. In the *Gītagovinda* (10.8) Krishna supplicates himself by commanding Rādhā to place her foot on his head in a symbolic gesture of victory. Or she assumes the top position during sexual intercourse, according to the poetic work of Śrī Hit Harivamś, indicative that she is in control and superior to her lord. Thus Rādhā is not always the subservient spouse, as is Śrī Lakshmī. In some works Rādhā retains her independence, even though her heart may ache at being separated from her lover.

With their arms around each other's neck and touching cheek to cheek, Rādhā and Krishna join the *rāsa līlā* (play), in which Krishna is traditionally partner to all the *gopīs* simultaneously by means of his command and control of *māyā* (creative, magical power). The circle dance brings the lovers to an ecstatic state, enabling them to transcend their bodies and ascend to a spiritual union. From a more theological viewpoint, the dance represents the wild energy of *prakriti*, which is synomyous with Rādhā, searching for the transcendent. The *rāsa līlā* is enacted in Mathurā in imitation of Rādhā and Krishna. The *rāsa līlā* consists of an initial dance followed by a one-act play based on any one of the multitude of Krishna's *līlās*, or deeds, which is performed in the courtyard of a temple or the privacy of a wealthy Vaishnava devotee's home. The circular dance and subsequent play are performed by young boys, who impersonate the *gopīs*, Rādhā and Krishna. The dance enables the participants to meet the absolute and to keep in touch with the source of creativity. The *līlās* are instructive lessons about the relationship between Rādhā and Krishna. In the *Prempanīkshā Līlā*, for example, Rādhā tests Krishna's loyalty by sending a *gopī* to inform him that there is a girl who would like to see him. Rādhā comes to Krishna after he replies that he will see no one but her. The *gopīs* warn Rādhā not to take a dancing lesson from Krishna in the *Mundariyācorī Līlā* because the god is a thief. Discovering that Rādhā's ring is missing at the conclusion of the lesson, the *gopīs* search Krishna and find the stolen ring. Seeking revenge, the *gopīs* steal Krishna's flute, crown, and cloak. Krishna, disguised as a lovelorn girl, approaches Rādhā hoping to retrieve his stolen goods. In an effort to console the girl, Rādhā dons the stolen property, and Krishna apprehends her. The *Vivāha Līlā* celebrates the marriage of Rādhā and Krishna. And the *Causar Līlā* depicts a chess game between the two lovers, with the loser becoming the slave of the winner. Krishna loses the game and binds himself to Rādhā as her slave.[29]

The love play (*līlā*) of Rādhā and Krishna is often depicted by poets in the color of *rāga* (passion), which literally means red. In the *Caurāsī Pad* of Śrī Hit Harivamś, Rādhā is, for instance, most often poetically represented with red eyes and cheeks, with a red streak in her hair, red dye on her feet, wearing a red garment, and casting red powder on Krishna. Associated with blood, health, vitality, and fire, red is a hot color. Thus Rādhā becomes, in the poet's mind, more intensely heated during separation from her lover, who is by contrast a dark blue color. Krishna's blue appearance is indicative of his control of body heat and gives him a cool exterior. This is also poetically expressed in the *Caurāsī Pad* by the yellow garments of Krishna, indicative of coolness. In a sense the love making of two deities results in the cooling of Rādhā, rendering her more pallid and less dangerous. The cooling of the goddess is an important motif in southern India. If the goddess is not made cool, she represents a danger to human beings. This is especially true of independent, unmarried goddesses who cannot release the sexual heat accumulated through sexual abstinence and must be cooled by ritual means.

In contrast to Rādhā, Śrī Lakshmī is often represented as yellow or golden. In Bengal a clay figure of Lakshmī is painted yellow. This cool color of the goddess represents her association with wealth in the form of gold and her connection with corn.[30] The *Caurāsī Pad* also represents Rādhā as possessing a golden face and body in order to emphasize her beauty, even though red is more often associated with her. Icons of Śrī Lakshmī can possess either a dark complexion (probably indicative of her identity with the earth) or a white color, and although the former color is rare, the latter color represents well-being and coolness. Lakshmī appears wearing white robes in the *Mahābhārata* (1.16.34) when she emerges after the churning of the ocean. The later *Vāmana Purāṇa* (49.36−39) relates that she is created in four colors— white, red, yellow, and blue—probably indicative of her connection with the four *varṇas* (castes). She is, however, associated with red in a fertility rite in Bengal, where a red cloth is placed over a symbolic representation of the goddess.[31] The red cloth is connected with the life-giving, creative aspect of her nature. Overall, cooler colors are associated Śrī Lakshmī, the subordinate spouse, and hot colors are mostly connected with Rādhā, the more passionate and independent figure.

## Conclusion

The sexual exploits of Rādhā and Krishna are those of experts in the art of love. It is not a game for novices because of its frenzied, erotic, and violent character. Śrī Lakshmī, the embodiment of chastity, virtue, and truth, is the devoted, humble, obsequious wife. An illicit love affair is uncharacteristic of her. This is not true for Rādhā, who steals into the night to be with her lover. Rādhā, although the wife of another, is willing to risk everything for her lover. Even as the wife of Krishna, Rādhā is still not the model of wifely virtue, as is Lakshmī. For example, the *Brahmavaivarta Purāṇa* (2.6.13−21) even depicts Lakshmī as the forgiving and understanding wife of Krishna when she condones unjealously her spouse's amorous affair. Rādhā is known for her jealousy and continuous testing of Krishna's faithfulness to her. This does not imply that Rādhā has a defective character. It is indicative rather of Rādhā's more independent nature and status in relation to her husband, even though the source of her being and activity is most often derived from Krishna. In comparison to Śrī Lakshmī, Rādhā is more of a free spirit. Rādhā, even when deified in the later Hindu tradition, retains a more human character, whereas Śrī Lakshmī represents more of a static, archetypical model of the devoted wife. Whereas Śrī Lakshmī represents to the Hindu mind a model for the ideal wife, Rādhā serves more as a model for the soul's odyssey in search of its beloved god.

This essay has been concerned not only with the historical development and nature of two goddesses; throughout, there has been implied a Hindu male conception of feminine sexuality (due to the fact that the primary source texts were exclusively composed by men). On the one hand, feminine sexuality is a very creative force symbolized by the good mother (cow). On the other hand, the power of female sexuality can become demonic, resulting in the destruction of everything that is previously created. To check the demonic aspect of feminine sexual power, it is necessary to restrain it. The male counterparts of these two goddesses act as restraining factors by means of the overwhelming dominance of their own power and authority or by safely channeling the sexuality of the goddesses through sexual pleasure, thereby rendering the potentially dangerous goddesses cool, safe, and sexually satisfied. On occasion, the male deities might even resort to a ruse to achieve their objective. Vishnu, for instance, turns Śrī Lakshmī into a child after she becomes upset at his sudden marriage to another. And Krishna turns into an infant in order to control Rādhā's sexual aggressiveness.[32] Vishnu's control of Śrī Lakshmī is, generally speaking, complete, whereas Krishna cannot entirely restrain Rādhā, the free feminine spirit always striving to assert itself.

## NOTES

1. Wendy Doniger O'Flaherty, *Women, Androgynes and Other Mythical Beasts* (Chicago & London: University of Chicago Press, 1980), pp. 90−91.

2. See Lawrence A. Babb, "Marriage and Malevolence: The Uses of Sexual Opposition in a Hindu Pantheon," *Ethnology* 9 (1970): 137−48, and C. J. Fuller, "The Divine Couple's Relationship in a South Indian Temple: Mīnānṣī and Sundareśvara at Madurai," *History of Religions* 19, no. 4 (May 1980): 321−48.

3. O'Flaherty, p. 117.

4. Jan Gonda, *Aspects of Early Viṣṇuism* (Delhi: Motilal Banarsidass, 1969), p. 180.

5. Although the contention that Śrī possessed an original connection with the Yakṣas is my own hypothesis, I am indebted to the following works for the historical development of the goddess and the derivation of her name: Gerda Hartmann, *Beiträge zur Geschichte der Göttin Laksmī* (Ph.D. diss., Christian Albrechts Universität zu Kiel, 1933); Gonda, *Aspects of Early Viṣṇuism;* Suvira Jaiswal, *The Origin and Development of Vaiṣṇavism* (Delhi:Munshiram Manoharlal, 1967); Hemchandra Raychaudhuri, *Materials for the Study of the Early History of the Vaishnava Sect* (Calcutta: University of Calcutta Press, 1920; reprint ed., New Delhi: Oriental Books Reprint Corporation, 1975); Daniel H. H. Ingalls, "Words for Beauty in Classical Poetry," in *Indological Studies in Honor of W. Norman Brown*, ed. Ernest Bender, American Oriental Series, vol. 47 (New Haven: American Oriental Society, 1962), pp. 87−107.

6. The best evidence of her independent status is contained in Buddhist literature. T.W. Rhys Davids, trans. vol. 2, *Sacred Books of the Buddhist*, *Dialogues of the Buddha, Part 1*, (London: Luzac & Company, 1969), 1.11; I.B. Horner, trans. vol. 1, *Milinda's Questions* (London: Luzac & Company, 1969), p. 191.

7. For the historical development of Rādhā, I have utilized the following sources: Barbara Stoler Miller, "Rādhā: Consort of Kṛṣṇa's Venal Passion," *Journal of the American Oriental Society* 95, no. 4 (October−December 1975): 655−71; Sadashiva L. Katre, "Kṛṣṇa, Gopas, Gopīs and Rādhā," in *Professor P.K. Gode Commemoration Volume*, ed. H.L.

Hariyappa and M.M. Patkar (Poona: Oriental Book Agency, 1960), pp. 83–92; Asoke Kumar Majumdar, "A Note on the Development of the Rādhā Cult," *Annals of the Bhandarkar Oriental Research Institute* 75(1955): 231–57; Charles S.J. White, *The Caurāsī Pad of Śrī Hit Harivaṁś* (Honolulu: University Press of Hawaii, 1979); Edward C. Dimock, Jr., *The Place of the Hidden Moon: Erotic Mysticism in the Vaiṣṇava-Shajiyā Cult of Bengal* (Chicago: University of Chicago Press, 1966); Charlotte Vaudeville, "Evolution of Love-Symbolism in Bhagavatism," *Journal of the American Oriental Society* 82 (1962): 31–40.; all references to the *Gītagovinda* have been taken from the following translation: Barbara Stoler Miller, trans., *Love Song of the Dark Lord: Jayadeva's Gītagovinda* (New York: Columbia University Press, 1977).

8. Cheever Mackenzie Brown, *God as Mother: A Feminine Theology in India* (Hartford, Vt.: Claude Stark & Co., 1974), p. 1.

9. Ibid., chaps. 8–9.

10. Stella Kramrisch, "The Indian Great Goddess," *History of Religions* 14, no. 4 (May 1975): 252.

11. Ananda K. Coomaraswamy, *Yakṣas*, 2 pts. (Washington, D.C.: Smithsonian Institute, 1929–1931; reprint ed., New Delhi: Munshiram Manoharlal, 1971), pt. 1:22; pt. 2:56; Heinrich Zimmer, *The Art of Indian Asia: Its Mythology and Transformation*, ed. Joseph Campbell, Bollingen Series 39 (New York: Pantheon Books, 1960), p. 175.

12. Gonda, p. 220; see also Heinrich Zimmer, *Myths and Symbols in Indian Art and Civilization*, ed. Joseph Campbell (New York: Pantheon Books, 1963), pp. 102–9.

13. Stella Kramrisch, *The Hindu Temple*, 2nd ed. 2 vols. ( Calcutta: University of Calcutta Press, 1956, p. 356; for numerous examples of the Gaja Lakshmī motif, see V.N. Hari Rao, "The Symbolism of Gaja Lakshmī," *Journal of Indian History* 48, pt. 1 (April 1970): 73–80. Other iconographical examples cited in this essay have been taken also from the additional following works: Coomaraswamy, *Yakṣas*; for a complete discussion of Lakshmī's iconographical symbolism see Ananda K. Coomaraswamy, "Early Indian Iconography: II Śrī Lakshmī," *Eastern Art* 1 (1928–29): 175–89; Zimmer, *Art of Indian Asia*; T.A. Gopinath Rao, *Elements of Hindu Iconography*, 2nd ed., 2 vols. (Delhi: Motilal Banarsidass, 1968).

14. Gonda, pp. 204, 220.

15. Ibid., pp. 236–37.

16. Kramrisch, "Indian Great Goddess," p. 252.

17. Radha Kumud Mookerji, *The Gupta Empire*, 4th ed. (Delhi: Motilal Banarsidass, 1969), pp. 31, 34.

18. Eric Neumann, *The Great Mother: An Analysis of the Archetype*, trans. Ralph Manheim, Bollingen Series, 47 (Princeton: Princeton University Press, 1955), chap. 4.

19. Paul Hershman, "Virgin and Mother," in *Symbol and Sentiments: Crosscultural Studies in Symbolism*, ed. Ioan Lewis (London: Academic Press, 1977), p. 279.

20. M.M. Underhill, *The Hindu Religious Year* (Calcutta: Association Press, 1921), pp. 59–63.

21. Lawrence A. Babb, *The Divine Hierarchy: Popular Hinduism in Central India* (New York: Columbia University Press, 1975), p. 164.

22. All numistic references in this section are taken from Mookerji, pp. 31, 53, 98.

23. For the Indian concept of kingship, I have relied on the following works: Jan Gonda, *Ancient Indian Kingship from the Religious Point of View* (Leiden: E.J. Brill, 1969) and J.C. Heesterman, *The Ancient Indian Royal Consecration* (The Hague: Mouton & Company, 1957).

24. White, pp. 31–32.

25. For a more complete discussion see Alf Hiltebeitel, *The Ritual of Battle: Krishna in the Mahābhārata* (Ithaca and London: Cornell University Press, 1976), pp.148–66.

26. All iconographic references to Lakshmī in this paragraph are noted by Rao, 1:374, 89, 90, 259.

27. Babb, *Divine Hierarchy*, p. 89.

28. See J. Gonda, "The Significance of the Right Hand and the Right Side in Vedic Ritual," *Religion: A Journal of Religion and Religions* 2, pt. 1 (Spring 1972): 1–23.

29. Norvin Hein, *The Miracle Plays of Mathurā* (Delhi: Oxford University Press, 1972), pp. 169–77.

30. Rai Bahadur, B.A. Gupte, *Hindu Holidays and Ceremonials*, 2nd ed. (Calcutta: Thacken, Spink & Company, 1919), pp. 126–27.

31. Ibid., p. 126.

32. Cited by O'Flaherty, pp. 103–4.

# 11

RICHARD L. BRUBAKER

*The Untamed Goddesses
of Village India*

F olk deities would recognize each other anywhere. Even so,
they would recognize many of the Hindu village goddesses
among them as a rather distinctive breed.

Folk deities are found in peasant societies; they belong to the
common people. Their powers are usually confined to small localities,
and the groups of people affected by those powers are seldom large.
Oral tradition supplies the stories told of them and governs how they
are represented and worshiped. Their priests, when there are such,
seldom belong to an official priestly class or receive any formal
training. The theology surrounding these deities is unsophisticated, if
articulated at all. Nonetheless, the significance of this theology
is routinely warped and massively underestimated by most outside
observers.

The realm of a folk deity—and the concern of someone approaching such a diety—is more practical and worldly than "spiritual." The
people of a peasant society, directly subject to nature's furies, working
long and hard to survive, bearing the burdens of family life and
negotiating the shoals of community relationships, striving for a measure of order and dignity in their lives and a few modest satisfactions
while guarding against capricious or hostile powers and coping with
tragedies—such people have many needs involving the "little" gods
and goddesses dwelling in their midst. There are occasions, of course,
for approaching the great deities with their grand temples and magnificent festivals, for awe or devotion to the ultimate rulers of the
universe and for contemplation of one's own destiny. But a folk deity,
however lacking in grandeur or high sanctity, can be stunningly powerful within local bounds; and, for dealing with the immediate burdens, hazards, and crises of life here and now, such a deity is a more
likely source of help. Furthermore, since the issue can be one of life or

death—or hope versus despair—there is plenty of room for a profoundly religious relationship.

Folk deities abound in rural India, where they appear in many varieties and share the scene both with greater gods and goddesses and with hosts of lesser spirits and demons. Amid this welter of "supernatural" beings, village goddesses stand out as striking figures. Especially prominent in southern India, they are powerfully ambivalent deities crucial to the welfare of their village. Whatever may have been going on in the meantime (and the pattern varies considerably), at times of village-wide crisis these goddesses "come alive" with a sudden intensity. The crisis may be caused by drought, flood, famine, or other disasters, but most typically by an outbreak of epidemic disease. The response is an orgy of ritual activity centered on the village's goddess (or on several of its goddesses). It is to her that the villagers turn, for she is responsible for the health and safety of the village as a whole—*and* because, in one way or another, she may have been responsible for the crisis in the first place.[1]

This highly concentrated ambivalence is an outstanding feature of many Indian village goddesses. We shall return to it shortly. But first, the various "supernatural" figures need to be sorted out.[2]

## Deities, Demons, and Others

Enshrined in many villages are images of one or more of the great deities of the Hindu pantheon, celebrated in sacred Sanskrit texts and worshiped in all parts of the country. These are regarded as possessing great purity and sanctity, are commonly attended by Brahmin priests, and are worshiped for the most part in a formal and decorous manner (though some of their annual festivals are wildly exuberant). Their purity is reflected in their "vegetarianism"—in their not being offered animal sacrifices, as local folk deities often are.[3]

Between the universal and the strictly local deities are gods and goddesses with a regional distribution, and they, too, are often represented in villages in their region. In character and in mode of worship these lie between the other two groups and can merge into either of them. Thus a deity may be, in important senses, both regional and local—for example, the goddesses Śītalā and Māriyamman. Māriyamman belongs to South India, especially to the Tamil-speaking southernmost state, where she appears in many villages, towns, and cities. Śītalā is found in most parts of the country except the south and is perhaps most prominent in Bengal. Both are goddesses of contagious disease, especially smallpox. Both are frequently found as guardian deities of individual villages, and in that capacity they may function just like a goddess found in but a single village. Yet in some places Māriyamman has acquired sizable temples, Brahmin priests, and other marks of a more-than-folk status; similarly, Śītalā in Bengal has given rise to published texts of mythology and devotion.

All such categories of deities are fluid over time, for any deity is first recognized as such in a particular place by a particular individual or group, and only gradually attains wider recognition. And in India this process continues today, with certain local deities slowly spreading over broader areas. In addition there are instances of a local deity coming to be identified as a manifestation of a universal god or goddess. Conversely, a local example of, say, the Lord Krishna can acquire a special local name, interact with events in local history, and take on a unique local character while remaining the universal Krishna. Every Hindu deity, in fact, combines some degree of transcendent significance with some measure of concrete particularity.

The situation is further complicated by numerous beings yet lower on the hierarchy. At the very bottom are the demons. Occasionally individualized, sometimes divided into categories, often lumped together, the demons range from mischievous to deadly. Tending to inhabit lonely waste places, they can possess individuals or otherwise cause individual misfortune. They can also harass an entire community; and in South India, as we shall see, much of the action at a crisis-time festival takes the form of the village goddess and her people mounting a struggle against a marauding horde of demons.

Again there is an in-between category, comprising a multitude of ghosts and various other spirit beings spanning the gap between the lowest-ranked deities and the demons. And again there is a continuum with no fixed boundaries between categories. Some of these beings are like petty deities in their capacity to provide benefits; others are capriciously or dangerously driven by desires; some are thoroughly malevolent. Here, as elsewhere along the spectrum, distinctions are made; but these are not standardized from one regional language to the next, nor is usage consistent, even in a given locality. Everyone knows the full range of extrahuman powers that, for good or ill, can affect life in one's village; but precision in defining them is less important than efforts to maximize the good and minimize the ill they can bring.

## The Village Cosmos

At the midpoint of the spectrum, as I have described it, stand the village deities, the local gods and goddesses linked to particular villages and intimately bound up with their welfare. In some ways these local deities are to their villages as great gods, such as Shiva or Vishnu, are to the universe. Each village is a kind of world in miniature—largely self-sufficient, largely self-governing, with its own intricate social structure based on the interdependence of its specific local castes—a world in which economics, governance, social interaction, and sacred tradition form an interlocking whole. And many communities, especially in the narratives and symbols surrounding their deities, nurture memories of the original creation of their village cosmos out of the surrounding wilderness.

Thus, villages depend upon their deities just as universes do. And in both cases the deities must repeatedly contend with demons who would return the cosmos to chaos in pursuit of their own ends. The difference is that great gods engage great demons in glorious battles set in mythic time, while a messy fight between the village goddess and a swarm of anonymous local demons may have happened last year and may break out again next week. The villagers know stories of some of the former struggles; in the latter ones they themselves throw bloody offerings to the demons while fending them off with shouts and sticks.

When a village goddess defends her people in a crisis, she is functioning as a goddess *of* the village, a guardian deity of the village as a whole. This is her central and decisive function but not necessarily her only one. Like the great deities who serve as guardians on a cosmic scale, she may also be adopted by a smaller group—a local caste, clan, or family—as its special protector or benefactor. Again like the universal (or regional) deities, though far more rarely, she may even become the focus of a devotional cult. In addition, like any other deity, she may be approached by individuals seeking help as needs arise.

Some village deities are not, in the same sense, deities *of* the village— some because they belong exclusively to a smaller group, others because their functions are too specialized to relate to a village-wide concern or a major crisis. Most village deities, however—indeed, most Indian deities at any level—have certain departments of life over which they preside or within which their power is especially effective. Thus, some village deities preside over marriage, conception, or childbirth; some aid in agricultural fertility; some protect herds, fields, wells, granaries, or the village boundaries; some have power to exorcise ghosts or demons; some guard against or heal snakebite or a specific illness—to name a few of the more common functions. In the distribution of such specializations from village to village there are both regional emphases and wide local variations. Regional and local traditions and circumstances also determine whether a deity with a particular specialization will also be linked with the overall health and safety of the total village cosmos, and thus—alone or with others—be invoked and dramatically worshiped by the whole village in time of peril. But in South India, where such village-protecting deities are most prominent, they are most commonly goddesses whose special concern is smallpox, cholera, or another of the major epidemic diseases.

Why the South? Why goddesses? Why epidemic disease?

## Regions and Genders

Southern India differs from the North in a number of ways. Its Dravidian languages constitute a family by themselves, quite distinct from the Indo-European languages of most of the country. The latter derive from Sanskrit, the language of the Aryans, an Indo-European people who began entering India through mountain passes in the Northwest around 1500 B.C.E. Originally seminomadic, the Aryans were an aggressively patriarchal people. And as their sacred texts, the Vedas, clearly show, the deities they invoked were overwhelmingly male. The most popular by far was Indra, an ecstatic warrior-hero. The Aryan arrival coincided with, and probably precipitated, the downfall of major centers of the Indus Valley civilization, a culture comparable to its contemporaries in ancient Egypt and Mesopotamia. In this long-settled agricultural civilization, female deities had a prominent place—especially, it would seem, as objects of domestic worship. The Aryans soon became dominant in the Northwest, and the masculinity of their religion set the tone for much of North India from then on. But they spread rather slowly and thinly to the east and even more so to the south, and it is not surprising that goddess worship remains strongest in the eastern and southern regions.

There were other peoples, many of them tribal, in India when the Aryans arrived, and the history of ensuing cultural interactions is complex and not fully understood. But there is increasing evidence of continuity, including linguistic continuity, between the Indus Valley civilization and the Dravidian culture of the South. The emergence of goddesses as major figures in later Hinduism reflects an ongoing interaction between Aryan and non-Aryan elements. But the humbler folk goddesses in regions outside the Aryan heartland seem to have been present, in one form or another, for millennia.

Thus questions about the prevalence of goddesses in the South turn out to be questions about their scarcity in the North. In India, village goddesses tend to be rare or of minor importance only in the regional strongholds of a vigorously male-oriented faith. And the same is broadly true for other goddesses as well, with the notable exception of those praised as dutiful wives of their divine lords. Nor is India the only place where the female aspect of the divine has suffered such a fate.

With few exceptions, Indian village goddesses are not anyone's wives. (On the other hand, as we shall see, they are not necessarily sexually inactive.) They are independent, they are powerful, and they can be hazardous to one's health as well as ultimately healing. Before we consider their involvement with disease, however, it would be well to look more closely at the relationship between the goddess and the village. Here, and in most of what follows, I want to concentrate on South India, where the patterns seem most fully developed and, despite endless variation in detail, most consistent.

## The Goddess and Her Village

I said before that each Indian village is a miniature world "in which economics, governance, social interaction, and sacred tradition form an interlocking whole." What goes on in each of these areas is shaped in large part by the caste system, by the patterns of interaction traditional to the particular mixture of castes present in a given village. In much of South India, though, as I have argued elsewhere, four specific castes are uniquely crucial to the functioning of village life in each of its major dimensions.[4] A brief look at the roles of these castes will suggest how closely knit into the fabric of village life its goddess is.

None of the four stands very high on the scale of purity by which castes are ranked, nor does any of them have the wherewithal to command much secular status. The four are potter, barber, and washerman castes and whichever caste of Untouchables has the responsibility for handling animal carcasses. It seems a curious grouping, but these four have a surprising amount in common.

Together with the dominant cultivating castes, they are the ones most closely tied to the land. In return for field labor, and especially for their specialized services, members of these castes have a hereditary right to a fixed share of the harvest plus various other benefits. Most others are simply paid daily wages, but these four castes are indispensable to an age-old system of reciprocal rights and obligations, the primary means by which a village feeds itself. The castes making up this system are also those most closely tied to the land in another sense: they have always inhabited agricultural villages, while various other castes are historically more urban-based or itinerant.

Ritual uncleanness is a deep and abiding concern in Hinduism, requiring an ongoing process of maintaining and restoring the degree of ritual purity appropriate to members of each caste. In this process, the hereditary occupations of certain castes are crucial, and none more so than those of our same potters, barbers, washermen, and scavengers. Potters replace polluted vessels, while the others remove various sources of defilement. And these tasks not only meet individual needs, practical as well as religious; they also serve to maintain the structure of the dominant community institution, the purity-ranked caste system itself.

Some of these pollution-management tasks are required in extra measure on ritual occasions. But along with them is a wide array of other services that these same castes are called upon to perform. Barbers, for instance, are often traditional go-betweens in marriage negotiations and usually perform major ritual duties at funerals, while the lowly carcass handlers lead all sorts of processions as drummers and musicians. Members of all four castes are virtually indispensable to the ritual life of the village.

Production and purification, social structure and ritual—these major dimensions of village life together make up a sacred system deeply rooted in the land and the traditions of a given locality. Contributing decisively to the working of this system in each of its dimensions is a small group of castes, themselves more deeply rooted than most. At the symbolic center of this sacred microcosm, often seen as its founder, always presiding over its destiny, stands the village goddess. It may not be surprising, then, to learn that she is served, on behalf of the entire village, primarily by members of these four castes.

Potters often make a temporary image of the goddess for use during her festival. Potters, barbers, or washermen commonly perform such tasks as carrying the image in procession, sacrificing sheep or goats, strewing blood-soaked rice to demons, and acting as presiding priests. Some of these roles may also fall to the Untouchables who handle carcasses, but their primary task is the traditional climactic act of the festival, the sacrifice of a water buffalo. Thus, those most immersed in the defiling actions of a bloody and tumultuous festival are the very ones who most serve purity and order in ordinary times. This is a paradox rooted in the paradoxical nature of the goddess herself. For the moment, let me just say that only castes regularly involved in pollution removal can handle such defiling tasks, just as only a goddess with a streak of the demonic in her can handle demons.

## The Festival and the Boundaries

The festival temporarily reverses the usual dialectic between purity and pollution, but the roles of our four castes in both situations underline the intimate, if paradoxical, relationship between the village's organic functioning and its goddess worship. Further emphasizing the bond between goddesses and village is the fact that the total community is usually expected to participate in the festival; similarly, each household is expected to contribute toward the expenses, and often to prepare its own individual offering to the goddess. As the other side of the same coin, many villages have not welcomed outsiders to their festivals, feeling their presence as a threat to the intense encounter taking place between the goddess and her own people—and no one has been allowed to enter or to leave the village during the few days the festival was in progress.[5]

Related to this is the importance of village boundaries. An Indian village includes not only its cluster or clusters of dwellings, shops, and the like, but also the surrounding fields and other lands belonging to the villagers, corporately or individually. Its outer boundaries are the limits of the goddess's domain. Beyond them, in many cases, lies the territory of adjacent villages; but symbolically (reflecting the conditions either of an earlier age or of the present) what lies outside the bondaries is wilderness. It therefore is frequented by demons, those dangerous and often hostile manifestations of the lawless no-man's-land in the midst of which the ordered, settled village has been carved out. When an epidemic sweeps into the village—which is to say, when the demons have been aroused to attack—the boundary takes on great importance in the ensuing festival.

The climactic event of the festival is the sacrificial beheading of a buffalo, representing the defeat of demonic power at the hands of the goddess. The buffalo is perfectly cast in this role. This powerful and unpredictably dangerous beast with a well-deserved reputation for brutishness is the one animal, it has been aptly said, on which domestication has made the least impression. The undomesticated variety, especially massive and savage, is also the one wild animal that will cross the village boundaries, stomp about in cultivated fields, and help itself to the crops in utter defiance of men trying to drive it off. Furthermore, and not surprisingly, brutish buffalo-demons are well-known in Hindu mythology.[6]

When the buffalo has been sacrificed, its head is placed on the ground before the image of the goddess, its right foreleg jammed crosswise in its mouth, its face smeared with its own fat, and a lamp filled with more of its fat set alight on its forehead—all this signifying the goddess's triumph. Near the end of the festival there is often a procession to the village boundary. In one of the festival's many variants, an Untouchable carries the buffalo head, as previously adorned, on his own head, his body smeared with its blood and some of its entrails draped from his neck; his shouting companions fend off the demons attracted by all the blood and guts and tumult, and the procession, collecting demons as it goes, makes its way to the boundary, on the far side of which the buffalo head is deposited. Finally, rice soaked in the beast's blood is strewn all along the village perimeter, serving to sanctify the boundaries and seal them against further incursion. Thus are the demons expelled from the village, the sacred precincts of the goddess, and confined to the anarchic outer spaces where they belong.

## Disease and the Goddess

A calamity strikes and a festival is held. The central actions of the festival emphasize the solidarity of the community, express the people's dedication to their goddess, and enact the defeat and expulsion of demons. Clearly the festival is intended to overcome the calamity, the demons are cast as its perpetrators, and the goddess is the source of power for their defeat. This scenario can apply to a variety of village disasters, any of which can be blamed on demons, but the outbreak of an epidemic has perhaps been the most common and the most widely feared. It is also the one that best fits the scenario, for three main reasons.

In the first place, an epidemic suddenly appears out of nowhere, invisibly and capriciously flits about the village, and subjects its victims to acute, debilitating, and even fatal attacks, their fevered bodies seemingly possessed by an alien force—just what one would expect from demons on the rampage. Second, in the ensuing festival the people are caught up in a contagion of intense and dramatic ritual action—action nearly as overheating, perhaps as delirious, and at least as defiling as the disease itself. In its festival the community behaves in many ways like the human body struggling to expel a virulent infection. And finally, of course, the goddess herself is closely linked with epidemic disease.

This link, as I have already indicated, is fraught with ambivalence and paradox. It is time now to examine it more closely.

In light of all that has been said about the goddess as village guardian and about the expulsion of disease-inflicting demons, it may be startling to learn that villagers often explain an epidemic as thrust upon them in anger by their own goddess—because they have neglected her worship or otherwise offended her. This has led numerous Christian missionaries, British colonial administrators, and even Western scholars to scorn such goddesses as little better than devils themselves. But a modest bit of reflection should show that Hindu villagers face exactly the same theological dilemma as every other worshiper. When suffering occurs, does one attribute it to God or not? If so, God seems evil (or arbitrary, at best); if not, God seems to have lost control. In strictly logical terms, no deity can be both all-powerful and totally beneficent. Thus Christians, in trying to deal with suffering, often vacillate between explanations that preserve God's goodness at the implicit expense of his power and ones that preserve his power at the implicit expense of his goodness. Hindu villagers do likewise.

There is a difference, however. While the logical dilemma is fundamentally the same, it is not likely to be the source of much agonizing for a Hindu villager. In the first place, he or she recognizes a multiplicity of divine (and demonic) beings whose powers can conflict with one another, and therefore does not expect any specific deity to be in total command at all times, even within the realm of that deity's special concern. And in the second place, Hindus acknowledge ambivalence and paradox as characteristic of most of their deities and do not expect perfect beneficence from them. Thus the villager has alternative images of the relationship between the goddess and the disease, and can go with whichever feels right at the moment.

In fact, there are more images than two. A third and distinctly different image virtually equates the disease with the goddess or sees it as her direct manifestation. This view is expressed especially in individual cases of, say, smallpox, which are often seen as instances of possession by the goddess.[7] Here the disease, far from expressing her wrath or punishment, is an act of special grace, however harrowing the experience may be. Around the patient's bed, acts of worship are performed and a reverent atmosphere maintained. The patient's fever, a prominent sign of possession, also shows that the goddess, too, is in an intensely heated condition; and both may be soothed by cooling foods and ritualized acts of fanning and bathing, offered either to the patient or to an image of the goddess.

This may seem close to suggesting that the goddess herself has come down with the disease. And in fact she sometimes has—but in a different context. Images of village goddesses (wondrously varied but usually simple and nonanthropomorphic) include unhewn stones, and some of these are naturally "pockmarked." Other images are adorned with red dots to indicate pustules, either as a regular feature or applied during an epidemic and its accompanying festival. Also, a good many local myths tell of the goddess contracting smallpox, either in her divine form or in a previous human existence.

The goddess defends her people against the disease, inflicts it upon them, manifests herself in its symptoms, and is herself its victim. Obviously she is deeply involved with it—so deeply that it takes at least four descriptions, partly conflicting, partly overlapping, to characterize the relationship. But where do these four leave us? Not, I think, with a clear sense of the whole. How do the pieces fit together? Is there a way of looking at them that brings this multiparadoxical form of divinity into sharper focus? I believe there is, but it involves finding a few missing pieces and turning around some of the ones we already have.

There is a fifth way of viewing the relationship between the goddess and the disease. It combines elements of each of the other four, together with certain intriguing phenomena that none of these four takes into account. The result is an interpretation not likely to be spelled out by a South Indian villager. But the villager's lack of interest in carefully examining the implications of his own traditional symbols need not prevent a fascinated outsider from attempting to do so.

## Sexuality and Violence

Consider the following facts. Demons in South India have a propensity for attacking and possessing humans of the opposite gender, as a means of satisfying sexual appetites. The deity representing the village is female, and it is nearly always male animals that are sacrificed to her; the buffalo whose sacrifice symbolizes the demons' defeat is always male. Numerous village goddess myths tell of a woman being wronged by a man (or men), often in the form of a buffalo, who has approached her lustfully.

Thus a common theme appears in several contexts involving or related to the village goddess festival—the theme of male assault, usually sexual assault, upon the female. This strongly suggests that the festival itself may be meaningfully viewed in the same terms. An enclosed, domesticated, sacred space personified by a divine female attracts and is penetrated and violated by a wilderness-roaming horde driven by distinctly masculine forms of lust and aggression. The village, in short, is being raped. And the festival, then, is the village's convulsive, expulsive response. In it the people relive the myth of their goddess defeating and repelling her male attacker.

So far this is simply our earlier picture of the goddess and her people fighting off the demonic bearers of their affliction, with the addition of a sexual polarization. But this addition creates problems. Surely an unrelieved enmity between female and male would be an untenable symbolic basis for a community's life. As it turns out, however, the goddess/demon relationship involves more than enmity. From the male or demon point of view, of course, there is the element of sexual attraction from the beginning. But here and there one finds clear indications that the goddess, too, is interested in sexual encounter.

In myths the sexual interests of the goddess vary widely. In some she is boldly, even incestuously, lustful, in which case the males in question tend to flee from her and she remains unsatisfied. In others (usually telling of a prior human existence) she is "properly" chaste and is either tricked into an illicit relationship or put to death on suspicion of one. And in yet other myths she is coyly inviting—in order to gain control over the male, here a demon, and destroy him.[8] Destruction is seldom final in Hindu myths, however, and the demon thus "destroyed" may then be transformed (as with other enemies noted earlier) into her sacrificial buffalo—or into a guardian, agent, or other subordinate of the goddess, who is sometimes represented by an image at her shrine. The subsequent relationship between the goddess and this male subordinate is often ambiguous, but in some places he is explicitly called her demon lover. Furthermore, in some villages an Untouchable (occupying the same position on the human hierarchy as a demon does on the "supernatural") is selected to spend the duration of the goddess's festival in the precincts of her shrine as her temporary "husband." Finally, the sacrificial buffalo itself is sometimes given the same euphemistic title.

The goddess's relations with males thus seem as varied and contradictory as her connections with disease. Her sexual encounters are always tinged with the illicit and always mingle eroticism with struggle and violence. The intense ambivalence implicit in all of this parallels the ambivalent intensity of her people's encounter with a goddess-linked epidemic and their festival response to that encounter. And this entire turbulent torrent of sexuality and violence, of divine and demonic, of village and wilderness, of attraction and repulsion, of agony and ecstasy, of grace and fury, of pollution and purgation—all this contrasts sharply with the normal everyday state of affairs.

In the self-contained little world of the village, the processes promoting purity and order proceed routinely, and the presiding goddess is quiescent. In many places, in fact, she and her inconspicuous shrine are virtually ignored. This is the usual situation, and it prevails for just as long as it can. Then, with a swift and uncanny shift in the winds of destiny, the goddess, the demons, and the people become extraordinarily aroused. Things mingle and merge that are normally kept apart; things carefully regulated overflow their usual bounds. And on the level of the symbolism pervading these events, it is perhaps above all the relations between what is male and what is female that surge beyond all restriction.

In the end order is restored, but in the process, life is rejuvenated: the village emerges with a fresh lease on life. To do justice to the struggle and risk involved, there is the imagery of battle between the divine and the demonic. But for the central meaning of the experience, for an ecstatic immersion in revitalizing depths, what better symbol could there be than sexual union?

## The Symbolism of Heat

We now have five ways of describing the relationship between the disease and the goddess: it is a demonic attack against which she defends her people; it is punishment she wrathfully inflicts upon them; it is her own awesome but gracious self-manifestation; it is a condition she herself suffers; and it is a kind of orgy she occasionally wills her people to join her in, in which her own divine order is temporarily inundated by demonic vitality for the sake of its own renewal. These five images give participants in the staggering experience of an epidemic (or any comparable crisis) a variety of options for understanding their expereience. And the Hindu tradition values such variety, for it recognizes that human beings vary, both from each other and within themselves. It recognizes that reality, though one, has many faces, not all of which can be seen at once.

Conversely, the typical South Indian village goddess, though she presents many faces, is one goddess. Profoundly paradoxical she is— for so is reality, or at least the human experience thereof. But a chaos of contradictions she is not. The multifarious symbols surrounding her are continually intersecting and weaving a web of connected meanings. Let me illustrate this by tracing some of the meanings of one symbol, that of heat.

We can begin with heat as a simple but vivid fact: the patient's fever. (There is also the fact that these feverish diseases and the festivals they occasion normally occur in the hottest season of the year.) When the goddess herself suffers the disease, she, too, is feverish. But beyond fever itself we encounter many other forms of heat. In South India all foods and many other substances are considered either heating or cooling, as are various physiological functions and emotional states, and proper balance, slightly on the cool side, is the norm for health and well-being.[9] Thus in folk medicine the diseases we are concerned with here are believed to be caused by an excess of heat building up within the body, and when the goddess inflicts them she does so by means of overheating her victims. Overheated also are those she chooses to possess, but here their fever manifests a different kind of heat: the heat of the goddess's arousal, of her newly intensified aliveness, of her prodigious energy, which the patient's body can scarcely contain.

With a slight shift in emphasis, the goddess's aroused energy becomes, of course, the heat of her sexual arousal. Both of these—energy and passion—are explicitly identified as forms of heat. And so is another kind of passion: the anger with which the goddess inflicts the disease as punishment—and equally the fury with which, alternatively, she battles disease-bearing demons. In some places the heat of her anger is symbolized by a pot of fire kept burning every night of her festival, alternating with a daytime pot of cool water symbolizing the beneficent side of her nature. More concretely, the firepot represents fire she once threw at a demon trying to seduce her. This latter action, a bit ironically, is a case of fighting fire with fire, for the demon was already burning with lust.[10]

In their assaults on villages the demons are also bearers of excessive heat—the heat of the disease they bring, the heat of their greedy appetites of all sorts (if not explicitly of the erotic variety), the heat of the frenzy with which they attack, and the heat of the pollution they spread (for pollution is yet another form of excessive heat). The festival response to all this is another case of fighting fire with fire, for it stimulates the people to vigorous activity, from fending off demons to the rhythmic dancing that invites possession by the goddess; it stirs people's passions and their devotional fervor; it sometimes includes a ritual of walking on a bed of incandescent coals; in numerous ways it multiplies the pollution already present, especially through the shedding and handling of blood (itself, of course, a hot substance); and all of this, for the moment, even further attracts and stimulates the overheated demons. As with sexual intercourse, the festival greatly intensifies the heat which led to it in the first place. And in both cases the aftermath is understood to be healthfully cooling.

## The Sacred and the Female

Heat is but one of the multidimensional symbols surrounding the goddess. But it illustrates especially well the intricate web of meanings linking her and her people and the demons. The epidemic and the festival may be seen as two dimensions of a singly extraordinary event, and in both dimensions of that event all participants—divine, human, and demonic—are supercharged, overheated. The meanings of this heating are multiple, but each of them enfolds the same profound paradox.

Heat is life, and an intensification of it can either enhance or threaten life. It can also create through destroying—which, in fact, the banked fires of ordinary life are doing continually, but less visibly, less starkly. Life, in other words, is a sacrifice to life. This reality finds a variety of expressions in the religions of the world, and to fathom its depths is to receive knowledge that is truly wise and sacred. In the festival that is an epidemic and in the epidemic that is a festival, the South Indian villager is at least confronted head on with this paradoxical and potentially liberating reality.

To say that life is a sacrifice to life is to express a theme that pervades the Hindu tradition. But it takes two basic forms, as visions of the sacred tend to do. On one side belong human actions of self-denial and self-control in pursuit of virtue, social harmony, and heavenly reward; rituals in which something is sacrificed for a greater good, whether it be material gain or the maintenance of cosmic order; and the deities who receive these offerings, provide these rewards, and sanction these values. However imperfectly individuals may meet their obligations, village life is steeped in this sacred ideal in which sacrifice bears its proper fruit in due season.

On the other side are those unseasonable irruptions of the sacred that can smash proprieties, overturn ideals, and occasion or force sacrifices of quite different kinds, ranging from shattering experiences of divine power to acts of spontaneous and ecstatic self-abandonment. Our village goddesses obviously belong to this side of the sacrificial theme, along with such fierce deities as the great goddess Kālī and (especially in some of his forms) the great god Shiva. But this is not their whole story.

*None* of their story can be heard if, demanding that the sacred be exclusively orderly and benevolent, one can see in them nothing more than disorder and malevolence. But the bloodthirsty Kālī offers an ultimately liberating knowledge: that the bright and dark sides of the sacred are but the human bifurcation of one holy reality. And on a humbler plane a village goddess confronts her people with the same transcendent unity. Thus a wise observer has written of smallpox outbreaks in the domain of the Bengali goddess Śītalā that "they are to be understood as an oscillation from the implicit to the epidemic form of grace."[11] In the case of the local as well as of the universal goddess, the shock of encountering her in all her power is proportional to one's habit of domesticating and sanitizing the sacred. Thus, again with reference to Śītalā: "It is through these events, called epidemics, that people, knowing little, wishing to know less, and tending to forget much, are made aware of her constant presence."[12]

Finally, why should the deities who most strikingly exemplify this union of what man has put asunder be female? The answer lies in the fact that traditional images of women are polarized in a way that parallels the polarization of the sacred. And in India this familiar split is found in extreme form.

In India the ideal woman is chaste, virtuous, and obedient to her husband. If a woman departs very far from this ideal she is in danger of being considered a slut—a reputation almost automatically acquired by any female who goes beyond puberty without marrying. Several factors deeply embedded in Indian culture account for this state of affairs, among them the belief that women have stronger sexual drives than men—drives which, if properly controlled and sublimated, can produce a saintliness beyond the capacity of the male, but which, if allowed to run rampant, can be very threatening to men.

Thus there are two kinds of Indian goddesses. One kind is married, subordinate to her husband, under proper control, and, so, a paragon of virtue. The other is unmarried, dominates any relationship with a male, and is therefore uncontrolled and dangerous. But it is easy to confuse the dangerous with the demonic and the safe with the sacred. Thus, it has been claimed of Indian deities: "When the feminine dominates the masculine the pair is sinister; when male dominates female the pair is benign."[13] The second half of the statement is true, but the first misses the point.

While far from wholly sinister, an uncontrolled goddess *is* dangerous. And part of her threat, part of her power, derives from a male fear of the female. But the greater part derives from a parallel human fear of the depths of the sacred. For perhaps the greatest danger she embodies is the possibility that human beings, "knowing little, wishing to know less, and tending to forget much," will find the comfortable categories to which they cling swept away in a flood of divine transcendence.

## NOTES

Most of what is presented here is documented and discussed more fully in the author's "The Ambivalent Mistress: A Study of South Indian Village Goddesses and Their Religious Meaning" (Ph.D. diss., University of Chicago, 1978).

1. What I am describing here is an age-old pattern, much of which remains intact in many villages. But village India is gradually changing. For one thing, public health measures have greatly reduced the incidence of epidemics (though not necessarily the severity of those that do break out). Partly for this reason and partly in imitation of other festivals in India, some village goddess festivals are now held annually rather than only in time of crisis. Nevertheless, the crisis symbolism continues to dominate the ritual; this and other aspects of the traditional patterns are the focus of this essay.

2. I place *supernatural* in quotation marks because, to a traditional Hindu, these figures inhabit the world as naturally as humans or animals.

3. The independent and fiercely dynamic goddess Kālī is the most important exception to this vegetarian pattern.

4. There are innumerable local variations, of course, but for present purposes they can be ignored. There is also much in what follows that is applicable to other parts of India as well, but the pattern as a whole applies only to the South. For a fuller examination of these matters, see my "Barbers, Washermen, and Other Priests: Servants of the South Indian Village and Its Goddess," *History of Religions* 19 (1979): 128–52.

5. Occasionally, on the other hand, a village spreads the word that its goddess has manifested herself with power, and enormous crowds gather for the festival. Likewise, crowds of one-hundred thousand or more converge on certain villages whose festivals have become annual affairs. This clearly reflects more of the Hindu pilgrimage tradition than of the archaic and fundamental meanings of village goddess worship.

6. The most famous is the world-threatening Mahiṣāsura, whose beheading by the great goddess Durgā, whom he had attacked, is celebrated in Sanskrit texts and widely portrayed in temple sculpture, especially in the South. There is little reason to doubt that the story of this encounter, which has been called "the archetypal myth of the goddess in India" (David Shulman, "The Murderous Bride: Tamil Versions of the Myth of Devī and the Buffalo-Demon," *History of Religions* 16 [1976]: 120), is based on the age-old practice of buffalo sacrifice at village goddess festivals.

7. During various festivals (village goddess festivals included) individuals from time to time are caught up in states of ecstatic trance, and these states may likewise be understood as divine possession and viewed with reverence. Demon possession, of course, is considered quite another matter.

8. This latter motif appears also in Sanskrit mythological texts telling of a great goddess and world-threatening demons.

9. See Brenda E.F. Beck, "Colour and Heat in South Indian Ritual," *Man*, n.s.4(1969):553–72.

10. Brenda E.F. Beck, "The Goddess and the Demon: A Local South Indian Festival and Its Wider Context," *Puruṣārtha* 5 (1981): 88-89, 95.

11. Edward C. Dimock, Jr., "A Theology of the Repulsive: The Myth of the Goddess Śītalā," in *The Divine Consort: Rādhā and the Goddesses of India*, ed. John Stratton Hawley and Donna Marie Wulff (Berkeley: Berkeley Religious Studies Series, 1982).

12. Ibid.

13. Lawrence A. Babb, "Marriage and Malevolence: The Uses of Sexual Opposition in a Hindu Pantheon," *Ethnology* 9 (1970):142.

# 12

## DIANA PAUL

# Kuan-Yin: Savior and Savioress in Chinese Pure Land Buddhism

T he beginnings of cultic devotion to Kuan-yin, the compassionate savior and bodhisattva, have not been definitely established. After the cult had become prevalent in Chinese Pure Land Buddhism, Kuan-yin was regarded as the principal teacher and next Buddha, after the decline of Amitābha's teaching.[1] Kuan-yin was conceived as a savior having an infinite lifespan whose actions consisted solely of saving sentient beings.

The purpose of this paper is threefold: to investigate what is the Buddhist notion of savior, to describe the historical development of the cult of Kuan-yin, and to present doctrinal reasons for the inclusion of the savior Kuan-yin in Pure Land Buddhist cult practices.

### Buddhist Notion of Savior

Before attempting to discuss the applicability of the terms savior or savioress to Kuan-yin in Chinese Pure Land Buddhism, the general notion of savior in the Buddhist context must be ascertained. In early Buddhism Śākyamuni, the historical Buddha, was regarded as the supreme teacher who had discovered an effective approach to realizing the truth but who could not cause the enlightenment of others. Enlightenment was defined as an internal process involving one's own effort: "One is one's own refuge, who else could be the refuge?"[2] According to Theravada Buddhism the Buddha was not a savior in the religious sense of one who answers prayers or bestows grace and love.[3] Nonetheless, even Theravādin Buddhism was eventually to incorporate a messianic figure, Maitreya, in its orthodoxy[4] and it may be argued that the Buddha was to some degree a docetic figure in popular religious practice.[5]

Generally speaking, however, the term savior, if it can be applied in any sense to Buddhist figures, either historical or mythological, seems most appropriately applied to those religious figures in Mahayana Buddhist teaching known as bodhisattvas. The Pure Land Buddhist cults as well as others have even been considered a "new religion"[6] because of their salvific doctrine of supplication to Buddhas and bodhisattvas as the means of assuring enlightenment. One of the most spectacular and popular bodhisattvas in terms of attributed powers and receptivity to prayers is the bodhisattva Avalokiteśvara (or, in Chinese, Kuan-yin), the bodhisattva who personifies the virtue of compassion.

All bodhisattvas were said to forsake their own justly deserved enlightenment by virtue of their compassion and intense identification with all sentient beings. As a result of this universal empathy, the bodhisattva professed vows to help others attain enlightenment to perform actions for the welfare of others. These self-sacrificing acts were due to past virtuous habits in the bodhisattva's previous lifetimes. In the first six to ten bodhisattva stages, the bodhisattva is said to be struggling to exemplify a very difficult ideal.[7] To the extent that an individual strived to follow the bodhisattva course of action, he or she was said to be beginning the bodhisattva career as a "good son" or "good daughter."

From the seventh stage of bodhisattva practice through the attainment of Buddhahood itself, the bodhisattva was no longer, strictly speaking, an individual struggling with forces and attitudes that hindered the attainment of spiritual perfection. It was at this level that this subset of bodhisattvas, often called "celestial bodhisattvas," became autonomous or semiautonomous deities who were endowed with countless miraculous and psychic powers to help those in distress. Several of these celestial bodhisattvas were the objects of cult worship, for example, Maitreya, Mañjuśrī, Kṣitigarbha, and Avalokiteśvara (or Kuan-yin). To the degree that these bodhisattvas were believed to be concerned about their faithful followers, to listen to their appeals, to fulfill their material and psychological needs, and to reside in or have access to a utopia, or "Pure Land," they may be said to be saviors. Stated otherwise, these figures were believed to satisfy all the needs of believers who were dependent upon them. These cult bodhisattvas were viewed as having nearly mastered the great powers of a Buddha. The devotees of these celestial bodhisattvas attributed names, spiritual and physical qualities, and specific functions to them.

In partial disagreement with Edward Conze, who states that "there is, however, nothing unique about Avalokiteśvara, and he does no more than all bodhisattvas are bidden to do,"[8] it may be argued that Avalokiteśvara, at least as the Chinese counterpart known as Kuan-yin, was indeed a very special celestial bodhisattva and was the object of considerable cult practice (and remains so today). Of all the various

Buddhas and saints in Mahayana Buddhism in China, Kuan-yin was nonsectarian and eventually the most popular of all cult figures. From the first traces of religious practice at the end of the Western Chin (ca. 313–17) through the Sung period (tenth through thirteenth century) and later, Kuan-yin was revered as the supreme savior or savioress in classical China.

## Redefinition of Faith by Mahayana Buddhism

The "taking refuge in the Three Jewels" of the Buddha, Dharma, and Samgha in Theravada and other early sectarian Buddhism implied a type of trust or faith in the Buddha as a teacher, on the one hand, together with a reinforcement of one's own commitment to pursue and follow the Buddhist teaching on the other. In contrast to this early view of faith or trust, Mahayana Buddhism developed the notion of an act of faith in a given celestial bodhisattva or Amitābha as a way of producing an enormous amount of merit for the person engaging in that act. Tremendous self-exertion was not required but rather an act, usually requiring visualization or recitation, acknowledging the externalized powers of the object of faith. The devout believer could than expect a rapid rate of growth in his or her spiritual development.

The critical difference between the trust or faith in the Three Jewels and that of faith in the bodhisattva or Buddha Amitābha is that the former stressed the Buddha Śākyamuni's role as a teacher while the latter emphasized the merits and spiritual powers of the given celestial bodhisattva or Buddha. The first type of faith resulted in a receptivity to the words of the Buddha in a slow culmination of spiritual growth. The second type of faith used the Buddha's words themselves for a rapid realization of spiritual growth and as a means for immediate gratification. Stated otherwise, trust or faith in the Three Jewels was inwardly directed, advocating a very high degree of self-reliance, while faith in the celestial bodhisattvas and in Buddha Amitābha was other-directed and relied upon the manipulation and distribution of merit by invoking the Buddha's words. Although the teaching was to be acknowledged and followed, it was equally important to have faith and trust in the merits and miraculous powers of the agent who could be invoked by calling out the name.

Since celestial bodhisattvas were personifications of religious ideals such as wisdom or compassion, one's faith in the ideal as being all-powerful and miraculous was enough to direct one's spiritual course of action. In the case of bodhisattvas as saviors, it was not the personality of a savior figure that came first in historical development, but rather the delineation and description of the powers, virtues, and merits that characterized all bodhisattvas or Buddhas. Individualized cult bodhisattvas evolved from the characterizations of specific bodhisattvas as "specialists" with regard to a certain set of virtues and powers. Their names were believed to be salvific because they invoked the power of the bodhi-sattva. It is in this sense that the celestial bodhisattva or Amitābha is a savior through invocation and assumes a special connotation in Ma-hayana Buddhism as contrasted with other salvific religious expressions.

In order to demonstrate that the term savior may be applied to Buddhist figures who were not so much personalities as purely spiritu-al forces, Kuan-yin, assistant to the Buddha Amitābha, will be investi-gated in terms of the historical development of both the texts describ-ing his or her powers and the subsequent cult practice vis-à-vis Chinese Pure Land Buddhism. Kuan-yin's historical development will be pre-sented, followed by a description of the evidence that attests to the popularity of Kuan-yin's cult practice. Finally, an account of the development of the cult-practice will be postulated.

## Development of the Mythology of Kuan-yin

### Background: The Indian Tradition
### of the Bodhisattva Avalokiteśvara

The mythology of celestial bodhisattvas has been compared with that of non-Indian, especially Iranian, gods to whom some of these Buddhist figures bear a striking resemblance. Avalokiteśvara, who is described in the twenty-fourth chapter, "The Universal Face," pos-sesses some of the attributes of the god Zurvan and of the god Srausha of the Zend-Avesta.[9] Playing a very important role as the great bodhi-sattva who embodied the virtue of compassion, Avalokiteśvara was even considered superior to any single Buddha in bestowing greater benefits and merits to faithful followers:

> ... the accumulation of pious merit produced by that young gen-tleman paying homage to so many Lord Buddhas, and the accu-mulation of pious merit produced by him who performs were it but a single act of adoration to the Bodhisattva Mahāsattva Avalokiteśvara and cherishes his name, are equal. ... So im-mense, a young man of good family, is the pious merit result-ing from cherishing the name of the Bodhisattva Mahāsattva Avalokiteśvara.[10]

According to the *Lotus Sūtra* there are seven powers that are con-jured with the invocation of Avalokiteśvara's name: extinguishing fires, stilling turbulent rivers and oceans, calming winds and storms, freeing the accused from executioners, blinding demons and spirits, freeing the imprisoned and enslaved, and disarming one's enemies. To women practitioners who invoke the bodhisattva's name, Avaloki-teśvara will bring a healthy child. In enacting these powers, the bodhi-sattva Avalokiteśvara, according to the text, assumes any one of sixteen apparitional male forms, in accordance with the station of the follower.[11] There are only passing references in the chapter "The Universal Face" to Avalokiteśvara's being the assistant to Amitābha.

In the extant Sanskrit recension of the *Smaller Sukhāvatīvyūha* there is no mention of Avalokiteśvara, although the *Larger Sukhāvatīvyūha* mentions Avalokiteśvara along with Mahāsthāmaprāpta as the two assistants to Amitābha and glorifies their merits and powers. In the *Amitāyur-dhyāna sūtra* (available only in Chinese), the two assistant bodhisattvas are also mentioned, first in Queen Vaidehi's vision and then as part of the Eighth, Tenth, and Eleventh Meditations.[12] The *Amitāyur-dhyāna sūtra* represents a systematic mythology of Amitābha and the two celestial bodhisattvas Avalokiteśvara and Mahāsthāmaprāpta.

The Buddhist literary tradition in India represents Avalokiteśvara as a powerful figure who assits Amitābha, has countless magical powers, and is glorified in the devotional and Tantric texts.[13] In China the magnitude of cult worship to Kuan-yin in Pure Land Buddhism was due, in part, to the introduction of the *Lotus Sūtra* to the Chinese people. Kuan-yin worshipers incorporated some of the Indian elements of invoking Avalokiteśvara with their own innovations, as will be demonstrated below.

### The Chinese Avalokiteśvara, Kuan-yin

At a very early date Kuan-yin's name appeared in Mahayana texts translated during the late Han. Exposure to Kuan-yin became widespread with the translation of the *Lotus Sūtra* (*Cheng-fa hua ching*) by Dharmarakṣa (Chu Fa-hu) of Western Chin in 276 C.E., but the popular cult practice of Kuan-yin did not appear during the Chin. Dharmarakṣa, the single most powerful translator before Kumārajīva, had developed a sphere of influence centered at Ch'angan, bounded on the east by Loyang and on the west by Tun-huang.[14] From the records of the eminent nuns and monks, it is evident that the *Cheng-fa hua ching* was quickly disseminated around Loyang and that the cult was beginning to flourish about the end of the fourth century.[15] Since Taoist thought was very popular during the Chin period, Prajñā literature, which was perceived to have an affinity with Taoism, eclipsed the study of the *Lotus Sūtra*. Gradually the study of the *Lotus Sūtra* and the appearance of cult practice to Kuan-yin began to emerge to a noticeable degree by the end of Eastern Chin (late fourth century C.E.).[16]

During the fifth century Kuan-yin's cult gradually rose to prominence with the composition of testimonial records (*chu-lu*) concerning Kuan-yin's miracles.[17] It was about this time that Kumārajīva translated the *Lotus Sūtra* (*Miao-fa lien hua ching*) (406 C.E.) and the twenty-fifth chapter, *P'u-men*, became popular as a separate text known as the *Kuan-yin ching* because of the focus on Kuan-yin. Under Kumārajīva's influence, his disciples conducted research on the *Lotus Sūtra*, resulting in the text's wide dissemination.[18] One outcome of this diffusion of studies on the *Lotus* was the fabrication of texts or "sutras" dealing with cult worship of Kuan-yin.[19]

One of the earliest texts to be translated by the end of the later Han and during Western Chin was the *Larger Sukhāvatīvyūha,* or *Pure Land Sūtra (Wu-liang-shou ching).* This text was translated at least two times[20] by Buddhist followers from central Asia (Yüeh-chih).

The *Larger Sukhāvatīvyūha,* which describes birth in Pure Land and explains the twenty-four vows of Amitābha, is one of the three[21] principal sutras upon which the Pure Land school in China was based. Although the practice of the Kuan-yin cult was being disseminated throughout China as a result of the various translations of the *Lotus Sūtra,* Kuan-yin was also described in the *Wu-liang-shou ching* as the assistant to the Buddha Amitābha in Pure Land literature. Some of the earliest Mahayana texts,[22] which were to have a close relationship with Pure Land Buddhist doctrine, were transmitted by central-Asian Buddhists, whose translations guided devotionalism during the Chin period. These texts played a part in the incipiency of Amitābha cult practice, which was to develop later. However, no cult practices seem to have developed by the end of Western Chin.

By the Eastern Chin period, Buddhist spiritual societies suddenly began to proliferate. Pure Land Buddhism was becoming attractive to Buddho-Taoists.[23] With the reading or recitation of the *Wu-liang-shou ching* both monastic and lay devotees increased their good Karma. Cult practice was beginning to be noticeable by the end of Eastern Chin, but not to the extent of influencing large segments of the population. Cult practice to Kuan-yin began to appear in association with the *Lotus Sūtra* but not with Pure Land.[24]

It is during the Six Dynasties (fifth through tenth century C.E.) that the cult practices among the general population began to emphasize devotion to Kuan-yin for present benefits in this world and as a future savior[25] who would carry the believer to Amitābha's Pure Land. Statues of Kuan-yin erected at this time almost always had a vow to be born in Pure Land inscribed on them.[26] T'ien-t'ai masters cited fabricated texts dealing with Kuan-yin's powers, which attested to the exceptional popularity of the various Kuan-yin cults.[27] The ten vows that Kuan-yin professed as a bodhisattva were known by this time. Most texts associated with Kuan-yin were translated during the period of the Six Dynasties, with only three or four translations appearing after T'ang (with the exception of Tantric-influenced texts, which were being translated in great numbers during T'ang and Sung).

*Popularity of Kuan-yin Cult Practices*

The degree of popularity of Kuan-yin cult practice may be attested to and from two principal sources: the number of translations of texts relating to Kuan-yin (especially "fabricated" texts) and the cave sculptures at Yün-kang, Lung-men, and other locations, which have examples of images of Kuan-yin as an object of worship.

As mentioned above, texts alluding to Kuan-yin's name date back to the late Han, but these texts primarily belong to the Prajñā body of literature. The first texts to describe and extol Kuan-yin's miraculous powers were the *Lotus Sūtra* in the *Amitāyur-dhyāna sūtra*. After these texts were translated, "fabricated sutras" discussing the "life stories"[28] or "birth tales" of Kuan-yin began to proliferate by the seventh century.[29] The relationship between birth tales and the development of cult practice is illustrated in early sectarian, pre-Mahayana Buddhism as well as in the Kuan-yin cults.[30] Many of Kuan-yin's birth tales appear during the Six Dynasties period.[31] One feature of these birth-tales is the mention of Mount Poṭalaka[32] as the residence of Kuan-yin in Pure Land cosmology. It is on Mount Poṭalaka that Kuan-yin is said to hear the prayers of the faithful, to wait until the time to stand by the devotee's bedside during the hour of death, and then to transport the devotee to Pure Land. While Amitābha ensured bliss in his Pure Land in the next life, Kuan-yin brought benefits in this world (Sahāloka), being a resident on Mount Poṭalaka, the very special environment of Kuan-yin in this world-system.

In the *Kuan wu-liang-shou ching* Kuan-yin is said to be the best friend of those who are mindful of the Buddha Amitābha.[33] As Amitābha's powerful assistant, Kuan-yin teaches the faithful about the coming of Amitābha at the hour of death. The sudden diffusion of the Kuan-yin cult occurred during the T'ang dynasty (seventh through tenth century), when belief in the power of Amitābha was at its zenith.

The people were preoccupied with the five[34] inauspicious features of the decadent age. With the practice of being mindful and invoking the Buddha Amitābha's name, the practitioner believed that he or she would transcend the life-death cycle and be born in the Western Paradise of Pure Land.

> A follower, whether or not he had committed sins, was believed to be saved by the deity and to be brought into the "Western Paradise" without judgement of his deeds. ... At least in popular belief, no repentance was necessary, only belief in grace.[35]

Kuan-yin was the good friend of those who practiced mindfulness and recitation of the name, offering protection to all faithful followers. The idea of "protection by a bodhisattva" in the present life became a feature of Pure Land Buddhism during this period.[36] Recognizing the sutra's teaching through the recitation of the name Amitābha was believed to protect against misfortune and to extend one's lifetime. Gradually, protection by the Buddha and bodhisattvas was also believed to increase one's longevity.

While Amitābha created countless images for those who were born in his Western Paradise, Kuan-yin, and to a lesser degree, Mahāsthāmaprāpta, always went to the practitioner's environment. In contrast to the distant savior Amitābha, Kuan-yin sat with the believer in the sphere of enlightenment in the believer's environment and then transported him or her on a white lotus to Pure Land.

For the general populace the intimate protection provided by the Buddha Amitābha and by Kuan-yin were desired and the Pure Land Buddhist scholastics could not overlook this need,[37] even for those who were most unworthy. The belief in a bodhisattva's protection probably dated back to the turn of the sixth century. Taoist-influenced notions of protection by spirits were most likely included in Pure Land Buddhist cult practices, since Taoist practice was deeply ingrained in the general popular beliefs. From the mid-seventh century Chinese Pure Land Buddhist scholastics accepted the immensely popular cult to Amitābha with its concomitant cult of Kuan-yin as established practices that focused on the protection provided by their great powers.

After Northern Wei (534 C.E.) the cult to Kuan-yin became immensely popular, as evidenced by inscriptions on cave scultpure remaining at Lung-men and T'o-shan. According to these inscriptions, many of the donors wished to be born on Mount Potalaka, Kuan-yin's residence.[38] From the Lung-men cave temples dating from the Northern Wei, it is evident that Amitābha and Kuan-yin, the compassionate savior bodhisattva, captured the hearts of the majority of the Chinese. If one studies the changes in objects of worship at Lung-men, the history of Buddhist cult practice becomes apparent. During the Northern Wei, statues that were privately constructed—that is, not constructed by commission of the imperial court—were overwhelmingly those of Śākyamuni and Maitreya. The majority of these statues were built by influential monks and by citizens of the upper classes.[39] A number of statues of Kuan-yin and Amitābha were constructed during the latter part of Northern Wei (525—527) which, in contrast to statues of Śākyamuni and Maitreya, were overwhelmingly the contributions of the general public.

According to the *Records of Statues Constructed during the Northern Wei*, Kuan-yin's representations were third in rank, with Śākyamuni being first and Maitreya second. Amitābha's images were fourth in number. The most noteworthy feature of the representations of Kuan-yin at this time is that Kuan-yin practice was guided by the teaching of the *P'u-men* chapter of the *Lotus Sūtra*, which had overriding influence in both the caves of Lung-men and Yün-kang during the Northern Wei period.[40]

It is only with the very beginning of T'ang that bodhisattva saviors, such as Kuan-yin, begin to appear as cult objects.[41] In contrast with the Northern Wei tradition in which Śākyamuni's perfection of wisdom and Maitreya's wisdom are represented, during the T'ang the central theme is the unlimited compassion of Amitābha and Kuan-yin. Kuan-yin as the merciful savior was being associated very closely with the Pure Land cult worship of Amitābha. Cult practice to Amitābha during T'ang gained considerable force, as evidenced by the over-whelming zeal illustrated in cave sculpture portraying devotees to Amitābha and Kuan-yin. Preempting Maitreya as the major cult bodhi-sattva, Kuan-yin was conceived as the compassionate savior or savior-ess[42] who appears in this world to all faithful believers and assumes a variety of apparitional forms.[43] Cult practice involved visualization of Kuan-yin and Amitābha at the hour of death as assurance of birth in Pure Land. In sharp contrast to Maitreya, who was living far away in the Tuṣita heaven to become the last Buddha at the end of this world-system, Kuan-yin was believed to be waiting on Mount Poṭalaka to rush to the aid of devoted followers. Kuan-yin became the most popular bodhisattva for the general population at this time, as an immediate savior and savioress for Pure Land Buddhists as well as for other Buddhists.

## Doctrinal Reasons for the Incorporation of Kuan-yin into Pure Land Buddhist Cult Practice

Unlike the religion of the influential monastic order and upper classes, the popular religious cults did not emphasize the wisdom of Śākyamuni and the bodhisattva Maitreya, as evidenced by class differences in selecting the subject matter for cave sculptures carved at Lung-men and Yün-kang. This difference was also evident in the cult practices initiated under the influence of the popularity of the *Lotus Sūtra*, which advocated universal salvation (*ekayāna*) regardless of individual capabilities or idiosyncratic behavior. In the *A-mi-t'o ching* the fear of death is addressed in terms of birth in Pure Land:

> If there are good sons and good daughters who hear Amitābha and cherish his name for seven days without a distracted state of mind then they will see Amitābha and his assembly before them. They will not have disturbed minds and will be born in the Pure Land of Amitābha.[44]

The association of peace of mind at the hour of death with the Buddha Amitābha's appearance does not seem to have occurred in early sectarian or even early Mahayana texts. This notion does appear, however, in even the earliest Pure Land texts.[45] The very first Chinese text to discuss the Buddha Amitābha's Western Paradise (*Pan-chou san-mei ching*) mentions that mindfulness of the Buddha (*nien-fo*), when practiced for seven days and seven nights, will ensure the appearance of the Buddha Amitābha first in a dream and then at the hour of death.[46] Besides the association with a serene death and subsequent birth in Pure Land, Kuan-yin cult practice was associated with immedi-ate protection in this world, due both to apparent Taoist influence and to the popularity of the *P'u-men* chapter of the *Lotus Sūtra*. Chanting Kuan-yin's name assured the elimination of any calamity or misfortune as well as the receipt of material, psychological, and spiritual benefits from Kuan-yin's infinite storehouse of merit.

While devotion to Śākyamuni and Maitreya appealed to the more intellectual Buddhists of the upper classes, devotion to Amitābha appealed to those who did not have a lifestyle that enabled them to cope more easily with the vicissitudes of the environment. For those devout followers a future utopia in the west was promised. Amitābha fulfilled one's needs for the next life by causing birth in Pure Land, but, at the same time, did not bestow present benefits in this lifetime. He was a savior of one's future destiny only. The general population, once introduced to the theory of the protection of the bodhisattvas that promised longer life in this world, desired to improve their circumstances in this lifetime as well as the next. It is with respect to present circumstances and tribulations that Kuan-yin played a critical role as the present savior for those in need. The mythology of Kuan-yin, from the period of its importation into China, had emphasized the bodhisattva's miraculous powers to change circumstances in this world as well as to assist the Buddha Amitābha in the next. Whereas Amitābha was centered on the "other world" of the Western Paradise, Kuan-yin, situated on Mount Poṭalaka, was much closer to the people's present concerns and needs. Undoubtedly, the belief that one's afterlife in Buddha Amitābha's Pure Land would automatically result from the recitation of the name allowed the practitioner's attention to turn to this world and to try to improve the quality of the present life as well.

The teaching of the bodhisattva savior Kuan-yin's merits and powers must have been tremendously good news for those who believed they were in the age of decline. A shift in emphasis in Pure Land cult practice seems to have taken place, and the reasons for this shift need to be explored in future studies. The focal point of Amitābha's worship was to abandon this decadent world and be born in Pure Land. The focal point in cult worship of Kuan-yin was to be free from suffering in this present world and to increase the "good things in life." If the practitioner wanted to remove the negative elements in this decadent world and try to change his or her lifestyle for the better, then development of a cult to a savior or savioress who would distribute benefits in accordance with devotion would be appropriate.

The general outline of the development of a present-day savior/savioress in Pure Land Buddhist practice began with central worship of Amitābha, sovereign of Pure Land, acknowledging only minor roles for Kuan-yin and Mahāsthāmaprāpta. From the earliest texts of Pure Land Buddhism translated into Chinese we have seen that these texts glorified Amitābha while relegating Kuan-yin to a secondary position.

Under the influence of the *Lotus Sūtra* in which Kuan-yin's special powers in this world preempted even the Buddhas as well as all other bodhisattvas, Pure Land Buddhist cult practice incorporated the miraculous powers of Kuan-yin in their glorification of Amitābha's Western Paradise. While *Lotus* cult practice in worship of Kuan-yin was in the ascendancy, Pure Land Buddhist practice of Kuan-yin's cult had also developed (as evidenced by various fabricated texts that modeled Kuan-yin's former lives on that of the Buddha Amitābha as the former bodhisattva Dharmākara (Fa-tsang). Along with these fabricated texts, testimonial records of miracles to verify Kuan-yin's power were included as part of devotion to Amitābha. Devotion to the future savior Amitābha, who appears at the moment of death, was united with devotion to the present savior, Kuan-yin, who guides the destiny of the faithful follower until the meeting at death with Amitābha.

In conclusion, what had developed first in terms of a notion of a savior in Pure Land Buddhist cult practice was the notion of a future savior, Amitābha, who allayed the fear of death by appearing to the practitioner immediately prior to expiration. After the notion of a future savior had become a tenet of belief, the idea of protection in this world by the bodhisattvas as a reward for practicing mindfulness prepared the way for devotion to the most popular savior in classical Chinese Buddhism, the compassionate savior/savioress Kuan-yin. Because of Kuan-yin's assurance that the present life will enable the devout Pure Land Buddhist both to fulfill his or her vow to be born in the next life in the Western Paradise of Amitābha and to enjoy security and freedom in this world to practice mindfulness, Kuan-yin most assuredly is the savior/savioress in Chinese Pure Land Buddhism.

## NOTES

1. *Kuan-shih-yin p'u-sa shou chi ching*, Taishō v. 12, n. 271, p. 357a 10—16.

2. *Dhammapāda* XII, 4. Cited in Walpola Rahula, *What the Buddha Taught* (New York: Grove Press, 1959), p. 1.

3. Winston L. King, cited in Edward Conze, "Buddhist Saviors," in *Thirty Years of Buddhist Studies* (Columbia, S.C.: University of South Carolina Press, 1968), p. 39.

4. Richard H. Robinson, *The Buddhist Religion* (Belmont, Calif.: Dickenson Publishing Co. 1970), p. 59.

5. Conze, *Thirty Years of Buddhist Studies*, p. 40.

6. Ibid., p. 38.

7. For example, the very sympathetic figure of the Bodhisattva Sadāprarudita in *The Perfection of Wisdom in Eight Thousand Lines and Its Verse Summary*, trans. Edward Conze (Bolinas, Calif.: 1973), pp. 276-300, and the Bodhisattva Sadāparibhuta in the *Saddharma-Puṇḍarīka, or the Lotus of the True Law*, trans. H. Kern (New York: Dover Publications, 1963), pp. 356—62.

8. Conze, *Thirty Years*, p. 34.

9. Marie-Thérèse de Mallmann, *Introduction à L'Etude d'Avalokiteçvara* (Paris: Annales de Musée Guimet, Presses Universitaires de France, 1967), pp. 85—104.

10. *Saddharma-Puṇḍarīka*, trans. H. Kern, p. 410.

11. In Kumārajīva's translation there are thirty-three forms, among which are nine females (T.v. 9, n. 262, p. 57a 23—b19); Dharmarakṣa (Chu Fa-hu) lists seventeen male forms (T.v. 9, n. 263, p. 129b 28—c6).

12. *Sacred Books of the East*, vol. 49, *Buddhist Mahāyāna Texts* (Oxford: Clarendon Press, 1894), pp. 176-86.

13. In later Sanskrit texts, e.g., *Kārandavyūha-sūtra*, the Bodhisattva Avalokiteśvara has immense magical power, embodied in the six-syllable mantra and suggesting that Avalokiteśvara is a supreme magician and yogin. Directions for iconographic representations of a mandala called "Amitābha's invisible mandala" are given in the text.

14. Tuskamoto Zenryū, "The Discovery of a Record of the Miraculous Efficacy of Faith in Avalokiteśvara, the *Kuan-shih-yin Ying-yen-chi*, by Hsieh Fu and Fu Liang, a Six Dynasties Document Hitherto Presumed Lost" (Koitsu rokki kanseon okenki no shutsugen), in the *Silver Jubilee Volume* of the *Zinbun Kagaku Kenkyushō* (Kyoto: Kyoto University Press, 1954), p. 245.

15. Tsukamoto, "The Discovery of a Record," p. 246.

16. For example, the *Kao-seng chüan* records a lecture which was a synthesis of the *Lotus Sūtra*, Taoist teaching, and the *Large Prajñāpāramita Sūtra* by Chu Ch'ien (d. C.E. 374). Yü Fa-k'ai, a contemporary of Chu Ch'ien, also lectured on the *Lotus*. Another monk, Chu Fai, became sick in 380 C.E. and was said to have been cured of his illness after invoking the name of Kuan-yin. Consequently, Kuan-yin cult practice probably gained momentum towards the end of the Eastern Chin. See *Kannon zenshū* (Tokyo: 1939–41), vol. 7, *Kannon shinkōshi*, pp. 49–60.

17. A list of testimonial records of miraculous events are found in *Kannon shinkōshi*, pp. 62–63. Also see Tsukamoto Zenryū, "The Discovery of a Record," pp. 234–49. For a translation of a Japanese record of Kuan-yin's miraculous events, see Yoshiko K. Dykstra, "Tales of the Compassionate Kannon—*The Hasedera Kannon* Genki," in *Monumenta Nipponica*, 31, no. 2 (Summer 1976): 113–43.

18. Kumārajīva's *p'u-men* chapter (T.v. 9, n. 262, pp. 56–58) corresponds to the twenty-fourth chapter, *Samantamukha*, of the *Saddharma-pundarīka*. Reasons for the popularity of the *Lotus Sūtra* are only partially attributed to Kumārajīva's reputation, however. On a popular level, the text's teaching of universal salvation inspired the general population to follow the Buddha's teaching.

19. Among the most famous of the "fabricated" texts (wei ching) are:

a. *Kao wang shih chü kuan-yin ching* (T.v. 85, n. 2898), composed in Northern Wei, according to Satō Taishun, *Shina bukkyo shisō ron* (Eihei-ji: 1970), p. 342.

b. *Kuan-shih-yin ch'an-hui ch'u tsui chou ching*, no longer extant; cited in chap. 5, *Jen-shou lu* (i.e., *Chung-ching mu-lu*, compiled by Yen-ts'ung of Sui in C.E. 602 (T.v. 55, n. 2147); chap. 5, *Ching-t'ai lu* (i.e., *Chung-ching mu-lu*, compiled by Ching-t'ai between 663 and 665 (T.v. 55, n. 2148); chap. 12, *Ta-chou k'an ting chung-ching mu-lu*, compiled by Ming Ch'üan and others in 615 (T.v. 55, n. 2153); chap. 14, *K'ai-yüan shih chiao mu-lu*, compiled by Chih-sheng in 730 (T.v. 55, n. 2154); and chap. 24, *Chen-yüan hsin ting shih chiao mu-lu*, compiled by Yüan Chao of T'ang in 800 (T.v. 55, n. 2157).

c. *Kuan-shih-yin shih ta-yüan ching*, no longer extant; cited in chap. 2, *Fa-ching lu* (i.e., *Chung-ching mu-lu*), compiled by Fa-ching in 594 (T.v. 55, n. 2146); chap. 4, *Jen-shou lu*; chap. 5, *Ta-chou k'an ting chung-ching mu-lu*; chap. 18, *Kai-yüan*; chap. 28, *Chen-yüan hsin ting shih chiao mu-lu*.

d. *Kuan-shih-yin san-mei ching*, no longer extant; cited in chap. 2, *Fa-ching lu*; chap. 4, *Jen-shou lu*, chap. 11, *Ta-chou mu-lu*; chap. 18, *Kai-yüan mu-lu*; chap. 28, *Chen-yüan mu-lu*.

e. *Kuan-shih-yin p'u-sa wang-sheng ching-t'u pen-y uan ching*, Dai Nihon zokuzōkyō, vol. 87, pp. 288–90; translation date attributed erroneously to Western Chin.

20. The two early Chinese redactions are (1) *Ta a-mi-t'o ching*, two *chüan* (T.v. 12, n. 362, pp. 300-318), translated by Chih Ch'ien of Wu between 223 and 226, and (2) *Wu-liang ch'ing-ching 'ping-teng chüeh ching*, four *chüan* (T.v. 12, n. 361, pp. 279–99), allegedly translated by Lokakṣema of Later Han between 147 and 186. A third

translation, *Wu-liang-shou ching* (T.v. 12, n. 360, pp. 265–79), usually attributed to Saṃghavarman of Wei, has been disputed by Kōtatsu Fujita, who claims that the *Wu-liang-shou ching* was jointly translated by Buddhabhadra and Pao-yun in 421. Cf. *Genshi jōdo shisō no kenkyū* (Tokyo: 1970), pp. 35–96. According to Tsukamoto Zenryū, *Shina bukkyōshi kenkyū* (Tokyo: 1942), p. 620, the *Ta a-mi-t'o ching* was probably translated by Lokakṣema, not Chih Ch'ien, but Kōtatsu Fujita explores the various proposed theories and claims Chih Ch'ien is the correct translator and the Pai-yen of Wei translated the *Wu-liang ch'ing-ching p'ing-teng chüeh ching* between 248 and 260. There was also an alleged Later Han translation of the *Wu-liang-shou ching*, attributed to An Shih-kao, translated between 148 and 170 C.E., according to the *K'ai-yüan* catalogue, chapter 14. Another edition, also entitled *Wu-liang-shou ching*, was translated by Dharmaraksa between 266 and 313, according to the *Chu san-tsang chi-chi*. Now no longer extant, the Dharmaraksa translation was probably similar to Lokakṣema's translation, *Wu-liang ch'ing-ching p'ing-teng; chüeh ching*, mentioned above. Cf. *Bussho kaisetsu daijiten*, vol. 10, p. 427a.

21. The other two texts are *Kuan wu-liang-shou ching* (T.v. 12, n. 365, pp. 240-346) (*Amitāyur-dhyāna sūtra*), translated by Kālayaśas between 424 and 453, and the *A-mi-t'o ching* (*Smaller Sukhāvatīvyūha*) (T.v. 12, n. 366, pp. 384–51), translated by Kumārajīva in 402 C.E. (variation 409) and by Hsüan-tsang (T.n. 367, pp. 348-51) in 650 C.E.

22. For example, *Pan-chou san-mei ching* (T.v. 13, n. 418), translated by Lokakṣema during the Later Han. Birth in Pure Land is promised to those who invoke Amitābha's name.

23. According to the *Kao seng chüan*, Chih T'un (315-70) of Eastern Chin was an active participant in arcane discussions (*hsüan-i ch'ing-t'an*) who influenced Buddhists with devotional tendencies; he was considered to be highly knowledgeable with regard to Taoism, especially the text *Chuang tzu*.

24. Occurrences of Kuan-yin's superpowers dating from Western Chin are recorded in the *Fa-yüan chu-lin* (T.v. 53, n. 2122), compiled by Tao Shih of T'ang. One account relates how an Indian monk, Chu Ch'ang Shu, was saved from a fire in Loyang after he read the *Kuan-yin ching* during the Yüan-k'ang (291–299 C.E.) and concentrated upon invoking Kuan-yin's name. However, the first known edition of the *P'u-men* chapter (i.e., *Kuan-yin ching*) as a separate text is that of Kumārajīva's translation in 406 C.E., at the end of Eastern Chin. Consequently, the account of Chu Ch'ang Shu is questionable. It is only in Kumārajīva's translation of this chapter that invocation (*i-hsin ch'eng-ming*) is mentioned (T.v. 9, n. 262, p. 56c7) Cf. *i-hsin ch'eng*, p. 56c 25. There is a similar passage in Dharmaraksa's translation corresponding to the line immediately following *i-hsin ch'eng-ming* when a crisis arises (T.v. 9, n. 263, p. 128c) (*ch'ih ming chih tsai hsin-huai*). Cf. *i-hsin tzu kuei*, p. 129a 1–2, 17–18; *i-hsin ch'eng-hu*, p. 129a 14. The *Fa-yüan chu-lin*, chap. 17, also mentions the incident of the first iconographic representation of Kuan-yin. In 408, when K'uo-hsüan Chih was imprisoned, he dreamt of Kuan-yin and paid reverence to the image in the dream. When he awoke he was suddenly released from prison. Based upon that dream K'uo-hsüan Chih made an image of Kuan-yin.

25. The epithet for Kuan-yin, "savior from suffering" (*chiu k'u kuan-shih-yin*) first appears on cave sculptures during T'ang. Cf. Tsukamoto Zenryū, *Shina bukkyōshi kenkyū*, p. 379, 593. Cult worship to Kuan-yin as the merciful savior was associated with cult worship to T'i-tsang (Bodhisattva Kṣitigarbha) and a peaceful death during the T'ang dynasty. *Chiu k'u* also had implicit Taoist overtones with regard to funeral rites.

26. Matsumoto Bunzaburō, *Bukkyōshi zatsukō* (Osaka: 1944), p. 271.

27. Matsumoto, *Bukkyōshi zatsukō*, p. 342.

28. For example, the *Pei-hua ching* (*Karuṇā-puṇḍarīka*), chüan 3 and 4 (T.v. 3, n. 157), translated by Dharmaksema of Pei Liang between 414 and 416, tells of one of the previous births of Kuan-yin as the eldest son of a Cakravartin ruler. The *Kuan-shih-yin p'u-sa wang-sheng ching-t'u pen yüan ching* also describes a former life; see n. 19 above.

29. *Kannon zenshū*, vol. 8: *Kannonkan no shujusō*, p. 62. Fabricated sūtras such as the *Ching-t'u san-mei ching* and the *Hu shên-ming ching* were also popularized, in part owing to the efforts of Tao-ch'o (562–645) and his emphasis on protection by the Bodhisattvas

and invocation to Amitābha as a regular practice in his work *An-le chi*. See Kyōshun Tōdō, "Shina jōdokyō ni okeru Zuisui yōgosetsu no seiritsu katei ni tsuite" in *Bukkyō shigaku ronshū* [Essays on the History of Buddhism], Tsukamoto Zenryū Festschrift (Kyoto: Jimbun Kagaku Kenkyūsho, 1961), pp. 502–513.

30. *Kannonkan no shujusō*, p. 13.

31. For example, the *Pei-hua ching* by Dharmakṣema.

32. The location of Potalaka has generally been considered to be a mountain or seaport in Ceylon where people gathered for cult worship to Avalokiteśvara as the protector from disasters at sea. Another probable place for cult worship was the Malabar range of South India, popular ca. 300 C.E., according to Fa-hsien. Cf. *Kannon shinkōshi*, pp. 25–28. The first textual reference to the name Potalaka occurs in the *Pu k'ung lo-so-chou ching* (T.v. 20, n. 1093), translated in 589 by Jñānagupta of Sui, according to Satō, *Shina bukkyō shisō ron*, p. 344. At the end of T'ang (916 C.E.) the Japanese monk Egaku constructed a temple to Kuan-yin at Ch'ao-yin Tung in the Chusan archipelago during his stay in China. This holy place came to be known as Potalaka.

33. *Kannon zenshū*, vol. 9, *Kyūsei kannon*, p. 91.

34. The five inauspicious features (*wu cho*) are (1) the occurrence of widespread famine, disease, and war during the period when the lifespan of the human race is less than 20,000 years; (2) unjust and false views becoming powerful; (3) the rampant proliferation of hate, greed, and delusion; (4) the decline in moral character of the human race; (5) the decreasing life expectancy of the human race until the lifespan only approximates ten years in duration. These characteristics of the decadent age begin as rather uncommon events and gradually become increasingly severe and prevalent.

35. Wolfram Eberhardt, *Guilt and Sin in Traditional China* (Berkeley: University of California Press, 1967), p. 19.

36. Protection by the Bodhisattvas may be related to the propitiation or *to suan* described in the Taoist text *Pao P'o tzu*, compiled by Ko Hung during the Chin dynastic period but used during Sui and T'ang. Propitiation was a means of being freed from demons and misfortune, as well as assurance of long life. This practice of *to suan* was so popular among the general population that Pure Land did not denigrate the practice. Cf. Kyoshun Tōdō, "Shina jōdokyō," pp. 506–12.

37. For example, T'an-luan of Northern Wei explained that even the criminal, at the hour of death, could be saved by reciting the ten mindfulness to Buddha Amitābha, based upon a scriptural passage from the *Kuan wu-liang shou fo ching* (T.v. 12, n. 366, p. 346a 12–26)

38. *Bukkyō Daijiten*, v. 1, p. 806c, 2.v. *Kwanseon bosatsu*.

39. Tsukamoto, *Shina bukkyōshi kenkyū*, p. 599.

40. Tsukamoto, *Shina bukkyōshi kenkyū*, p. 579.

41. For example, the name *Chiu k'u kuan-shih-yin* does not appear on cave art until T'ang. See n. 25.

42. When Kuan-yin emerged as a female celestial bodhisattva in China, the Tantric Buddhist pantheon, which included White Tārā, female consort to Avalokiteśvara, had been well-established in India and had been introduced into Tibet. Tārā was introduced into China during the eighth and ninth centuries. Hypothetically, the White Tārā was assimilated with Avalokiteśvara by Chinese Buddhists who superimposed Tārā's qualities onto Kuan-yin, perhaps believing that the White Tārā was a lower stage manifestation of Avalokiteśvara. This fusion of Tārā with Kuan-yin persisted, and the female forms of Kuan-yin continue to be the most popular and predominant representations throughout China and Japan. By 828 C.E. there was a statue of Kuan-yin in every monastery throughout China, over forty-four thousand statues in all. Several scholars have attributed the feminization of Kuan-yin to the fusion between Avalokiteśvara and the Taoist Queen Mother of the West (*Hsi wang-mu*) (*Hsi t'ien niang-niang*). The Taoist goddess was worshiped together with Kuan-yin in Taoist cult practice. Cf. *Kannon shinkōshi*, p. 128. See John J. Chamberlayne, "The Development of Kuan Yin, the Goddess of Mercy," *Numen* 9 (*January 1962*): 45–52; Henri Doré, *Recherches sur les superstitions en Chine*, vol. 6, pp. 94–196 (for a twelfth-century birth tale of Kuan-yin as

Miao-shan); and E.T.C. Werner, *A Dictionary of Chinese Mythology* (New York: Julian Press, 1961), q.v. *Hsi wang-mu*, pp. 163–65.

43. The thirty-three forms which are listed in Kumārajīva's translation became standard in China: (1) Buddha, (2) Bodhisattva, (3) Pratyeka-buddha, (4) Disciple, (5) Brahmā, (6) Indra, (7) Iśvara, (8) Śiva, (9) emperor, (10) Vaiśravana, (11) king, (12) merchant, (13) householder, (14) officer, (15) Brahman, (16) monk, (17) nun, (18) layman, (19) laywoman, (20) woman, (21) housewife, (22) officer's wife, (23) Brahman woman, (24) young boy, (25) young girl, (26) Nāga, (27) spirit, (28) Gandharva, (29) antigod, (30) birdlike being, (31) semihuman being, (32) great serpent, (33) Vajrapani.

44. *Smaller Sukavatīvyūha*: Kumārajīva (tr), T.v. 12, n. 366, p. 347 b 10–17; cf. Hsüan-tsang (tr), n. 367, p. 350a 7–14.

45. Kōtatsu, *Genshi jōdo*, p. 544.

46. T.v. 13, n. 418, p. 905a 6–27; cf. n. 417, p. 899a 9–20.

# 13

## KYOKO MOTOMOCHI NAKAMURA

# The Significance of Amaterasu in Japanese Religious History

The modern Japanese feminist Raichō Hiratsuka once wrote an essay entitled "In the Primordial Age Woman Was Once the Sun!"[1] This statement was so appealing that it became a slogan of the feminist movements in Japan. Lamenting the decline of vigor and vitality in women, she seems to have made an unconscious reference to Amaterasu, the mythological archetype of full personality.

Amaterasu, the supreme deity in Japanese mythology and the ancestor of the imperial family, is female, although she is androgynous enough to give rise to a theory of her masculinity.[2] While she is traditionally identified with the sun and considered the sun goddess, her myths reveal at the same time her other aspect as the priestess who serves the solar deity, or as a shamanistic woman possessed by the solar deity. Nobody will, however, deny the significant role Amaterasu has played as a symbol in the spiritual history of the Japanese, in which is found the long tradition of shamanistic women who have sometimes proved to be the innovative leaders of popular religious movements.[3] Accordingly, we can affirm that she offers an exemplary model in the spiritual history of the Japanese. This essay will discuss Amaterasu mythologically, historically, and symbolically.

### Genealogy of Amaterasu

When we refer to Japanese mythology, we acknowledge our dependence on the *Kojiki* ("Ancient Records")[4] and the *Nihonshoki* ("Chronicles of Japan")[5] as our main sources, particularly their earlier parts.

They were compiled in the late seventh and early eighth century with a clear intention to justify the new sociopolitical regime of the Yamato court, which had unified various tribes and established a centralized state for the first time in Japan. In the process of compilation, myths and legends were collected from all tribes and correlated into a mythological history; the continuity of the lineage from the primal couple, Izanagi and Izanami, and Amaterasu down to the reigning emperor was heavily emphasized.

The *Kojiki* version of the birth of Amaterasu is as follows: The primal divine couple, Izanagi and Izanami, created the great eight-island country. Then they gave birth to many deities, but in the birth of the fire deity, Izanami burned herself to death. Izanagi, therefore, descended to the land of the dead to ask Izanami to come back to the upper world with him so that they might continue the work of creation together. Izanami gave a favorable response to Izanagi's entreaty, but his breach of promise made her angry, and they broke their troth, remaining separated in the land of death and land of life. On returning home Izanagi purified himself in a river of pollution inflicted on the land of death. When he washed his left eye, Amaterasu-oho-mikami was born; and next, when he washed his right eye, Tsukiyomi-no-mikoto came into being; and next, when he washed his nose, Susanoo-no-mikoto came into existence. Izanagi rejoiced over the birth of these three noble children and assigned them, respectively, to rule the realms of the heavens, the night, and the ocean.[6]

The *Nihonshoki* gives several variants of this myth; its main text differs from the *Kojiki* in that Amaterasu was produced by both Izanagi and Izanami to be the lord of the universe after they had produced the eight-island country, that is, Japan. Another difference is the name given to the sun goddess; instead of Amaterasu-oho-mikami (heaven-illuminating-great-deity) she is called Oho-hirume-no-muchi (great-sun-goddess), although she is called Amaterasu in one version.[7] This apparent lack of consensus on the name of the sun goddess reveals that Amaterasu's myths were edited relatively late; Amaterasu was made unique and supreme probably when the mythology was in the process of compilation. It is said that Amaterasu is a common epithet of the solar deity and that it was made a proper noun when the imperial family monopolized the sun cult. In Japanese mythology the solar deity alone is made unique while other cosmological deities are all plural, being grounded in various local and tribal traditions.[8]

These versions, in spite of differences already mentioned, agree that Amaterasu was born from water. The deities who were born prior to her birth are related to water, and she also produced her offspring out of water. It is evident that Amaterasu is ritually celebrated in close relation to water. The Grand Shrine of Ise, as it stands today, is at the Isuzu River, while the former site of the shrine is the princess's palace at the Kushida River. Emperor Tenmu, who reigned 672–86, prayed to Amaterasu on the bank of the Tohogaha River when he was fighting for the throne.[9] In this connection Amaterasu is compared with Sarasvatī, Anāhitā, or the Scythian goddess as to her genealogy and function.[10]

It is widely known that water is the source of life and growth, and that water, moon, and women form the popular symbolical orbit of fertility.[11] We recall that the two brothers of Amaterasu are Tsukiyomi (moon-counting) and Susanoo (impetuous-man): the former is to reign over the world of darkness or night, while the latter the ocean or netherland. Accordingly, it seems that Amaterasu, Tsukiyomi, and Susanoo form a triad that is closely associated with agricultural life. Tsukiyomi, however, is not at all active in the mythology and remains a shadowy, obscure deity, although he is enshrined in the vicinity of the Outer Shrine of Ise. Susanoo, however, is a earthly Dionysian god, in sharp contrast to the serene Apollonian character of Amaterasu. We may point out here a remarkable tendency for dichotomy rather than tripartism. The deities are contrasted or paired, heavenly and earthly, male and female, good and evil, and the like. (In modern times many shrines are officially allotted various triads or divine couples in the official mythology, but they are often nominal and have no roots in the religious community. Parishioners, sometimes priests as well, are unaware of which deities are sanctified in the shrine. This phenomenon reveals the persistence of the tradition to make Amaterasu, the ancestor of the imperial family, unique and supreme and to introduce hierarchy among the eight-myriad deities.)

## Divinity and Femininity of Amaterasu

The image of Amaterasu was partly twisted and embellished by the seventh- and eighth-century historians[12] even to the point of blurring her nature, and modern scholars have been very interested in the divinity and femininity of Amaterasu. The relevant mythological accounts inform us that Susanoo was unhappy with his assignment to the ocean and ascended to the heavens to disturb his sister Amaterasu under a pretext of taking leave of her. Hearing his uproars Amaterasu suspected him of treason and greeted him defiantly, wearing masculine attire with arms. When she accused him of an evil intention to disturb the order, he proved his innocence by giving birth to three peace-loving daughters, while she begot five male children. Susanoo caused a series of offenses in the heavens until one weaving maiden serving Amaterasu struck her genitals against a shuttle and died. Amaterasu got so angry with his misdeeds that she closed herself in a rock cave. Consequently, darkness prevailed in the heavens and all heavenly deities consulted together, and they eventually succeeded in getting her out of the cave and regaining light. They took action to punish and expel Susanoo, who later became the lord of the earth. When Amaterasu sent her grandson Ninigi-no-mikoto to reign over the earth, Susanoo's heir complied with him and the hegemony of the imperial family was then established on earth.[13] One version of the *Nihonshoki* relates that the heavenly weaving maiden is Amaterasu herself, who died of the wound in the genitals and retired to the rock cave, the netherland.[14]

The crucial question, therefore, is whether Amaterasu is the solar deity or a priestess in the service of the solar deity? Scholars differ on this question, but most agree that Amaterasu is the deified priestess or consort of the solar deity. It is their presupposition, conscious or unconscious, that the solar deity should be male. Only recently, some have challenged this presupposition, asserting the original feminity of the solar deity Amaterasu by enumerating counterparts in other cultures and pointing out structural similarities in their myths.[15] Their hypotheses are all the more stimulating and informative because few documents are available on solar deities other than Amaterasu in Japan. It seems that the worship of solar deities is not limited to the imperial family but found in many local communities. They were, however, gradually suppressed and died out, while Amaterasu was transformed from a guardian deity into a unique deity for the imperial family—as the protector of their sovereignty during the sixth and seventh century, and, eventually, as the national ancestor in modern times.

The image in this myth of Amaterasu bravely confronting Susanoo in a military outfit has led to the theory of her masculinity. In the Japanese religious tradition, however, this was not a strange phenomenon: theocratic states were ruled by a shamanistic woman and a male administrator, often sister and brother. It seems that women monopolized the service of God in the early Japanese communities, and they used to join the camp to deliver oracles before military actions.

The *Nihonshoki* provides us with good illustrations of such women. During the long expedition of Emperor Keikō, the legendary twelfth emperor of the Yamato court, women were among the messengers sent to the heads of the clans along the route in order to negotiate peace. When Kamu-natsuso-hime (or Kamu-nashi-hime) received the Emperor Keikō's messengers, she broke off branches of a sacred tree and hung an eight-span sword on the upper branch, an eight-hand mirror on the middle branch, and a Yasaka jewel on the lower branch.[16] She was the chieftain of the local clan and surrendered to the Emperor Keikō with their guardian deity present. Any military action or political arrangement was invalid without divine presence, although we are not unaware of the editorial work to distribute the imperial regalia to a few local chieftains.[17]

When a priestess was not available in a long campaign away from home, a man might substitute for a woman in the role of mediator in a festival. This might be the origin of the priestly role. When Emperor Jimmu, the legendary first emperor, was about to celebrate an open festival in the camp, he asked his minister to preside over it in the person of Princess August.[18] Thus a female title was given to a man in order to invite the divine and administer the ceremony.

The most remarkable case of all is that of Empress Jingū, consort of Emperor Chūai, the legendary fourteenth emperor of the Yamato court. Empress Jingū is a duplicate of Amaterasu in arms. The tradition has it that Empress Jingū was possessed by Amaterasu and delivered an oracle to conquer Korea, and that the rationalistic Emperor Chūai was skeptical and ignored it, thus incurring a severe punishment entailing his immediate death. Keeping secret in the camp both his sudden death and her pregnancy, she led an expeditionary force to Korea in masculine attire. On a triumphant return from Korea she gave birth to a prince, later Emperor Ōjin, on the beach.[19]

Empress Jingū and Emperor Ōjin represent a form of mother-son deities, the various cults of which have been widely found in Japan.[20] None would argue about her femininity in spite of her valiant attributes, which seem to surpass those of Emperor Chūai, for she is a great maternal figure. In the case of Amaterasu, maternity is not depicted, although she has her offspring produced out of water and the descent of her grandson is one of the major themes in the Japanese mythology.

To our mind, the court historians tried to make Amaterasu ideal far above the eight-myriad deities with the possible influence of the image of other goddesses, such as the Empress Jingū. By adopting the deities of subdued tribes as Amaterasu's offspring or subordinates, the hegemony of the Yamato court and line of succession were legitimized, but Amaterasu in return suffers from a lack of reality and dynamic force. Although she is held in high esteem, she is far from dominant, but rather conciliatory. In fact she is complemented by Takamimusubi (high-producing-deity), who is also identified as Takagi (high-tree). He seems to be a commanding and judging deity among heavenly deities, and is given the epithet Ancestor of the Imperial Family.[21] He and Amaterasu are grandparents of Ninigi, who descends to earth to establish the sovereignty of the imperial family.[22]

A hypothesis may be offered to explain this complexity. Takamimusubi is the solar deity himself and Amaterasu the weaving maiden who dies because of Susanoo's wild misdeeds. She is deified as his consort even to the degree of overshadowing Takamimusubi, who is originally a functional deity and united with Amaterasu in his development into a personified god.

Hori reserves his comments on the theory of combining Amaterasu and Takamimusubi because of the obscurity of the relevant myths.[23] On the one hand, we agree with him, but on the other hand, we find the myth's meaning in a historical perspective. We know that Takamimusubi is venerated with Amaterasu, and that they were mutually complementary. Since every clan or locality had its respective guardian deity in early times, "eight-myriad deities" is no exaggeration. Many deities all over the country were correlated through marriage, birth, and adoption in the process of spiritual unification along with political unification of the country. The union of Amaterasu and Takamimu-subi may be regarded as a typical example of this unification.

Many contemporary historians would agree with this point, and question why Amaterasu is female? Or to put it another way, why did the imperial family make the female deity their ancestor? Most histori-ans share an unconscious presupposition that deities should be male and women should be their medium. Some answer that Amaterasu was made female because the courtly chronicles were edited in the reign of the empress. Some say that Amaterasu was made female to be distinct from other solar deities, who were mostly male. This is a mere conjec-ture because we lack enough documentation to prove it. Historians give us the impression that deities were invented arbitrarily. A more plausible answer is that there was in the courtly tradition a myth concerning mother-son deities that arrived from beyond the sea and that this maternal image was projected on that of a priestess, Amaterrasu.[24] Moreover, femininity is more significant if the divine act of procreation lies at the basis of Japanese mythology.

Symbolically, however, androgyny is an archaic and universal formu-la for expressing wholeness. Admittedly, the nature of Amaterasu was developed by the court historians, but the enigma of her origin and sex may be better understood as being androgynous. In traditional cultures all life was nothing but a manifestation of the sacred. Accordingly, the divinities of life and fertility represented sources of holiness and pow-er, and thus androgyny was confirmative.[25] Not only Amaterasu but many others are sexually ambiguous or not personified at all in the Japanese myths. Therefore, Amaterasu as the source of life was andro-gynous, and the question of her sex arose probably in the process of making her the ancestor of the imperial family.

## The Cult of Amaterasu

Tradition has it that Amaterasu was first sanctified at the imperial court sanctuary along with a local deity. The legendary tenth emperor Sujin made his daughter attend to Amaterasu at the sacred enclosure outside the palace for the first time because he was afraid of living so close to the divine in his palace.[26] In the following reign, Emperor Suinin assigned Yamato-hime to be an august attendant to Amaterasu. Looking for a proper place to sanctify Amaterasu, she made a pilgrim-age and covered the frontier until she was instructed to settle down at Ise by Amaterasu, who said, "I wish to reside in this province of Ise where the divine wind blows and the waves from the eternal land dash repeatedly against the shore successively."[27]

This account is often quoted as a legend on the origin of the Shrine of Ise, and Princess Yamato is the mythological archetype of the princess-priestess later institutionalized in the reign of Emperor Temmu.[28] However, historians doubt the founding of the shrine in honor of Amaterasu as early as that because the reigns of the emperors Sujin and Suinin are presumed to cover the late third and early fourth century, when the imperial family was not yet established in Yamato and surrounding areas. It is a general practice to place the founding of the temples and shrines at as early a date as possible in order to enhance their authority. Most contemporary scholars agree that the shrine was founded sometime between the late fifth century and the early sixth century, when the Yamato court became interested in the expansion to the eastern region of Japan. Nevertheless, we do not mean to ignore the fact that Amaterasu was venerated locally in the preceding centuries.

We may solve the problem of the gap between the mythological and historical accounts in the following way: the passages referred to above concerning the founding of the shrine may be examples of later interpolations designed to make the account seem older and more authoritative. There is a popular legend about the hero Yamato-takeru, who was sent to conquer the western and eastern provinces by his father, Emperor Keikō. Before departing, the prince asked for the spiritual protection of his aunt Princess Yamato, who was in the service of Amaterasu at Ise, thereby to gain divine favors.[29] No doubt this legend helped to establish Amaterasu as the guardian deity of the imperial forces in the eastern provinces, the frontier at that time. The route of Yamato-hime's pilgrimage encircled Yamato, the seat of the imperial court, from the west to the north and then to the southeast, and terminated at Ise, which is situated exactly east of Yamato, a port for boats bound for the eastern regions. Amaterasu's tour was meant to purify the land and establish the hegemony of the Yamato court solidly in the frontier. This aspiration is revealed in the hero's name Yamato-takeru (hero of Yamato).

The Grand Shrine of Ise consists of the Outer Shrine in honor of Toyouke-no-ohokami (bountiful-great-goddess), goddess of fertility, and the Inner Shrine in honor of Amaterasu. These two shrines stand independently in their respective precincts. Evidence shows that the Outer Shrine is older than the Inner Shrine, although the courtly chronicles are silent about its origin, and tradition dates the former later than the latter.[30] It is true that Toyouke appears in the *Kojiki* very briefly as the goddess of food, but no mention is made of her relation to Amaterasu or the Shrine of Ise.[31] We assume that Ise was originally the sacred site of the shrine dedicated to a local guardian deity. When the influence of the Yamato court was extended as far as Ise, the local influential family accepted the ancestral deity of the imperial family— Amaterasu—and subjugated theirs, probably another solar deity, to Amaterasu.

The first celebration of Amaterasu at Ise is recorded as follows: "When the princess-priestess Yamato-hime reached Taki, a sister and brother named Kishi-hime and Kishi-hiko dedicated the grove to sanctify Amaterasu together with rice fields and hemp fields .... they brought fresh shellfish for sacrifice to Amaterasu."[32] This account shows that Amaterasu was present in the grove or in a tree and that sacrifices were offered to it, and that this region was ruled by a sister and brother. It is generally known that Amaterasu's symbol is the mirror, one of the sacred regalia; Amaterasu said to her grandson Ninigi at the time of his descent to earth that he should venerate the mirror as herself.[33] To be exact, however, the mirror is a symbol of imperial sovereignty and not of the deity. The traditional way of sanctifying the divine is to set up a tree in a hedge or fix one in a grove, as noted above, to invite the divine onto it and then to offer sacrifices. When the princess sanctified Yamato and other frontier spots, she followed the tradition; the temporary sanctuary is encircled with hedges or rocks and the evergreen tree stands in the center. The sacred tree is the object of veneration since the divine is present in it.[34] This tradition has survived at older shrines where worshipers' veneration is directed to the sacred grove behind the shrine building. At the Shrine of Ise, however, it persisted in the form of the sacred pillar even after the introduction of the mirror as a symbol, although in many newer shrines the mirror replaced the tree or pillar.

The divine is often symbolized in human beings as well as in trees, pillars, rocks, mountains, or other natural objects and phenomena. Women once monopolized the service of the divine, as is still the practice in Okinawa. Accordingly, when Buddhism was transmitted to Japan, three unwed girls of originally immigrant families promptly renounced the householder's life to serve Buddha. They were venerated and paid tribute because they represented Buddha.[35]

As the society became patrilineal and professional and social status became hereditary, male household heads came to carry out all significant roles allotted to the family. The decline of female charisma is reflected in the nominal existence of the princess-priestess and the rise of powerful priestly families at Ise. It seemed that the princess-priestess originally sanctified Amaterasu in the palace at Ise. By the middle of the seventh century the shrine was founded at the present site, but the princess remained in the palace, holding aloof as a mere symbolical presence, while the shrine was managed by the two families, that is, the Outer Shrine by a local influential family and the Inner Shrine by a priest family appointed by the Yamato court. The princess paid a visit to the shrine three times a year, and later once a year, and her role in the daily service to Amaterasu was taken by a little daughter of the priestly family. Helped by her father the priest, the little girl cleaned the pillar and offered sacrifices to it.

Not only at Ise but elsewhere women gave place to men as the place of cult moved from open fields, woods, or waterfront to the shrines that became more and more institutionalized. Thus the religious activities of shamanistic women were gradually limited to the informal, popular spheres of religious life.

## Amaterasu as Archsymbol

Amaterasu as archsymbol, in spite of all vicissitudes, has played a significant role in the Japanese religious tradition, above all in modern times. Because of the imperial family's monopoly of Amaterasu's cult, common worshipers were banned from paying tribute to Amaterasu until medieval times, when the imperial court could no longer maintain the shrine financially. The Shrine of Ise had to open itself to popular piety when wars spread all over the country, even to the capital. In a feudal age when people did not have freedom to express themselves or to travel, pilgrimage to Ise no doubt provided them with opportunities to free themselves at least temporarily for self-realization and contact with the wider world. Ise-kō, voluntary religious associations for the pilgrimage to Ise, were organized in cities and villages and encouraged by some feudal lords. The Shrine of Ise became the focus of mass piety, and collective pilgrimages, triggered by some miracle wrought by the charms of the shrine, repeatedly took place in a spirit of mass hysteria. The increasing knowledge of Amaterasu and Japanese mythology stimulated the rise of modern shamanistic women and revived this age-old tradition in new forms, of which we will discuss three examples.[36]

Miki Nakayama (1798–1887) is the female founder of Tenri-kyō, which claims a membership of about two million. In 1838 she was possessed by Tenri-ō-no-mikoto (heavenly-wisdom-lord) and gradually won renown as the great healer in Yamato. She preached a radical theocentric life with salvation here and now. She revealed a unique cosmogonic myth: the universal gods, solar and lunar deities, created male and female models out of mud and named them Izanagi and Izanami, who cooperated in giving birth to their descendants, all human beings. To her understanding, Izanagi and Izanami are enshrined at the Shrine of Ise, since they were the primal parental deities. This myth is grounded on universal humanism, transcending the national framework of the Japanese mythology. After the Meiji Restoration in 1868, when sovereignty was restored to the imperial family, the government was extremely sensitive about any myth other than the mythology authorized in the court chronicles to legitimize national polity. Consequently, Tenri-kyō was persecuted repeatedly and persistently by the police, and the text of this myth had to be abandoned. According to the Tenri-kyō's cosmogonic myth, parent gods created men and women in order to see their happiness, that is, to see them lead peaceful, bountiful, and healthy lives. This myth was restored after the defeat of Japan in World War II, when the freedom of religion was guaranteed as a basic right of the people in the new constitution. Miki Nakayama impresses us with her universal gospel and strong sense of transcendence. She challenged the authorized mythology daringly, an event unprecedented in history.[37]

_ Another example is Nao Deguchi (1837–1918), who founded Ōmoto-kyō in 1892 on the basis of her revelation. Her message is eschatological, urging the realization of a kind of utopia, Maitreya's ideal world. She was possessed by a deity popular among local people, but her cosmological interpretation of the divine was very unique and opposed the authorized mythology. She was extremely critical of the society and the nation. Nao did not deny the supremacy of Amaterasu, but asserted that Amaterasu had retired and was no longer at Ise, for the whole country was too polluted for her to live in it. Consequently, the world was in a chaotic state until the appointed time when the eschatological deity would appoint legitimate rulers. Nao, like Miki, denied the major theme of the Japanese mythology, namely, the descent of Amaterasu's grandson Ninigi to earth as sovereign.

Onisaburō Deguchi (1871–1948) joined Nao's small group of followers and married Nao's daughter. He was an extraordinary charismatic figure with some theological education in the Shinto tradition. He edited Nao's message, organized her followers, and spread her teaching. The two, however, often disagreed and fought furiously over theological and practical problems. It is said that they were conscious of enacting the roles of Amaterasu and Susanoo; the deity that had descended into Nao was renamed by Onisaburō as Amaterasu's younger sister, while he played the role of Susanoo, the destructive power that occasionally presented a menace to Nao's theology and organization but eventually complied with her, becoming more constructive and cooperative. Thus Nao made use of Japanese mythology by transcending it in her own cosmology. She thought of herself as a man in the form of woman, and of Onisaburō as a woman in the form of man, emphasizing androgyny and her status above him.[38]

Because of the open challenge implied by Nao's revelation and Onisaburō's ideology, Ōmoto-kyō underwent a series of police interventions and persecutions, with its headquarters completely demolished in 1935. Nevertheless, it has survived and maintains the tradition of female succession in the Deguchi family.

Another example is Sayo Kitamura (1900–1967), the founder of the Tenshō-kōtai-jingū-kyō. The name of this organization itself reveals its close relation to Amaterasu and the Shrine of Ise: "Tenshō" is a rendering of Amaterasu and "Kōtai-jingū" the name of the Inner Shrine of Ise, where Amaterasu is enshrined. Sayo declared that she had been adopted by the supreme male deity, Tenshō-kōtai-jin, and his consort Amaterasu as their heir. The divine couple descended into Sayo's body, making it a temple for them, according to the tradition. As Nao Deguchi negated the authority of the Shrine of Ise, so Sayo Kitamura was critical of the shrine as well as of the reigning emperor because the divine couple had moved from Ise to her body and she was their chosen heir. She was luckier than her two great predecessors because she began missionary work after the end of World War II and was not persecuted, although she had had revelatory experiences before the war ended. She advocated radical theocentrism to those who suffered from the sudden collapse of old values and loss of self-identity. In spite of her radical teachings, she was fundamentally traditional in depending on the traditional symbols, such as Tenshō-kōtai-jin and Amaterasu, and affirming the legitimacy of the succession from them to the reigning emperor and to herself through adoption. It is true that she introduced the principle of selection into the rigid hereditary system exemplified by the imperial family, but she complied with the traditional means of adoption, legitimate means to secure the lineage when consanguinity fails.[39]

We have seen how these three women religionists were confronted with Amaterasu in their respective ways. Miki Nakayama interpreted Amaterasu as the primal model of man and woman, namely Izanagi and Izanami; but since the parent-god created them, Amaterasu's supremacy was negated. Nao Deguchi contrasted Amaterasu with Susanoo in parallel with the ideas of a man in the form of woman and a woman in the form of a man. It seems that she thought of a triad that consists of the supreme deity Kunitokotachi-no-mikoto[40] and the male and female deities embodied in Nao and Onisaburō. According to Sayo Kitamura, Amaterasu becomes the consort of the male deity Tenshō-kōtai-jin.

These three women are eminent religious leaders in modern Japan who were brought up in the traditional society when the Japanese mythology was taught as the glorious opening chapter of the national history, although neither Miki nor Nao had any formal education. They had to confront Amaterasu whether they liked it or not, since Amaterasu was the supreme national guardian deity. Amaterasu, however, was a taboo for modern Japanese, who were not allowed to discuss Amaterasu and relevant myths, even academically. If they wanted to talk about the divine outside the established tradition, they had to be prepared for persecution. New religious movements were destined for police intervention and persecution before 1945. Under such adversity they advocated the divine messages to their followers, who venerated them as the embodiment of the divine. We find in them the age-old tradition of woman in service of the living God. They all transcended femininity through their revelatory experiences, living the rest of their lives in devotion to the divine.[41]

## Conclusion

It is evident that Japanese mythology was made to reflect certain political views, and that Amaterasu suffered much from editorial embellishments designed to uplift her as the supreme deity and ancestor of the imperial family, and later of the nation. The extant mythohistorical documents, therefore, reflect society in the sixth and seventh century, when they were compiled, along with archaic mythical elements. Once they were fixed in writing, the mythological traditions offer exemplary models for the later creative impulses of the people.

Indeed, Amaterasu is a goddess who was intentionally made supreme but never dominant; rather, she was made complementary and conciliatory. In the ancient theocratic societies of Japan, a couple, often sister and brother, ruled in cooperation over communities where woman were to serve the divine. As society became more complicated and bureaucracy and professionalization developed under Chinese influence, patrilineal families transmitted professions in a hereditary system, and women gave place to men in many of their functions. In both Shinto and Buddhist establishments clerical professions and official titles have actually been inherited, nearly excluding women or allowing them niggardly, nominal existences. However, the tradition of female mediators and embodiments of the divine has survived informally and sporadically, in spite of feudalistic suppression and sexist prejudice.

It seems that divinity did not necessarily conflict with femininity; rather it was understood as the union of male and female principles or symbols of wholeness. In that sense it does not matter much whether Amaterasu is a god or goddess. In fact, crowds of pilgrims heading to Ise in the feudal age would not have known or cared who was enshrined there, for they were simply fascinated with miraculous stories and experienced a kind of catharsis in the act of pilgrimage itself. The pilgrimage to Ise was believed to be incomplete without paying visits to Buddhist temples in the same region.

Amaterasu's supremacy was questioned not only by academicians but also by others, including women religionists. However, Amaterasu as the one God seems to have lurked in their subconsciousness. Most women religionists transformed themselves from housewives to powerful androgynous personalities after their revelatory experiences, and they are often identified with the deity who had descended into them. In the traditional male-dominated society they are venerated as almost divine owing to their great psychic powers. We assume that the knowledge of Amaterasu served as a stimulant to them, but that they had to transcend Amaterasu as the imperial ancestor when they began advocating the faith in the universal God and the radical theocentric life. In contrast with the living God in themselves Amaterasu is a retired god that has left Ise.

## NOTES

1. Raichō Hiratsuka, "Genshi Josei ha Taiyō de atta," *Seitō* 1, no. 1 (September 1911):37–52.

2. Saukichi Tsuda, *Nihon Koten no Kenkyū* Vol. 1, *Tsuda Saukichi Zenshū* (Tokyo: Iwanami shoten, 1963), 1:370–84.

3. Ichirō Hori, *Folk Religion in Japan: Continuity and Change* (Chicago: The University of Chicago Press, 1968), chap. 5.

4. Donald L. Philippi, *Kojiki* (Tokyo: The University of Tokyo Press, 1968, pb., 1977).

5. W.G. Aston, *Nihongi: Chronicles of Japan from the Earliest Times to A.D. 697* (London: George Allen and Unwin, 1956).

6. For the myth see Philippi, *Kojiki*, 1:55–71.

7. For this version see Aston, *Nihongi*, 1:18.

8. Seishi Okada, *Kodai Ōken no Saishi to Shinwa* (Tokyo: Hanawa shobō, 1970), p. 398.

9. Aston, 1:307.

10. Atsuhiko Yoshida, Amaterasu no Genzō (Tokyo: Seidosha, 1980), pp. 44–77.

11. Mircea Eliade, *Patterns in Comparative Religion*, trans. Rosemary Sheed (New York: Sheed & Ward, 1958), pp. 188–215.

12. The *Kojiki* was completed in 712 by Yasumaro Ōno (d. 723); the *Nihonshoki* was completed in 720 by Prince Toneri (d. 735).

13. For the complete myth see Philippi, 1:79ff.

14. For this version see Aston, 1:122.

15. Contemporary comparative mythologists such as Taryō Ōbayashi and Atsuhiko Yoshida. For the latter see 10.

16. Aston, 1:192–93. The latter half is an account of inviting the divine, which coincides with the passage on the preparation to invite Amaterasu out from the rock-cave.

17. Hayatsu-hime, Asotsu-hime, and the like, female heads of local communities in Kyūshū. See Aston, 1:194 ff.

18. Ibid., 1:122.

19. Ibid., This legend lacks any historical evidence.

20. Ei'ichiro Ishida, "Mother-son Deities," *History of Religions* 4, no. 1 (Summer 1964):30–52.

21. For Takamimusubi see Aston, 1:64, 86, 90, 110, etc.

22.

```
        Amaterasu (female)              Takamimusubi (male)
              |                               |
    Amenooshihomimi (male)  ═══  Takuhatachiji (female)
                              |     (or Yorozuhata-toyoakitsu)

                        Ninigi (male)
```

23. Hori, p. 192.

24. Okada, p. 389.

25. Mircea Eliade, *Myths, Dreams and Mysteries*, trans. Philip Mairet (New York: Harper & Brothers, 1960), pp. 174–75.

26. For the full account see Aston, 1:151–52.

27. My translation. For a corresponding passage see Aston, 1:176.

28. For the institution of the princess priestess, see Robert S. Ellwood, "The Saigū; Princess and Priestess," *History of Religions* 7, no. 1 (August 1967):35–60.

29. For Yamato-takeru see Aston, 1:200–213.

30. The earliest source on the Outer Shrine, probably edited in the late eighth century, says that Emperor Yūryaku was instructed by Amaterasu in a dream and sanctified Toyouke at Ise to attend to Amaterasu. As his reign falls in the late fifth century and the traditional date of founding the Shrine of Ise is a century or two earlier, the Inner Shrine precedes the Outer Shrine in all official records.

31. Philippi, p. 12. It is said that Toyouke accompanied Amaterasu's grandson Ninigi from the heavens to the earth, but this account is suspected to be a later interpolation.

32. *Yamatohime-no-mikoto Seiki*, Series I, vol. 1, in *Zoku-gunshorui jū* (Tokyo: Zoku-gunshorui jū kankōkai, 1923), pp. 51–52.

33. Aston, 1:83.

34. Y.T. Hosoi, "The Sacred Tree in Japanese Prehistory," *History of Religions* 16, no. 2:95–119.

35. Aston, 2:101.

36. For the general history see Sheigeyoshi Murakami, *Japanese Religion in the Modern Century*, trans. H. Byron Earhart (Tokyo: The University of Tokyo Press, 1980).

37. For a good introduction and the founder's life, see H. Byron Earhart, *Religion in the Japanese Experience: Sources and Interpretations* (Encino, Calif.: Dickenson Publishing Company, 1974), pp. 238–44.

38. See Nao Deguchi, *Ōmotoshinyu*, vols. *Heaven* and *Fire*, Toyo-bunko nos. 347, 348 (Tokyo: Heibonsha, 1979) for her messages.

39. Kyoko Motomochi Nakamura, "No Women's Liberation: The Heritage of a Woman Prophet in Modern Japan," in *Unspoken Worlds: Women's Religious Lives in Non-Western Cultures,* ed. Nancy A. Falk and Rita M. Gross (San Francisco: Harper & Row, 1980), pp. 174–90.

40. Aston, 1:4.

41. Kyoko Motomochi Nakamura, "Revelatory Experiences in the Women's Life Cycle," *Japanese Journal of Religious Studies* 8, no. 3 (July-August 1981).

# 14

## JOSEPH M. MURPHY

# Oshun the Dancer

The African goddess Oshun (pronounced "aw-shoon") was born in the cool springs at the source of the river in Nigeria that bears her name. Like the river, Oshun brings her people life, plenty, and cool refreshment from the tropic sun. She enchants all who approach her. This essay introduces this most delightful of deities by examining her devotees, her character, and her incarnations.

### Oshun's Devotees

Oshun's first worshipers were the ancestors of the Yoruba people of present-day Nigeria. The Yoruba were and continue to be farmers, bringing large areas of their West African homeland under cultivation. The abundance of their crops has supported a complex urban civilization that is now at least one thousand years old. At their height Yoruba cities had elaborate and effective governments of kings and councils of elders. They boasted scores of temples, each with an established priesthood. And they produced some of the most beautiful brass and textile arts in the world.

But in the late eighteenth and early nineteenth century the political consensus that united the Yoruba city-states began to erode and the Yoruba were plunged into a series of disastrous wars with their neighbors and among themselves. As a result of these conflicts many hundreds of thousands of Yoruba men and women were enslaved and taken across the Atlantic to labor in the expanding mills and plantations of the New World. It is remarkable that despite some of the most bitter conditions imaginable they were able in some areas to maintain their devotion to the gods of their homeland. Particularly in the cities of Brazil and Cuba one can find many houses devoted to the gods of Yorubaland. With the exodus of Cubans to the United States since 1959 the worship of the Yoruba gods is firmly established and growing in America, especially in New York and Miami. Perhaps it is ironic that with the inroads of Christianity and Islam in Nigeria, there are now more devotees of Yoruba deities in the New World than in the Old.

Oshun is one of the most popular of the Yoruba deities on both sides of the Atlantic. After outlining the structural features of Yoruba religion we will concentrate on Óshun's myths and rites as they are celebrated in Cuba. It is the Cuban traditions of Oshun that are current in the United States and it is in Cuba that Oshun came to be identified with a different kind of goddess, the Catholic Virgin Mary. This "symbiosis"* of religious figures was brought about by the complex histories of religion and slavery in the Catholic colonies of the New World.

Under civil law, all slaves brought to the Spanish, Portuguese, and French colonies were to be baptized and instructed in the Catholic faith. Though some churchmen faithfully attempted to carry out this commission, the brutal realities of a society based on slavery vitiated their efforts. The slaves were indeed baptized and were obligated to practice the rituals of the church, but in their hearts they much preferred the responsive and humane gods of their homeland to the distant one of their oppressors. But recognizing the natural affinities between the gods of their homeland and the Catholic saints, they carried out African rites of devotion before the images and on the feast days of the Catholic saints. In Cuba their devotions came to be called *santería*, the way of the saints. *Santería* seemed to the authorities, when they recognized it at all, to be somewhat eccentric or ethnic celebrations of Catholic piety. But to the Africans and their descendants, it was the old religion in a new guise.

From the original purpose of disguising the African rites from Christian eyes, second and third generation *santeros* began to see the Catholic saints as genuine manifestations of the gods they worshiped. Oshun's devotees, for example, say that the Catholic Virgin, Our Lady of Charity, is really Oshun in one of her many forms. In this way the external forms of Catholic piety are incorporated into a system of worship that is essentially African. We must return to the Yoruba people for an outline of the religion that was so successfully transplanted in the New World.

Traditional Yoruba sources cite anywhere from 201 to 1,700 deities in the Yoruba pantheon, though most writers concede that these numbers are used symbolically to indicate plenitude.[1] The upper reaches of the pantheon are inhabited by Olodumare, God Almighty, the abstract and lofty personification of universal destiny. Nearer to human concerns are the *orisha* (pronounced "aw-ree-shah"), divine spirits manifest in human ceremonial life whose influence underlies the changes of human fortune. The favor of the *orisha* insures success

---

*I am indebted to Professor Leslie Demangles of Trinity College in Hartford for this useful term to describe the interpenetration of two religious systems without their merger.

in life: wealth, spiritual harmony, and many children. Their displeasure means nothing but trouble until amends can be made. The *orisha* are very close to their devotees and their worship demands the development of an intimate and enriching relationship between gods and human beings.

Yoruba theology admits a very wide range of interpretation for the nature of the *orisha*. They can be seen simply as spiritual personalities, "gods" in the plainest sense, who possess certain character traits and who are identified with certain natural phenomena. Thus we can recognize Shango, the forceful and fiery one among the *orisha*, whose voice is thunder and weapon the lightning bolt. Or Eshu, the mischievous trickster who delights in thwarting human presumption and who lives at the crossroads and thresholds of the community. Or our own Oshun, goddess of sensuous sweetness, who inhabits the river.

But initiates of the *orisha* reveal that the gods' natures are subtler than these anthropomorphic images. To them the *orisha* are names given to kinds of spiritual power in the world, power that inhabits plants, animals, and persons. From this perspective the *orisha* are archetypes, patterns of behavior or vibration that the adept can recognize flowing throughout creation and can channel in ceremony. This power is called *ashe* (pronounced "ah-shay") and indicates the effective aspect of the *orisha*'s presence. The historian of African art Robert Farris Thompson calls *ashe*, "the power-to-bring-things-to-pass."[2] In the ceremonies offered to the *orisha* the *ashe* latent in things is liberated and channeled. The *orisha* can be made present to strengthen their human children.

The priests of the *orisha* have developed a wide knowledge of the sacred taxonomies that align the vegetable, animal, and human worlds. Each *orisha* presides over and infuses his or her own cross section of these worlds. Through the appropriate ceremony, an *orisha*'s effective power (*ashe*) can be brought to bear on human problems. The anthropologist William Bascom gives us a picture of the vast system of classification that defines an *orisha*:

> For each of the hundreds of divinities there are appropriate songs, dances, rhythms, musical instruments, taboos, praise names, insignia, shrine carvings and other paraphernalia, leaves, sacrificial foods, and symbols through which they are fed.[3]

Like all living things the *orisha* must eat in order to live. A Yoruba proverb says, "Where there is no man there is no divinity."[4]

Human beings depend upon the *orisha* for grace and power (*ashe*) in meeting the problems of life. The *orisha*, in turn, depend on human beings for nourishment so that they will continue to be effective. Each *orisha* has his or her favorite sacrificial foods, which are consecrated to the *orisha* and consumed by the devotees at ceremonies. Thus the cults are organized on the sacrificial principle of *do ut des* ("I give that you may give").

This ritual relationship between gods and humans has implications for the spiritual growth of the devotee. As the devotee grows in this reciprocal exchange the gap that separates human and divine diminishes. The devotee sees the *orisha* less as an external personality to venerate and appease and more as an inchoate divine quality within himself or herself. This growth "in the spirit" is marked by progressive stages of initiation culminating in that of *orisha* priesthood, when the devotee becomes an *olorisha* (one who "has" or "owns" an *orisha*). The Yoruba scholar E.B. Idowu writes:

> A devotee is an *olorisha*—"one who possesses the *orisha*," ... there is something of the divinity in him and it belongs to his position not only that he should offer worship to the *orisha*, but that he should also absorb the *orisha* into his personality.[5]
> (Idowu's use of the masculine prounoun is purely formal for there are many priestesses of the *orisha* in Africa and a preponderance of women *olorisha* in the New World.)

Nowhere is the Yoruba mysticism of the indwelling of the *orisha* more dramatically demonstrated than in ceremonies of spirit possession. When the devotee becomes an *olorisha* the *orisha* that has been recognized and consecrated within him or her is made responsive to certain drum rhythms and songs. When this proper ceremonial context is achieved the *olorisha* goes into a trance. The *orisha* then emerges through the human medium to take possession of his or her faculties and dance and speak with the assembled devotees. Yoruba ceremony thus makes the gods present in the most dramatic way possible: by physically incarnating themselves among human beings, the gods bring humans into the divine world of peace and power.

From this sketch of Yoruba religion we can see that the tradition centers around a relationship with, and an incarnation of, the *orisha*. As spiritual powers that underlie all effective action, the *orisha* are conceived as divine personalities who are manifested in the human world through ceremonies. It is this system that survived slavery and gave to the enslaved a pathway to divine worlds of beauty and strength. We now turn to one of the strongest and most beautiful of all the *orisha*, the goddess Oshun.

## Oshun's Mythic Character

*Praise Poem to Oshun*
*Brass and parrot feathers*
*on a velvet skin.*
*White cowrie shells*
*on black buttocks.*
*Her eyes sparkle in the forest,*

*like the sun on the river.*
*She is the wisdom of the forest*
*she is the wisdom of the river.*
*Where the doctor failed*
*she cures with fresh water.*
*Where medicine is impotent*
*she cures with fresh water.*
*She cures the child*
*and does not charge the father.*
*She feeds the barren woman with honey*
*and her dry body swells up*
*like a juicy palm fruit.*
*Oh, how sweet*
*is the touch of the child's hand.[6]*

The goddess has her origin in the sparkling headwaters of the river and her identification with these cool sources does much to explain her vivacious character. Oshun is fresh and quick and her lively eyes have an infectious cheerfulness. She is the most beautiful of all the *orisha* and in one era or another each of the male gods has tried to make her his own. A story is told in Cuba that Oshun was born of a charming river maiden and Olofi, a primordial incarnation of God himself. She grew up in a river village, where she was beloved of all the inhabitants. Every order of creation—birds and fish, plants and animals—was charmed by her beauty and sweet temperament. The extravagant affection showered on his daughter made Olofi jealous, though he struggled against these feelings. Still, if he wanted to go out on the river in his canoe the current would not take him unless Oshun accompanied him. And if he went fishing the fish would not bite unless Oshun asked them to. Finally the devotion of all creation to his daughter at his expense sent Olofi into a jealous rage and Oshun was forced to flee for her life. She was taken by the fish to a cave beneath the waters and there grew to maturity under the care of Olokun, the goddess of the ocean's depths. From her cave Oshun traveled the waterways of the world, always coming to the aid of sailors who called on her. Eventually, after much searching and grieving, Olofi was reunited with his daughter and gave her full dominion over the earth's waters, especially those of the river from which she was born.

This mythic episode reveals Oshun's qualities as a beautiful nymph and siren of the ocean's depths. When the Yoruba slaves encountered in the Catholic churches the image of a beautiful woman calming the seas they recognized her as Oshun, though the Catholics called her Our Lady of Charity.

In her maturity Oshun's cheerful gaity blossoms into enchanting attraction. Men are overcome with the lushness of her figure and the way her hips sway so that her every movement is like the slow rolling of the river. As a woman of extraordinary sensuousness Oshun embodies the divine spark in the erotic life in human beings. She is truly an *orisha*, for it is in her form that the erotic mystery is recognized and venerated. The devotees of Oshun see her as a beautiful woman who reveals to them the wisdom of pleasure. She loves to receive rich gifts of silks and perfumes and sweet foods flavored with honey. She loves jewelry of coral, amber, and all kinds of red metals (copper, brass, and especially gold). Many myths of Oshun portray her winning the hearts of men by swaying her arms in slow rhythms and jangling her gold bracelets like the voice of the river. Her songs, too, captivate men like the sweet murmur of flowing water.

These powers of attraction, together with her love of pleasure, establish Oshun as a great coquette. She brazenly flirts with men and delights in their seduction. Her myths tell of different times when she was the wife of different gods, but none of them could hold her for any length of time. One myth relates her frustrations as the wife of Orunmila, the wise and grizzled god of divination. Though he was gentle and always thoughtful of his young wife, Orunmila was simply too old to meet Oshun's rather developed appetites. It seemed to him that everyday, at all hours, she was after what he could not give. Oshun's frustration led her to wander through the bush around Orunmila's compound looking for distractions. One day she came upon the compound of Ogun Areré, the fierce god of iron and warfare. Ogun was more accustomed to rape and pillage than to the patient arts of Oshun, but she enchanted him in her characteristic way. She oiled her body with the honey aphrodisiac *oñi* and danced slowly before him. He went mad for her. But every time he lunged she slipped through his fingers. She teased and tired him until he surrendered and when she finally gave herself to him he was so enthralled that he begged her to allow him to be with her everyday. She acquiesced, provided that he would bring her fine gifts and sweet cakes.

Meanwhile the venerable Orunmila consulted the Ifa oracle and confirmed what he had suspected about his flirtatious wife. He bought some parakeets and trained them to spy on Oshun and to report the truth to him. The next time Oshun returned from Ogun's compound her husband was not home but his parakeets were singing a strange song whose words became clearer as she approached: "Oshun is an adultress. She sleeps with Ogun Areré."

Horrified, Oshun gave the birds some of her enchanting *oñi* and for good measure some *aguardiente*, the fiery rum of the tropics. When Orunmila returned that night they sang with enthusiastic if slurred voices: "Oshun is very virtuous. She has never left the house."

Orunmila, suspicious of these protestations of Oshun's virtue, decided to settle the matter once and for all. The next day he told Oshun that he had already fed the birds and that they could eat no more that day. He didn't tell her that he had annointed their beaks with *epo*, the oil of truth telling. When Oshun returned home the next afternoon after her time with Ogun, Orunmila was not yet there. The birds, however, were uninterested in Oshun's offers of food and eluded her until Orunmila returned. Seeing him enter they fell into song: "Oshun is an adultress. She sleeps with Ogun Areré."

The myth, of course, never really ends, but we know that Oshun is brought shamefaced before the *orisha* and exposed as an adulteress. But one should not draw the conclusion that Oshun was in any way truly chastened. No man ever spurned her and her disgrace was shortlived. She remains as the myth reveals her: insatiable, delightful, and thoroughly uninterested in propriety.

Oshun's promiscuity and her sophistication in the arts of love have sometimes earned her the epithet La Puta Santa ("the whore-saint"). The great Cuban folklorist Lydia Cabrera says that the African goddess has become identified with a Cuban folk heroine, the lovely *mulata* ("half-caste").[7] In colonial times white men fantasized about the sexuality of black men and women as particularly exotic and satisfying. For the rich it became a kind of half-permitted fashion for gentlemen to maintain a pretty black woman as a mistress and lavish upon her every extravagance. Oshun often affects the haughty airs of this heroine—a charmer who lived by her wits and could get back something of what society had denied her brothers and sisters.

On more romantic grounds, some devotees resent the perception of Oshun's promiscuity as prostitution. They insist that she grants her favors only for love. She gives herself only at her pleasure, though, it is true, many things please her. As for her infidelities, some devotees tell the story of Oshun's devotion to Shango. The story goes that they were married and lived together for some time, but couldn't reconcile Shango's stormy temper with Oshun's love affairs and so they parted. Later Oshun heard that Shango's fortunes had turned for the worse. He had lost his military command, his wealth, and all his friends. She returned to him, cooked his meals, and washed his clothes. Her loyalty and courage inspired Shango to regain his lost glories. Oshun's devotees say that during this time she was so poor that she had only one white dress, which yellowed with repeated washings. (In honor of Oshun's sacrifice and loyalty to her husband her devotees wear yellow clothes today.) As the myth of the parakeets demonstrates Oshun's ability to use her erotic powers to tame the ferocious Ogun, this myth shows how the bravery of General Shango depends on her heart and strength. Oshun soothes the savage breast and inspires the despondent.

This tale of loyalty notwithstanding, no one can expect Oshun to be strictly monogamous. Her desires are too refined and her love too overflowing to be confined by social conventions. Many of her devotees do not object to her being called a harlot provided that one understands that she is filled with real love for those she pleases. Some even call her Puta Madre ("mother-whore"), juxtaposing two of the most powerful and paradoxical symbols of femininity. Like the hooker with the heart of gold, Oshun gives herself to her lovers as mothers do to their children. She patronizes them, protects them, and gives them self-worth.

These maternal aspects of Oshun are recognized in the titles Yéyé Kari ("mother of sweetness") and Iyalode, which can be translated as either "mother of fishes" or "mother of birds," representing her knowledge of the feminine powers of sorcery that are associated with creatures of the air. Like all the *orisha* Oshun has the power to give her devotees children and many women who were considered barren were able to conceive with her aid. Many consider her the patroness of women's reproductive systems and pray to her for help with ovarian and uterine problems. She is often called upon to help with difficult pregnancies and childbirth.

From her many love affairs Oshun has borne several children. In Africa she is considered to be the mother of the first king of Ode. By Shango she gave birth to the Ibeji, the divine twins of the Yoruba pantheon. Twins are considered to be a special sign of divine power and favor and many twins and their mothers become devotees of Oshun. Other myths liken the river waters to her womb and recognize her as the mother of all the creatures who draw their life from them. In her Catholic manifestation she is shown holding the Christ child, demurely dressed and radiating maternal compassion. But in the last analysis her children are her devotees who, for the pure and unqualified love that she offers them, forgive her her vanities and appetites.

These mythic images of Oshun's character are known to her devotees through stories that are told on all occasions: for amusement, as fables to edify or make a point, or as verses of prophecy to indicate a path of action to overcome a specific problem. Yet the stories are brought to life in ceremonies. In ceremonies of spirit possession, Oshun herself appears to act out her myths and to bestow her charm and advice upon her devotees.

## Oshun's Ceremonial Manifestations

*I bow to Oshun*
*Iyalode so very great, splitting the sands*
*She parts the sands to guard the money there*
*Shegéshé has coral combs in her hair*
*Elegant woman who has jewels of cast copper*
*There is no place where it is not known that*
    *Oshun is as powerful as a king*
*She dances and takes the crown*
*She dances without asking*
*A crownèd woman is rare*

*She goes with a haughty step*
*She is elegant and has money to amuse herself*
*She arrives and trouble is appeased*
*She shakes her bracelets to come to dance*
*She dances in the depths of richness*
*The water sounds like the bracelets of Oshun*
*We call her and she answers with wisdom*
*She can do what the doctor can't*
*The orisha who heals with cold water*
*We can stay in the world without fear.*[8]

What is so distinctive of the religion of the *orisha*, both in Africa and in the New World, is that the deities actually come to attend the ceremonies offered them. They are said to "descend" upon their human mediums in possession trance, to "rob the head" of the medium, and to "ride" him or her "like a horse." Astride their horses heads, the *orisha* dance and feast with their devotees at ceremonies that in Cuba are called *guemileré*.

One of the earliest descriptions of a *guemileré* is offered by Irene Wright, a traveler to Cuba in the first decade of this century. She describes the trance drama in this way:

> We returned to the dancing in time to see one apt performer throw a fit. "The saint" had entered into her. Immediately other women unbound her hair and removed her shoes. They hustled her into the other room and returned her clad in a garment which seemed to imitate the robes altar images of the virgins and saints wear. She wore gold and brass bracelets which jingled as she danced forth. She proceeded to salute all present by throwing her arms around the shoulders of men and women alike, one after the other, kissing them on the cheek, if they were women, and rubbing each of her shoulders to each of theirs, in turn, if they were men. As she went she collected offerings of pennies and dimes. She approached us, and with more or less good grace we, too, submitted to these caressings. It seemed to me the frenzied creature took particular delight in seizing hold of one of our number, a very precise and religious woman from Kentucky, whose face fairly froze with horror as she was smacked soundly on both cheeks. We were told that sometimes in this condition of hysteria those who had "the saint" prophesied and prescribed remedies for the sick.[9]

Wright's tone is condescending, but her description is a remarkably attentive bit of ethnography, considering the times. The possessing "saint" in question is, of course, Oshun. We recognize her by her gold and brass bracelets, unbound hair, and extravagant demonstrations of affection. It might be like Oshun, as well, to deliberately discomfort those who disapprove of her.

The "fit" to which Wright alludes is the opening stage of the trance drama of the *guemileré*, when the deity struggles with the medium for possession of the medium's faculties. Devotees maintain that it is the inexperience of the medium that causes him or her to resist the will of the deity to emerge. This is borne out by the facility with which senior priest and priestesses pass in and out of the trance. The nature of the trance itself is a cause of much controversy among scholarly observers and it has yet to be adequately explained by either sociological or psychological theories. From the point of view of the devotees themselves, the trance allows the emergence of the personality of an *orisha*, which was instilled in the medium at the time of his or her initiation. Pierre Verger, one of the greatest scholars of African religions, writes of this process:

> He [the initiate] carries within himself the latent image of the god, impressed at the time of initiation on a mind free of all impressions, and this image is revealed and manifested when all the favorable conditions are brought together.[10]

The favorable conditions are the essentials of the ceremonies themselves: the particular *orisha*'s favorite drum rhythms, songs, and foods gathered at the *guemileré*. Devotees say that the drums "call" the *orisha* and observers wonder whether the complex codes of the drum rhythms actually induce the psychological states of the trance. What is clear is that only ceremonial conditions "trigger" the trance so that the *orisha* emerges or "descends" to join in the festivities.

After the initial possession takes place the *orisha*-in-manifestation is taken into a separate room in the cult house, where the symbolic regalia of each *orisha* is kept. Here the *orisha* puts on the ceremonial clothes and picks up the sacred emblems which identify him or her to the community. In Wright's account we are not told what Oshun wears or carries, but she very frequently will emerge in a fancy gown of yellow silk and white-checked cotton. She adorns herself with jewelry, especially the famous gold, brass, and copper bracelets, and often carries a fan or a peacock feather.

These *orisha*-specific rhythms, dances, and emblematic accessories indicate that the trances are not random "fits" or "hysteria." Each action performed by the medium in a trance accords with well-understood and recognized acts of the *orisha* themselves. The medium enters a state of consciousness through which prototypical activities are performed in accordance with the mythological episodes of the lives of the gods. The activities of the possessed, from simple gestures to entire pantomimed dramas, are immediately recognizable to the congregation as reenactments of mythic themes.

When Oshun emerges into the dance her devotees know her by the force of her personality, the ritual objects and gestures that she assumes, and most of all by the mythic dramas she dances. Fernando Ortiz, a Cuban pioneer of Afro-American studies, likens the cere-monial appearance of Oshun to a "choreographic poem" of three stages.[11] In the first stage, Oshun dances the riverain rhythms of her birth. She sways from side to side in languid motions, sometimes spilling forward at rapids or spiraling gently in backwaters. Sometimes she will bring her arms up over her head, shaking her bracelets like the bubbling of springs, and then bring them down again along her body like the river crashing down from the highlands. The second stage reveals Oshun at her bath, washing and frolicking in the river water, combing her wavy hair and contemplating her reflection in the water. The final stage brings Oshun into the community of the *guemileré*, where she plays the coquette. Her body struts and sways, she flirts and kisses and laughs evasively.

Writing in 1951, Ortiz commented that the eroticism of Oshun's dances have been adapted by Havana's nightclub owners for commer-cial uses. Certainly seekers after the exotic could not be disappointed by the dances' sexual intensity, but the change of context from ceremony to performance deprives the viewer of the presence of the goddess herself and thus the healing wisdom that the eroticism conveys.

Almost as a footnote in her account, Wright mentions this most essential function of Oshun's incarnation. "Those who had the saint," she writes, "prophesied and prescribed remedies for the sick." The goddess is there to help people. She gives her devotees something of her power as she receives the sacrificial food and cultic attention that they have given her. Spirit possession opens up a direct chan-nel between human beings and the divine powers around them. The actual presence of Oshun, dancing in all her glory, assures her devo-tees that the divine can be approached, consulted, and brought to bear on their specific problems and hopes. Through possession-trance Oshun can hear petitions directly and offer divine counsel for the resolution of the petitioner's needs. As a coquette she responds to flattery and luxurious gifts, but her counsel and attention contain a primordial wisdom that will not lead her supplicants astray.

The particular gestures and dramas of each *orisha*-in-manifestation are known as *caminos*, an evocative word meaning "ways," "paths," or "roads." The *orisha* possess according to their *caminos*, that is, according to the gestures or episodes of their mythic lives. A useful comparison may be drawn between the *camino* of an *orisha* and an apparition or manifestation of the Catholic Virgin Mary. Catholics would agree that the Lady of Guadeloupe and the Lady of Fatima are different mani-festations of the same Virgin. They are the same archetypal Virgin though each is accorded a different cult and a different iconic repre-sentation. If a Catholic were to experience an apparition of the Virgin, the Lady's clothes, coloring, postures, and gestures would indicate which incarnation of the Virgin had appeared. In the worship of the *orisha*, these apparitions are fixed by the conventions of spirit possession. An *orisha*, too, is an archetypal spirit who is manifest according to particular forms, ways, or *caminos*. Oshun, we know, is the goddess of luxury and love, but when she manifests herself through the *camino* of Oshun Aña, she is particularly fond of drums and dancing, recalling her love affair with the great drummer Shango. Through the *camino* of Oshun Telargo she is shamefaced and modest, recalling her exposure before the *orisha* as an adulteress. As Oshun Yéyé Moró, she is the most "coquettish, cheerful, and licentious of all the orisha."[12] Lydia Cabrera counts over fourteen distinct *caminos* of Oshun in Cuba. Pierre Verger finds at least sixteen in Brazil.

For Oshun's devotees in Cuba, Our Lady of Charity, the beautiful patroness of the island, is herself a *camino* of Oshun, that is, a manifestation of Oshun recalling her role as the protector of sailors.

Each of these caminos represents Oshun in a different incarnation, bringing a different gesture or drama of her mythic life into the present time of ceremony.

In the trance dances of the religion of the *orisha*, the mythic world of the gods is made palpably present. The drums actually bring the divine figures to their devotees, and so, too, the devotees are brought into the world of the gods. The historian of religions Mircea Eliade argues that this process of making the mythic world of the gods present belongs to the nature of all religious ceremony.[13] By modeling human activity on that of the gods, the time and space that separate human and divine worlds are overcome, and human beings are regenerated by the contact. For the devotees of the goddess Oshun, ceremonies bring her among them, her lovers, to heal, bless, and delight them.

## NOTES

1. E.B. Idowu, *Olodumare: God in Yoruba Belief* (London: Longmans, 1966), pp. 67–68.

2. Robert Farris Thompson, *African Art in Motion* (Berkeley and Los Angeles: University of California Press, 1974), p. 200.

3. William R. Bascom, *The Yoruba of Southwestern Nigeria* (New York: Holt, Rinehart, and Winston, 1969), p. 97.

4. Idowu, *Olodumare*, p. 63.

5. Ibid., p. 130.

6. Ulli Beier, ed., *Yoruba Poetry: An Anthology of Traditional Poems* (Cambridge: Cambridge University Press, 1970), p. 33.

7. Lydia Cabrera, *El Monte* (Miami: Ediciones Universal, 1975), p. 37.

8. Pierre Verger, *Notes sur le culte des orisa et vodun* (Dakar: L'Institut Francais D'Afrique Noire, 1957), pp. 422–33. My translation and arrangement.

9. Irene Wright, *Cuba* (New York: Macmillan, 1910), pp. 147–48.

10. Verger, *Notes*, p. 72.

11. Fernando Ortiz, *Los Bailes y el Teatro de los Negros en el Folklore de Cuba* (Habana: Ediciones Cardenas, 1951), p. 251.

12. Lydia Cabrera, *Yemaya y Ochun* (Miami: Ediciones Universal, 1980), p. 70. My translation.

13. Mircea Eliade, *The Sacred and the Profane* (New York: Harcourt, Brace and World, 1959).

# 15

## ÅKE HULTKRANTZ

# The Religion of the Goddess in North America

**M**ost readers think of American Indian religions as father-oriented and dominated by a belief in the Great Spirit and in a horde of lesser spirits connected with nature (totemism was first discovered in North America). It seems that there is scarcely any place for a goddess in such a system. However, this view of North American religions is a misconception. The baffling fact is that the belief in a goddess, usually identified with Mother Earth, is found almost everywhere in North America.

I made the acquaintance of this goddess during my fieldwork among the Shoshoni Indians of Wyoming in the 1940s and 1950s. These Shoshoni were once a proud mounted Plains Indian tribe living off the buffalo and antelope of the plains, the elk and mountain sheep of the mountains, and the roots and berries of the valleys. Their social structure was that of a hunting people, and their political organization was formed after the manly Plains Indian pattern. And yet, there was a deep belief not only in a male supreme being, "Our Father," and in a good many atmospheric spirits and spirits of the vision-quest, but also in a powerful Mother Earth, "Our Mother" (*tamambia*), or "Our Mother Earth" (*tamso:gobia*). The Shoshoni think she is identical with the earth itself and that she produces all the things that living beings subsist on. However, Mother Earth is never mentioned in stories of vision-quest or in myths and legends. She is particularly hailed in two religious ceremonies, the sun dance and the peyote cult. In the sun dance she receives tobacco offerings toward the end of the ceremony, when the Shoshoni medicine man step forth to the central pole of the dancing lodge with an eagle wing in one hand and the sacred pipe in the other. He prays to Our Mother, and then turns the pipe and lets some tobacco fall on the ground. This is a smoke sacrifice to the progenitor of all living things.

Obviously, Mother Earth is not, as earlier generations of scholars thought, restricted to cultures with a matrilineal descent in an agricultural economy. She is not just a supernatural female prototype who invents horticulture and cultivates the fields. She is more than that, and her first appearance dates back to the days of the Paleolithic hunters in the Old World.

In order to understand her history in North America we have to look for her antecedents in Siberia. During the Ice Age a "steppe hunting culture" disseminated over the wide ice-free steppes in Europe, northern Asia and northern North America. These were the times when hunters pursued the "megafauna," or big game, such as the mammoth, the giant buffalo and other now extinct Pleistocene animals. Some twenty-five thousand years ago this hunting culture was associated with a religion in which the cult of female deities played a major role. Figurines in ivory, bone, and stone of such deities have been found from France to Lake Baikal, in Mongolia. So far no figurines of this age have been discovered in North America, although it is very likely that at this time Mongoloid hunters had already occupied a tiny part of North America.

The crude figurines of Europe and Siberia emphasized the sexual, procreative parts of the goddess. In a hunting milieu this meant that she was supposed to be a birth goddess, a mother goddess— perhaps not for humanity alone, but also for the animals necessary to human existence. All the evidence shows that this goddess has survived up to our own time. Ethnographic information on the peoples of Siberia informs us that until the Russian Revolution these peoples, who were then hunters, fishermen, and reindeer nomads, believed in birth goddesses that protected women during pregnancy and childbirth. We know of such goddesses all over northern Eurasia, from the Lapps to the Chukchi.[1] It has been pointed out that just as the men had their protective spirits that helped them in the hunt, the women had their set of guardian spirits (there could be several mother goddesses who each took care of a particular function associated with motherhood). However, the picture is more complicated because the Siberian tribes also believed in a mother of the wild animals, a spirit who gave her children to the hunter if he conformed to the hunting ritual, but withdrew the animals so he could not find them if he transgressed some taboo. The same functions usually pertained to the male master of the animals. However, as the producer of most living things, the great goddess might also (either as the goddess or in one of her manifestations) become the mistress of the wild animals.

It is this general concept of a mother goddess that penetrated North America with the arrival of the first Siberian hunters, who became the ancestors of the American Indians. Of course we have no sources on the goddess from those early days. Our first written information on

North American female divinities derives from Mexican codices from the days before the Spanish conquest and from ethnographic reports during the last centuries. By this time the old goddess had developed into multifarious forms, some of them retaining her original symbolism and others giving her entirely new meanings. To the former belongs the concept of the mistress of the animals that we find, for instance, among the Eskimo and the tribes of the Southwest. The idea of the goddess as Mother Earth, the producer of the vegetation in particular, also derives from the same general premises. This is the most common representation of the mother goddess in North America. It is possible that the peyote religion, which spread over North America from the 1880s, has contributed to the belief in Mother Earth among hunting tribes. However, this concept has had a natural anchoring in the areas where the collecting of plant foods by women constituted the main economic pursuit—among the tribes of the Great Basin and the Southwest that since 8000 B.C.E. belonged to the so-called desert culture.

About 2000 B.C.E., when agriculture came to prevail in Mexican Indian subsistence, a change took place in the conception of the mother goddess. Just as she had formerly protected game and vegetation in general, she now turned into a guardian of maize, beans, gourds, cucumbers, and all other cultivated crops. And just as the mistress of the animals was represented as identical with an animal, so the goddess or spirit of the corn was represented as identical with the ear of maize. For instance, archaeologists have disclosed beautiful miniature figurines of women at Tlatilco. They seem to portray both the ear of maize and the maiden of maize, who was provided with the long, mostly yellow hair of the maize. These are among the oldest known testimonies of the existence of the mother goddess in North America. They were the progenitors of later Mexican goddesses of the corn, like the Aztec Chicomecoatl and Xilonen.

Most anthropologists think that there was a gradual shift from the collecting to the cultivation of vegetables in America—an indigenous evolution that was not inspired from the Old World. Similarly, we may presume that the development of the old mother goddess into a goddess of the corn took the same course, independent of outside influences. We cannot be sure, however. There is evidence of occasional expeditions from Asia to America during the long prehistoric period, and even cautious anthropologists discover transpacific influences in American Indian cultural features. Thus, the southern Californian myth of the creation of the universe through the world parents, a father (or brother) god and a mother (or sister) goddess joined in coitus, has been linked indirectly to influences from Polynesian myth cycles.[2] This is a possible interpretation, although the idea of the union between a sky father and an earth mother as the stabilizing powers of the world occurs in several places in Indian North America—particularly in agricultural communities where social organization is arranged in moiety systems.[3]

Perhaps Betty Meggers is right when she calls attention to the context of diffusion. When agriculture had been established in the nuclear areas of America, she says, there evolved new forms of ritual, ceremonial structures, and so on. At this time, influences from outside American would have had a major chance for adoption.[4] We could, of course, also say that where agriculture was introduced a whole set of notions, rites, and myths naturally developed that for functional reasons would resemble agricultural religious complexes in other parts of the world. The change of the hunters' goddess into a goddess of agricultural fertility, her placement in a cyclical agricultural pattern, and her association with myths of a descent into the ground and later reappearance with the sprouting corn plants would naturally fall into place. This development is perfectly plausible.

However, the Danish scholar Gudmund Hatt chose the diffusional alternative when, in a paper on the American corn mother, he tried to account for the origins of the two basic myths surrounding this personage. The first and, according to Hatt, the oldest of these myths he called the "immolation myth." It describes how the corn goddess is killed and her body dragged around on the ground to fertilize the ground and give rise to the new crops.[5] This myth reminds us of the Hainuwele myth of Indonesia, well-known through the writings of Adolf Jensen.[6] According to this myth, the culture hero, or *dema*, is slain and dragged on the ground, and from the blood-stained ground sprout forth all the tubular roots on which the tropical people live. This is obviously a ritual fertility myth, and the same thing can be said about its American Indian counterpart: human representatives of the fertility divinity, usually war prisoners, were killed in great rituals among the Aztecs and the Pawnee (of Nebraska). Some Indian tribes performed this fertility rite in a less bloody way. Thus, in order to secure good crops the Ojibway woman at Lake Superior went out nude on a dark night and proceeded around the cornfield, dragging her best garment after her.[7]

Hatt thinks that the mythic versions in America and Indonesia are historically related, and perhaps they are. However, such a mythic pattern that describes the planting process seems in a way to have been stimulated by agriculture, and consequently may have originated independently in both places.

The second fertility myth Hatt mentions is, he says, younger; it reminds us of the Old World myth of the descent of the fertility goddess to the netherworld. For some reason the corn goddess goes away. As a result people can no longer live on maize. However, her husband seeks her and receives from her both corn and the necessary rituals, and she agrees to return. The mythic versions may vary, but they all contain the flight motif and the restoration of the goddess, that is, the maize.[8] In the New World this myth is known only in North America. It is clearly linked with corn cultivation. Whether it stems from the Old World is difficult to decide. The arguments that were presented for the immolation myth hold also in this case.

Indigenous or not, the corn goddess developed in North America the character of a goddess of the dead, which she often had in the Old World. The reasons for this transformation are obvious. The seed of the plant is buried in the ground, as are people. The goddess who rules the plants is in charge of the germinating powers of the underworld and the subterranean realm of the dead. It is therefore natural that we find a female divinity of the dead among agricultural tribes in north-western Mexico, the Southwest, and the eastern woodland. It is more surprising that we encounter such a goddess of the dead among the hunting-and-collecting tribes in northern California and Oregon. The lunar mythological affiliations of this goddess may indicate that here we are dealing with quite a different type of goddess, the original birth goddess connected with woman's menstrual cycle. The moon dies and regains life and, during its dead period, is presumably the mistress of the dead in underworld.

In post-Columbian times the old mother goddess has sometimes merged with the Virgin Mary or with other female saints. A good example of such syncretism is the Virgin of Guadalupe, in Mexico. She is counted by Christians among the manifestations of the Virgin Mary, but her first revelation occurred at a place that was formerly dedicated to a Mexican goddess.

If, in retrospect, we examine the influence of the goddess in North America, we may single out three important traits.

First, the goddess is characteristically the patron of women, a religious symbol of the qualities of womanhood in a bilateral hunting-and-collecting society. She is often the partner of the male supreme being, and is occasionally depicted as his spouse. Particularly in agrarian cultures the goddess is the professional guardian, inventor, and, except in the Southwest, main agent of agricultural work. Second, the goddess in her capacity as birth goddess may, through her sexual union with the sky father, give impetus to the idea of creation through emanation. She may even stand out as a kind of supreme being, sometimes usurping the role of, or merging with, the male supreme being. This may explain the occurrence of bisexual high gods in North America, like the Zuni Indian Awinowalona. Third, as Mother Earth and fertility divinity the goddess is intimately associated with the germinating underground powers. Within the agricultural system she is linked to the idea of a subterranean realm of the dead, often gloomy in comparison to the rather superterrestrial afterworld of hunting peoples.

## The Mistress of the Sea Animals: An Eskimo Goddess

Among the goddesses who have both given birth to and protected the game and fish, the Eskimo Sea Woman occupies a conspicuous place. Although the Eskimo are not Indians in a strict sense, they share many of their religious concepts with the Indians, such as that of the masters and mistresses of the animals. The importance of this concept among the Eskimo relates, of course, to their life as hunters and fishermen. We shall discuss the Sea Woman as a religious conception, as a center of myth building, and as a focus of ritual action.

Like all hunting and fishing peoples, the Eskimo believe in supernatural owners of the game. There are many of them. Some are nameless spirits associated with certain landmarks, such as the big rock on the Sentry Island mentioned by Birket-Smith.[9] Among the western Eskimo, the Moon Man is the lord of the game, in particular the sea animals, except along the Pacific, where there are two mistresses of the game, one for the sea animals and one for the land animals. (The Eskimo make a very strict separation between what pertains to the land and what pertains to the water.) On Labrador the owner of the land animals is female, the owner of the sea animals male. The Caribou Eskimo on the tundra west of Hudson Bay believe in a master of the reindeer who is sometimes male but most often female. However, for most of the Eskimo—from the Asiatic Eskimo to the South Greenland Eskimo—the Sea Woman rules the animals and fishes of the sea.

The idea of a goddess as mistress of the sea fauna and even the sea itself is widely dispersed among the so-called paleo-Asiatic peoples in eastern Siberia. Since we can trace Eskimo cultural origins from the coasts of the North Pacific, it seems legitimate to presume that the goddess derives from these regions. In a larger perspective she is a representative of the North Eurasian mother goddesses mentioned before.

The Eskimo Sea Woman is known by many names. In the Far West she is called Nulirahak, "the great woman," and west of Hudson Bay Nuliajuk, "the dear wife." Her name on Baffinland is Sedna, "the woman of the depth of the sea." This last name has been adopted by scholars as the scientific name under which she has become known in anthropology, folklore, and religion, and I use the same name here.

According to the Greenlanders, Sedna lives at the bottom of the sea in a big domed house (an exceptionally beautiful house, say the Central Eskimo). It is guarded by seals standing on their rear flippers who bite intruders. In and out of the house are swimming all sorts of water creatures: whales, seals, fish, and sea birds. Inside is seated the frightening goddess, angry and awful to look at. She is, some reports say, one-eyed, just like some divinities connected with death in the Old World. It is not surprising then to learn that she is also in charge of the dead. Their dismal abode is adjoined to her living quarters at the bottom of the sea.

The Sea Woman is the central person in the most famous Eskimo myth. This myth is diffused over the whole Eskimo area and, not surprisingly, has many versions.[10] The basic pattern is the story of a girl who for some reason, usually a refusal to marry the man her father has chosen for her, is thrown by her father into the sea from a boat. When she clings to the gunwhale, her father chops off her fingers, and she sinks to the bottom of the sea. Her fingers turn into the animals and fish of the sea, whose protective mistress she becomes. This myth has become mixed with two others among the Eskimo of Canada. One is about a woman who married a dog from whom the various races of humankind spring. The other is about a woman who married a fulmar. The dog-husband myth is widely disseminated in Siberia and northern North America, whereas the tale of the marriage with a fulmar is restricted to the Eskimo.

The central Eskimo version is a hybrid of the Sedna and fulmar tales, and is perhaps the one which is best-known among general readers. It tells how Sedna, a handsome girl, coldly rejected all suitors until a fulmar wooed her with his enticing song. He promised her much food and a bed of soft bearskins. She could not resist him, and followed him on a long journey to the distant country of the fulmars. However, when she arrived she found that she had been deceived; she was forced to sleep on hard walrus hides, eat miserable fish, and live in a home of fish string. A year later her father visited her and she asked him to take her back. The outraged father killed the fulmar and took Sedna into his boat and departed for home. The other fulmars pursued them and stirred up a heavy storm. The father became scared and threw Sedna overboard as an offering to the birds. She held on to the boat, however, so her father cut off her fingers, which then swam away as whales, seals, and ground seals. When the storm subsided he allowed Sedna to return into the boat. She was angry, however, and had the gods gnaw off his feet and hands so that he looked like a seal. He then cursed both himself and his daughter, and the earth swallowed them.[11]

The crucial thing in this myth is that genetically the marine animals are part of Sedna. Therefore, what happens to the animals happens to her. This is of great interest when we come to the rituals surrounding her.

These rituals are based on the presumption that scarcity of game, which results in hunger and disease, is due to the fact that the Sea Woman refuses to release the animals for the hunters to kill. When this happens the humans are supposed to have transgressed some hunting taboo; for instance, they might have cooked together the flesh from sea animals and land animals. Such a transgression results in pollution of the animals, who feel a great pain and return to their mistress, Sedna. She is furious with rage, for she shares their passion— they are her own fingers! Moreover, her whole body is covered with dirt, in particular her hair, which hangs in a tangled, filthy mess down her face. In order to make her release the animals, the shaman has to dive down in an ecstatic dream to the Sea Woman's place.

Knud Rasmussen, an acute observer of Eskimo customs, has provided us with a dramatic account of what happens at the shamanizing of the Iglulik Eskimo. The lamps of the lodge are extinguished and the shaman sits on the ground, calling his helping spirits. They arrive and his voice turns weaker, for he now is supposed to disappear underground with his spirits. After a while his soul reaches the realm of Sedna, where the terrible lady is seated with her back toward the pond in which she keeps all the sea animals. It is the task of the shaman to free her from her dirt, which, since she has no fingers, she cannot remove. The shaman therefore combs her hair and speaks soft words to calm her down. Soon she becomes friendly and happy and releases the sea animals. The shaman can safely return to his body. As soon as he has arrived back in his lodge, he orders the assembled to confess their taboo transgressions. All of them loudly announce all their "sins."[12]

There is a remarkable parallel between Sedna, who has no fingers to touch her unclean hair, and the situation of the menstruating or childbearing Eskimo woman, who is not allowed to touch her hair because it is here that her uncleanliness is concentrated. We could say that Sedna is the prototype of the woman who is ritually unclean. She is, in other words, like her Paleolithic progenitor, still the goddess of women.

## The Culture Heroine: The Dakota Buffalo Calf Woman

Although the culture hero is a common figure in North American Indian pantheons, the culture heroine is not. Still, there is a supernatural figure among the Dakota (Sioux) Indians that deserves this title, and this is their Buffalo Calf Woman. She is rather complicated. Some of her traits remind us of the mother goddess: she has a certain relationship to the animals and appears as a white animal, as does the master of the animals in many places; and she is a giver of new institutions, as is the ordinary male culture hero in other tribes. The Dakota know no male culture hero.[13] In his absence a female spirit plays such a role.

She is primarily associated with the legend of the sacred pipe, which is told in many versions. According to the version of Black Elk, holy man of the Oglala Dakota, one morning long ago two Indian hunters, looking out from a hill for game, saw a mysterious being approaching them from a distance. As it came closer it turned out to be a beautiful woman dressed in white buckskin with a bundle on her back. One of the young men was seized with passion for her. She called him over, and a great cloud covered them. When it lifted, the man had been transformed into a heap of bones. The mysterious woman now announced to the other man that he should tell his chief to assemble the people in a tepee and wait there for her arrival. He did so, and the people put on their best garments and waited in great excitement. The mysterious woman arrived in a magnificent manner, brought forth her bundle, opened it, and showed to the assembled a sacred pipe. She instructed them to smoke the pipe in relation to all the beings of the universe, for she said, "all send their voices to Wakan Tanka, the Great Spirit. When you pray with this pipe, you pray for and with everything." She also told them about the seven rites in which the pipe should be used, and admonished them always to remember how sacred it is. She pointed out that the bowl of red stone represents the earth that is sacred, and that the carving in this stone depicts the buffalo calf "who represents all the four-leggeds" that live on Mother Earth. Then the mysterious woman went out of the tepee, and as she withdrew she turned first into a red and brown buffalo calf, then into a white buffalo, and finally into a black buffalo. She bowed to the four sacred directions and disappeared over the hill.[14]

The connections of the sacred Buffalo Calf Woman with the buffalo and the earth are interesting. The buffalo is the symbol of animal food among the Plains Indians; it "contains" the earth and dwells inside the earth when it disappears. Such beliefs point to the buffalo's close association with Mother Earth, clearly referred to in the legend. The relatives of the Oglala, the Hunkpapa Dakota, have special ceremonies for those who kill a white buffalo. They believe that the white buffalo is "the chief or sacred one of the herd," and is important because "from the buffalo comes our animal food and this gives life and strength."[15] The white buffalo is the master of the game, just as the white caribou is the master of animals among the Cree. At the same time it is linked to Mother Earth, who plays a conspicuous role in the Hunkpapa white buffalo rites.

From all this we can conclude that the Buffalo Calf Woman is the mistress of the buffalo, related to Mother Earth, and a culture heroine as a consequence of her one-time appearance as a visionary spirit.

## The Female Creator: A Shawnee Goddess

The Shawnee of the eastern woodland have made the mother goddess their supreme being and creator, which is uncommon for a goddess. "Our Grandmother," as she is called, lives in a typical Proterozoic bard house (wigwam) in the sky. She has a sky window through which she looks down on earth to see that her children, the human beings, are obedient to her. She is occupied with weaving baskets, making a fire, and cooking. Some people think that she is so big that she can pick up grown men and hide them in cracks in her lodgepole. It is also said that the moon is her shadow—probably an indication of the old connection between the mother goddess and the moon. She has great mental powers: according to the legend, when some people visited her she answered their thoughts before they were expressed. People born with divinatory gifts, like the Shawnee prophet Tenskwatawa (brother of the famous chief Tecumseh), received them from the goddess when they dwelled with her before their birth. Our Grandmother is the abode of the dead, over whom she also rules. It is rather exceptional in North America that a supreme being is also the ruler of the dead.

Carl Voegelin has observed that Our Grandmother is integrated in those parts of Shawnee religion that are communal rather than individual.[16] Thus, in the annual ceremonies people worship her to preserve humankind and the whole world. Negligence in performing ceremonies is punished by the goddess, usually through diseases. However, she plays no role in the guardian-spirit quest, which is the affair of a single individual. Only when the guardian spirit becomes a matter of collective concern does Our Grandmother enter the scene. Tecumseh received a war dance in about 1800 from his guardian spirit, the buffalo. Those who dance it today claim that they do so to worship Our Grandmother.

In mythology the goddess is described as the creator of the world, of the other divinities, and of human beings. (She is supposed to have created only good people and good animals; how their bad counterparts came about remains a mystery.) One of her creations is the corn goddess, who is thus separate from Our Grandmother. The corn goddess once fled from the earth to her mother but was persuaded to return to feed the Shawnee. This myth is an evident parallel of the Persephone (Kore) and Ishtar themes of Greece and the ancient Near East.

Of particular interest is the story of the world creation. We are told that the great goddess descended from above and created a turtle for the earth to rest on. She was assisted by her grandson, Rounded-side. He slayed dangerous monsters but also released impounded water, thus flooding the world—he was, in other words, a typical exponent of the American Indian culture hero who is also a trickster. The goddess herself has traits of a culture hero: she taught people how to live and how to hold ceremonies, cultivate the corn, hunt, build houses, and make laws.

The origin of the world through an old woman and her culture-hero son or grandson is a motif well-known among the Iroquois and the Huron Indians. This opens new perspectives. Shawnee statements from the 1820s reveal that the supreme being was then a male high god of a kind we meet among other Proterozoic Indians. The goddess and her grandson are mentioned, but they are subordinated to the high god, who alone is the creator. It is obvious that the goddess represents the intrusion of Iroquois myth motifs, possibly associated with the adoption of agriculture.

The strong position of the goddess brought about a revolution in the pantheon: the old god became obsolete, the Iroquois "grandmother" usurped his place as highest divinity and creator, followed by her grandson.[17] This case demonstrates how quickly, under favorable conditions, a god may be supplanted by a goddess.

## The Corn Goddess of the Iroquois and the Hopi

It would be easy to imagine that with the introduction of corn it was Mother Earth that became the corn goddess. However, this was not always the case. In the eastern woodland there was a mother-daughter relation between the great goddess and the corn spirit, just as in ancient Greece Demeter (possibly originally *gē meter*, "earth mother") was the mother of Kore, "the girl." Because of this relationship the corn goddess is mostly represented as a young woman. This applies, as we have seen, to the Shawnee, and it applies to the Iroquois as well.

What Lewis Morgan has called "perhaps the most beautiful conception in the mythology of the Iroquois" is the notion of the three sisters, the spirits of corn, beans, and squash. It is said of them that they are very attractive, each clothed in the plant they guard and decorated with its flowers. They like to be together, an expression of the fact that formerly they were planted on the same hill. The sisters come to dwell among their respective plants in the growing season. The spirit of the corn was once more fruitful than today. The bad heavenly twin (a grandson of the mythological old woman mentioned above) sent a devastating blight over her fields, which thus lost their original richness. "To this day, when the rustling wind waves the corn leaves with a moaning sound, the pious Indian fancies that he hears the Spirit of Corn, in her compassion for the red man, still bemoaning, with unavailing regrets, her blighted fruitfulness."[18]

There are several myths, sometimes mutually contradictory, surrounding the corn goddess. One of them says that the corn plant sprang from the bosom of the great primeval female divinity who obviously functioned as Mother Earth. Another myth tells how a good hunter was joined by the corn goddess, who spent the winter with him. She had received the seeds of corn from the "master of life," and the next spring she distributed them among the people and gave instructions for planting them. When the crops were ripe for the harvest she taught the people how to gather them and how to make bread from them. The story goes on to describe how in the spring she returns down into the earth where her children—the plants to come—cry for her.[19] The cycle of the plant—growth, death, new life—is thus mirrored in the fate of the corn goddess. She is at once the corn itself, its spiritual protector, and the patron of humans who cultivate the maize.

She is also represented in the cult. When the planting season comes she is called upon. Before dawn of the first day of the planting, a young virgin is sent out to the fields. She scatters some grains of corn on the earth, invoking the assistance of the corn goddess.[20] From all appearances the young girl is not only the priestess of the corn spirit, she also represents the corn spirit. The three sisters receive the thanks of the people at the harvest festival and the midwinter feast. On the latter occasion Mother Earth is thanked for her willingness "to yield so plentifully of her fruits," and the three sisters for being "the main supporters of our lives."[21]

The Southwest, the stronghold of corn cultivation, abounds with fertility spirits of all sorts. Many of them are male germinators, for in Pueblo societies men usually cultivate the ground, and the spirits supporting men are often male. However, there are also plenty of goddesses connected with the earth, corn, vegetation in general, the underground, and so on. It seems that even the Athapaskan hunters from the north, the Apache and Navajo, have taken over the Pueblo goddess figure. Among them she is known as Changing Woman, a goddess of the moon for the Apache, a goddess of verdure for the Navajo.

Let us concentrate on the Hopi pueblos in Arizona, with the oldest continuously inhabited site in North America, Old Oraibi, which dates from the twelfth century. Hopi fertility divinities have a certain affinity to those of the Rio Grande pueblos but also show a character of their own. It is not always easy to identify them or to measure their importance, for they are almost hidden in the intricate ceremonialism of Pueblo religion. The famous specialist in this religion Elsie Clews Parsons even thought that they were negligible in this ritualism. This is not true, however, as we can see from recent writings, in particular *Book of the Hopi*, written from information collected by Frank Waters from the Hopi themselves.

Waters admits the Hopi religion "is a belief whose core is not spoken, but expressed by the abstract ritualism and symbolism embodied in the great annual cycle of intricate ceremonies."[22] This quality makes the religion difficult to understand. We may even get the impression, as did Hamilton Tyler, that Hopi religion is devoid of earth and corn goddesses.[23] Much of the confusion arises because different clans have different myths.

According to one myth, the world was created by command of the sun god. There was also Spider Woman, who gave life to the world, creating plants, birds, animals, and finally human beings out of the earth and out of herself. So, although human beings have human parents, the real parents are Mother Earth (Spider Woman), from whose flesh all are born, and Father Sun. It is apparent that Mother Earth is symbolized by Spider Woman, Sand Altar Woman, and other female spirits conceived to be the mothers of all living things. This mother is represented in the cult by the *sipapuni*, the opening in the floor of the underground ceremonial chamber, or *kiva*, for the *sipa-*

*puni* is the womb of Mother Earth, just as it is the hole through which humankind originally emerged from the underworld.

The corn goddess is obviously mostly identical with Mother Earth. She is also a mother of man, for man has built her flesh into his own. In ritual she is represented by a perfect ear of corn whose tip ends in four full kernels. This ear is also called Corn Mother. Such an object is used not only at maize festivals, but also on other occasions, such as childbirth (the fetish then stands for the mother goddess in a wider sense). Corn meal and corn pollen, representing the sacred in general, are used at a great many ceremonies.[24]

## A Universe of Mothers: Huichol Goddesses

The Huichol Indians of Jalisco and Nayarit in Mexico are known for their accomplished artistry in yarn and for their annual pilgrimages into the desert of Wirikuta, where they fetch the sacred peyote. As we know, the eating, drinking, or smoking of peyote induces colorful visions. Such visions may have contributed to the beautiful coloring of the Huichol world of goddesses. These Indians believe in a whole universe of goddesses that encloses their daily life. The goddesses are called "Our Mothers" and are all associated with motherhood, growth, fertility, and water. They are typical representatives of an agricultural pantheon. The Huichol are maize farmers, but they also hunt animals, first of all deer, and gather plants and roots, the peyote cactus in particular.

To a certain extent this pantheon with its female dominance (of male gods only Father Sun, Grandfather Fire, and Brother Deer seem to play significant roles) could be likened to the pantheons that preceded the complicated theological systems of the Maya, Toltec, and Aztec high cultures. Maybe the Huichol religious structure is, at least in part, a leftover from those ancient times, but there is no consensus on this point.

The great goddess of the Huichol, the earth goddess, is known in many forms. She is "Our Great-Grandmother," Nakawe, a towering goddess who occasionally also appears as a male—one of those androgynous divinities that so frequently turn up in high cultures. She brings life and fertility and is therefore associated with sacred wells and with birth, growth, and planting. An interesting trait is that she is depicted surrounded by snakes. We are here reminded of the Aztec goddess Chiuacoatl, "Serpent Woman," who was also a goddess of the earth and of childbearing women. Snakes are symbols of the earthbound—chthonic—essence of the goddess.

The earth goddess's bearing on the fertility and growth of the plants is manifested in her appearance as Our Mother Urinanaka. This is Mother Earth after the sun has warmed her and the rains have soaked her, the earth that is ready for the planting of the maize. As Our

Mother Utuanaka, she stands both for the earth that bears the maize and for the maize itself. The three representations of the earth goddess in close connection with the phases of agriculture remind us of the so-called *indigitamenta* gods of ancient agricultural Roman civilization.

Just as there are several earth mothers—or rather, several aspects of the earth mother—so there are several rain mothers and several corn mothers. The maize mother is one, Our Mother Kukuruku, manifested in the corn cob but also in the wild dove (that says "kukuruka"). However, she is also divided into five young corn goddesses, personifying the yellow, white, red, blue, and speckled corn. This oscillation between one and many in the perception of divinities is typical of American religious conceptions. We may, for instance, think of the Maya rain god, Chac, who could also be divided into four Chacs.

There is information on other Huichol goddesses: for instance, the mother of the Pacific Ocean, the waters that separate the living from the dead. Enough has been said, however, to support the view that this is truly a religion of goddesses.[25]

I have mentioned that the Huichol are ardent peyotists. It was from these regions of Mexico that the peyote religion spread over the centuries to the Indians of the United States. Today this "peyote cult," as it has been called, is firmly rooted among many North American tribes. All over its area of diffusion the sacred cactus is known as a representation of the divine. Often it is referred to as "Peyote Woman," a divinity probably created after the pattern of Mother Earth, with whom she is occasionally identified. Those who take peyote during a peyote ritual may hear her sing, as I did once when I attended a peyote ceremony. Certainly, Indian goddesses also appear to white people.

## NOTES

1. See G. Rank, "Die Hausgottheiten der Frauen und das Geschlechtstabu bei den nordeurasischen Volkern," *Ethnos* 13, nos. 3–4 (1948):153–70.

2. A.L. Kroeber, *Handbook of the Indians of California*, Bureau of American Ethnology Bulletin 78 (Berkeley: University of California Press, 1925), pp. 677f.

3. Åke Hultkrantz, *The Religions of the American Indians* (Berkeley, Los Angeles, and London: University of California Press, 1979), pp. 111ff.

4. B.J. Meggers, *Prehistoric America* (Chicago: Aldine Publishing Company, 1972), pp. 176f.

5. G. Hatt, "The Corn Mother in American and in Indonesia," *Anthropos* 46 (1951):853–914.

6. A.E. Jensen, *Myth and Cult among Primitive Peoples* (Chicago: University of Chicago Press), pp. 88ff., 166ff.

7. W.M. Beauchamp, "Indian Corn Stories and Customs," *Journal of American Folklore* 11 (1898):195–202.

8. Hatt, pp. 856ff.

9. K. Birket-Smith, *The Eskimos*, 2nd ed. (London: Methuen & Company, 1959), pp. 170f.

10. E. Holtved, "The Eskimo Myth about the Sea-Woman," *Folk* 8–9 (1966–67):145–53.

11. F. Boas, *The Central Eskimo* (Lincoln, Neb.: University of Nebraska Press, 1964), pp. 175ff.

12. K. Rasmussen, *Intellectual Culture of the Iglulik Eskimos*, Report of the Fifth Thule Expedition, 1921–24, 7:1 (Copenhagen: Gyldendalske Boghandel, Nordisk Forlag, 1929), pp. 123ff.

13. A. van Deursen, *Der Heilbringer* (Groningen: J.B. Wolters, 1931), pp. 182ff. The spider (Iktomi) is sometimes compared to a culture hero, but less convincingly.

14. J.E. Brown, *The Sacred Pipe* (Norman, Okla.: University of Oklahoma Press, 1953), pp. 3ff.

15. A.C. Fletcher, *The White Buffalo Festival of the Uncpapas*, The Sixteenth and Seventeenth Annual Reports of the Peabody Museum (Cambridge, Mass.:1884), pp. 260–75.

16. C.F. Voegelin, *The Shawnee Female Deity*, Yale University Publications in Anthropology 10 (New Haven: Yale University Press, 1936), p. 3.

17. C.F. and E.W. Voegelin, "The Shawnee Female Deity in Historical Perspective," *American Anthropologist* 46, no. 3 (1944):370–75.

18. L.H. Morgan, *League of the Ho-de-no Sau-nee or Iroquois*, 2nd ed., 2 vols. (New York: Dodd, Mead & Company, 1901) 1:152f.

19. D. Jenness, *The Corn Goddess and Other Tales from Indian Canada* (Ottawa: National Museum of Canada, 1956), pp. 1ff.

20. H.M. Converse, *Myths and Legends of the New York State Iroquois*, New York State Museum Bulletin 125 (Albany, 1908), p. 66.

21. Morgan, 1:211.

22. Frank Waters, *Book of the Hopi* (New York: Ballantine Books, 1976), p. 411.

23. H.A. Tyler, *Pueblo Gods and Myths* (Norman, Okla.: University of Oklahoma Press, 1964), pp. 116, 125, 131.

24. Waters, pp. 4ff., 8ff., 30, 164ff.

25. B.G. Myerhoff, *Peyote Hunt: The Religious Pilgrimage of the Huichol Indians* (Ithaca: Cornell University Press, 1974); K. Berrin, ed. *Art of the Huichol Indians* (New York: Abrams, 1978).

# 16

## RITA M. GROSS

# Hindu Female Deities as a Resource for the Contemporary Rediscovery of the Goddess

For some time now, the lack of feminine symbolism in the theistic and, therefore, anthropomorphic symbol system of Western religions has seemed somewhat bizarre to me. These religions stress the personal dimension of their symbols of the ultimate, and stress that the ultimate should be conceived of and related to as if it were a personal being in relationship with other persons. But this personal god is always symbolized and addressed as a male person in the three major religions of the West, and male forms of symbolization and address are adamantly maintained. This seems somewhat strange, and the strangeness is significantly enhanced when one realizes that, while anthropomorphic symbol systems are quite common in the world religions, only the symbol system of Western monotheism has ever attempted or valued the expulsion of feminine symbolisms. Most of the symbol systems that have utilized anthropomorphic symbols have also utilized bisexual and androgynous symbolism. Furthermore, it is undeniable that the male symbolism of deity has been a major contributor to the exclusion of women from positions of respect and authority in Western society and religion.[1]

These facts must raise some obvious questions, must be the impetus for a significant recasting of the religious vocabulary. In this essay I will suggest some approaches to what I consider the most compelling solution to the problem of a deity imaged solely in masculine terms—the second coming of the goddess. However, it is one thing to know that the goddess must return and another to know where to find her. The problem of resources for goddess imagery is one of the most difficult facing those working on her thea-logy.[2]

Thus far, three major sets of resources have been suggested. Feminist theologians most often turn to experience as the final arbiter and most trustworthy resource. I agree with this position but I see experience not so much as the sole creative source for imagery of the goddess but as the final arbiter of the value of specific goddess imagery, no matter what its source. In fact, I think it is rather dangerous to rely solely on our own experience to create appropriate imagery. We may simply not have the experience to conjure up some of the most fruitful and compelling images of the goddess, though we easily recognize their validity or reject them as unhelpful when we come into contact with them in other contexts.

Many feminist theologians also utilize the hidden tradition of female imagery of deity found in the Western traditions, as well as the numerous and fascinating goddesses of the ancient world, who seem to have survived in some form to the present day. These resources are much richer than is generally suspected. However, they are not without problems, for they represent a tiny inroad in a largely patriarchal tradition, or, in the case of the ancient goddesses, they are very removed from us.

For these reasons, I suggest looking to another resource that has been underutilized thus far in our search for goddess imagery. Living goddess traditions are much more extensive than people usually expect, and Hinduism presents one of the richest sets of images of the goddess. Therefore I will discuss how we might utilize the Hindu female deities as a resource for the contemporary rediscovery of the goddess.

As I make this suggestion, I am not unaware of significant problems. There is the problem of cultural distance between Western and Hindu forms of religion. A wholesale transplant will not work because of that cultural distance, but such a transplant is not what I suggest. I am more concerned with another problem. As is the case with any culturally unfamiliar material, Hindu materials are easily susceptible to misinterpretation. As a scholar of the Hindu tradition, I find that even a favorable misinterpretation is unacceptable. Perhaps I am suggesting that some real scholarly competence with these materials is a prerequisite, but I am also suggesting that if approached critically and carefully, and if intelligent selection and borrowing are utilized, the Hindu goddesses can be the greatest stimulant to our imagination and to our speculation about the meaning of the goddess. Specifically, I want to suggest six basic images of the goddess that I think are fundamental in her thea-logy, all of which can be significantly enriched by meditating on the Hindu goddesses.

I will begin with a discussion of the fundamental bisexuality of deity in Hinduism. This aspect of Hindu theism has not received as much attention from scholars of Hinduism as it should. Bisexuality is the foundation of modern Hindu theistic images, with independent status and activity of both female and male deities springing from this foundation. The scholarly lack of emphasis on this fundamental bisexuality can easily be explained. First, the bisexuality is a relatively recent phenomenon. Everyone knows that the Vedic pantheon was largely male and everyone who writes about Hinduism makes a few comments about the resurgence of the goddess sometime after the beginning of the Christian era. One gets the impression that many commentators simply don't know what to make of this resurgence and do not appreciate its true significance and scope, being content to treat the significant female sides of Vishnu and Shiva as a shadowy composite third, the great goddess. Furthermore, the evidence for a foundational image of bisexuality is much more obvious in the iconographic materials than in the texts—and scholars of Hinduism have tended to leave iconography to art historians.

There are several significant icons connected with the image of divine bisexuality. First there is the icon of deity-as-couple, and the closely related phenomenon of female counterparts corresponding to every male manifestation of deity, from the most significant to the Trimūrti itself.

The image of the divine couple is so common in Hinduism that little needs to be said about it. This image pervades both the Shaivite and Vaishnavite traditions, though it is somewhat more noticeable in Shaivite tradition. However, the Vaishnavite tradition has also been significantly touched by the metaphor of the divine couple, though the Vaishnavite couple tends to be more patriarchally male dominant than the Shaivite couple, with a diminutive Lakshmī rubbing Vishnu's feet in proper wifely submission. However, that tendency is not universal in Vaishnavite imagery, as the icons in the central shrine of the Lakshmī-Narayan temple in New Delhi show. The two members of the divine couple stand side by side, Lakshmī only slightly shorter than Vishnu. The tradition of deity-as-couple also occurs in the materials regarding Vishnu's *avatārs*. It is sometimes said that Vishnu is always incarnated as a couple. In any case, the later Krishna materials present striking examples of the divine couple. The history of the Krishnaite materials also presents a strong example of the refeminization of Hindu traditions, for Krishna begins his career as a male hero who gradually becomes the archetypal lover. The image of Krishna as lover, of course, represents something of a resurgence of feminine symbolism but even more instructive is the gradual ascendence of Rādhā from a nameless human lover to Krishna's divine counterpart.[3]

Closely related to the image of the divine couple is the fact that in classical and modern Hinduism, every manifestation of divinity, from insignificant spirits to the great gods themselves, has a female as well as a male manifestation. We may begin with Nāgas, serpentine beings of folklore and popular mythology who become Nāginīs and Nāgas, their tails sensuously intertwined beneath their male and female heads and torsos. More interesting is the fact that the remnants of the old Vedic male gods suddenly receive female counterparts, Indranī and Varunanī, for example[4] (relatively late in the development of Vedic tradition). These female counterparts of major male gods were not important during the height of the Vedic period, when the male deities were prominent. Therefore, it seems that their appearance in late Vedic tradition and in iconography can be due only to the new power of the image of divine androgyny. However, it is not just minor deities that are portrayed in female guise. Abstractions of divinity like Bhuvaneśvarī and Maheśvarī appear in female form.[5] One also finds icons of goddesses with all the major attributes of Vishnu and Shiva, as well as Bhairavī, the female form of Bhairava,[6] a manifestation of the destructive side of Shiva. The entire Trimūrti also takes on female form on occasion.[7] In conclusion, it perhaps would be worth noting that the refeminization of the tradition was so strong that it significantly affected not only all anthropomorphic figures within Hinduism, but also Buddhism and Jainism, despite their nontheistic teachings.

Two other icons demonstrate even more graphically the androgynous image of deity. The *linga-yoni* icon is, if anything, even more widespread than the image of the couple; often being the central icon in Shaivite temples and found in many other places as well. Though it is generally called a "Shivlinga" and there is much stress on its phallic component, both on the part of scholars of Hinduism and Hindus, everyone knows that the *linga*, or phallic component, rests in the base of the *yoni*, or stylized vagina, and that one rarely finds a *linga* without a *yoni*. The fact that the *yoni* tends to be overlooked is typical of the way androgynous images often are discussed, as if they were purely androcentric images.

The second image I wish to discuss as an even more obvious demonstration of divine bisexuality than the couple-image is subject to some of the same problems. Generally called the Shiva Ardhanārī icon, or "Shiva as half-woman" icon, it is an icon of a single being who is obviously male on one side of the body and female on the other side, down to the minutest details. The image itself is obviously much more bisexual than its title. This icon is not as common as others I have discussed, but it is by no means rare, occurring quite early at Elephanta and Mahabalipuram,[8] in the later style of South Indian bronze casting (a copy of which sits on my coffee table[9]) and in the style common to late North Indian painting.[10] An especially interesting occurrence of this icon is a Nepali carving of Vishnu as a hermaphrodite,[11] interesting because the hermaphrodite icon is almost always associated with Shaivite tradition. The occurrence of this icon in Vaishnavite tradition, even rarely, is significant and demonstrates once more the attractive power of the image of bisexuality.

This bisexuality of deity strikes me as indicative of a basic sanity—of a fundamentally healthy and whole way to approach the need for personal imagery. It is quite reassuring to study and contemplate it and I suggest it as a foundation for any attempt to reimage the goddess, taking care, of course, that the imagery is not used to express or perpetuate sexism in either direction.

However, while I think it is crucial to stress the androgynous foundation of sane theistic imagery, I am obviously more interested in the independent status and activity of the goddess springing from this foundation. The independent manifestations of the Hindu goddess offer five more very significant suggestions for the reimaging of the Goddess.

First, perhaps the most noticeable feature, as well as one of the most significant for us, is the goddesses' obvious strength and capability, their transcendence and dynamic creativity. This quality is somewhat difficult to convey apart from the icons but it is omnipresent in representations of the goddess. However, it is most obvious in the stories and icons of Durgā Mahisāsura Mardinī—Durgā, the slayer of the buffalo demon—a very widespread icon of the goddess. The classic text itself[12] reveals patriarchal overlay, attributing the origin of Durgā to the male gods, who recombine their energies to create the goddess. A modern calendar picture, reversing this story and showing the three great male deities of present-day Hinduism springing from a ray of light emanating from the goddess's palm, probably reflects a more primordial perception. In any case, even in the text Durgā is called upon to accomplish that which none of the male deities can accomplish—the destruction of a very powerful embodiment of evil. Without a moment's hesitation, with consummate grace, calmness, and beauty at all times, Durgā mounts her lion and easily defeats the buffalo demon in physical combat. She is often portrayed in the midst of the battle as capable, strong, calm, and exceedingly beautiful. This icon has been exceedingly widespread and popular from relatively early times (the classic Mahabalipuram relief[13] is from the seventh century) to the present. In many of the icons the buffalo demon recedes in importance and all the stress is on Durgā herself, masterfully standing on his head, as in relief in use today in a South India temple in Kanchi. This emphasis on Durgā as deity has given rise to a very widespread and popular icon of Durgā riding her lion or tiger, displaying her attributes and dispensing boons with no reference whatsoever to the buffalo demon. It seems she has acquired more and more significance and universality. It is important to note that these icons portray her carrying the emblems of *both* major Hindu theistic traditions, the Shivite (trident, sword, etc.) and the Vaishnavite (solar disk, lotus, club, etc.). This is certainly a powerful indication of universality. It is important to note that except for the composite creation of Hari-Hara, a figure that is half Shiva and half Vishnu, this is the only icon that *combines* the attributes of both major streams of theistic imagery. And Durgā is certainly infinitely more popular and well-known than Hari-Hara.

I am always especially struck by the combination of strength and beauty, since we are used to seeing these two qualities as mutually exclusive, especially in women. This element of the goddess is the perfect counter to the objection that God must be male, since God must be strong, and capable of engendering trust and confidence—an argument that I often hear from naive people who expect that a goddess would directly embody the qualities currently expected of females and therefore expect a goddess somehow to be passive, ineffectual, and weak. Since I think theistic imagery must contain images of strength and capability that produce trust and confidence, and since these are qualities not usually associated with females in our current repertoire of images, I find it highly instructive to contemplate this element of the Hindu goddesses. The other element of this icon that is of most significance for us is the modern portraits of Durgā carrying the emblems of both major traditions. I am struck by the fact that it is a female image of deity that demonstrates this kind of universality. One would expect such universal significance and completeness to occur with the second coming of the goddess.

The second major characteristic of the goddess that I wish to discuss is a characteristic she shares with the male Hindu deities, a characteristic that seems to me to be exceedingly important in theistic imagery but one that also seems to be very weak in current Western religious imagery. All Hindu deities, female as well as male, demonstrate a symbolism of the coincidence of opposites, perhaps most brilliantly demonstrated and commented on by Danielou.[14] At its most basic level the coincidence of opposites is a coincidence of creation and destruction, of good and bad looked at from the point of view of the ego's needs and self-interest. This dimension of the Hindu symbol and the symbolism of the destructive goddesses and gods is quite susceptible to misinterpretation, to the painfully wrong conclusion that the goddess is demonic because she promotes death as well as birth. However, many commentators have begun to decipher this kind of symbolism, noting its realism and wisdom. Both poles are an inevitable part of experience; it is shortsighted to look only at increase, continuity, and well-being. Rather, this symbolism looks beyond the gratification of immediate needs to the necessity of death for life in a closed ecosystem. Not only is this kind of symbolism necessary, but it seems fundamental that in a theistic symbol system, the deities should incarnate and embody this symbolism. If both poles are necessary and inevitable, then both must characterize the gods.

In the Hindu context, the destructive side of the coincidence is more than just something we recognize as inevitable and life-giving in the long run. The destructive manifestations of deity, both female and male, with their swords and severed heads dancing in the cremation ground, demonstrate cutting away finite attachments, thus demonstrating the way to the ultimate goal—liberation. The process of cutting away all resting places, all finite attachments, though difficult and painful, is inevitably necessary for release in most Indian views. Therefore the deities most closely connected with death and destruction, Kālī and Shiva, are also intimately connected with revelation and release. This dimension, this function of the destructive side of coincidence-of-opposites symbolism has been much less noted, though Danielou has buried some intimations of it in his discussion of Shiva,[15] and Kinsley sees the same functions of this symbolism in connection with Kālī, doing a masterful job of drawing forth its implications.[16]

Both levels of coincidence-of-opposites symbolism are valuable and, since the Hindu goddesses manifest both kinds of coincidence-of-opposites symbolism, these goddesses have much to teach us. Let me say only that this is perhaps the area in which we most need outside help in reimaging the goddess, since it seems unlikely that any of our present resources prompts us to develop this symbolism. Perhaps we should also remember that the ancient European and Middle Eastern goddesses seem to have this same ambiguity. Therefore we seem to be tapping into an extremely primordial tradition, one toward which we need to be passively receptive.

It remains only to discuss the specific manifestations of coincidence-of-opposites symbolism in the Hindu goddesses. To do so at the deepest level would require a discussion of all the goddesses, the "beneficient" goddesses Durgā, Pārvatī, Lakshmī, Sarasvatī, etc., as well as the "destructive" goddesses, particularly Kālī. In this context I want mainly to discuss the destructive side of the pole, dealing in a general way with the broadest coincidence of opposites by pointing out a relatively rare scene that combines the mild, young, beautiful Durgā with Kālī at her worst—naked, black, fierce, sword in hand—both of them awaiting a huge multitude.[17]

I want to focus on the second figure in this scene, who is sometimes portrayed in a totally mild manner. One sometimes hardly notices the skull in her headdress, but it is there and the noose she holds is ominous. Nevertheless, her hands form the comforting *mudras*, "granting peace" and "granting a boon," and she sits in the relaxed teaching pose—a subtle but significant sign. What is she trying to teach us? It becomes more obvious in her most familiar portraits.[18] She is black, her eyes are fierce and terrible, her tongue reaches well past her chin, eager to lick up the blood of her victims, and she carries a severed head and a curved knife in two of her four arms. Neophytes usually overlook the peace-giving and gift-giving *mudras* of the other two hands, the beautiful hair and the halo. That balance is crucial. It must not be overlooked.

In modern iconography it is common to portray this dark Kālī dancing on the prone body of Shiva. Though there is little textual evidence about this particular icon of Kālī the icon itself can be found in relatively early times, for example on the walls of the temples of

Belur and Halebad dating from the twelfth or thirteenth century, and from a wide geographic area within India. In one very surprising painting, the whole imagery is transferred to Vishnu and Lakshmī, which comes as quite a shock to anyone used to Vaishnavite symbols.[19] Transferring this whole icon to the Vaishnavite context, even if rarely, demonstrates dramatically the power and attractiveness this icon attains. In contemporary India the Kālī-Shiva version is surprisingly popular. In some paintings Shiva watches Kālī in rapt fascination, his head propped up by his hand and arm. This behavior contrasts significantly with the text [20] about this incident, which narrates how Kālī danced madly out of control on the battlefield until Shiva threw himself among the corpses. When Kālī danced on him, Brahmā pointed out that it was inappropriate for her to tread upon her husband, and Kālī, rebuked, stopped dancing. The difference between the text, which subtly snubs Kālī, and the icon, which catches her at the moment of her exultant dance upon a cooperative, fascinated, unreproachful Shiva, indicates how important the tradition of visual Hinduism is. In other modern paintings, Kālī's dance occurs in a cremation ground and the divine couple is surrounded by funeral pyres, cracked bones, skeletons, and jackals, and Kālī is irresistibly beautiful. The balance is clear and perfect, down to the frequent boon-giving and peace-giving *mudras*.

Another fascinating well-known portrayal of a goddess contains much of the same symbolism. Chinnamastā, the sixth of the ten *Mahāvidyās*, or forms of the energy of the Goddess,[21] sits or stands on the lotus throne, holding her self-severed head in her hands.[22] Three streams of blood, representing the three *gunas*, or basic strands in the phenomenal world, nourish her and two female figures flanking her. Rawson says that each of the three females should be in intercourse, but I have seen only paintings with the entire lotus throne above or on a copulating couple, with female in the superior position, of course. The coincidence of life and death, the bloody presence of the mother of the world, could hardly be more obvious.

The third set of resources for reimaging the goddess that are found in connection with the Hindu goddesses, the image of God as mother, is one of the most difficult to deal with, both from the point of view of assessing how the image is utilized in the Hindu context and from the point of view of determining how this imagery should be used in revalorized goddess symbolism.

The problem we face in revalorizing God the Mother is double-edged. On the one hand, it is crucial to revalorize images of birthing, nurturing, and mothering. They have been banished and denigrated for far too long. On the other hand, this revalorization must be done without excessive glorification and without giving credence to the notion that because divine motherhood is so significant, human motherhood itself is a sufficient role for women. This is a particularly difficult situation for us, since the transcendent significance of birthing and mothering have been denied at the same time as women have been trapped in and confined to mothering, caretaking roles, solely responsible for the care of young children. A more pervasive dead-end is hard to imagine, and I am afraid that the only significant Western female deity, the Virgin Mary, at times helps to foster that confinement, since she usually functions in relation to and in dependence upon the divine child. However ambiguous the Hindu images of God as mother may be, they clearly present one idea that is extremely helpful for us. The motherhood of God, while real and strongly expressed, is basically metaphorical. Though there are a few icons of the goddess giving birth,[23] the mother-and-child icon is conspicuous in its absence. Nevertheless, references to the life-giving creative motherhood of God are omnipresent. Participating in the goddess's creative potential, female religious leaders frequently have the title "mother" appended to their names, despite the absence of biological children. Thus it seems obvious that motherhood in this case means something more subtle than the role of cosmic housewife and diaper-changer. It seems instead that any act carried out by a female that produces positive results of some sort merits the title mother. This really should not be so hard to grasp, since we use language that way all the time in reference to God the Father, whom no one expects to be a cosmic universal inseminator (at least not anymore). Why then should God the Mother be an infinitely fertile perpetual birth-giver and caretaker of young children? I doubt that the goddess ever was *only* that, even when fertility (as opposed to creativity) was an important part of her symbolism. That kind of literal motherhood does not now constitute the motherhood of the Hindu God-Mother and it certainly would not be the kind of motherhood that is revalorized by the second coming of the goddess.

We can get some further clues for revalorizing the mothering aspects of the goddess by noting that not only do creative things done by females justify the title mother, but also any kind of creativity or bestowing of life seems to evoke a symbolism of motherhood. This correlation explains the common practice of calling the rivers "mothers," a custom that is most noticed in the case of Mata Gaṅgā, but is common for other rivers as well. The same habit of thought is expressed in the very common and widespread notion that the male pole of the male-female dichotomy represents passivity and potentiality, while the female pole represents activity and actuality. Called Māyā-Shakti, this version of the goddess is responsible for the manifest, manifold world of our experience, while her passive consort represents only the potential for existence. This notion is extremely widespread, especially in later and/or Tantric versions of Hinduism. Visually, it is most vividly expressed by a development of the familiar motif of Kālī dancing on Shiva. Everything is familiar except that Kālī dances on two figures of Shiva, one above the other.[24] The bottom Shiva is a *sava*, a corpse, the wordplay that gave rise to the icon, while the top Shiva shows signs of life and attention. He is in contact with the feet of Kālī, which is paradigmatic of the relationship between the absolute and the manifest, the male and the female. There is a world only because of Kālī. Without her everything would slip back into primordial void. It must be pointed out, however, that this symbolism is more ambiguous in the Hindu context than it would be in the Western context, since *Māyā* is often regarded as demonic and Shakti as *prakriti*, or materiality, is negatively assessed in some Hindu philosophies. Nevertheless, there is real ambiguity about this point, for the philosophical traditions that denigrate Māyā-Shakti—as philosophical ideas, not as personifications or images—have probably been overemphasized in Western perceptions of Hinduism. The icons and many less well-known traditions do not present a negative portrayal of Kālī as Māyā-Shakti. In any case, the image could function positively for us regardless of its connotations in its original context, and I think it has much to offer.

The Hindu methods of dealing with the motherhood of God offer a final suggestion. It seems that there is a keen perception of the awesomeness of female sexuality and the female sex organs, particularly the *yoni* but sometimes the breasts. They are venerated in and of themselves as awesome and creative. Sometimes this veneration is represented abstractly, as in the painting that portrays the perhaps stereotypical Hindu creation scene—Vishnu on the cosmic serpent, with Brahmā sitting on a lotus that grows from Vishnu's naval and creating the world, while Lakshmī rubs Vishnu's feet—all occurring within a *yoni*.[25] However, the veneration does not remain so abstract. The actual *yoni* of the goddess is venerated and the goddess presents her *yoni* in a highly exhibitionist pose.[26] In some cases, the devotees' veneration in touching the goddess's *yoni* has worn an indentation in the carvings. In other cases, icons of abstract or graphic *yonis* are utilized for veneration. The breasts are emphasized and venerated less often, but one finds icons of the goddess drawing attention to her breasts by holding them or by holding one breast while pointing to her *yoni* with the other hand.[27]

I have repeatedly been met with stunned, slightly uncomfortable silence when presenting and discussing these icons. The correspondence between feminine and divine imagery, to say nothing of the explicit veneration of female sexuality and its creative potential, seems to unnerve people. It is the visual corollary of the verbal God-She, and teaches us the same lesson: it is good to be female.

Another lesson that might be learned from the symbolism of the Hindu goddesses is relatively straightforward and simple, though of great significance. The goddesses are involved with the broad range of culturally valued goals and activities. Their connection with mother hood and female sexuality does not confine or exhaust them. In this case, it is the general principle rather than any specific examples that are most instructive, though it is easy to demonstrate the general principle in the Hindu context by pointing out that Lakshmī distributes wealth and good fortune, while Sarasvatī promotes learning and cultured, artful living. Subtler clues in her icons demonstrate the general point more thoroughly. Sarasvatī assumes the cross-legged meditation pose and teaching *mudras* without sacrificing any of her explicitly female form, just as Durgā is strong and capable without compromising her femaleness. The combination portrayed by Sarasvatī has the same stereotype-breaking power as Durgā's power and is therefore important. In addition, Pārvatī presents herself in the posture of a teacher and Kālī destroys finite attachments, feeding on those attachments, symbolized as the entrails of a victim on whom she dances. Nor should this universal range of activities be surprising; it is consonant with goddess symbolism in other religions. However, it is important to point out this universal range of activities again and again, since femaleness is often interpreted as a limiting condition.

The goddess will not necessarily involve herself in her second coming with the same activities she has undertaken in past or current goddess religions. She may, but she may also manifest solutions for totally new problems. For example, metaphors of rulership and heirarchy have always been crucial in Western religious imagery, but I doubt that those images are of central concern today. Therefore, while the goddess involves herself in the broad range of our culture's values and goals, I don't look for her to manifest herself as a female lord or ruler. (Note the absence of a true female counterpart for the term lord. Lady simply does not carry the same connotations.) Instead I expect her to be involved in more egalitarian, mutually sharing and giving manifestations, to which feminine imagery should have much to contribute.

My last comments and suggestions concern the reintroduction of sexuality as a significant religious metaphor. If deity is bisexual, explicit sexual symbolism becomes unavoidable. It is important to note that it is only the explicitness that is new, since God the Father has always been an implicitly sexual symbol, as is the notion of his begetting the Son. So it is actually only female sexuality and the male-female sexual relationship that are unfamiliar images, and they have much to offer.

Sexual metaphors are present in all the images of the goddess and of divine bisexuality that I have already discussed. The motherhood of God involves veneration of female sexuality and the many versions of the divine couple are laden with implicit sexuality. All that remains is to point it out explicitly. Rādhā-Krishna metaphors are laden with implicit sexuality as the lovers' eyes meet, and with explicit sexuality as they make love in paradisical settings. The *yoni* and the *linga* abstractly embrace each other. Kālī dances on a longing, impressively erect Shiva not only with her feet but also with her *yoni* as all the imagery accompanying the icon of Kālī dancing on Shiva or Shiva-Shava are transferred to icons of Kālī sitting on the erect penis of Shiva or Shiva-Shava with her sword and severed head, her *mudras* of peace-giving and gift-giving, in the midst of the cremation ground.

There is no need to document further the pervasive sexuality in Hindu images of the goddess and of deity in general. Indeed the explicit and pervasive sexuality of Hindu images is often either confusing and alienating or titillating to outsiders. Yet it seems bizarre that theistic, personal imagery of the absolute could have so neglected or defused a basic dimension of personal experience, especially in a religious context that pays so much attention to the other basic bodily experience of eating. Furthermore, the loss of this imagery is especially problematic for an image system that turns on personal relationships both for imaging intradivine relating and the divine-human relationship. To invest so heavily in relational metaphors and then to limit the metaphors to *one* of the four parent-child relationships while completely excluding and denying the most basic human relationship as well as the other three parent-child relationships seems a bit strange, to say the least.

This final suggestion about the meaning of the goddess—the reintroduction of sexuality as a significant religious metaphor—seems to me to be commonplace and obvious by now, especially since, like the coincidence of opposites and the life-giving properties of the female, sexuality is stressed in the symbolism of the ancient goddesses. However, I consistently find that this set of images is among the most perplexing and surprising of all the images involved in reimaging the goddess. The reluctance or relief with which people respond to the notion of sexuality as a religious metaphor reveals much about a lingering uncomfortableness about our embodied condition. Therefore, the reintroduction of the goddess, which demands the reintroduction of sexual metaphors, represents a basically sane and healthy turn of events, helping us to move beyond the lingering body-spirit dichotomy and consequent hatred of the body. The resultant coincidence of sexuality and spirituality has much to offer.

In the end, some sort of vision of the goddess does begin to emerge—fuzzy and indistinct, waiting for more revisionings, drawing upon other resources. But she is a lot clearer and more distinct than she was when I wrote my first essay of female god-language three years ago, and ended unable to get beyond articulating why God-She was a theologically sound and sociologically necessary idea, totally unable to see any imagery of the goddess. As I look at her now, what seems most significant is not her similarity to or difference from the images of male deities, though there are plenty, but her sheer presence *as female*. By being there as female she validates me as I am. Her limitlessness is exemplary for me. It is good to be in the image of the goddess. That is the most important of her many meanings.

## NOTES

1. The most widely quoted recent statement of this thesis is George Rutland's statement:

> A priest is a "God symbol" whether he likes it or not. In the imagery of both the Old and New Testaments God is represented in masculine imagery. The Father begets the Son. This is essential to the *givingness* of the Christian faith, and to tamper with this imagery is to change that faith into something else.
>
> Of course, this does not mean God is a male. The biblical language is the language of analogy. It is imperfect. Nevertheless, it has meaning. The male image about God pertains to the divine initiative in creation. Initiative is, in itself, a male rather than a female attribute.
>
> The recent Roman Catholic decision against the ordination of women as priests turns on the maleness of Jesus. This is only the most recent example of the use, for the past 2,000-3,000 years, of the symbolism of a male deity to exclude and denigrate women. The ways in which this symbolism functions to exclude and denigrate women is most obvious when one engages in role-reversal fantasies. Then what is normally done to women becomes intolerable and unbearable, simply because it is being done to men instead. The most effective published role-reversal fantasy that I know of was written by Nelle Morton and is published in Hageman, *No More Silence: Sexist Religion and Women in the Church* (Association Press, 1974), pp. 29–31.

2. The term was coined by Naomi Goldenberg.

3. C.M. Brown, *God as Mother: A Feminine Theology of India* (Hartford, Vt.: Claude Stark & Company, 1974), pp. 119–98.

4. Mario Bussagli and Calembas Sivaramamunti, *5,000 Years of Indian Art* (New York: Abrams, n.d.), p. 207; and Zimmer, Heinrich, *The Art of Asian India*, 2 vols., Bollingen Series 39 (n.p.: 1955), plate 243.

5. Bussagli and Sivaramamunti, pp. 191, 197.

6. Ajit Mookerji, *Tantra Asana: The Way to Self Realization* (Basil: Ravi Kumer, 1971), plate 93.

7. Curt Maury, *Folk Origins of Indian Art* (New York: Columbia University Press, 1969), p. 43.

8. Zimmer, *Art of Indian Asia*, plates 256, 258.

9. Bussagli and Sivaramamunti, p. 254.

10. Zimmer, *Art of Indian Asia*, plate 70.

11. Ernst Waldsmidt and Leonare Rose, *Nepal: Art Treasures from the Himalayas* (New York: Universe Books, 1970), plate 20.

12. Heinrich Zimmer, *Myths and Symbols in Indian Art and Civilization* (New York: Harper Torchbooks, 1962), pp. 189–97.

13. Zimmer, *Art of Indian Asia*, plates 284, 285.

14. Alain Danielou, *Hindu Polytheism* (New York: Bollingen Foundation, 1964), pp. 5, 190–92.

15. Ibid., pp. 188–90.

16. David Kinsley, *The Sword and the Flute* (Berkeley: University of California Press, 1975), pp. 141–59.

17. Philip Rawson, *The Art of Tantra* (Greenwich, Conn.: The New York Graphic Society, 1973), plates 87, 104; and Zimmer, *Myths and Symbols*, plate 57.

18. Philip Rawson, *Tantra: The Indian Cult of Ecstasy* (New York: Bounty Books, 1973), plate 15.

19. Philip Rawson, *Erotic Art of the East* (London: Waldenfeld and Nicolson, 1968), plate 8.

20. Kinsley, p. 108.

21. Danielou, pp. 268–88; and Rawson, *The Art of Tantra*, pp. 132–33.

22. Rawson, *The Art of Tantra*, plate 86; Rawson, *Erotic Art of the East*, plate 110; Mookerji, *Tantra Asana*, plate 47; and Mookerji, *Tantra Art* (Basil: Ravi Kumer, 1972), plate 64.

23. Rawson, *Tantra: The Indian Cult of Ecstasy*, p. 99; Mookerji, *Tantra Art*, plate 74.

24. Zimmer, *Myths and Symbols*, pp. 197–16.

25. Rawson, *Tantra: The Indian Cult of Ecstasy*, p. 101.

26. Maury, plate 23: figs. 133, 134.

27. See books by Rawson; and Bussagli and Sivaramamunti, plate 110.

# 17

## CAROL P. CHRIST

# Symbols of Goddess and God in Feminist Theology

### Symbols and Society

God," Paul Tillich wrote cryptically, "is a symbol for God." For years, the meaning of that statement eluded me but now Tillich's aphorism seems a perfect introduction to feminist work on the symbol of God, for it expresses the central thesis I will explore here: that "God" is a symbol which may have outlived its usefulness as an exclusive mediator between humans and the ultimate reality that grounds and sustains their lives. I believe we are living in a revolutionary time when new religious symbols are being formed by a process of syncretism and creativity that includes discovering new meanings in biblical and nonbiblical symbolisms, tapping the unconscious through personal and communal dream and fantasy work, trusting intuition and poetic inspiration, and even bringing the process of symbol creation to consciousness. It is my belief that the work that feminists are doing to transform the image of God has profound but subtle and not easily observable consequences for social life.

The subject of this paper can be threatening. To those without theological training the word "God" refers to the Father and Lord of biblical tradition. This God may be accepted or rejected, but to play with, change, or transform the image or word God is something most people never consider. Even theologians who have rejected naive biblical faith often hold symbols in a kind of reverence, asserting that they arise by mysterious unconscious or poetic processes that elude the rational mind. While they will question theological dogmas and muse on alienation from biblical symbolisms, such people often grant an honored status to other previously created symbolisms, such as those found in Greek mythology, Jewish kabbala, medieval alchemy, or the works of some modern poets. If someone suggests that people do not need to cite the authority of past tradition or poetic genius for symbols, many liberal scholars of religion become almost as quick to cry heresy as biblical literalists.*

Theologians' views about the process of symbol creation are often derived from Freud and Jung via Tillich, and therefore these men's views need to be considered. Following Sigmund Freud, Carl Jung asserted that symbols often arise from a deep part of the mind that is below consciousness and never fully subject to conscious control. This depth dimension of the mind, the unconscious, is a repository of imagery and feelings, many but not all of them stemming from childhood experiences or traumatic experiences of later life that our conscious minds have repressed because they do not coincide with conscious self-images. These symbols emerge in dreams and fantasies and become expressed in the myths and symbols of a culture. While Freud had a unidimensional method of interpreting symbols, Jung believed that a symbol's ability to express more than could be put into words was essential to its meaning. Jung developed the theory that dreams and cultural symbols often express the human quest for meaning, the desire for connection to a wellspring of life power and creativity deeper than that offered by modern science. He believed that modern life was truncated by a slavish adherence to rationality and that people needed to be open to an irrational and mysterious dimension of life in order to find meaning. For Jung, connection to symbols is connection to a meaning that transcends rationality, a depth dimension in life.[1]

Jung and many of his patients were alienated from the symbols found in institutional religions, but derived solace from connection to transpersonal mythic patterns that emerged in their dreams and fantasies. While Jung remained open to the notion that symbols connected individuals to divine power existing outside themselves, his primary focus was on the divinities or powers of symbol creation within people. Though Jung encouraged his patients to create new symbol systems through attention to their dreams and fantasies, the second generation Jungians rigidified the notion of archetype and used it to stifle the creation of new symbols.[2]

While Jung emphasized the inner meaning of symbols, Protestant theologian Paul Tillich[3] stressed their transcendent reference. He

*The idea of creating new symbol systems raises the specter of ideological control over the arts and religion. Symbols do arise from the unconscious, but they can be created by those who are open to the unconscious. People who feel a need for new symbolisms can stimulate their imaginations through reading mythologies from other cultures and can learn to listen to their dreams and to use guided meditations to unlock the symbols that are forming in the unconscious. As new social situations begin to emerge, the need for new symbolisms is felt, and symbols emerge from the unconscious to fill that need. New feminist symbols need not be ideological constructs, but rather may reflect the new vision of a "general order of existence" in which feminist visions of social change are rooted.

asserted that humankind's ultimate concern must be expressed symbolically because symbolic language alone is able to express the ultimate. The influence of depth psychology can be seen in Tillich's definition. Like Jung, he believed that symbols transcend rational analysis, arise from the unconscious, and mediate meaning in human life. But for Tillich it is not enough to say that symbols arise in the soul, it must also be said that they point to and participate in transcendent reality. For Tillich, this transcendent reality, which he prefered to call humankind's "ultimate concern," is not simply a shared human sense of meaning, but is grounded in Being itself, that which traditional theology has called God. For Tillich, Being is not an entity existing outside humans, but is more appropriately understood as the ground of Being, which transcends finite existence, but in which finite beings participate and without which they would not be. Because humans are finite and their ultimate concern is infinite, it is impossible for them to adequately represent their ultimate concern. Thus for Tillich, primary religious language must be symbolic, because symbolic language points beyond itself to that which can never be fully or finally expressed. Tillich also believed that symbols cannot be produced intentionally, but grow and die by mysterious unconscious processes and therefore can never be subject to human control or conscious manipulation.

The insistence of Jung and Tillich on the importance of symbols in the human quest for meaning underscores the importance of feminist work on symbols. While the differences between Tillich's and Jung's views of the ultimate referent of symbols is not important for the purposes of this paper, the insistence of second generation Jungians on the eternal archetype and Tillich's proposition that symbols cannot be consciously manipulated must be demystified if feminist symbol creation is to be understood. For feminists are engaged in the process of creating symbols that deviate from the so-called archetypes, and they are doing so consciously.

What is left out in the Tillichian and Jungian analyses of symbols is the interaction between symbol systems and culturally relative systems of value. Cultural anthropology fills in these gaps in symbolic theory. According to Clifford Geertz, religious symbols establish "powerful, pervasive, and longlasting moods and motivations" in people which make their social and political arrangements seem inevitable.[4] Religious symbols are both models "of" divine reality and modes "for" human behavior. Moreover, religious symbol systems enforce attitudes and behaviors by labeling those who deviate from them outside the divine order. Geertz's theory of the reciprocal relation between social and political attitudes and behaviors and religious symbol systems does not postulate a rigid one-to-one correlation between religion and politics, but it does alert us to the social and political ramifications of all symbols, even of the eternal archetypes of the Jungians and the "broken" symbol discussed by Tillich.

Putting these theories of symbols together, we can see that symbols are tremendously important in human life. If Jung is correct, rational life is but the tip of our total life, and many of our deepest feelings and attitudes stem from the unconscious, which is a repository of symbolic thinking. Both Tillich and Jung agree that symbols are the mediators of meaning in life and that life is truncated without symbols. Geertz tells us further that symbols affect behavior and social attitudes and policies.

Recognizing the importance of symbols calls attention to a feminist dilemma, because the primary symbol systems of both religious and secular culture in the modern West are male-centered. If symbols are important, then the lives of modern feminists are impoverished and conflicted if they are not grounded in a compatible symbolic order. Feminists have alleged that the symbol of God as male, Father, Son, Lord, and King, induces powerful, pervasive and longlasting moods and motivations that are contrary to feminist values. Those who are influenced by the symbol of God as (exclusively) male are led to believe that men should rightly have all significant and legitimate power in society. Reciprocally, the fact that men hold most of the significant and legitimate power in society reinforces the notion that God is most appropriately symbolized as male.

After recognizing the influence of biblical religion on social policy and attitudes, feminists might well conclude that the demise of religion would be the best thing that could happen in Western society. But if symbols are important in human life, then this solution is inadequate. Humans have a need for symbols that can express the depth and ultimacy of life and ground their strivings in what Geertz has called "the conception of a general order of existence." Feminists who focus exclusively on social-policy issues may experience that emptiness and meaninglessness which Jung said occurs in a life without symbols, or alternatively may experience profound conflicts between the symbol systems that provide depth in their lives and the social changes they strive to achieve.

Thus the cultural and symbolic dimension of feminism is critically important. The creation of new symbolisms in art, literature, music, religion, and ritual will make feminist goals easier to achieve. Instead of a discontinuity between symbols in the deep mind and desired social change, there will be a continuity and reciprocal reinforcement. If a feminist symbol system were created, then feminists might be able to overcome the feeling they sometimes have struggling against the stream of nature and history, against, as it were, the "general order of existence." Instead of being devalued in songs, stories, rituals, and symbols, feminist moods and motivations would be reinforced by cultural symbol systems. Instead of remaining unarticulated, feminist conceptions of a general order of existence could be expressed. Feminist songwriters, artists, and writers, like Holly Near, Cris Williamson,

Mary Beth Edelson, Judy Chicago, Adrienne Rich, Marge Piercy, and others, are listening to their inner muses in conscious knowledge that they are engaged in the process of creating new symbols that will express feminist visions. Feminist work on language and symbol in religion is an important part of this process.

## Feminist Work on God Symbolism

*Critique*

The feminist critique of the God symbolism in the biblically based religions of the West includes two principal arguments. The first is that in religions in which God is primarily imaged in language associated with the male gender, maleness is deified as the source of all legitimate power and authority. Proponents of this argument ask that genderized God language be eliminated in favor of sex-neutral or androgynous language or that genderized language associated with the female sex be included alongside male generic language. The second feminist argument is that the attributes associated with God, both in biblical symbolism and in philosophical tradition, are based on a model of perfection derived from alienated male experience that distorts the concept of divinity. According to this argument, changing the gender of the language associated with God would not be sufficient to overcome the sexism in the symbol of God. Other aspects of both biblical imagery and the philosophic concepts associated with God would also have to be changed. While these two arguments are fundamental to feminist work on the symbol of God, some feminist theologians focus more attention on one or the other of them.

Mary Daly is well-known for her articulation of the first argument about God symbolism. In "After the Death of God the Father" and in *Beyond God the Father*,[5] she argued that the identification of divinity with maleness through the relentless use of masculine pronouns and genderized titles, such as Father, Son, Lord, and King, in Scripture, liturgy, and theology communicates a message to the deep mind that male power is divine. Daly is of course aware that philosophical and theological traditions alike doggedly assert that God transcends sexuality, that God does not have a long white beard or a penis, and that God is not a member of the male sex. Her quarrel is not with philosophic conceptions of deity (at this point), but rather with what may be called the core symbolism of the tradition. Daly cited McLuhan, "the medium is the message"—the message communicated by the language of tradition is that maleness is divine.

A response to Daly's argument might draw on Tillich's notion that a symbol points beyond itself to the transcendent ground of being in which it participates. The male pronouns and titles point beyond human male power to a notion of infinite power that judges all finite power, including that of human males. Without denying that the symbol of God as father may *on occasion* point beyond itself, Daly would respond that the symbol of God as father in most cases functions as an idol and does not point beyond itself, but instead allows humans to deify a finite power. "God" in Tillich's terms is no longer a symbol for the genuine, ultimate God.

A second premise implicit in the first argument is that as male power is legitimated, female power is denigrated by the image of God as male. Elizabeth Janeway has brilliantly argued (in a different context) that female power is not altogether denied in patriarchy, but is not recognized as legitimate power. Power that is not recognized as legitimate cannot be openly and directly expressed. Janeway has further noted that power which can only be expressed deviously, secretly, or through manipulation is always suspected of being dangerous or evil. The illegitimacy and danger of female power within the Western tradition is epitomized in the story of Eve, which is the fountainhead of a woman-hating tradition within biblical religion. In Genesis, Eve's power is outside the law and commandment of God and is perceived as evil in exegetical tradition. Within the biblical traditions, there are only two ways in which the power of women can be positively affirmed: when it is subordinated to the power of males—as loyal daughter, wife, or mother of sons—or when it is neuterized. In several of the Gnostic gospels and in the writings of some of the church fathers the notion that a woman must become *vir* ("man") before she can enter the kingdom of God is expressed. Since that which most obviously makes a woman female is sexual relationships and the bearing and nursing of children, it was a tenet of early Christian and medieval theology that a woman who denied her sexuality and remained virgin became like a man, not tainted with the evil and malignancy of her sex. The Virgin Mary and the female saints, symbols of female power in Western religion, are revered because they have transcended female sexuality. But Western religious tradition has never been able wholly and fully to affirm female power as female.

It might be argued that biblical religion has never been about the affirmation of the power of any creature, whether male or female. Some would point out that the biblical tradition affirms the transcendence and power of God above all, and affirms human male power only insofar as it is subordinated to the divine will. But this argument fails to recognize the dual trajectories of Christian God symbolism. One is to point to the absolute transcendence of God, and the other is to point to the participation of finite beings in the divine ground. God symbolism couched in the male generic does not point equally to the participation of females and males in the divine ground. Male language allows males to participate fully in it, while females can do so only by abstracting themselves from their concrete identities as females. Even the notion of God as transcendent other who limits the power of finite beings affects males and females differently, for if both males and females are limited by the power of God, they are limited in different ways. Though limited by God, male power is also affirmed by the generic language used in God symbolism—men can see themselves as "like God" in their relationships to women and children. Women receive no such compensation, and thus their power is doubly denied.*

The second feminist argument against traditional God symbolism makes the point that even if all the male generic language were corrected, the symbolism of divine power would still be distorted because it is based on an alienated male experience of power. This argument is spelled out in a variety of ways. For example, it might be argued that the image of God as a holy warrior, leading his people out of Egypt with a mighty arm and destroying the horses and chariots of the Egyptians, cannot be salvaged with a simple change of genderized language. A female or neuter holy warrior would still be an alienated image of deity based on the male glorification of conquest and domination, not an image which appropriately describes the nature of divine power. The problem with the symbol of God is deeper than the comparatively simple matter of changing genderized language.

Rosemary Ruether[6] has developed this argument into an important critique of what she calls the alienated dualistic and hierarchical mentality that has informed Western theology. According to Ruether, the breakdown of tribal and national cultures, increasing urbanization, and centuries of imperialistic domination produced a spirit of world negation that gave rise to a dualistic habit of thought. Transcendent and immanent, rational and irrational, spirit and flesh, soul and body, spirit and nature, male and female, were conceived of as opposites and ordered hierarchically. Much of Reuther's work has shown how the negative image of women in Western tradition is rooted in the fact that women were identified with despised flesh, nature, and irrationality. But she has also noted that these dualisms gave rise to an alienated paradigm of divine power, a paradigm of domination requiring subjection. It could be argued that this image of God is integrally linked to the authoritarian and oppressive attitudes that feminists have labeled patriarchal. Moreover, power so conceived was not merely transcendent but alienated from the powers of the body and nature that had been celebrated in earlier religions. This alienated image of God gave rise to distorted notions of sexuality that led to the notion that only the celibate are truly holy. It also made possible the

*In her book *The Mermaid and the Minotaur* Dorothy Dinnerstein provides an intriguing explanation of why both males and females find it comfortable to defer to the power of men in religion and society. According to Dinnerstein all mother-reared children develop a deep ambivalence toward the power of women because of their early intimate dependence on women for food, clothing, comfort, relief from dirty diapers— quite literally, for life. As they begin to assert their independence of the mother, mother-reared children wish to forget their total dependence on her, and thus they willingly transfer their allegiance to the father, whose power, because it is more distant and less connected to intimate bodily dependence, seems more manageable.

domination of nature that has produced the ecological crisis. These dualisms became the pattern used to dominate women and other groups such as Jews, blacks, and third-world peoples, all of whom, like women, are perceived by the dominant males to be less spiritual and rational as well as more carnal and natural. According to Ruether, the key to the cultural transformation that feminists seek is the overcoming of classical dualisms and the alienated, hierarchical mentality they have produced.

Mary Daly has elaborated Ruether's critique of the dualistic, hierarchical mentality that informs Western theology and images of God. In *Beyond God the Father*, Daly argued that the distorted image of divine power has given rise to a mentality of conquest and domination, which she labels an "unholy trinity" of rape, genocide, and war at the base of Western culture.

The two arguments that we have examined are the basis of the feminist critique of God symbolism found in the work of feminist thinkers as diverse as Mary Daly, Rosemary Ruether, Sheila Collins, Letty Russell, Virginia Mollenkott, Phyllis Trible, Elisabeth Schüssler Fiorenza, Naomi Janowitz, Maggie Wenig, Judith Plaskow, Rita Gross, Starhawk, Christine Downing, Z. Budapest, Naomi Goldenber, and myself.

*Solutions*

Feminist theologians agree on the outline of the critique of God symbolism, but they propose different solutions to the problem. Feminist theologians differ both in their assessment of and allegiance to Scripture and tradition, and in their visions of what God symbolism ideally should be. Because of these two variables, it is difficult to chart feminist theologians neatly on a scale of conservative to radical, for some feminist theologians might be considered conservative in their allegiance to tradition, but radical in their vision of what tradition has been and can become (or vice versa). The views of tradition held by feminist theologians fall into three main types: in type 1 tradition contains an essentially nonsexist vision or intentionality that becomes clear through proper interpretation; in type 2 tradition contains elements of an essentially sexist vision: the nonsexist vision must be affirmed as revelation, while the sexist vision must be repudiated on the basis (warrant) of the nonsexist vision *and* the contemporary experience of the full humanity of women; and in type 3 tradition contains an essentially sexist vision: and must therefore be repudiated and new traditions must be created on the basis of present experience and/or nonbiblical religion. (It should be noted, however, that some feminist work on God symbolism brackets this last issue).

On the issue of visions of what God symbolism ideally should be, feminist theologians hold four views. Type A: male symbols of God (and Jesus) may be interpreted in nonoppressive ways because what is oppressive is not the language associated with the male gender, but the notions of domination and oppression often associated with male symbolism. Type B: God language should be neuterized or made androgynous because language associated with one sex or the other inevitably is oppressive and also fails to symbolize the transcendence of God. Type C: female symbolism for God as discovered within tradition or found outside it and/or Goddess symbolism must be introduced alongside of male God symbolism because the transcendence or bisexuality of God is best symbolized by dual imagery. Type D: male symbolism for God must be abandoned and/or deemphasized as the female God or Goddess returns to ascendency.

Individual feminist thinkers may propose more than one of these solutions, or different solutions in different contexts or at different stages of their thinking about the issue. I will discuss the various feminist positions on God symbolism in light of these basic solutions.

Letty Russell, Virginia Mollenkott, Phyllis Trible, and Leonard Swidler are Christian thinkers who consider the tradition to be essentially nonsexist if properly interpreted. While not denying that there are sexist elements within tradition, they attribute these elements to the patriarchal cultures in which the Bible arose, and claim that the core vision or intentionality of the biblical faith is salvific and liberating for all people. Sexist elements within tradition do not need to be repudiated, but properly interpreted. Rosemary Ruether, Elisabeth Schüssler Fiorenza, the early Mary Daly, Rita Gross, and others hold a more complex view of tradition. They believe that tradition includes an essentially liberating vision, but acknowledge that elements of sexism have crept into this vision. Freeing tradition of sexism is not simply a matter of being faithful to biblical or traditional intentionality, but also of repudiating parts of Bible or tradition on the basis of present experience and theological insight. Elisabeth Schüssler Fiorenza[7] stated the hermeneutical principle of this group most radically when she said that only those parts of Scripture that are free of sexism can be considered authentic revelation. Clearly this is not a hermeneutical principle that can be derived from Scripture itself. Rather, it is based on Fiorenza's experience and interpretation of what is revelatory within Scripture—on theological principles that are informed by, but not wholly derived from, Scripture itself. The middle and later Daly, Naomi Goldenberg, Starhawk, Z. Budapest, Merlin Stone, Christine Downing, myself, and others fit into the third group, which, while not denying elements of nonsexism within Scripture and tradition, sees them as essentially or fundamentally sexist. This group claims that the core symbolism and the preponderence of teachings within tradition add up to an intentionality or vision that is essentially and profoundly sexist. This group argues that the attempt to transform tradition on the basis of selected liberating passages is doomed to failure.

Within the first group (type-1 thinkers) who believe that Scripture or tradition is essentially nonsexist, different views of the solution to the problem of God symbolism are held. Many thinkers in this group are influenced by Phyllis Trible's discussion of feminine symbolism of God within biblical tradition.[8] While admitting that the Bible comes from a patriarchal culture, Trible argues that the existence of elements within tradition that challenge patriarchal norms testifies to a biblical intentionality (1973) or alternative vision (1978) that transcends sexism. This intentionality or alternative vision is found, for example, in certain passages from the Hebrew Bible in which God is imaged in terms derived from women's experience or traditional roles, including giving birth, nurturing children, and providing clothing or food. For example in Isaiah 66:9 Yahweh speaks of himself as a mother giving birth:

> Shall I bring to the birth and not cause to bring forth? says the Lord? Shall I, who cause to bring forth, shut the womb? says your God.

That such imagery could arise at all within a patriarchal culture such as that of ancient Israel is astonishing, and is evidence, Trible argues, of a fundamental biblical insight that God transcends sexuality.* Trible thus finds a biblical warrant to justify a theology and liturgy in which God may be symbolized in both male and female terms.

Letty Russell[9] and Virginia Mollenkott[10] hold theological positions that are strongly biblically based and similar to Trible's. According to Russell, the biblical message is essentially one of liberation, but this liberating potential has been partly obscured for women by patriarchal language. While not denying the need for female God language and the biblical warrant for it, Russell's constructive proposals tend to emphasize the need for an inclusive neutral or androgynous language in which pronouns are eliminated altogether by repetition of words like God; neutral terms like Creator, Redeemer, Liberator, and Ruler are substituted for the traditional Father, Lord, and King. Virginia Mollenkott, a Protestant evangelical, likewise claims biblical warrant for feminine imagery for divinity, but also focuses on the sex-neutral solution to the problem of God symbolism. The work of Tom and Sharon Neufer Emsweiler[11] in creating nonsexist liturgies illustrates the position defended by Russell and Mollenkott. In their liturgies, for example, female imagery is occasionally used, but more often, male imagery is neuterized. For example, in the confession of faith, the

---

*The fact that such imagery was commonly associated with Goddesses who were worshiped throughout the ancient Near East and even in the official cult of ancient Israel, to my mind, weakens Trible's argument. A simpler explanation is that the biblical writers attributed qualities associated with Goddesses to Yahweh, in attempts to weaken the power of Goddess symbolism in the hearts and minds of the Hebrew people.

Emsweilers speak of "the living God, the Parent of humankind," instead of "God, the Father Almighty," and of "God incarnate on earth," not "his only begotten Son."

(The reluctance of these theologians whose work is strongly based in the Bible to insist on the necessity of female God language may perhaps be attributed to their loyalty to the Bible. They are aware that the number of places in which the Bible uses female imagery for God is small, whereas there is certainly no dearth of male imagery for divinity in the Bible. The requirement that female God language be used more than occasionally in liturgy constitutes a more fundamental alteration of the Biblical pattern than these authors seem ready to embrace. The regular use of female language for God would require a radical change in the image people hold of the reality to which God symbolism points. The change to a sex-neutral language eliminates the direct offense to women created by male God symbolism without necessarily forcing people to change their understanding of divinity. One can use sex-neutral language and still imagine that God is male or abstractly neutral, but when female language and symbolism is introduced, people's minds are jarred and they are forced to think about the positive inclusion of the female in the nature of God and also to rethink their prejudices about women's roles in society.)

Jesus presents an important challenge to feminist theology because tradition holds that he is both a historical figure and the decisive incarnation of divinity. Because of his alleged historicity, Jesus' maleness cannot be neutralized or supplemented with female imagery, and this seems inevitably to point to the notion that God is also to be identified with the male sex. Several sectarian leaders of the nineteenth century, including Mother Ann Lee, founder of the Shakers, and Mary Baker Eddy, founder of Christian Science, solved this problem by asserting that in the second coming the messiah would be female. While a few feminist theologians have proposed that the second person of the Trinity could be referred to as the Daughter as well as the Son of God, neither this nor the nineteenth-century solution has had much appeal to contemporary feminist theologians. Instead, following the lead of Leonard Swidler,[12] they have called attention to Jesus' alleged feminism and a purported absence of sexism in the early Christian movement. Swidler's argument is that even though Jesus is a male figure, the New Testament tradition never identifies him with the hierarchical, authoritarian symbolism associated with patriarchy, and it never pictures him as expressing negative attitudes toward women. Following the line of thinking about God symbolism discussed here as type A, Swidler alleges that the maleness of Jesus as a historical figure is not problematic, since Jesus' life points beyond sexist ideology to a vision of the world in which sexism is transcended. Views similar to Swidler's are adopted and elaborated by Russell, Mollenkott, the Emsweilers, and by type-2 thinkers, such as Ruether, Fiorenza, and others.

A number of interesting solutions to the problem of God symbolism are proposed by type-2 thinkers, who view the tradition as both sexist and nonsexist. Rosemary Ruether,[13] whose important theories on dualism and hierarchicalism have already been discussed, has sketched out a reinterpretation of the alienated symbolisms of transcendence that have been associated with the male symbols of God and Christ. Ruether argues that the sexist symbolism of domination, which compared Christ to a male patriarch and the church to his obedient bride and which can be found in the New Testament itself, must be repudiated by Christian feminists. But she believes there is also a "feminist Jesus" who points toward a nonsexist, nonalienated God. According to Ruether, Jesus' model of community (which she finds in the New Testament) was one in which the "orders of domination and subjugation are replaced by a community of brothers and sisters related to each other in mutual service." She even speculates, in a radical reinterpretation of the Greek doctrine of *kenosis* ("self-emptying"), that, in Jesus, God overcomes the modeling of God's power on "male leadership class domination" and "overthrows the masculine alienation of the divine by being poured out with the flesh." Ruether suggests that it is not the maleness of God and Christ that give rise to sexist attitudes, but rather the patriarchal models of maleness as dominance and femaleness as subjugation. If understood in nonsexist ways that stress the giving up of power on the part of the male, then the maleness of Jesus and even of God need not be alienating for women.

Ruether[14] has stated that she thinks of God as the "Great Matrix [which] is neither male nor female" and prefers to think of "Her as She in personal prayer," though she "would not want to dogmatize that preference." Nonetheless, Ruether has shown much less interest in female symbolism for God than most other feminist theologians. Perhaps her studies of Marian traditions and ancient Goddesses—and the ways they have been used to support patriarchal societies—have convinced her that the medium is *not* the message.

Much feminist work on God symbolism clusters in type 2C, and is an attempt to introduce female God symbolism into Christianity and Judaism. The thinkers in this group draw on the work of Trible and others that provides biblical and traditional warrant for female God symbolism. They often call attention to the work of Jewish or Christian mystics who have used feminine imagery for God. An essential tenet of type 2C is that while the Bible and tradition provide warrants for female symbolism, both have distorted the image of God through primary use of male symbolism. These thinkers believe further that it is not enough to neuterize the image of God, but that female imagery must be positively included if women are to become full members of the worshiping community and the society it projects. A stated or unstated premise of this position is that (at least at this point in religious history and in the development of the English language) sex-neutral language used about God is still likely to conjure up the image of a male God that has been firmly fixed in the unconscious by repeated use of male symbolism for God within the Jewish and Christian traditions. If the being of women is to be affirmed by God language, then female symbolism must be positively included. A 1e-cent psychological study[15] confirms the allegation of some feminist theologians that sex-neutral language does not include women. When asked what image was connoted for them by supposedly sex-neutral terms like *student*, most female subjects drew a blank, while most male subjects imagined a male like themselves.

Rita Gross has argued for the introduction of female God language into Jewish ritual.[16] Her views and those of Wenig, Janowitz, and Plaskow, discussed below, can also be applied to the critique of Christian symbolism. She argues that though the deity may transcend sexuality, language does not. Since Jews are committed to the notion of a personal God who may be addressed in prayer and ritual, they are committed to personal or anthropomorphic language. The exclusion of female God language from traditional Jewish practice means the exclusion of women from full participation in the religious communi-ty. Though advocating that change begin with pronouns, Gross predicted that further changes in core symbolism would follow. Her prediction has been proved correct with the publication by Maggie Wenig and Naomi Janowitz[17] of some of the prayers used in a Jewish women's *minya*, or worshiping community, at Brown University. Not only is God referred to as she, but startling and profoundly important imagery of the female body and female experience is used to point to-ward God. In one of the prayers, the women say:

> *Blessed is She who spoke and the world became.*
> *Blessed is She.*
> *Blessed is She who in the beginning gave birth.*
> *Blessed is She who says and performs.*
> *Blessed is She who declares and fulfills.*
> *Blessed is She whose womb covers the earth.*

In this rewriting of a traditional prayer women reaffirm the traditional notions of creation and covenant, but they affirm them of a God sym-bolized as female, thus allowing women to picture the qualities of power and faithfulness as part of their own being. And they also introduce the notion of a female God who gives birth through her womb into Judaism, thus allowing women to see that the creativity of their own bodies points to the divine creativity. Such affirmations of female power, creativity, and faithfulness are especially important to women who have been taught to subordinate themselves to a male God (and to fathers, hus-bands, and sons who reflect his power), who have been taught that they are unclean during menstruation and following childbirth, and who have been told stories of the faithlessness and treachery of women.

In "The Right Question Is Theological,"[18] Judith Plaskow has taken the Jewish feminist discussion of female God language a step further, by arguing that the word *Goddess* must be spoken again within Judaism. Acknowledging that for some this raises "the specter of paganism," Plaskow poses the following challenge:

> While it might seem that we are now distant enough from paganism to understand the suppression of the Goddess without feeling the need to refight this struggle, the deep resistance called forth by naming her indicates that the needs she answered are still with us. It is precisely because she is not distant that the Goddess must be recognized as part of God. For the God who does not include her is an idol made in man's image, not the relativizer of all gods and goddesses who nonetheless includes them as part of God's self. Acknowledging the many aspects of the Goddess among the names of God becomes a measure of our ability to incorporate the feminine and women into a monotheistic religious framework.

Catholic theologian Elisabeth Schüssler Fiorenza[19] has pointed out the resources in Marian symbolism for a female language and imagery of divinity. With Mary Daly, Rosemary Ruether, and others, she argues that though every Catholic schoolchild is taught that Mary is not God, on an emotional, imaginative, and experiential level Catholics experience the love of God in the symbol of Mary, and thus they experience Mary as a symbol of God. Catholic feminist theologians are rightly aware of the destructive elements in Marian tradition, particularly its function as one pole of the virgin/whore, virgin/witch polarity that has been used to oppress women. Also they recognize that Catholic doctrine has limited the power of Mary by insisting that Mary is mother of God, but not God the Mother—a figure whose power is derived from her relationship to the Father and the Son. Catholic theologians have yet to articulate a full theology of Mary as symbol of God from a feminist perspective and to show how they will reconcile new interpretations of Marian symbolism with Catholic tradition and dogma.

Sheila Collins,[20] following the arguments of Ruether and Daly concerning male language and authoritarian symbolism for God, has elaborated the feminist argument that God symbolism is distorted by the exclusive use of symbolism derived from the male experience. She urges women to learn about the history of the Goddess worship that preceded Christianity and Judaism and to use it as a resource for resymbolizing God. She also argues that women must not reject the so-called feminine qualities of emotionality, intuitiveness, relatedness, and closeness to nature, which have been denigrated as the negative side of the classical dualisms, but rather must reclaim those qualities and integrate them into a holistic value system and symbolism of divinity that transcends the classic polarities. She argues that pre-patriarchal, premonotheistic cultures where Goddesses were wor-shiped have much to teach about the integration of so-called masculine and so-called feminine qualities. The great Goddesses were not only birth givers, but also the givers of just law and the arts of civilization.

Collins's work is in many ways transitional between type 2C and types 3C and 3D. She does not clearly state whether the revisioning of God that will come about through renewed contact with ancient God-desses will reform biblical religions or whether it will move beyond the boundaries of Judaism and Christianity into a new religious future. This refusal to draw clear boundaries may be a virtue in a transitional phase of religious history that may result in the renewal of traditional faiths, the creation of new religions, or both.

Type-3 thinkers have been called revolutionaries because they nei-ther claim allegiance to the biblical faiths nor attempt to transform them. They consider the essential core or intentionality of biblical religions to be essentially linked with male dominance in society. They believe that to strip away or transform the male images of God or salvation in these traditions would change them so profoundly that they would not be the same religions.

In *Beyond God the Father*, Mary Daly argued that sexist language and symbolism was essential to the core of Judaism and Christianity and proposed that women abandon those religions. At that time she ar-gued that androgynous or sex-neutral language replace the male God language of tradition. Emphasizing the transcendent divinity spoken of by philosophers and pointed to in the mystical traditions of *via negativa*, she did not see the clear need for female symbolism for God. Instead she proposed that God be named Verb in order to point to the dynamism of Be-ing, which is always moving toward transcendence. In her later book *Gyn/Ecology*,[21] Daly has embraced gynomorphic symbol-ism for divinity, including the ancient term Goddess.

Other thinkers and symbologists, such as Christine Downing, Nelle Morton, Rita Gross, Merlin Stone, Starhawk, Z. Budapest, and myself, have also advocated the reemergence of the symbol of the Goddess in Western religious consciousnesss. Those who call for the reemergence of Goddess in modern life have different visions of the symbolic context in which Goddess imagery will emerge. Some believe that the Goddess is the most adequate symbol for divine reality, or include her son as a distinctly secondary figure. Others believe that the Goddess and God together point toward a single divine ground that transcends sexuality. Others believe that images of God and the Goddess reflect an ultimately plural reality. But in order to avoid misunderstanding, let me state that envisioning the Goddess does not necessarily imply substituting the Goddess for God and thereby creating yet another single-sex symbol system.

The suggestion that the Goddess be reintroduced into Western religion sounds strange to many. Even the word *Goddess* seems to have only a vague and shadowy meaning, connoting perhaps a fertility fetish, a Greek myth, or the beliefs of primitive peoples. What do feminists mean when they say *Goddess?* They have in mind a bas-relief painted perhaps eight thousand years ago on the walls of a shrine in Çatal Hüyük, which pictured her with legs spread wide, giving birth. Or the image of the lady who was invoked by peoples throughout the ancient world:

> Hear O ye regions, the praise of Queen Nana; magnify the Creatress; exalt the dignified; exalt the Glorious One; draw nigh to the mighty Lady.

> In the beginning was Isis: Oldest of the Old, She was the Goddess from whom all becoming arose. She was the Great Lady.
> (Egypt, fourteenth century B.C.E.)[22]

They have in mind also the Goddesses of all lands including those of Africa and Asia as well as the more familiar Goddesses of Greece and the ancient Near East.

In *When God Was a Woman* Merlin Stone discusses the power ancient symbols of the Goddess can have for modern women. She believes that the discovery that "at the very dawn of religion, God was a woman" can aid modern women's quest to liberate themselves from beliefs and attitudes of female subordination fostered by patriarchal religion. Learning that God was a woman can help women to view themselves as being in the image and likeness of the Goddess, as creators of their own destinies and responsible for their own lives.

In "Persephone in Hades" and in *The Goddess*,[23] former president of the American Academy of Religion Christine Downing discussed her lifelong connection to the myth of Demeter and Persephone, the story of mother and maid that was central to the religion of Greece for several thousand years. Downing tells how the story of Persephone, the daughter born with the spring flowers and taken away to the underworld by a male god, gave depth to her own experiences of girlhood, sexual initiation, and depression, while the story of Demeter's grief at the loss of her beloved daughter helped her to accept her feelings of anger and loss when her own children grew up. Knowing that her life fit a mythic pattern helped Downing to accept its rhythms of joy and grief, anger and depth. It is important for women, she argues, to connect mythic stories of female divinities whose experiences elucidate women's lives more completely than stories of gods and heroes can.

The recent interest in Goddesses is part of a widespread grassroots movement of women's spirituality that has emerged spontaneously in the United States and elsewhere during the past several years. In 1974 *Woman Spirit* magazine[24] emerged out of the women's movement as a center where women could share the imagery and symbols of their spiritual experience. In 1975, eighteen hundred women gathered in

Boston to celebrate power and share information about spirituality. In 1978 a conference at the University of California at Santa Cruz called "The Great Goddess Reemerging" drew a sell-out crowd of over five hundred. Feminist symbol creators and ritualists like Z. Budapest and Starhawk have begun to develop new syncretistic religions that combine the insights of ancient folk religions, Goddess worship, and feminism. Z. Budapest is high priestess of the Susan B. Anthony Coven Number One in Los Angeles and founder of the Sisterhood of the Wicca, a modern religion described in *Holy Book of Women's Mysteries*,[25] which integrates the insights of Hungarian witch traditions that she inherited from her mother with feminism. Starhawk is author of *The Spiral Dance* [26] and the first president of the Covenant of the Goddess, a union of pagan and Goddess traditions, which is officially recognized as a church in California. These women and others like them invoke the Goddess as the symbol of the life-and-death power of the universe, the energy of waxing and waning power incarnate in all nature, and particularly evident in the seasons of the sun and phases of the moon. They believe that cultural creation as well as natural creation follows rhythms of waxing and waning. Since the life-and-death powers are graphically incarnate in women's bodies in the cycles of menstruation, pregnancy, lactation, and menopause, female symbolism is seen as particularly appropriate for divine power. But the Goddess is not only the creator of physical life, she is also known as the giver of just law and the arts of civilization. The image of the Goddess that is reemerging in the psyches of modern women is symbolic of women's sense that the power which they are claiming for themselves through the women's movement is rooted in the ground of being itself. This movement is also discussed by Naomi Goldenberg in *the Changing of the Gods*, and its widespread influence is considered in *Heresies* and in *The Politics of Women's Spirituality*.[27]

Though funded by ancient symbols of Goddesses from around the world, women's imagination is by no means subject to the authority of the past. Instead, modern women joyfully discover what is useful to them in the past and reject what is not. They understand that many symbols of the Goddess have come down to them from patriarchal cultures, and, using feminism as a principle of selection, they reject those aspects of ancient mythologies that picture Goddesses as legitimators of the power of men. In a spirit captured by Monique Wittig, they seek to remember a past where women were not slaves, but what they cannot remember, they invent joyfully, recognizing that modern women can create symbols that express their quest for authenticity and power.

Several feminist scholars have begun to analyze the significance of the emerging Goddess symbol. Drawing on her expertise in Hinduism, Rita Gross[28] argued that the symbol of the Goddess has five things to teach modern Westerners. First, the Goddess's obvious strength, capability, and transcendence validate the power of women as women that has been denied in Western religion and culture. Second, Goddess symbolism involves the coincidence of opposites—of death and life, destruction and creativity—that reminds humans of the finitude of life and points to its transcendent ground. Third, Goddess religion values motherhood as symbolic of divine creativity, but without limiting female power to biological destiny. Fourth, Goddess symbolism also associates women with a wide range of culturally valued phenomena, including wealth, prosperity, culture, artful living, and spiritual teaching. Fifth, the Goddess requires the explicit reintroduction of sexuality as a religious metaphor in a symbol system where God is imaged as both male and female.

In "Why Women Need the Goddess,"[29] I discussed four meanings of modern symbolism of the Goddess in the women's spirituality movement. First, the Goddess is symbol of the legitimacy and beneficence of female power in contrast to the image of female power as anomalous or evil in biblical religion. Second, the Goddess validates women's bodily experiences, including menstruation, birth, lactation, and menopause, and validates the human connection to finitude, which has been denigrated in Western religions. Third the Goddess symbol in the context of feminist Goddess worship values the female will, which has been viewed as the origin of evil in biblical mythology. Fourth, the Goddess points to the valuing of woman-to-woman bonds, including the mother-daughter relation, which is celebrated in the story of Demeter and Persephone but which has scarcely been mentioned in the religion and culture of the past several thousand years. The symbol of Goddess, I argue, legitimates and undergirds the moods and motivations inspired by feminism just as the symbol of God has legitimated partriarchal attitudes for several thousand years.

In "Beloved Image"[30] Nelle Morton argued that the experience of women that has been articulated for centuries is the source of a new imaging of humanity and divinity. In a final section of her paper she argues that the titles God the Mother and Goddess have a metaphoric power that God the Father lacks today. God the Father is taken for granted and assumed after centuries of use in a male-dominated culture, whereas God the Mother or Goddess points to the new and requires change and movement on the part of the speaker and hearer. While not claiming that God the Mother or Goddess will be the final resting point in the transformation of religious language occurring today, she argues that using the titles Goddess and God the Mother is probably the only way to shatter the hold of idolatrous male God on the psyche.

## Conclusion

While not denying the importance of all the feminist work on the symbol of the Goddess, it seems to me that the challenge posed by God the Mother and by the Goddess is the one most important to the success of feminist theology. The absence of the Goddess in biblical religion is no mere oversight, nor can it be blamed on the cultural milieu in which the biblical canon was shaped. The active suppression of symbols of the Goddess and God the Mother is at the heart of the process of the formation of the Hebrew and Christian Bibles, as I have argued elsewhere.[31] Both the victorious Yahweh-only groups within ancient Hebrew culture and the victorious Christian groups did battle with Goddess religions and suppressed them. Moreover, as Elaine Pagels[32] has shown, one of the characteristics of the groups labeled heretical by emerging orthodox Christians was their use of femal symbolism for divinity.

The symbol of the Goddess was not merely omitted from the Jewish and Christian cannons, but forcibly evicted from them. This suggests to me that there is an unanswered question at the heart of the biblical traditions. This question is why the symbol of the Goddess was suppressed and what was the meaning of that suppresion. The suppression of the symbol of female power cannot have been without consequence for women and men within those traditions. While there is no convincing evidence to support the theory that the transition from God the Mother and the Goddess to God the Father and King reflects a simple transition from matriarchy to patriarchy, the widely held theory that the transition was from the orgiastic excesses of nature religion to the higher morality of a religion of covenant and history seems tainted with apologetic pleading. (The reason for this historical change is beyond the scope of this paper.)

What is significant here is the meaning of the reemergence of the symbols of God the Mother and the Goddess today. Whatever God the Mother and the Goddess may have meant in ancient cultures, today God the Mother and the Goddess symbolize the emerging power of women, the celebration of the powers of the female body, and an acceptance of humankind's rooting in nature and finitude. It seems to me that these three issues—female power, the female body, and finitude—have been consistently denied in Western religion and that the symbol of the Goddess forces their recognition more clearly than any other symbol. God the Mother and God-She have considerable power to bring these issues to consciousness, as the liturgies of Janowitz and Wenig suggest; but I would argue that the word *Goddess* must also be spoken. As long as Goddess remains unspeakable, female power is not fully expressed. God-She jars the imagination, but God-She is still a hybrid symbol, made up of the word god (which in common usage will connote maleness) and a female pronoun. Goddess is a more clear validation of the legitimacy and autonomy of female power. Some might object that it is unwise to press this argument, since God-She and God the Mother might become acceptable symbols within Christianity and Judaism, but Goddess never will. If this is so, and I do not believe it *must* be so (since historical traditions can change), then it may mean that the conscious rejection of the symbol of female power in the formative periods of these religions means that they will never be able to affirm female power or the participation of women in the divine ground fully and wholeheartedly.

The symbols of God the Mother, God-She, and the Goddess have the power to begin to transform deeply held attitudes and beliefs. It would be foolish to argue that the reemergence of God the Mother, God-She, and the Goddess will alone ensure equal rights for women. Clearly, there are many contemporary and historical societies in which God-desses are or were worshiped and women were or have not been granted full social equality. Nonetheless most feminists who are interested in the symbols of God-She and the Goddess have an intuitive sense that the reemergence of God-She and the Goddess will not be without enormous social and political consequences. These women talk about how their connection to the symbols of God-She and the Goddess have enabled them to integrate feminist beliefs and ideals on a deeper level. They say that the Goddess and God-She have made them more comfortable in accepting their own power and the power of other women, and that their unconscious needs for male approval have lessened as the Goddess and God-She symbols begin to transform the hold of the male-father-savior on their minds. They say that they no longer feel that the feminist political struggle is against the tide of history and the course of nature, that they feel more confident about eventual feminist success, since they have discovered a symbol that points to the rooting of feminism in the nature of being.

Perhaps what we can safely say about the symbols of God-She and the Goddess is not the grandiose claim that they will ensure equal rights for women, but the more minimal—but certainly not insignificant—claim that they will help to bring the attitudes and feelings of the deep mind into harmony with feminist social and political goals, *and* reciprocally, that they will express and bring to articulation the feminist intuition that the struggle for equal rights is supported by the nature of reality.

## NOTES

1. Carl G. Jung, *Psychological Reflections*, ed. Jolande Jacobi (New York: Harper & Row, 1961).

2. Naomi Goldenberg, *The Changing of the Gods* (Boston: Beacon Press, 1979).

3. Paul Tillich, *The Dynamics of Faith* (New York: Harper & Row, 1957).

4. Clifford Geertz, "Religion as a Cultural System," in *Reader in Comparative Religion*, 2nd ed., ed. William Lessa and Evon Vogt (New York: Harper & Row, 1972).

5. Mary Daly, "After the Death of God the Father," *Commonwealth*, 12 March 1971; reprinted in *Womanspirit Rising*, ed. Carol P. Christ and Judith Plaskow (New York: Harper & Row, 1979); and *Beyond God the Father* (Boston: Beacon Press, 1973).

6. Rosemary Ruether, *Liberation Theology* (New York: Paulist Press, 1972); and *New Woman/New Earth* (New York: Seabury Press, 1975).

7. Elisabeth Schüssler Fiorenza, "Feminist Spirituality, Christian Identity, and Catho-

lic Vision," *National Institute for Campus Ministries Journal*, Fall 1978; reprinted in *Womanspirit Rising*.

8. Phyllis Trible, "Depatriarchalizing in Biblical Interpretation," *Journal of the American Academy of Religion* 41, no. 1 (1973): 31, 33; partially reprinted in *Womanspirit Rising;* and *God and the Rhetoric of Sexuality* (Philadelphia: Fortress Press, 1978).

9. Letty M. Russell, *Human Liberation in a Feminist Perspective* (Philadelphia: Westminster Press, 1974); and *The Liberating Word* (Philadelphia: Westminster Press, 1976).

10. Virginia Mollenkott, *Women, Men, and the Bible* (Nashville: Abingdon, 1977).

11. Tom and Sharon Neufer Emsweiler, *Women and Worship* (New York: Harper & Row, 1974), p. 61.

12. Leonard Swidler, "Jesus Was a Feminist," *Catholic World*, January 1971; and *Biblical Affirmations of Woman* (Philadelphia: Westminster, 1979).

13. Rosemary Ruether, "Christology and Feminism," *WomanSpirit*, Summer 1977. p. 42.

14. Rosemary Ruether, "A Religion for Women," *Christianity & Crisis*, 10 December 1979.

15. "Ms. Gazette," *Ms.* magazine, August 1978, p. 24; the study by Wendy Martyna was published in *The Journal of Communications*.

16. Rita Gross, "Female God Language in a Jewish Context," *Davka* 17, reprinted in *Womanspirit Rising*.

17. Naomi Janowitz and Maggie Wenig, "Sabbath Prayers for Women," in *Womanspirit Rising*, p. 176.

18. Judith Plaskow, "The Right Question Is Theological," in *How Feminism Is Transforming Judaism*, ed. Susannah Heschel (New York: Schocken, 1982).

19. Elisabeth Schüssler Fiorenza, "Feminist Spirituality, Christian Identity, and Catholic Vision," in *Womanspirit Rising*, pp. 136–48.

20. Sheila Collins, *A Different Heaven and Earth* (Philadelphia: Judson Press, 1974).

21. Mary Daly, *Gyn/Ecology* (Boston: Beacon Press, 1978).

22. Merlin Stone, *When God Was a Woman* (New York: Dial Press, 1976).

23. Christine Downing, "Persephone in Hades," *Anima* 4, no.1; and *The Goddess* (New York: Crossroad, 1981).

24. *Woman Spirit* magazine, 1974, Box 263, Wolf Creek, Oregon.

25. Zsuzsanna Budapest, *Holy Book of Women's Mysteries*, vols. 1 and 2 (Los Angeles: Susan B. Anthony Coven no. 1: 1979, 1980).

26. Starhawk, *The Spiral Dance* (New York: Harper & Row, 1979).

27. Naomi R. Goldenberg, *The Changing of the Gods* (Boston: Beacon Press, 1979); *Heresies*, Summer 1978, Box 776, Canal Street Station, New York, N.Y. 10013; Charlene Spretnak, ed., *The Politics of Women's Spirituality* (New York: Doubleday, 1981).

28. Rita Gross, "Hindu Female Deities as a Resource for the Contemporary Rediscovery of the Goddess," *Journal of the American Academy of Religion* 46, no. 3.

29. Carol P. Christ, "Why Women Need the Goddess," *Heresies* (Summer 1978); reprinted in *Womanspirit Rising*.

30. Nelle Morton, "Beloved Image," published as "Deo/Dea immagine dilleta" in *La sfida del femminismo alla teologia*, ed. Mary E. Hunt and Rosino Gibellini (Brescia: Queriniana, 1981).

31. Carol P. Christ, "Outsiders & Heretics," *Soundings*, 61, no. 3.

32. Elaine Pagels, *The Gnostic Gospels* (New York: Random House, 1980).

# Suggestions for Further Reading

**Prehistoric Goddess**

Gimbutas, Marija. *The Gods and Goddesses of Old Europe*. London: Thames & Hudson, 1974.

Hawkes, Jacquetta, and C. Leonard Woolley. *Prehistory and the Beginnings of Civilization*. New York: Harper & Row, 1962.

James, E.O. *The Cult of the Mother Goddess*. London: Thames & Hudson, 1959.

Levy, G. Rachel. *Religious Conceptions of the Stone Age and Their Influence upon European Thought*. New York: Harper's, 1963.

Mellaart, James. *Çatal Hüyük*. London: Thames & Hudson, 1967.

————. *Earliest Civilizations of the Near East*. New York: McGraw-Hill, 1971.

Stone, Merlin. *When God Was a Woman*. New York: Dial Press, 1976.

Thomson, George. *The Prehistoric Aegean*. London: Lawrence and Wishart, 1949.

**Mesopotamian Religion**

Batto, Bernard Frank. *Studies on Women at Mari*. Baltimore: Johns Hopkins University Press, 1974.

Cumming, Charles Gordon. *The Assyrian and Hebrew Hymns of Praise*. 1934. Reprint. New York: AMS Press, 1966.

Enheduanna. *The Exaltation of Inanna*. Translated by William H. Hallo and J.J.A. VanDijk. New Haven: Yale University Press, 1968.

*The Epic of Gilgamesh*. Translated by N.K. Sandars. Middlesex, England: Penguin Books, 1960.

Jacobsen, Thorkild. *The Treasures of Darkness: A History of Mesopotamian Religion*. New Haven: Yale Universtiy Press, 1976.

Kramer, Samuel Noah. *The Sacred Marriage Rite*. Bloomington and London: Indiana University Press, 1969.

————. *Sumerian Mythology: A Study of Spiritual and Literary Achievements in the Third Millennium B.C.*, rev. ed. Philadelphia: University of Pennsylvania Press, 1972.

Ochshorn, Judith. *The Female Experience and the Nature of the Divine*. Bloomington: University of Indiana Press, 1981.

Oppenheim, A. Leo. *Ancient Mesopotamia: Portrait of a Dead Civilization*. rev. ed. Chicago and London: University of Chicago Press, 1977.

Pritchard, James B., ed. *Ancient Near Eastern Texts Relating to the Old Testament*. 3rd ed. with supplement. Princeton: Princeton University Press, 1969.

**Egyptian Religion**

Bleeker, C.J. *Hathor and Thoth: Two Key Figures of the Ancient Egyptian Religion*. Leiden: E.J. Brill, 1973.

_____. "Isis and Nephthys as Wailing Women." In *The Sacred Bridge*. Leiden: E.J. Brill, 1963.

_____."Isis as Saviour Goddess." In *The Saviour God*, edited by S.G.F. Brandon. Manchester: Manchester University Press, 1963.

_____. "The Position of the Queen in Ancient Egypt." In *The Sacral Kingship*. Leiden: E.J. Brill, 1959.

Breasted, J.H. *Development of Religion and Thought in Ancient Egypt*. New York: Scribner's, 1912.

Cerny, Jaroslav. *Ancient Egyptian Religion*. London: Hutchinson's University Library, 1952.

Frankfort, Henri. *Kingship and the Gods: A Study of Ancient Near Eastern Religion as an Integration of Society and Nature*. Chicago: University of Chicago Press, 1948.

_____. *Ancient Egyptian Religion*. New York: Columbia University Press, 1948.

Gardiner, Alan H. *Egypt of the Pharaohs: An Introduction*. Oxford: Clarendon Press, 1961.

Morenz, Siegfried. *Egyptian Religions*. Translated by Ann E. Keep. Ithaca: Cornell University Press, 1973.

**Greek Religion**

Butterworth, E.A.S. *Some Traces of the Pre-Homeric World in Greek Literature and Mythology*. Berlin: Walter de Gruyter & Co., 1966.

Downing, Christine. *The Goddess: Mythological Representations of the Feminine*. New York: Crossroad, 1981.

Farnell, L.R. *The Cults of the Greek States*. Chicago: Aegean Press, 1971.

Guthrie, W.K.C. *The Greeks and Their Gods*. Boston: Beacon Press, 1955.

Harding, Esther. *Woman's Mysteries*. New York: Bantam Books, 1973.

Harrison, Jane. *Prolegomena to the Study of Greek Religion*. New York: Meridian, 1957.

Kerenyi, Carl. *The Gods of the Greeks*. London: Thames & Hudson, 1979.

Nilsson, Martin P. *A History of Greek Religion*. New York: W.W. Norton, 1964.

Otto, Walter. *The Homeric Gods*. Boston: Beacon Press, 1964.

Pomeroy, Sarah B. *Goddesses, Whores, Wives and Slaves*. New York: Schocken Books, 1975.

Slater, Philip. *The Glory of Hera*. Boston: Beacon Press, 1968.

Spretnak, Charlene. *The Lost Goddesses of Early Greece*. New York: Harper & Row, 1978.

**Roman Religion**

Bieber, Margaret. *The Statue of Cybele in the J. Paul Getty Museum*. J. Paul Getty Museum Publication no. 3. Malibu, Calif., 1968.

Cumont, Franz. *The Oriental Religions in Roman Paganism*. 1911 English ed. Reprint. New York: Dover, 1956.

Duthoy, Richard. *The Taurobolium: Its Evolution and Terminology*. Leiden: E.J. Brill Press, 1969.

Ferguson, John. *The Religions of the Roman Empire*. Ithaca: Cornell University Press, 1970.

Godwin, Joscelyn. *Mystery Religions in the Ancient World*. London: Thames & Hudson, 1981.

MacMullen, Ramsay. *Paganism in the Roman Empire*. Ithaca: Cornell University Press, 1981.

Neumann, Erich. *The Great Mother: An Analysis of the Archetype*. Bollingen Series, vol. 54. Princeton: Princeton University Press, 1956. 2nd ed. New York, 1963.

Pomeroy, Sarah B. *Goddesses, Whores, Wives and Slaves: Women in Classical Antiquity*. New York: Schocken Books, 1975.

Showerman, Grant. *The Great Mother of the Gods*. Bulletin of the University of Wisconsin, no. 43. Madison: 1901.

Vermaseren, Maarten J. *The Legend of Attis in Greek and Roman Art. Études Préliminaires aux Réligions Orientales dans l'Empire Romain*, no. 9. Leiden: E.J. Brill Press, 1966.

_____. *Corpus Cultus Cybelae Attidisque. Études Préliminaires de Réligions Orientales*, no. 50. Leiden: E.J. Brill Press, 1977.

_____. *Cybele and Attis: The Myth and the Cult*. London: Thames & Hudson, 1977.

**Canaanite-Hebrew Religion**

Brown, Raymond E. *The Gospel According to John*, Vol. I, Appendix II. Anchor Bible Series, no. 29. Garden City, N.Y.: Doubleday, 1966.

Cassuto, Umberto. *The Goddess Anath*. Jerusalem: Hebrew University Press, 1971.

Heidel, Alexander. *The Gilgamesh Epic and Old Testament Parallels*. Chicago: University of Chicago Press, 1949.

Jonas, Hans. *The Gnostic Religion*. Boston: Beacon Press, 1963.

Patai, Raphael. *The Hebrew Goddess*. New York: Avon Books, 1967.

Pope, Marvin H. *Song of Songs*. Anchor Bible Series, no. 7C. Garden City, N.Y.: Doubleday, 1977.

Pritchard, James B. *Palestinian Figurines in Relation to Certain Goddesses Known through Literature*. American Oriental Society, 1943.

_____, ed. *Ancient Near Eastern Texts Relating to the Old Testament with Supplement*. 3rd ed. Princeton: Princeton University Press, 1969.

Reed, William L. *The Asherah in the Old Testament*. Fort Worth, Tex.: Texas Christian University Press, 1949.

Scholem, Gershom, *Major Trends in Jewish Mysticism*, New York: Schocken Books, 1941.

_____. *On the Kabbalah and Its Symbolism*, New York: Schocken Books, 1965.

Von Rad, Gerhard, *Wisdom in Israel*. Nashville, Tenn.: Abingdon Press, 1972.

**Christianity**

Adams, Henry. *Mont-Saint-Michel and Chartres*. New York: Houghton Mifflin, 1904.

Budge, E.A. Wallis. *One Hundred and Ten Miracles of Our Lady Mary*. Oxford: Oxford University Press, 1964.

Graef, Hilda. *Mary: A History of Doctrine and Devotion*. 2 vols. New York: Sheed & Ward, 1963.

Greeley, Andrew M. *The Mary Myth: On the Femininity of God*. New York: Seabury Press, 1977.

O'Meara, Thomas A., O.P. *Mary in Protestant and Catholic Theology*. New York: Sheed & Ward, 1966.

Ruether, Rosemary Radford. *Mary—The Feminine Face of the Church*. Philadelphia: Westminster Press, 1977.

Schillebeeckx, Edward. *Mary, Mother of the Redemption*. Translated by N.D. Smith. New York: Sheed & Ward, 1964.

Turner, Victor and Edith. *Image and Pilgrimage in Christian Culture: Anthropological Perspectives*. New York: Columbia University Press, 1978.

Warner, Marina. *Alone of All Her Sex: The Myth and the Cult of the Virgin Mary*. New York: Knopf, 1976.

## Gnosticism

Brown, P. *The Making of Late Antiquity*. Cambridge: Harvard University Press, 1978.

Foerster, W., ed. *Gnosis*. 2 vols. London: Oxford University Press, 1972.

Jonas, H. *The Gnostic Religion*. Boston: Beacon Press, 1963.

Layton, B. *The Rediscovery of Gnosticism vol. 1: The School of Valentinus*. Leiden: E.J. Brill, 1980.

MacMullen, R. *Paganism in the Roman Empire*. New Haven: Yale University Press, 1981.

Pagels, E. *The Gnostic Gospels*. New York: Random House, 1979.

Perkins, P. *The Gnostic Dialogue: The Early Church and the Crisis of Gnosticism*. New York: Paulist Press, 1980.

Robinson, J.M. *The Nag Hammadi Library in English*. San Francisco: Harper & Row, 1977.

## Hinduism: Kālī

Avalon, Arthur [John Woodroffe], trans. *Hymn to Kālī: Karpūrādi-Stotra*. 2nd ed., rev. and enl. Madras: Ganesh & Co. 1953.

Danielou, Alain. *Hindu Polytheism*. Bollingen Series 73. New York: Random House, Pantheon Books, 1964.

Kapera, Constance. *The Worship of Kali in Banaras: An Inquiry*. [Delhi: Motilal Banarsidass, 1966?]

Kinsley, David R. *The Sword and the Flute: Kālī and Kṛṣṇa, Dark Visions of the Terrible and the Sublime in Hindu Mythology*. Berkeley and Los Angeles: University of California Press, 1975.

M. [Mahendranath Gupta]. *The Gospel of Sri Ramakrishna*. Translated by Swami Nikhilananda. New York: Ramakrishna-Vivekananda Center, 1942.

Nivedita, Sister [Margaret E. Noble]. *Kali the Mother*. 2nd ed. Mayavati, Almora, Himalayas: Advaita Ashrama, 1953.

*Rama Prasada's Devotional Songs: The Cult of Shakti*. Translated by Jadunath Sinha. Calcutta: Sinha Publishing House, 1966.

Saradananda, Swami. *Sri Ramakrishna, the Great Master*. Translated by Swami Jagadananda. 4th ed. Madras: Sri Ramakrishna Math, 1952.

Woodroffe, John. *Shakti and Shākta: Essays and Addresses on the Shākta Tantrashāstra*. 3rd ed., rev. and enl. Madras: Ganesh & Co., 1929.

Zimmer, Heinrich. *Myths and Symbols in Indian Art and Civilization*. Edited by Joseph Campbell. Bollingen Series 6. Princeton: Princeton University Press, 1946.

## Hinduism: Śrī Lakshmī and Rādhā

*The Brahma Vaivarta Puranam*. 2 vols. Translated by Rajendra Nath Sen. *The Sacred Books of the Hindus*, vol. 24. Allahabad: The Panini Office, Bhuvaneshwair Ashram, 1920. Reprint. New York: AMS Press, 1974.

Brown, Cheever Mackenzie. *God as Mother: A Feminine Theology in India*. Hartford, Vt.: Claude Stark & Co., 1974.

*The Caurāsī Pad of Śrī Hit Harivaṃś.* Translated by Charles S.J. White. Honolulu: University Press of Hawaii, 1979.

Coomaraswamy, Ananda K. "Early Indian Iconography: II Śrī Lakṣmī." *Eastern Art* 1 (1928–29):175–89.

Gonda, Jan. *Aspects of Early Viṣṇuism.* Delhi: Motilal Banarsidass, 1969.

Hartmann, Gerda. *Beiträge zur Geschichte Göttin Lakṣmī.* Ph.D. dissertation, Christian Albrechts Universität zu Kiel, 1933.

Jaiswal, Suvira. *The Origin and Development of Vaiṣṇavism.* Delhi: Munshiram Manoharlal, 1967.

Jayadeva. *Love Song of the Dark Lord: Jayadeva's Gītagovinda.* Translated by Barbara Stoler Miller. New York: Columbia University Press, 1977.

Katre, L. "Kṛṣṇa, Gopas, Gopīs and Rādhā." In *Professor P.K. Gode Commemoration Volume*, edited by H.L. Hariyappa and M.M. Patkar, pp. 83–92. Poona: Oriental Book Agency, 1960.

*Lakṣmī Tantra: A Pāñcarātra Text.* Translated by Sanjukta Gupta. Orientalia Rheno-Traiectina, vol. 15. Leiden: E.J. Brill, 1972.

Majumdar, Asoke Kumar. "A Note on the Development of the Rādhā Cult." *Annals of the Bhandarkar Oriental Research Institute* 76 (1955):231–57.

Miller, Barbara Stoler. "Rādhā: Consort of Kṛṣṇa's Venal Passion." *Journal of the American Oriental Society* 95,4 (October–December 1975):655–71.

## Hindu Village Goddesses

Babb, Lawrence A. "Marriage and Malevolence: The Uses of Sexual Opposition in a Hindu Pantheon." *Ethnology* 9 (1970): 137–48.

Beck, Brenda E.F. "The Goddess and the Demon: A Local South Indian Festival and Its Wider Context." *Puruṣārtha* 5 (1981):83–136.

Bhattacharyya, Asutosh. "The Cult of the Village Gods of West Bengal." *Man in India* 35 (1955):19–30.

Dimock, Edward C., Jr. "A Theology of the Repulsive: The Myth of the Goddess Śītalā." In *The Divine Consort: Rādhā and the Goddessess of India*, edited by John Stratton Hawley and Donna Marie Wulff. Berkeley: Berkeley Religious Studies Series, 1981.

Dube, S.C. "Ritual Structure." In *Indian Village*, chap. 4. New York: Harper & Row, Colophon Books, 1967.

Elmore, Wilber Theodore. *Dravidian Gods in Modern Hinduism: A Study of the Local and Village Deities of Southern India.* University Studies of the University of Nebraska, vol. 15, no. 1. Lincoln: University of Nebraska, 1915.

Freed, Ruth S. and Stanley A. "Two Mother Goddess Ceremonies of Delhi State in the Great and Little Traditions." *Southwestern Journal of Anthropology* 18(1962):246–77.

Harper, Edward B. "A Hindu Village Pantheon." *Southwestern Journal of Anthropology* 15 (1959):227–34.

Hiltebeitel, Alf. "Rāma and Gilgamesh: The Sacrifices of the Water Buffalo and the Bull of Heaven." *History of Religions* 19(1980):187–223.

Shulman, David. "The Murderous Bride: Tamil Versions of the Myth of Devī and Buffalo-Demon." *History of Religions* 16(1976):120–46.

Wadley, Susan S. "Śītalā: The Cool One." *Asian Folklore Studies* 39 (1980):33–62.

Whitehead, Henry. *The Village Gods of South India.* 2nd ed., rev. and enl. Calcutta: Association Press; London: Oxford University Press, 1921.

## Buddhism

Chamberlayne, John J. "The Development of Kuan Yin, the Goddess of Mercy." *Numen* 9(January 1962):45–52.

Gross, Rita, and Falk, Nancy eds. *Unspoken Worlds: Women's Religious Lives in Non-Western Cultures*. New York: Harper & Row, 1980.

Horner, I.B. *Women Under Primitive Buddhism*. London: George Routledge, 1930.

Paul, Diana Y. *The Buddhist Feminine Ideal: Queen Śrīmalā and the Tathāgatagarbha*. Missoula, Mont.: Scholars Press, 1979.

————. *Women in Buddhism: Portraits of the Feminine in Mahāyāna Tradition*. Berkeley, Calif.: Lancaster-Miller, 1979.

Schuster, Nancy. "Changing the Female Body: Wise Women and the Bodhisattva Career in Some *Maharatnakutsūtras*." *Journal of the International Association of Buddhist Studies* 4, 1(1981):24–69.

Tay, C.N. "Kuan-yin: The Cult of Half Asia." *History of Religions* 16, 2(November 1976):147–77.

Wayman, Alex, and Wayman, Hideko, trans. *The Lion's Roar of Queen Śrīmalā*. New York: Columbia University Press, 1974.

## Japanese Religion

Anesaki, Masaharu. *History of Japanese Religion*. London: Kegan Paul, Trench, Trubner, 1930. Reprint. Rutland, Vt.: Charles E. Tuttle, 1963.

Aston, W.G., trans. *Nihongi: Chronicles of Japan from the Earliest Times to A.D. 697*. 1896. Reprint. London: George Allen & Unwin, 1956.

Blacker, Carmen. *The Catalpa Bow: A Study of Shamanistic Practices in Japan*. London: George Allen & Unwin, 1975.

Earhart, H. Byron. *Japanese Religion: Unity and Diversity*. Belmont, Calif.: Dickenson Publishing Company, 1969[1], 1974.

————. *Religion in the Japanese Experience: Sources and Interpretations*. Encino, Calif., and Belmont, Calif.: Dickenson Publishing Company, 1974.

Ellwood, Robert S. *The Feast of Kingship: Accession Ceremonies in Ancient Japan*. Tokyo: Sophia University, 1973.

Hori, Ichirō. *Folk Religion in Japan: Continuity and Change*. Chicago: University of Chicago Press, 1968.

Kitagawa, Joseph M. *Religion in Japanese History*. New York: Columbia University Press, 1966.

Murakami, Shigeyoshi. *Japanese Religion in the Modern Century*. Translated by H. Byron Earhart. Tokyo: University of Tokyo Press, 1980.

Philippi, Donald L. *Kojiki*. Tokyo: University of Tokyo Press, 1968.

Tsunoda, Ryusaku, et al. *Sources of Japanese Tradition*. New York: Columbia University Press, 1958.

## Afro-American Religion

Barrett, Leonard E. *Soul Force*. Garden City, N.Y.: Doubleday, Anchor, 1974.

Bascom, William R. *Ifa Divination*. Bloomington: Indiana University Press, 1969.

————. *The Yoruba of Southwestern Nigeria*. New York: Holt, Rinehart & Winston, 1969.

Bastide, Roger. *African Civilizations in the New World*. New York: Harper & Row, 1972.

————. *The African Religions of Brazil*. Baltimore: Johns Hopkins University Press, 1978.

Deren, Maya. *Divine Horsemen*. New York: Dell, 1972.
Gleason, Judith. *Orisha: The Gods of Yorubaland*. New York: Atheneum, 1971.
Idowu, E.B. *Olódùmarè: God in Yoruba Belief*. London: Longmans, 1966.
Métraux, Alfred. *Voodoo in Haiti*. New York: Schocken Books, 1972.
Thompson, Robert Farris. *African Art in Motion*. Berkeley and Los Angeles: University of California Press, 1974.
_____. *Black Gods and Kings*. Bloomington: Indiana University Press, 1976.
Walker, Sheila S. *Ceremonial Spirit Possession in Africa and Afro-America*. Leiden: E.J. Brill, 1972.

## American Indian Religion

Alexander, H.B. *North American Mythology*. Mythology of All Races, vol. 10. Boston: Marshall Jones, 1916.
Brown, J.E. *The Sacred Pipe*. Norman, Okla.: University of Oklahoma Press, 1953.
Hatt, G. "The Corn Mother in America and in Indonesia.' *Anthropos* 46(1951):853–914.
Holtved, E. "The Eskimo Myth About the Sea-Women.' *Folk* 8–9(1966–67):145–53.
Hultkrantz, Åke. *The Religions of the American Indians*. Berkeley, Los Angeles and London: University of California Press, 1979.
Jenness, D. *The Corn Goddess and Other Tales from Indian Canada*. Ottawa: National Museum of Canada, 1956.
Thompson, S. *Tales of the North American Indians*. Cambridge: Harvard University Press, 1929.
Voegelin, C.F. *The Shawnee Female Deity*. Yale University Publications in Anthropology 10. New Haven: Yale University Press, 1936.
_____, and E.W. "The Shawnee Female Deity in Historical Perspective. *American Anthropologist* 46,3(1944)370–75.
Waters, F. *Book of the Hopi*. New York: Ballantine Books, 1976.

## Contemporary Rediscovery of the Goddess

Bhattacharyya, N.N. *The Indian Mother Goddess*. Delhi: D.K. Agencies, 1977.
Brown, C.M. *God as Mother: A Feminine Theology in India*. Hartford, Vt.: Claude Stark & Co., 1974.
Christ, Carol, and Plaskow, Judith, eds. *Womanspirit Rising*. New York: Harper & Row, 1979.
Kinsley, David. *The Sword and the Flute: Kālī and Kṛṣṇa, Dark Visions of the Terrible and the Sublime in Hindu Mythology*. Berkeley and Los Angeles: University of California Press, 1975.
Mookerji, Ajit. *Tantra Art*. Basil: Ravi Kumer, 1972.
Rawson, Philip. *The Art of Tantra*. Greenwich, Conn.: New York Graphic Society, 1973.
Zimmer, Heinrich. *The Art of Indian Asia*. 2 vols. Bollingen Series 39. Princeton: Princeton University Press, 1955.
_____. *Myths and Symbols in Indian Art and Civilization*. New York: Harper & Row, Torchbooks, 1962.

## Feminist Theology

Christ, Carol P., and Plaskow, Judith, eds. *Womanspirit Rising*. New York: Harper & Row, 1979.

Collins, Sheila D. *A Different Heaven and Earth*. Valley Forge, Pa: Judson Press, 1974.

Daly, Mary. *Beyond God the Father*. Boston: Beacon Press, 1973.

_____. *Gyn/Ecology*. Boston: Beacon Press, 1978.

Downing, Christine. *Goddesses*. New York: Crossroad, 1981.

Goldenberg, Naomi R. *The Changing of the Gods*. Boston: Beacon Press, 1979.

Mollenkott, Virginia. *Women, Men and the Bible*. Nashville, Tenn.: Abingdon Press, 1977.

Ruether, Rosemary R. *New Women/New Earth*. New York: Seabury Press, 1975.

Russell, Letty M. *Human Liberation in a Feminist Perspective*. Philadelphia: Westminster Press, 1974.

_____. *The Liberating Word*. Philadelphia: Westminster Press, 1976.

Trible, Phyllis. *God and the Rhetoric of Sexuality*. Philadelphia: Fortress Press, 1978.

Spretnak, Charlene. *The Politics of Women's Spirituality*. New York: Doubleday, 1978.

Starhawk. *The Spiral Dance*. New York: Dial Press, 1976.

Stone, Merlin. *When God Was a Woman*. New York: Dial Press, 1976.

Swidler, Leonard. *Biblical Affirmations of Woman*. Philadelphia: Westminster Press, 1979.

# Contributors

Anne L. Barstow teaches medieval history and women's religious history at SUNY College at Old Westbury. She has published *Married Priests and the Reforming Papacy: The Eleventh-Century Debates* and a feminist study, *Joan of Arc: Heretic, Mystic, Shaman*.

C. J. Bleeker is professor emeritus of the University of Amsterdam. His numerous published works include *Die Geburt eines Gottes, The Sacred Bridge, Christ in Modern Athens, Egyptian Festivals, Hathor and Thoth*, and *The Rainbow*.

C. Mackenzie Brown is professor of Religious Studies at Trinity University, Texas, and author of *God as Mother: The Development of a Feminine Theology in India* and the soon to be published *Rādhā, Wife and Mistress: A Study of Rādhā Devotionalism through the Sixteenth Century*.

Richard L. Brubaker has taught at Vanderbilt University and Davidson College and has contributed articles to *Anima* and *History of Religions*. He has contributed to *The Divine Consort* and is editing a book on female and male symbols in Hinduism.

Carol P. Christ is professor of Women's Studies and Religious Studies at San Jose State University. She is the author of *Diving Deep and Surfacing* and co-editor of *Womenspirit Rising*. She received an NEH Fellowship in 1981-82 to work on a book devoted to the problem of goddess and god in feminist theology.

Steve Davies is professor and chairperson of Religious Studies at College Misericordia. His most recent publications are *The Revolt of the Widows: Social World of the Aprocryphal Acts* and the soon to be published *The Gospel of Thomas and Christian Wisdom*.

Christine R. Downing is professor and chairperson of the Department of Religious Studies at San Diego State University and a senior core faculty member of the California School of Professional Psychology. Her most recent work is *The Goddess: Mythological Images of the Feminine*, and she is currently working on images of sisterhood in Greek mythology and German fairytales.

Rita M. Gross teaches in the Department of Philosophy and Religion at the University of Wisconsin at Eau Claire. She has edited *Unspoken Worlds:*

*Women's Religious Lives* with Nancy A. Falk and *Beyond Androcentrism: New Essays on Women and Religion.*

Åke Hultkrantz is professor of comparative religion and head of the Institute of Comparative Religion at the University of Stockholm. He is the author of more than two hundred articles on American Indian religion and his latest books include *The Religions of the American Indians, Praire and Plains Indians, Belief and Worship in Native North America,* and *The Study of American Indian Religions.*

E. Ann Matter is professor of Religious Studies and director of Women's Studies at the University of Pennsylvania. She is the editor of *De partu Virginis* of Paschasius Radbertus, and has published on medieval spirituality and exegesis in *Traditio* and the *Revue Benedictine.*

Joseph M. Murphy teaches comparative religion at St. Joseph's University in Philadelphia. He has studied African religious tradition in Nigeria and New York and is the author of several articles on African and Afro-American religions.

Kyoko M. Nakamura teaches in Tokyo, Japan and authored *Ryoi-no-sekai* (The World of Wonders) in Japanese. She has also published *Miraculous Stories from the Japanese Buddhist Tradition* and contributed an essay to *Unspoken Worlds: Women's Religious Lives in Cross-Cultural Perspective.*

Judith Ochshorn is professor and director of the Women's Studies Program at the University of South Florida. She has contributed an essay to *The Lost Tradition: Mothers and Daughters in Literature* and authored *The Female Experience and the Nature of the Divine.*

Carl Olson is professor of Religious Studies at Allegheny College and author of many articles on Indian religion, philosophy, and history in journals in America, Europe, and India.

Diana Paul is professor of Religious Studies at Stanford University and author of *Women in Buddhism: Images of the Feminine in Mahāyāna Tradition* and *The Feminine Ideal: Queen Śrīmālā and the Tathāgatagarbha.*

Pheme Perkins is professor of Theology at Boston College. Besides her numerous journal articles, she has published *The Gospel of John, Reading the New Testament: An Introduction, The Johannine Epistles, The Gnostic Dialogue, Love Commands in the New Testament,* and two forthcoming works, *Resurrection* and *Revelation.*

Michele Renee Salzman is professor in the Department of Classical Studies at Boston University. She has published articles on classical Rome and has received a research grant from the American Council of Learned Societies to prepare *Studies on the Calendar of 354 A.D.* for publication.